For He is an Englishman
Memoirs of a Prussian Nobleman

For He is an Englishman
Memoirs of a Prussian Nobleman

by
Charles Arnold-Baker
or
Wolfgang von Blumenthal

JEREMY MILLS
PUBLISHING LIMITED

Published by Jeremy Mills Publishing Limited
www.jeremymillspublishing.co.uk

First Published 2007
© Charles Arnold Baker

The moral right of Charles Arnold Baker to be identified as the author of this work has been asserted. All rights reserved. No part of this book may be reproduced in any form or by any means without prior permission in writing from the publisher, except by a reviewer who may quote brief passages in a review.

ISBN 978–1–905217–44–1

Front cover pictures: the author and Fanny his wife
Back cover pictures: the author's son Henry von Blumenthal and grandson Alexis

Charles passed away on 6th June, 2009 Aged 90

CONTENTS

Chapter 1	First Persons	1
Chapter 2	Parental Engagement	17
Chapter 3	New Life	23
Chapter 4	Ancestry	29
Chapter 5	Staffelde – A Pomeranian Manor	47
Chapter 6	World War I in Germany	65
Chapter 7	Munich, Switzerland and Me	75
Chapter 8	Defeat	87
Chapter 9	Revolution and Divorce	93
Chapter 10	The Transition	101
Chapter 11	Whooping Cough, Margate and Beatenberg	109
Chapter 12	Edwardians and Matrimonial Muddle	117
Chapter 13	Elmau and Confused Education	123
Chapter 14	The Real Divorce	133
Chapter 15	Hither and Thither	141
Chapter 16	More Anglicised	151
Chapter 17	Winchester	161
Chapter 18	Hitler	177
Chapter 19	Venice and Oxford	185
Chapter 20	St Tropez and French Degradation	195
Chapter 21	Love	203
Chapter 22	Odd Military Scenes	209
Chapter 23	M I 6	225
Chapter 24	Bombing and Normandy	235
Chapter 25	Belgian Politics, Girls, Bombs and Spies	245

Chapter 26	Intrigues and Norway	261
Chapter 27	Sweden	273
Chapter 28	The Bar	285
Chapter 29	Parishes	295
Chapter 30	Underneath Parliament	303
Chapter 31	Local Government Reorganisation	313
Chapter 32	Disillusion and CBH	327
Chapter 33	Personal and Public Transition	339
Chapter 34	Siam	343
Chapter 35	Three Cables and my Father's Suicide	359
Chapter 36	Four Countries and Some Hospitals	367
Chapter 37	Last Blast	399
	Continuation	404
	Index	405

Chapter 1

FIRST PERSONS

There was a wonderful place called Clapham where Betty Robinson had a friend. It shed a golden glow over some vaguely located suburb, and Betty went there whenever she had an afternoon off. Later, I learned that when it rained in Clapham it did not necessarily rain in the Boltons, and much later, that it had an Omnibus on which there was a Man. Seeing that I never went there from the Boltons, it played a remarkably prominent part in my life. The reason was that she habitually brought it into conversation with the cook. I do not remember going there until January 2001 when I delivered a copy of *The Companion to British History* to an address near Clapham South. Save that the cook wore red and blue feathers in her hat when she took an afternoon off, there was nothing memorable about her. Betty, who was much less flamboyant in brown and beige was memorable because she was kindness personified. She became a treasure and was passed from aunt to aunt. We got her back, still beige, for a couple of days fifteen years later for my 21st birthday to 'do the cloakroom'. She originally came from a foggy place called Stafford which seemed to be on the way to one or more of the aunts. A treasure is a person who can be reliably retrieved from aunts or found in Stafford. The Good Lord must have done it long ago.

I originally set out (in a train to Colchester) to write these memoirs for my children, who feared that otherwise my experiences would be lost. I thought that a chronological treatment would be sensible and began at My Birth on 25th June 1918 (that is, during World War I) in Berlin. This in itself required some explanation, so I went back several centuries and began my chronology then. If I had baskets on my desk, they would be labelled 'In', 'Out', 'Too Difficult' and 'Bores Me'. With that version consigned to 'Bores Me', I tried again. Much the same happened to the second version, so this time, instead of extrusion through a tooth-paste tube, I have decided to let it out in Blomps (something between Blots and Lumps).

This seems a good moment to make a preliminary
ANNOUNCEMENT

My competent genealogical son Henry says that I am descended from Charlemagne on the wrong side of somebody's blanket or perhaps polygamous, and so from his ancestor Pepin of Heristhal, mayor of Austrasia, who died in 639. Pepin's son had been married to the daughter of St Arnulf, Duke and Bishop of Metz, whose ancestry is said to stretch back to a third century senatorial family of Narbonne. With a saint in the family, I can claim a certain respectability, which, however, is not to be compared with that of the Queen of England, who is descended from three Gods. Through more recent connections with the Austrian Khevenhüller family, I can claim relationship with Bartolemeo Colleoni whose statue by Verrocchio in Venice remains the finest equestrian monument in the world, and through my German grandmother, with the artist Lucas Cranach the Elder.

At this time we were living at 13, The Grove, The Boltons in Kensington. My stepfather, Percival Richard Arnold Baker, had bought it when he married my mother in 1923. As well as he, and Betty and the cook, the household comprised Wilhelmine, my mother, and my elder brother Werner. My stepfather was known in the family as Uncle Percy and in the Wide World as Monkey Baker, but we called him Pater to distinguish him from our absent father, who was called Father. I was called Wolfgang but also Charles, and the Bakers, being very British, called me Charlie. These little details may provoke speculation, and it will come as no surprise that I was brought up in two languages and four clans. Also six schools, eventually three universities and an army figured in the process which went on until at 60, I was quite well informed, though I am not sure that I ever learned to think. After, say, 65 I began to forget things, especially at awkward moments. I sympathise with Bishop Spooner's 'I know your name but I've forgotten your face' or the exasperated Bishop Fitzgerald's 'If I haven't got a ticket, how do I know where I'm going?'

Actually, Werner, my mother and I scrambled our way to the Boltons by way of Freiburg im Breisgau, Munich, Berlin, Pomerania, Holland and Hythe. We were surnamed von Blumenthal, Wilhelmine having married Albrecht von Blumenthal in June 1912.

English false modesty has no place in estimating the Blumenthals who, as I shall show, were amongst the most distinguished families in Europe. Henry has rightly expressed astonishment that they have received little notice from historians. The sixteenth century Elector Joachim I of Brandenburg described them as a family of the highest nobility. Frederick the Great called them 'une trés bonne famille qui a toujours servi avec distinction à moi et mes ancêtres'. In 1779 two Blumenthals were made Counts together expressly in recognition of the public services rendered by the family. So far as I know, no other family in the world has received such an honour. Another, also made a Count as well as a Field Marshal, won three nineteenth century wars.*

The wedding took place at, of all places, Bonchurch (Isle of Wight). My mother was older than he, so I will start with her. She was one of the six children of Abimelech Hainsworth and his cousin Elizabeth Gaunt. They were West Riding baptists, living at Farsley near Leeds — he being an industrialist who made that splendid scarlet cloth for the British army. As all the army, not merely the Guards, then used it, Abimelech was rich. He was not the first in the Hainsworth family to be called Abimelech and this is very odd because these Bible thumpers did not apparently know that both the biblical Abimelechs were mass murderers.

The French would have classified the Hainsworths as *des originaux*. Abimelech smiled upon the world through a considerable grey beard and believed in self sufficiency and independence. He sent his two sons, Gaunt and Charles round the world with £100 each. They reached San Francisco just in time for the Great Earthquake. At Basel station he sent Wilhelmine off on some errand. He made no comment when this fourteen year-old girl took a tram across the city and caught up with him at the other (Baden) station, of which, previously she had never heard. It would be easy to fill up this chapter with Abimelechiana: the second hand zoo which he bought (a bargain), his failed attempt to use steam wasted from his mill to heat his workpeople's houses, his habit of passing round peppermint humbugs in church, his refusals to describe his symptoms to doctors. Unconventional he certainly was, but not, I believe, eccentric. Everything he did had a rational, if sometimes unusual base. Not surprisingly the village respected him and the dogs adored him. His cat was called Tiglath-Pilezer IV.

His wife, a mathematician, had however, a genuine streak of eccentricity. My youngest aunt, Helena (pronounced like the island) recalled a frying pan flying past her ear, and Elizabeth was seen one morning in the garden wearing a jaunty hat, with an umbrella at the slope singing 'Onward Christian Soldiers'. She differed politically from Abimelech. He stood for parliament as a liberal-unionist: she read nothing but Moneypenny and Buckle's *Life of Disraeli*. Apart from the Bible, it was the only book in the house. With such parents life must have been hard for the eldest, called Ethel, a small fireball who never in her long life spoke anything but the truth and, naturally, was detested by one and all. She and my mother enjoyed a lifelong feud, but when Wilhelmine heard that Ethel, at 98, was dying, she made up her mind to seek a good Christian reconciliation. The attempt was not wholly a success. When she approached the deathbed, the semi-moribund Ethel opened one eye and said 'Hullo, Wilhelmine, when are you leaving?'

* For the family's vast collective landed possessions see Annex, p. 15 below.

My mother came after Gaunt and Charles, and then there was Harriet. She was the closest to my mother in age and temperament, being intelligent, an excellent linguist in French, German and Italian, but a born shop steward. At Fulneck, the distinguished Moravian settlement where both girls were at school, the bread was bad. Harriet showed a sample to her father. He got into his trap and faced the headmistress with it. Upheaval! Special School Assembly. 'Harriet Hainsworth, COME HERE'. I find it strange that the headmistress thought it right to take it out on the child. Wilhelmine was Head Girl at the time.

Gerda von Rheinbaben now appeared. Helena and she had been at school together at Chateau D'Oex and someone had asked Abimelech to take her so that she might learn English. She was a phenomenon. She was handsome, seductive, charming and clever, her father being a Doctor both of classics and of engineering, besides head of the Prussian diplomatic service. Not surprisingly she learned all that the Hainsworths could teach her in a couple of months. Soon after she went home, came a return invitation for Wilhelmine and Harriet. Little did they realise what was in store. They had failed to appreciate the full significance of the address when they showed it to the cabby at the Anhalter Station. The surprise at the Wilhelmstrasse was mutual. The Rheinbabens had meant to send a carriage, for unchaperoned girls did not take taxis in the Berlin of 1908; Yorkshire girls, per contra, did not expect the grandeur and flunkies of a full blown Prussian palace.

But they settled down somehow, and for several months they became entangled in the social life of the great houses. They could scarcely have had a better introduction, for old George von Rheinbaben, with his ancestry, his abilities and his official position, moved in the highest levels, while Gerda was the toast of Berlin. Subalterns fell over each other to be within her line of sight. The Emperor had to forbid at least one duel. She was at last, hustled to the altar by a Herr von Hohberg-Buchwald amid the plaudits of *le tout Berlin*.

It was at this time and at more than one point that Blumenthals entered my mother's life. In the first place one of them was found in bed with Gerda. In the social explosion that followed, the Emperor had to forbid another duel; the newspapers were full of the ensuing deliciously salacious divorce; and Gerda returned in disgrace to the unsympathetic arms of a Prussian mother, who asked dinner guests whether they objected to sitting next to her divorced daughter. Not surprisingly she escaped by marrying – a Blumenthal, but I am not sure if it was the same one, and left the Wilhemstrasse for Potsdam. They produced in due course, two accomplished and beautiful daughters, Alexandra and Marion who spoke English as well as their mother.

The social disasters broke poor Gerda. Born out of her time, she should have been a diplomat, a politician or a company director, but this was impossible in the Prussia of 1908. She was projected into a life of unhappy illness for which the birth of her daughters was no cure. Prussia was in some ways a terrible place. After the fall of the monarchies in 1918, the Prussian outlook seems to have softened. Berlin in the 1920s became reputedly a Sodom and Gomorrah, and the Reichswehr a Theban Golden Company, whose elegantly dragged soldiers were seen at balls with their officers. At any rate Alex and Marion became friendly with the Hohberg-Buchwalds. I do not know how he earned his living but with the rise of Hitler he became head of the Mounted SS. I gathered from Marion, with whom I became well acquainted in later life, that this was no more than a social and athletic club. I can well believe it, because in all the literature there is hardly any reference to it, and I have seen no pictures of it on parade. All the same someone in Hitler's entourage seems to have taken a different view, for during the 1933 *Putsch* against Rhoem and the SA, a squad appeared at the door. Alexandra and Marion happened to be staying with the Hohberg-Buchwalds at the time. They saw him cross the garden to the summer house with the officer in charge, and heard the pistol shot.

The combination of government by murder and the mutual dislike of Hitler and the aristocracies boded ill for Europe, which, however, failed to read the signs.

As the manner of 1908 was, the great houses organised house parties. These houses were huge establishments, usually with a Home Park or garden (though not on the lavish scale of the English) surrounded by immense farming acres dotted with hamlets, villages, and pine plantations. The soil of Brandenburg, Pomerania and Prussia is poor sandy stuff, and it needed large estates to make much of an economic impression. The north German landowner was rich, but not as rich as he seemed, for much of his apparent wealth came, still, in the form of services. This was feudal-seeming, though it was not true feudalism.

Thus the two Yorkshire girls found themselves, with Gerda, staying for weeks on end at country houses. The idea that a guest might stay for weeks, or even months, was, in that time and society, unremarkable. As late as 1937, my aunt Astrid von Kleist-Retzow asked whether she could come and stay at our Wentworth house for three weeks. The houses entertained, particularly by throwing balls. The families invited each other, and of course, each other's house guests.

These assemblies were major operations. The distances, a long half day's drive, had to be covered by convoys of carriages, the men and girls in the best of them, their valets and lady's maids with the luggage in the others. There would be tea, and then, in anticipation of a strenuous night, everyone would go to bed. 'Everyone' does not include the servants, who would be laying out. In the early evening there was a general bustle of dressing and washing, perfuming and chatter. The girls wore the long ball dresses with their widely flowing skirts: if they had been presented at court, these were cut fairly low. The men, apart, perhaps, from a few foreigners and a few (or many) officials, statesmen or diplomats, wore uniforms, for this was Prussia, a land without frontiers other than the ranks of her defenders, a land of regimentation and, unintelligible to civilian English imperialists, of military conscription. The uniforms were gorgeous: the Hussars with their pelisses and cording, the Garde Uhlan in blue with red facings, the Leibgarde zu Pferd in heavy white with thin blue threads and immense silver eagle-topped helmets.

The proceedings began with dinner at which, like as not, everyone ate and drank from silver. The ladies were allowed nothing but Champagne in my German grandfather's household: the gentlemen were expected to have a more delicate palate, and were served the finest Rhenish and Moselle, besides Burgundies halfway through, and the Champagne later on. This was a curious and too seldom remarked feature of aristocratic Prussia: the military brutes which were its symbol, were expected to have aesthetic and even romantic susceptibilities. Was not the All Highest, the Emperor and King, the arbiter of taste and the inspirer of a style? It was at such a dinner, given by Count Poninski, that every guest was presented with a vase of flowers. The blooms came, no doubt, from his hothouses: the vase was the finest blue-glazed Copenhagen. I have my mother's now.

These assemblies were not the idle extravagances of a pampered caste. They were a manner of conducting business and politics and the family alliances which were a common feature of both. Scandal, rumour, political and economic information circulated in the drawing rooms, while the couples waltzed and flirted in the halls. The great men, abetted by their wives and mothers, made deals between cigars and hands of *Skat*. Nor, actually, were the young people idle either. The arrangements and the detailed work was not left to the servants, who anyway had their daily routines. My father's sister, Nora von Lettow-Vorbeck, recalled how she used to spend all her spare time in the preceding fortnight making and bottling strong coffee which the dancers consumed by the gallon. Daughters of these houses, even if they were Susana Krafft von Delmensingen or the Countess Annette von Katznellenbogen, were highly trained as cooks, housekeepers, accountants, seamstresses and were often kept hard at work by stoney faced duennas, sewing, sewing, sewing. Meanwhile their brothers were *on Service* as cadets or subalterns on the square at Potsdam, Königsberg or Küstrin, learning their arduous vocation and laying the girls. *Dienst*, called service in the dictionaries, meant military service and nothing else. A notice at the Berlin Cadet School read, and for all I know still reads: 'Gentlemen should not necessarily expect a practical return from the ladies to whom they pay their attentions'.

My parents first met at one of these routs. My aunt Nora wanted my mother to talk English to her brother. He was not a tall upstanding cavalryman at all, but a spare civilian, the youngest son of a landowning Junker and a wealthy Hamburg patrician mother. He was handsome in the narrow faced dark way, common in Frenchman and Italians. He spoke both languages perfectly. He was a Rhodes scholar, the last ever nominated by the Kaiser, at Lincoln College, Oxford. They fell in love; and everybody said 'Why him?' He was *too* aesthetic and too little a brute for the Prussian taste. In England, of course he was a foreigner: worse still he was six years younger than she.

German connections with England had been close. In 1837, when Salic Law separated the Hanoverian and British crowns, my relative, Leonhard von Blumenthal, later Field-Marshal and Count, married a Miss Vyner, and the court with its matrimonial ramifications among the protestant German ruling houses, set an example among the bankers and other cosmopolitans like the Rothschilds. Such natural influences are still commemorated in pub and place names, like the *Prince of Teck* in the Earls Court Road, and Mecklenburgh Square, and they were not confined wholly to London. The Delius family came from Hamburg to Bradford: the Barings to Exeter.

All the same, they did not think much of it in Yorkshire. My mother's family were West Riding weavers. There had often been marriages between Gaunts, Yorkshiremen of Flemish extraction (Gaunt = Ghent), and Hainsworths who had lived in the West Riding since the sixteenth century. The charm came from the Hainsworths: the physical solidity through Elizabeth Gaunt. They had heaven knows how many brothers and sisters each, and the Hainsworth ones were mostly in need of help. The children of Farsley village were taught, for example by Hannah, an alarming dame whom Abimelech set up in a school house so that she could earn a living. Educationally it was not brilliant, but it kept Aunt Hannah out of Bim's hair and off the parish. Then there was the gentle sweet old Uncle Littlewood, who would appear at intervals because, somehow he found it difficult to pay his debts…

Abimelech and Elizabeth settled in a large house called 'Claremont' and while he developed the mill at the bottom of the village into his successful fine cloth business, she had her six children at the top. Facially this brood was striking rather than handsome, and in particular, my aunts had remarkable snub-nosed features which have shown up persistently in their descendents. Their attractiveness must have lain in speech and movement. My mother could dance like an angel, and she was all vivacity into middle life. Her childhood seems to have been happy. The mill hands all knew them, and they used to play up in the sorting lofts and bounce about on the bales, or sit beside the man whose job it was to scrutinise and perfect the cloth, pulled in ten-foot lengths over a beam, against the light.

All the same there were alarms: the Mill, like many others long since converted to steam, still had its pond, in which brother Gaunt was found floating face down. They hauled him out and dried him, and he lived until he was over 70.

And then there were the holidays. Abimelech may have been a demanding Victorian father but he was not oppressive and had money and imagination. He bought a farm at Pateley Bridge. The children were given animals – rabbits, guinea pigs, ponies – on the strict instruction that they looked after them themselves: the more animals, the less mischief. One, or perhaps several summers, they took a ramshackle house at Killiney, near Dublin, and rattled and bumped along the roads in, or rather on those back-to-back jaunting cars, then a feature of Irish life. The house was old, in beautiful scenery and full of mice, which scampered unconcernedly across the beds at night.

Mr Thomas Cook, a Baptist temperance campaigner, had run his first railway excursions in 1841, in the interests of sobriety and thrift. Abimelech, who was a teetotaler, and Elizabeth who was very much a Baptist, knew him and used his admirable facilities from time to time. He died in 1892, but there remained a friendly relationship with the concern. Hence an early package visit to Switzerland for all the family. Cooks laid on everything from rail tickets to hotel bookings, with picnic hampers where there was no restaurant car. They stayed at the Victoria Hotel at Beatenberg, an ornate brown wooden building with carved eaves, the likes of which have mostly disappeared.

Thus commenced my mother's roving habits, which were to give her a speaking familiarity with porters and sleeping car attendants all over West Europe, as well as a remarkable knowledge of foreign towns. I remember often getting off the train at some probable or improbable place and marching with total confidence round six corners into a hotel, a restaurant, a chemist or, on one occasion a locksmith. In the same *genre* strange railway officials addressed her by her name.

Abimelech seems to have started something. Other West Riding industrialists were soon organising travelling parties abroad. One of these, which Wilhelmine did not join, went to Italy. Brother Gaunt boarded the train at Stanningley and found it crowded to the eyes. An elderly man made a seat for him by taking his teenage daughter onto his knee. The object of sending Gaunt on this expedition was to find him a wife amongst the tribe of relatives which composed it. He naturally fell for the only stranger in the party. By London they had no thought for anyone else. Father must have had an uncomfortable journey. Gaunt married Gertrude about eighteen months later. They lived as nearly idyllic an existence as is possible in this imperfect world, until she died of some painful illness, a few years before he did.

The highlight of this time was Queen Victoria's diamond jubilee. Abimelech took rooms in Queen Victoria Street to watch the processions coming up the slope from Blackfriars. It took an enormous time, and they had to get to their rooms very early, before the excited and exalted crowds closed the approach. My mother handed down few details of that event, for she, poor thing was wracked with toothache, and Abimelech was furious because her misery prevented full appreciation – and besides, the whole affair, horse, foot and guns from five continents was so vast and extraordinary with its bands and bagpipes, its rajahs and nawabs clattering splendidly on their Arabs and barbs, and here comes the Prince of Wales, and Oh Lord! The German Emperor (the Queen's grandson), both in military splendour on either side of the six-horse landau in which SHE sat. She was a tiny figure in black, holding up a tiny lace parasol against the fierce Queen's weather sun and bowing jerkily to right and left while everybody yelled their bloomin' 'eads off. She seemed embarrassed by her triumph, or her long heart-broken seclusion had got her out of practice. It was rumoured that her seat had a special spring so that she was propelled forward to another bow whenever she leaned back. Toothache or no, the Jubilee remained a feature of the furniture of Wilhelmine's mind.

This procession and others had one thing in common. No motor vehicles. Yet Pater had seen his first car in Oxford in 1894, Wilhelmine hers at about the same time on Pateley Moor. They were soon common enough to be unremarkable. Perhaps there were horseless carriages in the Great Procession but perhaps too, in moments of high ceremony or deep reverence, mechanical, inorganic things have little place, and the human psyche reaches back to an older and more primitive level. The Roman priest (like his caveman ancestor) wore little, if anything, on *dies fasti*. Your modern high church parson at his altar, dresses up like a Roman official.

My stepfather was born in 1875, the eldest son of Frederick Arnold Baker and Helen, née Nairne. When I was reading law at Oxford, I stumbled across a case of 1777. The solicitors involved were Baker and Nairne, and at the time of Percy's childhood, his father – *The Governor* was the senior partner, and their offices were at Crosby Hall. I do not know when the Bank of England ceased to open new private accounts; but Baker and Nairne's account was always at the Bank, and they used those distinctive cheques directed to the Cashier of the Bank, beginning with the words 'Pray pay …'

Percy was the most unassuming of men: so unassuming indeed, that when he went to Winchester from Sandroyd in 1888, he entered the bottom class, and when, six years later instead of the usual five he left, he had not only not reached the top form but became nothing more important than the junior house praefect.

He was a very small man with long arms, hence 'Monkey Baker' and by reason of his small size, he coxed the house and school four, and, with his long arms and being no fool, he was an inspired fielder at cricket and a joy to watch in later life, for to field really well requires, besides a quick eye and an agile body, an instinct for the psychology and mechanics of the game. He knew where the batsman was going to hit the ball; when the bowler delivered it, Percy would be seen walking towards the spot where, if the batsman was at all likely to hit it in his quarter, he and the ball would meet. Sure as fate, they met. He almost never had to run for it.

Such a man was not likely to be ambitious or showy, and though he was not intellectual, he got himself, as I have said, into Oxford where because of the family legal background, he read law. He also, on one occasion, drove down the High St in a carriage and pair playing the trombone. I discovered the instrument under a bed. He would otherwise never have mentioned the fact. He had a number of small but distinct talents. He played tennis and golf rather well, and croquet, and he was a good shot. He had a passion for fishing – trout in Hampshire or, if he could get it, salmon on the Spey. He could play most card games, and he never let on how the three card trick worked. Besides the trombone, learned for the occasion, he played the piano very passably by ear, and the mandolin, the banjo and other instruments of that family. I have even seen him play the 'British Grenadiers' successfully, after half an hour's fiddling around, on a fife. Another of his pleasures, an ability inherited from the Nairnes, was to paint water colour landscapes. He did it only for fun, because he was brought up to think that art was not really a very serious profession, yet, if John Sell Cotman is anything by which to judge, he might have earned a passable reputation and perhaps a living as an artist. In fact, he used this talent as people now use a camera.

Percy's background was, like so many nineteenth century Englishmen's partly Indian. His mother's uncle, Sir Charles Nairne was Commander-in-Chief in India before he died in 1899, and some eighteenth century relatives, the Smarts, had had a shipyard at Millwall: the Bakers had a splendid picture, all cloudscape, of this Thames reach, with a Danish pink in full sail in the foreground, and a couple of ships abuilding on the Millwall slipways. I think that there were East India Company connections as well, because Percy's family houses were full of oriental things – gold, lacquer, ivory, carpets and so forth, and it was never said that all these things came by way of Sir Charles.

This sensible and assiduous person as usual, was in demand, and coxed the Magdalen eight with great success. He passed his Law Moderations. Then, with a remarkable sense of proportion, bearing in mind his skill and passion for sports, he refused a Blue. They wanted him to cox the Oxford boat. He thought that his law degree might suffer, for he wanted a Second. He sent himself to a crammer and got one. He was elected to the Leander Club, just the same. This was the year of the Jubilee, when he began his Articles in the firm. His father was irascible and domineering, and Percy, who never mentioned the subject, had a bad time even though he was actually articled to his father's Nairne partner.

My mother meanwhile had reached a finishing school at Southport. She was, by the standards of the day, well trained, and therefore needed nothing save polite accomplishments. It was a curious feature of her complex character that she was habitually exhibited to show off the school's advantages as a ballroom dancer; that she rapidly became Head Girl, as a person of character, who respected and was respected by the staff, and yet that she was so tortured by nerves that she could not utter a speech, nor pass a piano examination which all assured her that she could take in her stride.

It was at this moment that the first bolt fell from an almost clear sky. Her adored father was concussed on cobbles by a cyclist, and was unconscious for six weeks. When he came to, his genial oddities had turned into obstinate eccentricities. He was persistently furious with the newspapers for abruptly dating themselves six weeks later. He stopped paying the workpeople, who threatened to go on strike. He was evidently ill, but not so ill as to be certifiable. In these circumstances the household at 'Claremont' fell to pieces. Ethel was already married and set up. Gaunt and Charles were trying to keep the business afloat with a prematurely ageing backer, who had to be trapped into signing cheques. The two youngest sisters were not old enough to be much help. The strain was too much for Elizabeth. She had insisted on staying in the hospital where Abimelech was; the sight of so much suffering affected her overcharged mind. She became violent and hysterical. The faithful but unpaid servants stuck it out as long as they could and then, in a body, left. Wilhelmine was called suddenly from her schoolgirl success to a house of despair.

The first morning, she got up at five to do the housework. A major housemaid's chore, which I have done myself, was cleaning grates and laying fires. The job was tiresome and back breaking; you had to kneel, and the cold ash was apt to disintegrate into a fine dust which got all over the room. If the kitchen range had gone out, it had to be cleaned and relit first, because no cooking was possible until it was burning properly; but the stones inside it might be hot from the night before, and one might burn one's hands in the process of relaying it. There were no rubber gloves or firelighters. There was a special art in laying crumpled newspaper on the bars, and then dry sticks with some small coal on top and some more handy. You lit the paper and hoped that the wood would catch. Sometimes you had a bellows, which if indiscretely used, blew the whole lot out – or a back draft did it. Either way, or both, you had to start again.

After about 40 minutes, just as the range was beginning to burn properly, she heard her mother stumping down the stairs. It had for some time been the rule not to make any room fires at all. Elizabeth appeared like a tatterdemalion in the doorway, strode across the kitchen, filled a bucket, hurled its contents towards the range, filled another and hurled that, and then another and another, while Wilhelmine stood paralysed by the belief that interference might bring worse. The huge kitchen was half an inch deep in water and ash. Satisfied with her work, Elizabeth walked up the stairs chuckling. It took several days to dry the place out.

Abimelech recovered little by little, nursed by my mother and occasionally others while Elizabeth sat by, silently listening to the talk until she was tired. Then she would say 'rubbish' or 'why not?' or something equally laconic and walk out. Occasionally, as I have already mentioned, she behaved more strangely. Abimelech was, after a while, sufficiently recovered to be understanding about her condition. The trouble was that he was not invariably sound himself. Fecklessness and poverty had made a deep impression on his youth, and he had decided never to be dependent or poor. His brothers and sisters were not so determined, they constantly came forward to remind him of a past which he preferred to forget. His father, by the way, had been a widower, and on the day that he was married again to a local village girl, all the children, including Abimelech, left him.

Some of these habits of mind were exaggerated by the effects of his accident. Should people be self-reliant? 'Yes'; hence Wilhelmine's Basel adventure. Should money be saved? 'Yes', so the tradespeople went unpaid, and the house was besieged by brokers' men. He had a passion for bargains. 'Will-of-mine', my mother would apprehensively hear, 'Look outside and see what I've got for you?' Obediently she would look out, to behold a hearse and funeral carriages purchased 'very cheaply' at a bankrupt sale. Once he came home with 3,000 lithograph prints. He admired, rightly, the faculty of quick decision: 'Will-of-mine'. 'Yes, Father?' 'Will you come to Italy with me after lunch?' He would sulk if you showed the slightest hesitation, so they went to Italy. When they arrived his wallet was stolen. He was so incensed that they both went straight home again.

In later life my mother was rather like this. At breakfast one day, when I was thirteen, she said 'Let's go to Switzerland'. So we packed, rang a message to Percy's office, and caught the afternoon train from Victoria. Next day, at Zürich, it was pouring with rain. She got the Baur-au-lac to ring south to Chiasso. Pouring there too. She said, 'Let's go home'. So we went. We struggled from Victoria across to Waterloo, and caught a 5.30am workmen's train down to Virginia Water. Then we walked. We had forgotten to bring our keys, so I climbed in through the larder window. We made a great deal of noise and giggling, which brought down Percy with a shotgun.

Abimelech's long drawn out recovery continued to be punctuated by escapades. He could vanish. Somehow if you wanted 'Bim, and 'Bim did not want to be wanted, 'Bim was not there. In those days of sectarian intolerance and righteous indignation, he, a freethinker, invited the shepherds of all the rival flocks to tea. As the Vicar, the Roman Catholic priest, the ministers of the various embattled nonconformists, the clerk of the Quaker meeting, the Rabbis, grew more and more uncomfortable in the drawing room, Wilhelmine found, without surprise that the French window of his study was open. Fortunately there was enough tea to go round. It was the same when a cheque had to be signed or an awkward decision taken.

Things got better. This was partly due to the kindness of the Gaunt relations, especially of Elizabeth's hypochondriac brother John William. The Victorian horror of madness, divorce and bankruptcy exerted an immense pressure upon the rising moneyed society, which stood upon a floor so that it could concentrate on business. These things were disgraceful because they introduced the unpredictable into routines justifiable because they ministered to security: but supposing that there was no security anyway? The attitude to divorce and bankruptcy were of a piece. You kept your engagements. In the case of marriage, it was 'for better or for worse'. No decent person ever attempted to escape from it, however unreasonable, immoral or downright bad the other party might be. The husband might be drunk (with gin at 6d a pint) or spendthrift (gambling was rampant), or violent and with prostitutes everywhere, often adulterous or like Lord Randolph Churchill, syphilitic. The wife put up with it. She might be a slattern, cruel to the children, a termagant or a whore. He put up with it. Divorce was a scandal reflecting on 'innocent or guilty' alike. Some cast this idea into a theological mould, but Roman Catholic and protestant agreed with passion, if for different reasons on it. It subverted the moral as well as the physical foundations of life.

This attitude was not wholly dead in the 1950s when divorces were running at 40,000 a year. An acquaintance of mine refused to send his son to a particular house at Winchester because the housemaster, Ronald Hamilton, whom we both knew and liked, had been the *innocent* party in a wartime divorce.

To bankruptcy a similar stigma was attached. The word itself, like the four-letter words of the 1960s, was never spelled out. The stigma clung to families, which ritually cleansed themselves by despatching erring relatives (like my uncle Bob), to the colonies. During the second World War, an officer who failed to pay his mess bill within a week could still be ordered to resign his commission. A gentleman paid his debts. Quite right too.

Very little was known about madness. Nowadays Elizabeth would probably have got over it very soon. It involved no personal breach in the rules of society. Yet the unpredictability of the dotty was alarming and out of place. Vast numbers assumed that it was a visitation: the enlightened, which included, by then, most educated people, no longer thought this, but still did not know what to think. All the same, a family with someone who was 'not quite normal' was deemed unfortunate in a rather conspicuous and shaming manner.

So when the twin disasters stared the Abimelech Hainsworths in the face, Elizabeth's side of the family rallied round. The sons borrowed and borrowed from the Gaunts until the head of the family was able to manage. Morally, they had some claim, for Reuben Gaunt & Sons had profited immensely from Abimelech's early support, but it was touch and go, and Abimelech was never again completely reliable. I am not clear about what happened, but 40 years later, the interests had undergone a reversal. The Hainsworths and their descendents had important holdings in Reuben Gaunt & Sons, while A W Hainsworth & Sons was owned almost entirely by Gaunts. I suppose that the money could be repaid only by selling the shares to the creditor relatives, but that Abimelech's interest in the Gaunt firm was retained (perhaps he never got round to signing the transfers), and descended to his children.

At any rate, things began to calm down, and my mother resumed her interrupted education. She had music teachers, and became quite a competent player. Harriet and Helena reached school leaving age and came home to look after Father and Mother. Life was difficult but not impossible, and a little of the old magic sometimes returned. That life *was* comparatively normal can be shown by the fact that they had guests. Mother was quiescent. Father was charming. Hence the appearance of Gerda von Reinbaben.

Annex

The family's vast collective possessions are summarised in the following table, the product of research done in 1982. It does not include estates owned before 1299.

DISTRICT	NUMBER OF NAMED PROPERTIES 1299–1945
<u>Mark – Brandenburg</u>	
Prignitz (East)	10 plus 21 scattered hides
Old Mark	2
Prignitz (West)	3 plus 8 separated villages
Elsewhere	12
<u>Lower Lusatia</u>	3
<u>Mecklenburg</u>	2
<u>Halberstadt area</u>	2
<u>Silesia</u>	1
<u>Pomerania</u>	16
<u>West Prussia</u>	2
TOTALS	53 29

The least considerable was my father's estate at Schlönwitz near Stolp (600 acres): the richest, Vehlow in the Prignitz now has 80,000 inhabitants. Paretz (Potsdam) and Steinhofel (East of Berlin) are still palatial. Horst was held for 600 years before 1833. Varzin and Wendisch Puddiger were sold to Bizmarck, Suckow and Paretz to the Hohenzollerns. The rule of equal partition between sons prevented all the properties being in one hand, but battle and disease kept the numbers of inheritors down. Everything was lost in 1945. The communists wrecked nearly all the manors and desecrated the churches.

Chapter 2

PARENTAL ENGAGEMENT

Wilhelmine and Harriet did a good deal of miscellaneous travelling in middle Germany. Our lives are full of coincidences. This was before she got to know my father's family. One of her friends was a sweet girl, later by godmother, called Irene Kühne. Irene invited her to stay at Wanzleben, the family farm near Magdeburg. This estate had been connected with the history of the Blumenthal properties some centuries before: and very recently a Blumenthal had worked there. Incidentally, the crest of the Blumenthal arms is, like the famous blazon of the nearby city of Magdeburg, a girl holding up a virgin wreath.

Wanzleben, a fortified hamlet, became the central office under the communists of an agricultural cooperative. It was in rich well watered lands and in my mother's time, the family, servants, farm labourers, bailiffs, horses and agricultural equipment were all housed within. Erich Kühne's bedroom was over the gate: if he was not already up by 5.00am the carts on the way to work soon drew him to the window. Sometimes people evaded this watchful patronage. My mother once told an obscure story, of how she and Irene escaped on a night ramble. I never got to the bottom of this, but I sometimes wonder how much rambling they really did.

This was not a Prussian household, and one of the differences between Prussia and Saxony was that the aristocracy was much less in evidence in the latter. The Saxon landowner might be as demanding and autocratic as his Prussian colleague, but he lived much more closely with his tenants and workpeople, and, like Erich Kühne, he was often untitled, and had no society distractions. The difference was illustrated daily in almost dramatic fashion.

At the Wanzleben mid-day spread; father Kühne sat at one end of a huge table: his sons and daughters were ranged in order of age down to the youngest in its highchair next to mother Kühne. Beyond them, but still at the same table, were the bailiff, one or two other senior farm servants, and perhaps factors and visiting trades people. Opposite the family were the guests. Erich dispensed food and talk intermingled with chaff and reproof to the children and shouted instructions to the bailiff, while a kitchen hand brought beer brewed in the house. It was patriarchal, co-operative and a trifle steamy. 'Sowass gibts nicht in Hinterpommern'. 'That sort of thing isn't done in Upper Pomerania' was the equivalent of 'we don't think much of that in Yorkshire'. In Prussian households of exactly the same economic purpose, the principal meal would be formally announced in the evening. The bailiff, if he ever ate in the house at all, would eat in the kitchen and report to the Lord in his study. The atmosphere was cooler and the butler brought wine. There was a gap between the masters and men in both countries, but it was socially emphasised in Prussia. The difference can be illustrated in another way. The Prussians respected their kings, but it never occurred to them that they might be likeable – even when, sometimes, they were. Some Prussian rulers preferred to speak French rather than German, though the story that Frederick the Great could not speak German at all, is as my family archives prove, a myth. The Saxon monarchs, on the other hand, managed to be at once more cultivated and more down to earth. Augustus, demurely called the Strong, inspired most of the glories of Dresden Baroque, and the exquisite products of Meissen. He also had nearly 300 children. The last king of Saxony spoke broad dialect even in public, to the proud amusement of his people, yet Leipzig and Dresden, under court patronage, were the chief musical centres of Germany, where you heard the best music and sat at the feet of the best teachers; where, except for Mittenwald violins, they made the best instruments, and where they printed most of the world's supply of scores.

Everyone brings to his view of a country, the prejudices, the assumptions and the blind spots of his own. The English view of Germany is unsurprisingly coloured by the twentieth century wars. The consequent misinterpretations have included an assumption that she is one country. Despite tyranny, migrations and defeats, she is not a unity now and was still less in 1900.

Linguistically unified written prose was achieved only at the end of the eighteenth century with Goethe, but the common speech remained fragmented into often mutually incomprehensible dialects, no one of which had a leading status. By 1900, the best that anyone could manage was to use the Hanoverian as a kind of *lingua franca*, and it is this which is taught in foreign schools and used in the media. It was, indeed, the kind of German which I learned myself, but in Hanover the dustmen and the Dukes speak it without a second thought. To speak in dialect is neither quaint nor socially embarrassing, but it still creates difficulties. The spoken *Platdeutsch* of the Baltic coast and the *Boarisch* of Upper Bavaria differ as much as Danish and English.

One of the misfortunes of Germany was the fragmentation into unimportance of Saxony. The Kings of 'Saxony' were kings only of a territorial rump. Erich

Kühne's predecessors were 'Musspreussen' – compulsory Prussians – in the Prussian province of Saxony, but for Erich the memory of the King over the border was growing weak; and further south, the impotent Thuringian principalities, such as the Saxe-Coburgs, served to ensure that the Saxons could no longer make the political running, or restrain the Prussians, and eked out their perilous autonomy by exporting maps, genealogical almanacs and marriageable Highnesses.

Modern Prussia was a miniature empire within an empire. It sprawled across two thirds of imperial Germany, but the sprawl contained large subject populations, not all in tune with the ruling power. The absence of genuine frontiers and its peculiar history, made it in some ways cosmopolitan. Berlin and Hamburg contained many people of Huguenot origin and French words in their dialect; most of the eastern landowning families, if not actually Polish, had Polish ancestors – I have myself. In Pomerania there were Swedish aristocrats, not to mention Scots. The regimental marches of most of the units based on Königsberg were Russian. The Moltkes, archetypal Prussian staff officers came from Mecklenburg. Even the Province of Saxony was not uniform: Magdeburg had fallen to Prussia in the seventeenth century, but the southern part, annexed only in 1866, still resented it. There were also semi-submerged pockets of Obotrites and Wends, some still coherent enough, as late as 1935, (as at Cottbus) to retain their own incomprehensible language. Moreover since 1740 there had been frequent changes and rearrangements of territory and sovereignty, so that a family might never move house, yet have three different nationalities in as many generations.

There was, besides, the Diaspora. The Baltic provinces of Russia were ruled by German planters descended from the crusading Knights who retained their Teutonic habits and intermarried with their cousins across the frontier. They gave German names to people and things. If you meet someone called Erdwurm (worm) or Holzwurst (wooden sausage), he will probably be a Latvian or Estonian, whose servile ancestor was whimsically named by his knightly lord. The new Russian capital, St Petersburg, had a German name and so had the local constellation of places (Kronstadt, Schlüsselburg, Oranienbaum) echoing the villages of Catherine the Great's native Anhalt. She, after all was wholly German and many of her bedfellows and advisers were German too. The Balts provided talent for the bureaucracy, graded (as it still is) on the model of a German army, as well as the officers for the British trained, Russian navy. Thus the foreigner of German origin, though not a Prussian, was a cousin or a friend, in whose affairs one had a natural concern. The Habsburg empire was maintained by a German minority. A Hohenzollern occupied the throne of Roumania. Prague, Riga, Temesvar, Cracow and Trent figured unconcernedly in the conversation.

Wilhelmine got on well in German society, and she and a Prussian fell in love. The Prussians were used to foreigners and to English marriages from the Emperor Frederick and Daisy Pless down to the Blumenthals themselves. All the same, there was opposition in both families.

On the Prussian side, this stemmed from xenophobia. That the Prussian aristocracy could be both cosmopolitan and xenophobic is not a paradox. Knowledge and understanding do not necessarily bring people close together; you may dislike a person once you perceive or think you perceive his real character. The Prussian cornflower was not so much a patriotic as an anti-French symbol. The, doubtless apocryphal, story of its origin is as follows. The heroic Queen Louise of Prussia was hiding with her children in a field of standing corn from French dragoons. To keep the children quiet, she set them to picking cornflowers. They kept quiet. The dragoons passed and Prussia was saved. The Brandenburg-Prussian state was organised as a reaction to conflict with the Swedes. Russian troops occupied Berlin in 1759 as well as 1945. Indeed it might be said that Prussia was an institutionalised xenophobia. My son Henry has observed that unlike Italy and India which at times have been geographical ideas, Prussia has always been an idea without a place.

The Yorkshire opposition had a different character. It was not knowledge but ignorance of foreigners, with their funny ways, peculiar talk and probably immoral proclivities which stood in the way, but alongside this was the companionship which had grown up between Abimelech and Wilhelmine.

He was not provincial, nor did he entertain the irrational prejudices common in Yorkshire at that time and since. His trouble was that his wife was too withdrawn to be companionable, and he had more in common with Wilhelmine than with his other children. He was a brave, odd, honourable man facing the threat of loneliness.

When Albrecht came up to Farsley in 1911 to ask for my mother's hand, Abimelech's first reaction was to challenge him to a game of billiards. In reply to a question, Albrecht told him that his own father was against the alliance too. Neither side, as will appear, had anything against the other beloved's intended. Albrecht made himself very agreeable to everyone, and took Elizabeth for silent, hour-long understanding walks. Eventually Abimelech laid it down that if the pair would refrain from seeing each other for a year, and remained of the same mind, he would withdraw his opposition. Wilhelmine accepted this, though at 28, she could have defied him. Albrecht's father agreed.

The two fathers were at cross purposes. Abimelech was postponing a step which would become irrevocable at some future date; but in Prussian social practice, the important step was the engagement, which a subsequent wedding only served to confirm. Albrecht's father was thus confronted with a problem of much greater immediacy than Abimelech's had been. A broken engagement was as scandalous in Prussia as a divorce in England.

Chapter 3

NEW LIFE

I believe that during the year of separation Albrecht first came into the orbit of the well known poet Stefan George (pronounced Gay-Orgë). Germany is full of masters and disciples, and George was a person who needed a following. Being a strong personality and magnificently handsome. Wilhelmine was, after the end of the close season, jealous, though interestingly, I am told that the *Georgearchiv* at Stuttgart contains not only many letters from Albrecht but a number from her.

I am not much of a judge of poetry (too frivolous) but I would have thought that his kind would have appealed to the German country-bound aristocracy. I wonder if eventually it did, but not before the end of the First World War. The trouble was that they more than half suspected him of seducing his young friends, and so allowed scandal to blind their literary critical faculties. Perhaps, anyhow, this was why my German grandfather decided to welcome the marriage. English she might be, but at least she was the right sex.

I must now give notice that there will be more about Stefan George later in this account, for, as it turned out, the aristocrats, let alone Wilhelmine and my grandfather grossly misjudged the man. The aristocracy was the only real and practical opposition to Hitler, ultimately in the shape of the failed July 1945 conspiracy. With a country infested by informers, the participants were secretive and their moves and conversations necessarily unrecorded, save a little (and prejudiced) by their enemies, but so far as I can see, George was the inspirer, perhaps the unforeseen brain of the movement. He had got into the good books of the better aristocrats. Count Stauffenberg and Adam von Trott zu Solz were friends of his, and friends of my family; indeed Werner stayed with the Stauffenbergs in 1935, and my father was, I believe an active and at the last a martyred collaborator in the conspiracy.

The wedding trousseau was enormous. Abimelech had sized up these Prussians and did his daughter proud. It reminds me of the Swiss hotel proprietor turned mercenary called Bluntschli in *Arms and the Man*. he, you will remember, asked his Balkan hostess how many table cloths she had, and when she said 'about a dozen', he said cheerfully, 'I've got 3,000'. I have some of it still. Everything in double-dozens, sheets, cutlery, even boot-bags had to be marked with the Blumenthal B surmounted by the seven-spiked baronial coronet (five for nobles by patent, who wrote out the 'von' in full, seven for the ancient families who only wrote 'v', nine for counts. After that you started on arches). The damask table-napkins were specially woven. I reckon that they still, with luck, have another 50 years of life. There was furniture, glass, china, not to mention clothes, and the whole lot was enclosed in packing safely carpentered, for delivery in Germany.

Then there were the social negotiations. Albrecht's father did not want to come to Farsley, and obviously, if the wedding were there, Abimelech would have had to be present. But he did not want to differ from his opposite number more than he could help: it might create problems for Wilhelmine later, and it might be interpreted as an admission of inequality.

The ceremony had to be in England, because of the rigid rule that weddings were given by the bride's parents, so Albrecht and Wilhelmine settled upon Bonchurch. Albrecht established a nominal residence there, and there they were married at an Anglican church; and as the parents were absent, my mother was given away by her brother Gaunt. The occasion was remarkable in another fashion. This teetotal family, all of which had signed the pledge drank Champagne provided by a naughty cousin. Then Albrecht and Wilhelmine stayed on for their honeymoon, and had their first quarrel.

The trouble, I think, was that their mutual attraction was physical, and the year's moratorium had prevented them from getting to know each other really well. Had they had better opportunities for commitment, they might have had fewer dangerous commitments, for such there were. In the first place, my mother wanted ardently to retain her British nationality: indeed she had an interview, abortive of course, at the Home Office. In the legal circumstances of the time it was inevitable that she would, at the altar, become a German. But supposing that it had been otherwise, it would have strengthened with legal realities, the matrimonial reservations which they both felt. Secondly, he was sexually experienced but she was not. It seems that he conducted their first love-making with delicacy and charm, but the whole thing represented an entry into a new life, which was unfamiliar and too difficult for her to understand until long after it was too late. In the third place, there was an issue of good faith. She had been bitterly affronted by her new father-in-law's opposition. Abimelech had been, so one is told, extremely courteous in his. Albrecht, however, had shown Wilhelmine some of his father's letters on the subject. I have no idea what they contained, but as a result Wilhelmine had tried to impose a condition, that she should never be expected to stay under the same roof with him. When people are in love, they do strange, and sometimes unwise things: Albrecht should never have shown her the letters, which must have been confidential. It was a breach of faith towards his own people. The habits of Prussian society were well known, by now, to Wilhelmine, and she must have known that the condition was unreasonable. She believed (though I do not) that Albrecht accepted it. In entering the matrimonial state, she hoped to tear Albrecht up by the roots.

Albrecht was in some ways ready to be torn. His dead mother, it is said, had spoiled him, and at some period, probably when he was at the university, he had already fallen out with his father. The Stefan George connection doubtless had something to do with it, and he had Jewish friends. This touched the Blumenthals on the raw, because Blumenthal without the inconspicuous 'v' is by the effect of the Josephan Decree, a Jewish name. Until about 1783 almost all Jews in the Holy Roman Empire were called Israel. In requiring them all to take differentiated surnames, the decree laid down that if a Jew wanted to take a surname already used by a Christian, he had to pay the Christian for the right to do so. The v. Blumenthals of the period did well out of this trade, and some, just before the French revolutionary wars, became rich on it.

My ancestors were not anti-Semitic[*] but there was a certain atmosphere of anti-Semitism in Prussian life, and they did not want to suffer its disadvantages. On top of all this, Albrecht was a learned person too much caught up with the attitudes of the German Academe, in whose groves the initiated congratulated each other on not being as other men are. Between most of the professors and most of the rulers, there was a deep gulf, kept open by, respectively, intellectual and aristocratic contempt. The Professor in Germany was a respected figure, who rather like Stefan George, deliberately courted a popular following, and, since universities were in towns, this following had an urban character. The title 'Professor' is common and signified simply one who taught on the staff of a university. The German townsmen could rise to affluence through trade, but aristocratic tradition forbade the nobleman to trade in anything save the produce of his own land. Then there were the student corporations which regulated the duelling. You always accepted an ordinary challenge, for fun; it only involved getting your face cut open. A challenge after a quarrel was more serious. Reconciliation apart, the parties fought stripped to the waist. Injuries were often serious: deaths, however, very rare. This barbarism maintained a strong grip on public opinion, for it provided, in facial disfigurement, a lifelong red badge of courage and it also represented a defiance of academic ideals. It died hard. The Weimar Republic made it illegal, but it continued to flourish merrily and almost openly, until the Nazi government legalised it again. The

---

[*] When the German Conservatives adopted anti-semitism, a Blumenthal alone spoke against the motion.

academics retaliated. The fine flower of German civilisation was in its towns. The Reich might need an army to defend that civilisation. If that army chose to have a facially scarred hereditary officer caste, that was its own affair. Civilised people did not become professional soldiers anyway. Moreover the army was getting too big for its boots. Its function was ancillary to the society which it was supposed to protect. The aristocratic relatives of its officers were far too brutal and stupid to rule sensibly.

The Emperor William II, the notorious Kaiser Bill, attempted, in his ham-handed fashion, to moderate these hatreds. He upset the court nobility by giving social countenance to Jewish financiers and businessmen, some of whom he ennobled. There was, perhaps is, a family of von Blumenthals as well as a family of v. Blumenthals. He honoured the occasional artist, and he took a clumsy and wrong-headed interest in academic affairs. As I have already said, he encouraged an aesthetic style. It is customary nowadays to denigrate the taste of the Wilhelminian era, and I find it oppressive, but it had a unity, like the Empire style of the first Bonaparte. It was assertive, difficult to ignore, and over ornamented. In Berlin the Victory Column and the *Kaiser Wilhelm Gedächtniskirche* (The memorial church to his father) are flamboyant, if wildly dissimilar examples of it. You find it, too, in the jewellery, glass, furniture and porcelain of the time. We had a patriotic vase, possibly capable of holding a bunch of snowdrops: it is in white and cornflower blue and gold, with a very demanding black Iron Cross on the front which would kill any flowers that one was unwise enough to put in it.

Moreover, the Emperor was himself a misfit, straining after effects too. His withered arm apparently stunted his character, particularly by inducing a pushing flamboyance. This view was widely held among the aristocracy, many of whom, of course, knew him well, and disliked him personally. It seems a plausible theory but cannot be proved because it involves a historical might-have-been. Had William been physically normal, would he *not* have put his private regiment in to search his mother's correspondence? Would he *not* have signed the *Bjorko* convention? Would he *not* with constitutional punctilio have dropped the pilot?

Now my father, with his own withered arm was an aristocrat who had strayed into the bourgeois academic field. I imagine that he must have been lonely; his background would have militated against full-blooded acceptance by his chosen associates, while his choice alienated him from his relatives. Yet he had to make his way, like his Emperor, and he was proud of his country and its people and achievements. Hegel, Goethe, Savigny, Mommsen were emblazoned on the breast of his eagle, as well as *Gott mit Uns*. And, of course, being a German academic, he was sometimes maddeningly pedantic.

When I knew him, he had developed Dupuytren's contracture of the left hand. The cause of this condition, first described in the 1830s was and (2002) is, still unknown, and modern surgery can alleviate, but cannot guarantee to cure it. Before World War II such surgical techniques did not exist at all, and the sufferer's hands, beginning with the one least used, closed over the years into a tight lock. My brother had to have both hands operated, and lost a finger. I have been luckier. Only one hand has had to be done so far. It is a painful operation, and afterwards one lives in one's bed with the affected hand, suspended day and night above one's head on a gantry.

And so back, by way of social etiquette, to their first evening at Bonchurch. They were sorting out the wedding telegrams after dinner. He said that he would reply to them. She said that she would. He insisted. So, you will not be surprised to learn, did she. She said that in England wives always did such things. He said that England or no England, she was now German, and such business was always done by German husbands. They had a flaming row, in which, no doubt, she became more and more strident, and he, according to her, more and more prissily withdrawn. She often alluded to it in later life. All the same, she had a strong feeling for duty, and she was madly in love.

The surrender of that first night was a commitment which led to others. In due course, they went to Germany and Albrecht took her to his father's house. She later said that she went unwillingly, and held it against him as a breach of faith: but I think that this represented a view from the other end of the bridge. In fact, it was a tremendous and rare celebration, and I believe that my grandfather staged it, not only as a public recognition of his new foreign daughter-in-law, but as a reconciliation with his estranged youngest son.

German brides wore their wedding dresses at functions for a year after the wedding, and took precedence of other women of equal rank. Albrecht and Wilhelmine arrived in high feather by train at Tantow. They were met by an open carriage procession with outriders, and made their way towards Staffelde, the main family estate. Other people's villagers turned out to watch. There was the bailiff under a decorated arch, with respectful greetings, to the Baroness. She had forgotten that that was what she now was, though the Blumenthals never used the title in reference to each other.

Then on they went – to the village with more arches and cheering tenants, and then up the hillside to the Schloss, with Vally v Blumenthal, Lord Over Staffelde, at the top of the steps. Smiles, open arms, tears of emotion, and so through the door into the panelled hall. Here were Albrecht's brothers and sisters to be introduced, and all the servants in a semi-circle headed by Olweg the butler, Selli the cook, and Lila, my lady's maid, to be presented. And so finally, upstairs to the bridal suite to prepare for dinner.

On a velvet cushion was a diamond and platinum pendant of such delicacy and aesthetic tact that, again one wonders what kind of people these Prussians were. It is supported on a chain as strong and insubstantial as that other chain, composed of the sound of cats' footsteps, which for aeons bound Fenris the wolf. Vally had seen to it himself, with Friedländer, his jeweller, and had composed a graceful message to go with it.

Of course Wilhelmine wore it at the evening's banquet.

Chapter 4

ANCESTRY

Leonhard von Blumenthal, Count and Field-Marshal, one of the ablest men of his generation, in the intervals of winning wars, began a family history, and another Count in the family, Oscar, finished and published it in 1903. Leonhard's purpose was to bring members of the family together by giving them a common knowledge of each other and their achievements. I have seen two pictures of him. One, an official portrait of a great soldier – with something, just a hint, behind. The other occurs in Anton von Werner's ceremonial tableau of the founders of the Second Reich, with the Emperor William I, Moltke and Bismarck sitting sternly at the council table, the Crown Prince Frederick on his feet romantically exalted, Roon and Steinmetz standing weightily and grave, and then, out of keeping with the others, a puckish Leonhard in a posture so odd that it must have been characteristic: his short stiff beard is thrust ahead and he is leaning forward so far that one wonders if he is about to fall flat on his face.

This was the man who, as an Army Chief of Staff in 1866 and again in 1870 used, for the first time, the dangerous combination of strategic penetration and tactical flexibility which, allowing for the absence of motor vehicles, tanks and aircraft, was the *Blitzkrieg* of its day. The historian Willamowitz-Möllendorf has plausibly said that Leonhard was the only *Feldherr*[*] in either war who understood what he was doing. I think that he overstated the case: but other generals, whether Prussian, Saxon, Austrian or French, stuck to the military patterns already in use. Only Leonhard broke the mould. People of originality are apt to express themselves simply: At Hiller's on the Unter den Linden the Duke of Ujest thought that the Austrian infantry would be better than the Prussian in wooded country. 'No', said Leonhard, 'our officers are better trained than theirs'. 'And what about the open plains'? Said the Duke, 'I'm sorry for them, for we shall just shoot the poor fellows dead'.

In the 1970s the family history was taken up by Robert von Blumenthal, a doctor at Gundelsheim on the Neckar, and, on his death by his doctor son Ewald, who also died. Robert believed that he had traced the family origins back to

---

[*] I dislike this Anglicism of the difficult word *Feldherr*. The word has tactical or strategic not political implications, and might be rendered 'battlemaster' or, by contrast with Slavs lurking in bogs or forests, 'Lord of the Open Field'. Of many combinations consider *Feldzug*: campaign. *Schlachtfeld*: battlefield. *Feldwebel*: serjeant. *Feldzeug*: Military equipment.

a moment in 1180 when it acquired vineyards on the River Weser near Bremen. Climatically this is possible because the average temperature was higher in North Germany than it is now. It apparently abandoned its coat of arms to the Amendorfs for those which it uses now. The escutcheon shows a vine stock with leaves and grapes: a maiden, suggesting a connection with Magdeburg, as a crest, came later.

Henry and I both regarded Robert's account with some scepticism. It is not easy to account for a total historical blank between Bremen in 1180 and the family's reappearance in 1241 as witnesses to a margravial grant of lands to the Abbey of Lehnin near Kyritz in the Prignitz 150 forest miles further east, or the fact that there was at this time and still is a village called Blumenthal near Kyritz. Henry and I have visited it and stayed in a nearby hamlet called Rosenwinkel, later a family estate. It seems likely (certainly not impossible) that the family took its name from Blumenthal, not Blumenthal from them.

At this period they had the more Dutch sounding form of the name, that is Bloemendal, and there is to this day a village called Blomendal in the Rhineland. There is also a Blumenthal, not to mention a Brandenburg, in the Grand Duchy of Luxemburg. The confused evidence is by no means simplified by the established fact that the Germans migrated aggressively if slowly eastwards on a broad front at right angles to the Baltic or by a tradition that they had already reached the Prignitz in the tenth century. The area was bitterly contested for generations with the indigenous Wends, and was first reduced to order after King Lothar installed Albert the Bear as Margrave in 1134. He imported knightly families who built castles while his coadjutor, Bishop Anselm of Havelberg imported priests and built churches. The family's original seat at Blumenthal soon included Kyritz with Vehlow and Horst.

Henry has developed a theory about this. Horst, name of the family castle and mansion for about six centuries is amongst other things a word meaning a mount or artificial hillock on a coast, and this may corroborate the view that the family started from some point on the Dutch or Flemish coast. The area is very wet and interleaved with lakes, and land drainage was a necessity for substantial settlements. Hence, the argument runs, the Margrave may deliberately have imported colonists who were not only knights but people with experience of land drainage, as the coastal inhabitants of Holland and Flanders undoubtedly had. It is, after all, common for immigrants to name a place after something which they knew back home. I met an American once in the train who looked out of the window and said 'Gee you've got a Boston too'. Land drainage does in fact figure considerably in the family history and archives.

There is however, a splendidly flamboyant legend about them which it is fun to quote. After the murder, in the third century of the soldier emperor Florian, his sons fled across the Alps and introduced viticulture to the hitherto beer-swilling aboriginals. It was then prophesied that after a thousand years 'an emperor of the Romans would arise from the seed of Florian, who would place judges over the Parthians and Persians, subject the Franks and Germans to Roman law, drive the barbarians out of all Asia, appoint a governor over Ceylon, who would give the law to all the Sarmatians (Poles? Russians?). He would subject to his rule all the conquered peoples of the earth, but would then return the sovereignty to the Senate and rule according to the laws of the Republic. He would live for 120 years and die without heirs'.

Theodor Mommsen sent the text of this prophecy to Leonhard and it, and the rest of the legend contain, let us face it, difficulties. The only so-called emperor Florian was a praetorian prefect, who was proclaimed emperor by some mutinous troops in Asia Minor and murdered after a few months in 276. The prophet's ambitious political programme seems to have gone wrong somewhere. Various Blumenthal's certainly administered Roman law over a few Germans from time to time, and gave the law to the odd Sarmatian, though the nearest that any of them got to Ceylon was my uncle Bob on his Lloyd-Amerika passages (First class out, steerage home) between Hamburg and New Guinea.

All the same the story *does* seem to have one connection with something real. There was a castle called Blumenthal in the Lugnez valley near Ilanz in the Swiss Engadine, and a family of Blumenthals still living there at the end of the nineteenth century. In 1881 Vally got in touch with them. He stayed with a Colonel v Hess-Castelberg at Disentis. The colonel had married Lady (Freiin) Anna v. Blumenthal and there was a small number of relatives living round about. In 1273 their ancestor Christian Peter was brought in by Rudolf of Habsburg as a feudatory and hereditary sheriff. They later became vassals of the bishops of Chur. Another tradition said that they went on a pilgrimage to Rome, and decided not to go all the way home. These two versions add up, but do not square with the heraldry, for the Swiss Blumenthal arms (three horns issuing from mounds) do not remotely resemble mine. I doubt if it matters. In 1996 Henry contacted their descendants, who preserved the memory of Vally's visit. They asked Henry whether he could help them to bid for some Scotch heifers, which he did. It shortly emerged that, outside Britain, the only centre of Mad Cow disease was in this Swiss canton. It is natural to hope that this is a mere coincidence.

The family history is intimately connected with the manors and estates which its members bought, managed, cultivated, inherited and sold or gave away. I have found it convenient to deal with the various branches of the family under the names of these places, beginning with Horst and ending with Staffelde. All of them were in the new Poland or in a communist East Germany, so the family lost all its lands at the end of World War II.

HORST

It would not be surprising if the Swiss Blumenthals had not wanted to go home. True, the Blumenthals farmed their lands, cleared new acres and lived at Horst for six centuries, but the area was disputed between the Ascanian Margraves of Brandenburg, with whom the Blumenthals threw in their lot, and Slav or Wendish Mecklenburg. The wars in the Prignitz went on and on. In 1320, when the Ascanians died out, Germany was in dynastic confusion: the northern areas were being ravaged by Polish armies, there were Papal interdicts, and the partisans of the False Waldemar added to the general terror and rapine. During these hard times the Blomendals were showing a largely military talent for survival, turning imperceptibly into Blumenthals and enlarging their estates. In 1411 the Emperor Sigismund appointed the Burgrave of Nuremberg, Frederick of Hohenzollern governor of the Mark. He held an assembly of the nobles other than the Havellanders and with the assistance of the Archbishop of Magdeburg and some shrewd bargaining, he won enough support to put the Havellanders down.

The powerful Blumenthals had already been in Brandenburg for two centuries before the Hohenzollerns appeared, and they acted for Frederick who was invested Elector at the Council of Constance in 1416. In 1420 Otto (I) v Blumenthal negotiated a three year truce on the western (Mecklenurg) frontier while Frederick was fighting a northern war with the Pomeranians. The spasmodically renewed truce was a trifle thin. Both sides lifted cattle and burned each others villages. Such raids represented the earliest contacts between the Moltkes and the Blumenthals,* who also kidnapped Reymer v Plessen. The forays continued at least till 1478 and the family did well out of them. By 1441 Frederick I had mortgaged Arneburg, a strategic castle on the Elbe to the sons of Otto (II), so evidently they were in the money. In 1486 the Elector Albert Cicero gave the brothers Otto (III) and Hans (I), five new manors, and the family accumulation came into the hands of Hans (II) who married Ottilie v Bredow. She gave birth in 1490 at Horst to the remarkable George, their second child.

The Elector Albert Cicero founded Prussian success even if no 'Prussia' was recognisable at the time, for he conceived with George the educational policy which eventually made the local aristocracy the best educated and most successful in Europe. He was sending his nobles to South German and Italian universities to read

---

* But the latest was in 2001when the Moltkes gave an organ to the Temple Church in London. I went to the ceremony.

law so as to supply the state with civil servants and judges. He planned a new university at Frankfurt-on-the-Oder but died before it could be set up, and his son Joachim I founded it in 1505. George was one of its first students, besides acting as the Bishop of Lebus' university treasurer. He became Dean of Lebus in 1512 and in 1513 Rector of the university besides a Doctor of Both Laws, a lifelong friend of Joachim I whom he accompanied to Imperial diets.

He made more than a local impression, for in 1520 the chapter of the vacant see of Havelberg elected him Bishop and the Papacy confirmed the election. Joachim however, would have none of it. In his view, Havelberg and Brandenburg should be held together, so George had to wait. In 1524 he was elected to Lebus and presently too to the islanded Prince Bishopric of Ratzeburg to the west of Mecklenburg, with its fortress cathedral and its seat, as of right in the imperial diet.

George looked more like one of the Gloriana's desperadoes than a clergyman, and led his troops, for example, in the Danish war of 1526, but he was a convinced Romanist in that particularly riotous period of the Reformation, and was twice besieged in his Episcopal fortresses. He died, in his bed, however, in 1550.

His brothers' descendents included politicians, diplomats, and heiresses. There was at this juncture and for nearly 150 years no organised army so soldiers came later. Meanwhile the family extended its estates by reclamation, or improved productivity by scientific husbandry, and they took their wives from and married their sisters and daughters into other similar families. The names have persisted: for example Königsmarck (one of whom was murdered for going to bed with King George I's Queen), Hindenburg, Jagow (diplomats), Plessen (old enemies), Kleist and Schlegel (literary families), Bonin (explorers), Lettow and Podewils (politicians and landowners). Not all the connections were Prussian. The Seidlitz were Silesians, a Blumenthal married in Sweden, and Leonhard and my father married Englishwomen.

PRÖTTLIN

While accidents, war, health or sterility shifted the descent of property from one line of noble inheritance to another, the Elector became King in Prussia in 1701. A distinctively 'Prussian' state, however, had been emerging from the pressures of disorder for nearly a century, and a Blumenthal was again at the bottom of it. This was Joachim Frederick (I) who at a very early age became, in effect if not in name, war minister, and in 1639 was involved in a military fiasco. Hitherto the Electorate had always relied on the feudal host, or on hired troops. Joachim Frederick was thus really an overseer of contracts. He appointed his Saxon wife's father as general. The General turned out to be lazy, incompetent and corrupt and his men ill disciplined.

When the Great Elector assumed the Bonnet in 1640 he abandoned the hitherto pro-Austrian policy, so Joachim Frederick resigned in 1641 and offered his services to the Court of Vienna, which snapped him up. He became their minister of war and was also involved in the complicated affairs of Cleves, Jülich and Berg. These with their Rhenish tolls, and huge brown-coal quarries were to form an important element in Prussian history. He was a great success with the Austrians: he led their diplomatic mission in the Westphalian negotiations and became an imperial Baron (*Reichsfreiherr*) in 1646, but stayed on good terms with his Prince, for whom he performed occasional services. Hence, when he came home he was made governor of Halberstadt, and his talents were put to wider use on the Elector's Council.

Peace was the commonsense objective. He analysed the financial confusion of the state, and propounded a package of solutions which evolved from a first trial at Halberstadt and held good for three centuries. The nobility became permanently liable for the land taxes without any right to refuse supply, but received in return a duty and a monopoly of paid commissioned service in the army, and virtual autonomy in the civil administration of their estates. Free movement being incompatible with this, the tenantry became serfs attached to the land, and the towns were closed to immigration save by foreigners.

The state could now pay its debts, but the changes were not as oppressive upon the rural population as they seem. There would be an army to protect it from such horrors as the Thirty Years War, and in the new tranquility there was plenty of timber to be exploited and land to be reclaimed. When the war really ended (1648-1651) there was, as after World War II, a universal desire to get on with the job, and if the legal status of the tenantry was technically depressed, they shared in the long land boom. Hence they never tried to rebel. The military institutions reflected this situation. The aristocratic officer could theoretically assault an underling as much as he liked as long as he did not kill or maim him or rape her. Frederick the Great's father habitually treated his son thus. Yet Voltaire, who had been thrashed by the bravoes of the Chevalier de Rohan, escaped to Berlin because it was relatively liberal. In the army a blunt sword called a *Klinge* was used for beatings, but a trooper called Wille who had had altogether at least a thousand strokes of the Klinge, performed prodigies of bravery to rescue his Blumenthal colonel at the Battle of Lobositz. Frederick the Great had no difficulty in animating his small army before his spectacular victory at Leuthen. Thus the law may have sanctioned barbarities, but actually they were neither common nor burdensome.

On the other hand, a very high standard of leadership and courage was expected of the nobles. With war at a range of 60 feet, the advantages of their commissioned monopoly were limited. I know of eleven Blumenthals at the least, who fell in battle between the relief of Vienna in 1683 and the end of the Franco-Prussian War of 1870-1. There were undoubtedly others. In addition Count Hans-Jürgen was hanged in 1944 for his part in Oster's plot against Hitler, and my cousin Ruthger, a naval officer, was blinded when the *Scharnhorst* and *Gneisenau* passed the Straits of Dover in 1942.

For a policy of recovery, a compact and well equipped army was a useful shield, but the Elector and Waldeck his minister, had wider ambitions. In 1651 they put the troops into Cleves, Jülich and Berg, and in 1653 sent Joachim Frederick to argue about it with the Austrians at an Imperial Diet. To him it was a hateful and wrong-headed task. Why did he accept the job? The answer is a human one. He was better at managing other people's affairs than his own. He had been away too long from his estates and they, unsupervised, were not paying. He told Waldeck that if he died tomorrow, his wife would only just be able to buy his coffin. Meanwhile his diplomacy failed. He secured nothing for his Prince, and returned empty-handed to live out the short remainder of his life at Halberstadt, whose cathedral he adorned with an immense silver candelabrum.

Before he died, he had sent his son, Christoph Caspar on one of the earliest known Grand Tours to Italy, Sicily and Malta – on which he wrote a still extant book – and so home via Spain and France. The hard-headed Elector made him a Councillor (he was 23) and he became a well-known European career diplomat. He was twice ambassador to France and got to know Richelieu, Mazarin and especially Marshall Turenne. He also became a Lord of the Bedchamber to the Elector-King of Saxony-Poland and astonishingly negotiated the settlement of the War of the Polish Succession by rearranging *Italy* in the Habsburg interest; but the Blumenthals in the next generation were much caught up in Austrian affairs; one, Ludwig became a Count of the Holy Roman Empire and, served under Prince Eugene at Blenheim, where he fell.

VEHLOW

Between 1442 and 1486 the family had acquired a group of estates at Vehlow in the shallow flood basin of the Elbe, which they proceeded to drain. Hans (IV) and his son Hans (V) were between them Captains of the Dykes for nearly a century, and, again Blumenthals were the guiding influences in a paramount aspect of (later) Prussian society – this time land drainage. Agricultural prosperity created the sinews of the state, and new land provided building sites for the new towns (for example Berlin) while new canals ultimately channelled Polish resources westwards and prepared for the Polish Partitions.

Hans (V) died in 1716 leaving a very dotty widow Sabine (née v. Barnewitz) and a son Hans (VI) aged four. There followed a muddle of curators, interfering relatives and flopped engagements ending in 1739 with Hans marrying Anna Dorothea v. Wedel, but in 1755 a Captain Frederick v. Blumenthal appeared. He had married Louise v. Platen, daughter of one of the former curators and he now challenged the marriage on the ground that Hans (VI) was as dotty as his late mother. He was supported by his cousin Ludwig (II) who was a minister of state. There must have been a conspiracy: the properties were, after all, worth it. Within a week a Herr v. Bülow had the curatorship and Hans was confined in the fortress of Spandau. Anna Dorothea fought back by petitioning for a suspension of proceedings because Bülow was wasting the property. The Seven Years War had just started. A lunacy commission declared Hans unfit but replaced Bülow with a Königsmarck. Hans, however, was eventually allowed home.

KRAMPFFER AND HORST AGAIN

The Krampffer Blumenthals inherited the Vehlow complex in 1772, but by then the Captain had sold Krampffer itself to the Möllendorf's and gone to live with the extraordinary Hussar General v. Ziethen, his wife's relative, in Berlin. The Captain's son Hans (VIII) eventually inherited all the properties and died in 1823.

I must now return to Ludwig (II), the suspect intervener in the dispute of 1755. Actually he was really Minister of War (had the job been so named) in the great opening events of the Seven Years War. He died in 1760 and in 1763 his eldest nephew Joachim (VIII) stepped into his position. In 1772 the Second Polish Partition and the canals gave Prussia a stranglehold on the Polish economy. The great King died in 1786. One of his many oddities had been a maniacal hatred of Counts yet he was considering conferring the title on the Blumenthals. His son liked Counts. He made Joachim and Ludwig's son Hans Counts in a single and unique patent, with precedence with the senior family of the same rank, reciting as the reason the long family record of service to the state.

As Joachim's only son predeceased him, his countship was the third to die out, but the family of Hans, constantly threatened with extinction, made it into the twentieth century. Of his eleven children, seven were girls, and three boys died young. The survivor Henry (VIII) also had eleven children; seven died young or childless, three had children who were either girls, or died young. The eleventh, Bernhard, died in 1866. Only one of his five children, Oscar, had offspring, and of his four, two boys died young, leaving a girl and Hans (X), the family historian, alive in 1905. I have to encapsulate a point, run ahead of myself. Joachim had two daughters; Frederika married a Count Podewils, while Charlotte married the Marshal of the Court, Valentin v. Massow the patron of Hegel.

The Podewils connection, intermittent in the eighteenth century, had some interesting results in the nineteenth, but my son Henry did some work on the Massows with whom there were matrimonial connections before Valentin. Biologically, the modern Blumenthals are more Massows than anything else, and most of them are Blumenthals because of the insertion of a single Blumenthal at a strategic point in the Massow genealogy.

Count Henry (VIII) was born in 1765, after his father retired from the army and had become governor to Prince Henry of Prussia. He was brought up with his contemporary, Prince Frederick William, later King, and accompanied him on his grand tours. He became a knight of St John at the age of twelve and married and succeeded to his father's estates at thirteen. His wife Frederica v. Plessen, brought him lands near Strelitz. At fifteen he became simultaneously a chamberlain (*Kammerherr*) at the courts of Prussia and Macklenburg, and at twenty he acquired a lucrative lay prebend at Magdeburg, where he bought a house. He had an estate in Potsdam, called Paretz, which Frederick William, now Crown Prince, bought from him at this time, and he reinvested the money. In 1800 he was one of the biggest landowners in Germany, with fourteen huge manors in the Mark and two in Mecklenburg, houses in the Wilhemstrasse and in Magdeburg, the lay prebend already mentioned, and the tithes in much of Halberstadt. He had modern ideas, too, on estate management, and was beginning to arrange the cash commutation of boon work with his serfs.

FALL OF THE HORSTS

The first revolutionary wave now suddenly submerged the fortunes of the most anciently established Blumenthal family. The Prussian army was rounded up at the twin battles of Jena and Auerstedt. The glittering Bonapartist horde surged northward across the defenceless land, pillaging as it came. Europe, by now, knew all about French military practices: and particularly about the habit of looting as a substitute for pay and supply. This French habit was maintained long after. In 1941 an acquaintance who served in the *Chasseurs Alpins* related how, at Narvik in World War II, he had quite lawfully helped himself to a gramophone, which he had espied through a window. He had to break in the door with his rifle-butt, and there were two frightened old people in the place. 'I carried that damn gramophone about in my pack for a week, and then I had to pitch it into the harbour when we embarked'. There was a refugee stampede. Henry removed his large family from his Prussian to his Mecklenburg property, but in the confusion, Blücher and his cavalry, the only survivors from the debacles, were driven through the mob, and the pursuit herded them all into Lübeck. Lübeck surrendered, and Henry returned to Horst. In six months the swarming French soldiery had robbed the barns down to the seed corn and the turnips; horses and cattle had been requisitioned or eaten, and many of the tenants had simply disappeared. Inquiries with the French senior officer brought nothing but abuse. Outrages were a daily occurrence and rape-pregnancies common. Naturally, the desperate country-folk were turning to banditry and guerilla. In the summer of 1807 the mayor, the bailiff and a shopkeeper at Kyritz were taken out and shot, because the townspeople had not turned out against their own friends. Other countries, besides Czechoslovakia and France, have their Lidices and Oradours.

The Peace of Tilsit (July 1807) made things worse. Onto the ruined farms, still burdened with foreign troops, there was now piled heavy taxation to defray the war indemnity. Moreover Bonaparte-inspired social decrees abolished vassalage, the heritable jurisdictions, and with them the formal apparatus by which the landowners controlled the rural population. The confusing effect of this was sharp, but luckily short. The landowner, under such conditions, could no more get an income from his land than his tenant could get a living; and the peace had for practical purposes, turned the government into an ally of the enemy. Henry was suddenly poor, with a family, a crippled mother and no certain income save from the prebend at Magdeburg. The family made its laborious way thither. The Kingdom of Westphalia had come into existence, and Magdeburg was in it. The Bonaparte King Jerome faced Henry with alternatives: he could return to the Prussian court, where he was, of course, a Lord of the chamber (*Kammerherr*), in which case he would forfeit the prebend or he could become *maire* of Magdeburg at a salary of 10,000 Francs. For the time being he took the latter.

Within months, it seemed that there might be a general uprising. He resigned and was promptly deprived of his job and his prebend; but the hope was premature, and he was now destitute of private income. He began to sell his impoverished estates for ready money. Meanwhile, King Jerome was using the financial pressures to force local notabilities into his court. In the end, Henry became his first German *kammerherr*, and governor of the castle-palace of Wilhemshöhe (temporarily called Napoleonshöhe!) near Cassel, a son became an officer in the royal army, and two others joined his Bonapartist Majesty's Corps of pages. Napoleonshöhe (renamed) was the place where Napoleon III was kept in six months luxurious custody, after he capitulated at Sedan in 1870.

I suspect that Henry's idea of poverty and, for instance, mine, would not be the same. Expenses at French courts since Louis XIV have been apt to be high. In any case, he could not cross the Elbe to look after his Prussian property. It would be natural to sell something: but Horst and Blumenthal with their outliers fetched 110,500 Thaler (about £30,000 in the currency of the time) from Count Wartensleben, at a period when a quartern loaf cost 1d. Yet he sold all his Prussian estates. The proceeds kept him going till he was able to rejoin his own King in 1813 after the uprising.

His childhood friend was helpful, and promised commissions in the Guards for his sons, and so it came about that he had sons fighting on both sides. But the long term effects were to alter the balance of the family. The senior branch, recently so resplendent, was now poor, with nothing but the royal promise of commissions. The notion that a landless gentleman could earn a living only at court or in the army (and they were becoming much the same thing) had taken deep root in that rather self righteous protestant community. The army was now not only the frontier of the country: nationalism had arrived, and the army embodied the national spirit. Who led the Army? The nobility. Patriotism and poverty all pointed in the same direction.

The Blumenthals of Horst became a purely military family. I do not mean that the other, Quackenburg, branch was not military: far from it as we shall see, but there is a radical difference between officers with solid assets, and officers with little but their pay; and if the assets are as solid as land, the difference can be very great. You generally knew where the Quackenburgs were: with the Horsts you could never be sure. They might, like the first family historian, be in foreign parts, in Mainz, or like his father, in Stuttgart. And come to that, they had an asset: their good looks. The Horsts had a roving eye for handsome girls, especially (if not always) with bank balances. There was the egregious Conrad (1856-1922) who got through eleven wives, and whose descendents are not admitted to the Blumenthal family association.

Moreover, just because they were so helplessly involved in the service, they probably thought about it too little. The most distinguished modern soldiers came from the Quackenburgs. They could afford to resign.

QUACKENBURG

The conscientious uninspired Count Joachim acquired Quackenburg and died in 1800, taking his title with him. His younger brother George (IV), took Egsow and Cummerzin, and became a Lieutenant General. He exchanged the dependent copyholds in Schlönwitz for some farms owned by Reinhold v. Krokow (like the Massows, of Polish origin but from Graudenz, now Grodno), and, though a busy military man, applied his mind and personal inclination to cattle breeding with some profit. His interest seems to have been a trifle obsessive: he habitually greeted disasters with the words 'I'd have given my last cow for that not to happen!'

SUCKOW AND VARZIN

His younger son Werner (II) was made of equally solid stuff. The elder brother had died on service, and Werner picked up the estates and the cattle. What was more, he picked up yet another Podewils, and when the old Count, his father-in-law, died, the extensive Podewils properties passed to him. These included Varzin and Wendisch-Puddiger near Stolp, besides Suckow near Schlawe.

Here follows a blomp. Varzin, of course, has a separate interest of its own for in 1867, with Wendisch-Puddiger, we sold it to Bismarck. The house is still intact. Henry, Nieves and I went there in 1994. We had been to nearby Dubberzin. My great grandmother, the Countess Krockow had been brought up and had married Hermann von Blumenthal there. It was she who brought Schlönwitz back into the family. Dubberzin was a wreck. The church and house had vanished, and the village resembled nothing so much as one of those Mexican social films with idle bystanders, dirty children, gravel and chickens. We fled and made for Barzino on the map. A priest in a biretta said that Varzin was ten kilometres further on. We found a no-admittance sign in Polish at the gate, so of course, we drove in. Once they understood why, they were very friendly. The Director, almost invisible behind a vast brown beard, got his pretty daughter, who had some English, to show us round.

The house stands as an L with a pillared portico in the right-hand arm and a clock tower over the angle. We found undamaged *Art Nouveau* ceilings, an impressive but not grandiose staircase, and a remarkable heptagonal drawing room with a heavy black coffered ceiling and a huge green-tiled fireplace and mantlepiece occupying one wall from top to floor, and a deeply recessed corner window. It could not be exactly opposite because this was a seven-sided room. The mantlepiece was adorned with the arms of Prussia, Bismarck and Puttkammer. The room is large but not enormous, and it combines a German stolidity with that element of the irrational which Germans so elusively show. My grandfather Vally must have known it well, for his mother died while giving birth to him, and the Bismarcks invited Vally over every weekend from early childhood until he went into the army. Bismarck called Vally his Sunday-child.

Varzin is now a forestry school, the resident students being accommodated in a filing cabinet up the hill. The building itself is used for libraries, laboratories and lecture rooms, which keep it unharmed, and the Director, we discovered, was interested in the building and its history, and had started a restoration fund – to which we contributed. There were Blumenthal graves in a thicket on the hillside and Bismarck graves behind the house. There is also a full sized plaque on the side of the house commemorating Schmetterling (Butterfly), Bismarck's favourite horse. The whole is deeply embowered in trees.

Returning to George (IV) and Werner (II) and the latter's accumulated properties and cows, his aunt Elizabeth, who had married yet another Lettow, now left him the enormous manor of Natzlaff near Kösternitz. 'Tu, felix Austria, nubes'. He was now as great in Pomerania as his ill-starred cousin Henry had been in the Mark. Only a nine-pointed coronet was missing. This, King Frederick William IV obligingly supplied at his Pomeranian Acclamation in 1840.

In contrast with the double elevation of 1786 this patent was granted simply because Werner had a lot of land: and the title was limited to inheritance by eldest sons of aristocratic mothers and only so long as they held Suckow. He became the Count of Blumenthal-Suckow. He died at Varzin in 1844, and was succeeded by his son Werner (IV).

We are now approaching the era of popular politics and industrialisation. The hated French had been driven home in 1815, but had left their ideas behind. The power of these had been enhanced rather than reduced by the ineffectual oppressiveness of Metternich's Holy Alliance. You have to shoot a lot of people to suppress an idea. Metternich & Co, being civilised, hardly shot anyone, but they provided enough of a challenge to evoke a mighty response. The modernist movement's overwhelming champion was Britain. She refused to have anything to do with the Holy Alliance. She supported liberation movements in America and Greece, where brigands hurriedly christened themselves Themistocles, and the colossus Byron bestrode the mighty world, or at any rate the beach at Missolonghi, in a toga (this is not merely playing with words: for a century, Byron was the only English poet who sprang naturally to the continental mind). Above all, Britain had been the powerhouse of industrial innovation, whose products were everywhere.

For example, English cloth was made on machine looms at a constant and predictable tension. Therefore English tailors could make suits so that they kept their shape, and with English cloth one could rely on cut rather than ornament (sometimes bizarre) to achieve distinction. You either bought English machinery or did without, and English engineers built continental railways, many of which, to this day keep to the left. In Switzerland shunters still signal with bosun's pipes. There was, too, a growing trade in strong beer to the Baltic. 'Porter' is still advertised in Sweden, and Jim Sillem, a friend from MI 6 was the manager of the 'Russian' stout brewery at Tallin when the Russians took it over in 1940.

It was perfectly possible for a patriotic, that is, an anti-French Prussian to reject the ideas of the revolution while embracing the liberating ingenuities of English modernism. We thus find that in 1848, the conflicts which shook every continental throne and toppled some, were fought out in Prussia not so much between progressives and reactionaries or between different classes, as between generations who shared each others' convictions, but in different proportions. Everyone wanted things 'made in England': practical experience of 'Liberté, Egalité, Fraternité' had devalued those glorious concepts. All the adult Blumenthals supported the monarchy in suppressing 'The Trouble'. Several took charge of units before disaffection contaminated them. Rural landowners and their households sent loyal addresses to the King, and patrolled the villages. Three were at the decisive suppression in Berlin. The whole thing was over in no time – or was it?

Count Werner (IV) was a more modern man than his father, though, I suspect, something of a sybarite with expensive tastes, but where others of his kind held aloof from the new limited parliamentary constitution (Made in England), he got himself elected to parliament. Moreover, he thought that industry might be a better investment than Prussian potato lands. He began to sell off his estates.

Bismarck was the same kind of man. He was no democrat, but saw the uses of parliamentary fora. He had little time for the aristocracies from which he came, or for the royalties through whom he worked. But he had seen as a young man, the practical advantages of such simple administrative arrangements as the North German Customs Union (*Zollverein*) and of technical advances like the railways. With his instinct for recognising safety limits, he sailed the ship with its purblind sailors through the European shoals, while the engineers were still constructing the engines.

Every public action of that extraordinary man has been dissected, and I, of course, cannot refrain from doing it too. Bismarck's major purpose always was to set up a Germany in which Prussia was not only supreme, but controlled the avenues to the ocean. For this, it was necessary to dominate, at the isthmus of Schleswig, the entrances to the Baltic, and by way of the Ems, Weser, and Elbe valleys, the ports (The Jade, Emden, Bremen, and Hamburg) on the North Sea coast. The key to both these sets of doors was the Kingdom of Hanover, separated in 1837 by Salic Law from the formal but not the social or economic English connection, when its crown passed to the unlovely and autocratic Ernest Augustus, Duke of Cumberland. The Hanoverian territories divided the post-Vienna Prussian Kingdom, but, more importantly, through their ports and along their rivers, British goods moved restlessly into the heart of Europe. Hence the pertinacity with which Bismarck interfered in the affairs of Schleswig-Holstein, and, when Hanover's

Austrian backer had been defeated, the determination with which, against opposition and intrigue, he destroyed Hanover altogether. Other German states, after that, were small beer. Even Saxony need not be wholly swallowed, and Bavaria, after the defeat of France, could be left to Wagner and the *Dämmerung* of its homosexual King; but Hanover and Schleswig-Holstein he would have. Modernisation, and the huge industrial investment which it implied, was simply not feasible until Germany could physically control her own tariff policy.

Apart, possibly, from Count Werner the Blumenthals played no direct part in this at all but their military contribution was considerable. It began with Leonhard, a mere captain in 1849 with the staff of the Schleswig-Holstein force against the Danes. There was a Prussian relative, the not very able General v. Bonin, in command. The Chief of staff was killed, and Leonhard, called to take his place, carried his general on his back brilliantly. In the Danish War of 1864 the Augustenburg claimant's centre was on the island of Alsen. Leonhard inspired the daring dawn coup-de-main, by which the Prussians crossed the strait to Alsen, and ended the war. This earned him the third *Pour le Mérite*, the supreme Prussian military award in the family.

SCHLÖNWITZ

Now Bismarck and the Blumenthals were close acquaintances in Pomerania. It happened thus. My great grandfather Hermann, a Quackenburger with whose lineage I will not trouble, was not a military minded sort of person at all. He married Waleska, Countess Krokow, and she brought him Schlönwitz, part of which George (IV) had sold to her ancestor all those years ago. Hermann went into the army because, by 1828 everybody did. His heart was not in the business. His military record could scarcely be equalled for lack of distinction. He entered the twelfth infantry regiment as a second lieutenant, and seventeen years later he was still there as a second lieutenant. Then he made the acquaintance of the beautiful Waleska. He threw up his boring old commission and they retired to idyllic Schlönwitz. They had a daughter, who died in her second year, and then in 1848 my grandfather Vally. The birth was a tragedy, it killed Waleska. Hermann, whose true vocation was academic, retreated into learned seclusion. Vally, from his tenderest years had to make do with second best.

Fortunately, he had four useful uncles. One of these had also married a Krokow, but Robert (I), the most distinguished, had disgraced himself by marrying a commoner. Tut-tut! But it did not prevent Robert, in the new Germany, from rising to very high rank in the Prussian civil service. He became, under a private arrangement between the Prussian and the Sigmaringen Hohenzollerns, administrator of Sigmaringen. The Krokow aunt did her best – and so, as already mentioned, did Bismarck who lived just down the road.

In 1866 lots of Blumenthals went off to Bismarck's war with Austria. Leonhard was the Chief of Staff in the Crown Prince's Second Army which advanced into Bohemia from Eastern Silesia. Beginning with the Battle of Nachod, he brought the second army by way of engagements at Skalitz, Trautenau, Soor and Schweinschädel, onto the exposed right wing of the Austro-Hungarians at Sadowa and so converted the threatened defeat into brilliant and decisive victory. Others of the family fought in half a dozen battles in the seven weeks. Vally, who at eighteen was a Porte-Epée Fähnrich (a sort of military midshipman) with the Blücher Hussars, fought in the furious action at Gitschin, then at Münchengrätz and finally at the bloody end at Königgrätz, where he was involved in the muddled cavalry battle in which at one point, two Prussian regiments fought each other until staff officers disentangled them; then he was commissioned on the field. According to him, it was a glorious picnic; it launched him into the military life of his early manhood. German promotion was always inefficiently slow, but he kept his mind alive and maintained other interests. He spoke French well because, he said, the way to learn it was to have an affair with a pretty *parisienne*. Later he became military attaché in Bern. Hence his contact with the Engadine Blumenthals.

It was after the Austrian War that Bismarck decided that he wanted a *Rittergut* (knight's fee) like his in-laws the Puttkammers. Count Werner's brother wanted, as we already know, to dispose of Wendisch-Puddiger and Varzin, so the deal was struck.

Eighteen Blumenthals now went off to the 1870 war. They served, between them, in every rank from corporal to lieutenant-general. One spent the war commanding a baggage column. Two brothers were killed. Nine got second-class Iron Crosses, Vally a first-class one. Werner (V) was in the great cavalry engagement (six regiments a side) at Mars-la-Tour. Leonhard won the battles of Weissenburg and Wörth. Several were in at the kill at Sedan. And then they helped to found an empire. The brilliance of the early operations, which overthrew the Bonapartist regime in a month, and the sensational mostly political events which took place in Paris on the French side and at Versailles on the German, have distracted foreign attention from the longer haul which constituted most of the war. Two brothers met their deaths at the two-day battle of Cravant in December 1870, three months after Napoleon III had capitulated; and Gustav (V) was in *six* battles after the same event. The French denied Bismarck his quick war, saved the fortress of Belfort, and founded the Third Republic on a desire for revenge which Bismarck, with all his common sense, was unable to assuage.

The German word *Schadenfreude* has no equivalent single word I believe, in any other language. It means 'pleasure in other people's misfortune'. Connected with it is a derisive noise – *Aetsch* – with which Germans, and not only children, were apt to express triumph over the unlucky. I remember this in childhood. A bootlace came undone while I was running. I fell headlong into a puddle. Splash. Peels of laughter. The puddle was full of jagged stones, and I got covered with blood and mud and half a dozen cuts on elbows and knees. Shrieks of mirth. I was hurt and furious. 'Aetsch!'

This posture would not fail to make the French (with all their memorials of Napoleonic triumph) grind their teeth with the hope of retaliation. Bismarck did his best. Amongst other things, he checked his extremists. He took most of Alsace and only part of Lorraine between the Rhine and the crest of the Vosges, but no more. They became imperial territory (*Reichsland*), an international bone of contention. They acquired this character because it suited successive French governments that it should. The ricketty republic had to have a foreign enemy to distract its voters from its own inadequacies. This was a kind of diluted Bonapartism, for which it is hard to blame the French statesmen of the time. A second Empire Marshal, MacMahon, after all, became President of the Republic.

Now, rights and wrongs do have some relevance to politics, even if only as persuaders. The French made such a noise about Alsace-Lorraine because their case was weak. The Rhine valley from Basel, perhaps indeed from Bregenz, northwards to the Dutch frontier, is an obvious unity. The area should be in a single hand. In whose hand? In fact, most of it is in German territory anyway, and though the most authoritative school of French phonology has long been at Strasbourg university, the natives of Alsace-Lorraine speak a very broad German dialect, akin to Swiss German, at home. Bilingualism was forced on them by the French educational system: but they are *Mussfranzosen*. Nor is this particularly surprising. The area was Germanic in speech and part of the Holy Roman Empire (of the German Nation!) from the earliest middle ages. At one stage, places like Colmar and Mulhouse were federated with Swiss republics. French power arrived only when Louis XIV seized Strasbourg by a ruse and in peace time in 1681.

Two stories about being a disputed border territory have come my way. I shared a table in a restaurant car with a professor, on the way to her annual philological seminar at Strasbourg. She and I agreed aggressively about the limitations of the military mind. 'Would you believe it', she said, 'but the French Railway administration has never yet been allowed to electrify the Strasbourg railway line beyond Saverne'. 'Why not' I asked. 'General staff fighting the last war but one, as usual' she said with a contemptuous toss of her Gallic head. So at Saverne, I stuck my head out of the window to admire the steam monster which would shortly pant its way with us for the last few miles. Not a sign. The story was quite untrue. Indeed, it was obvious that the line had been electrified for years.

As for the other story: M. Pflimlin, *maire* of Strasbourg, told me that electric bulbs were the curse of Alsace-Lorraine. The French use bayonet sockets: the Germans, screw sockets. Within the memory of everybody over 40, the entire population had had to change all its bulbs and sockets three times.

The new Europeanism is eroding some of this nonsense. The *départements* of Haut and Bas Rhin (French Officialese for Alsace-Lorraine) have special regimes, which allow for concessions to local culture, and there is Trans-Rhenanian co-operation between local authorities. The bridge at Kehl is no longer wired and guarded by mutually hostile pickets, as it was in 1919 when Wilhelmine was allowed briefly to talk to Harriet across the barrier. Indeed, these days the *hausfraus* of Kehl pop over to Strasbourg to do their shopping.

So they all came home in triumph, and time marched inexorably on. The Hohenzollern-Sigmaringen family trust wanted to buy a north German estate. Ruling the principality was such a bore, and could be safely left to Robert (I). Count Werner (IV), now in the imperial parliament, wanted to sell Suckow. The patent of 1840 stood in the way. So Werner applied for a new condition that if the sale went through and if Werner set up a trust fund in favour of the heirs, of at least 200,000 Marks before he died, the title could be attached to the fund rather than the land. So, in 1874 the Hohenzollerns got Suckow – an exceptionally beautiful estate – but Werner never set up the fund, and so the fourth title of the kind ended when he died in 1883.

In 1980 I shared a table at Elmau (which will appear hereafter) with a survivor of the Hohenzollern-Sigmaringens, a composer prince brought up at Suckow, and his mistress. Enter, meanwhile, fairy godfathers. The emperor William I made Leonhard a Count (No. 6) and, for good measure, the Emperor Frederick made him a field-marshal. Vally left the army as a cavalry captain (*Rittmeister*) and went to Hamburg. He had, or had made, some money. He bought the great estate of Staffelde, and married (tut-tut) Cornelia (Nelli) Keyser, the daughter of a Hamburg Patrician. The Keysers were fabulously rich.

So far (in 2001) by the way, Leonhard's title has survived. The present incumbent lives at Obergrainau on the Zugspitze.

Chapter 5

STAFFELDE - A POMERANIAN MANOR

Staffelde, then, was no ancestral home. Its stuccoed octagonal tower, crenellations and its pitch-pine panelling proclaimed the rural daydream of some industrial or commercial magnate. Vally bought it from a Frau Ebart, but the manor had belonged to the v. Wussows who had sold it to the v. Wilichs in 1771, and Vally's purchase only returned it to the sort of people with whom the tenants had been familiar. The atmosphere, however, was traditional. Nowadays it would, erroneously, be called feudal. It was the people who made for this relatively modern place a feeling of something older than itself.

According to the visitor's book, I was there in 1923 when I was five. It had a wonderfully beautiful situation. A drive which went diagonally up the ridge, curved in a second leg below the stone balustrade of an immense terrace, which stretched away from the warm façade along the ridge. Over the brow, the woods and clearings sloped down to the wide Oder which, with its occasional sandbanks, disappeared into the smoky horizon of a summer's day towards Stettin. Beyond the great river, the plain of Greifenhagen with its villages and cultivation petered out flatly to a distant eastward horizon. My brother described the inside as 'pitch-pine with unpleasant ancestral portraits'. My own recollection, I have read, is a common type of experience among young children, but one which is normally censored by conscious rationalisation. I ran down a narrow green glade, which went perhaps half the way to the water level. Then I turned round and ran up the steep grass. There was the tower rising above the terraced skyline, and there was I standing at the top of the slope. I was running up the hill towards myself, and standing at the top watching myself doing it. There was somebody else there, with another sort of voice, but who it was I do not recollect. It is not the slightest use arguing with me about this: my memory of being both people at once is as crystal. It was, by the way, rather damp underfoot.

We are however, back in 1912. Vally had five children by Nelly who died in 1908. She was one of four sisters, Keysers of Hamburg, two of whom married Blumenthals and two Counts Oeynhausen. One of the Oeynhausens, Susanna, known to all north

Germany as *Tante Su* (Aunt Sue) was another of my godmothers. She was dignified, energetic; and could always be consulted in trouble. Hamburg had been not only an independent state, that is to say a different country, but until 1866 it was distanced from Prussia by the width of another country, namely Hanover. It ceased to be legally independent when it joined the new Reich proclaimed in 1871. Before then, a Hamburg businessman could not have bought a Pomeranian *rittergut* because even if he were accidentally noble, he was not a Prussian. The creation of the Second Reich made all the difference.

The long-rich Hamburg *patrizier* regarded themselves as the equals of the Venetian nobility. The Burgermaster was second to none in the world. Only once in history has a burgermaster descended his town-hall steps to receive a visitor, and that visitor was not the Kaiser or the Federal President but the Queen of Great Britain. So when the aristocrats of the German monarchies started looking for brides with well balanced portfolios, the proud Hanseatic patricians somehow seemed to be more noble than anyone had previously thought. In this, as in other things, William II upset people by being ahead of his time, but my god-mother Tante Su did things in a style which impressed even his detractors. When she travelled, at the very least she took two compartments – one for the servants and one for herself. She had carriages shunted into her private siding so that her people could line out the seating with her own linen. She often went to Russia, which involved changing trains at the frontier because of the different gauge. Servants travelled ahead for this. Once her steward, as in duty bound, declared 70,000 cigarettes to the Russian customs and, as he was not believed, got the whole lot through for nothing. How are the mighty fallen! She had a palatial house on the Alster, the lake in the centre of Hamburg. She and a grandson were killed by a direct hit during the British bombing of the city, and the site of the house is now part of a public park.

Of the five children, the eldest was Bob (Robert III). He was the sort of Hussar subaltern who habitually sowed wild oats. Vally looked at his eldest calmly, and after he had paid his debts several times, he offered him a Hobson's choice. He had no right to consume the shares of his brothers and sisters. He could resign his commission, have his debts settled for the last time, and find himself a place in the colonies, or he could go on as he was and take the consequences. The consequences, of course, involved a court-martial.

So Bob wisely kissed his mother, and spent two years in the Marshall Archipelago. In the summer of 1901 Staffelde was electrified by a telegram from Hamburg. They would not let him off the ship until he had paid his debts. Vally laughed and paid. There was still something in Bob's share, but this time there would be a real investment. Vally picked up two estates for him near Rabaul called Kuragakaul and Natava. Rabaul, the tin roofed capital of the Bismarck archipelago was in New Pomerania, now called New Britain.

I would like to imagine Bob as a brutal lounging European, cracking his whip in the veranda while boys trotted about with brandies and sodas. Actually, he was not like that at all. He seldom applied his mind to any one thing, like clearing a plantation, for long, and was too kindly to crack a whip – save to shake the dust out of it. So, of course, after five years there was another telegramme from Hamburg. Vally laughed again, and everyone was very happy. In due course, Bob redisappeared and five years later, just before Wilhelmine and Albrecht were married, there came another of the customary telegrammes. Hence Bob managed to be present at Staffelde on the great day. He gave Wilhelmine a spectacular necklace of corals, dredged up probably for very little, when he was in the Marshall islands. She gave it, in 1976, to my wife.

His sister, Waleska, two years younger had married Fritz v. Kleist-Retzow, who now lived at Damen, a huge agricultural concern, employing much seasonal labour. Seasonal labour was, indeed, common on Pomeranian estates. The flat north European plain, stretching all the way from Hamburg to the Urals, was divided only by the shifting frontiers of European politics, which, in their personal lives, the populations tended to ignore, but the German customs houses controlled the movement of goods on the Vistula and the Niemen, and ensured that Russian Poland should be poor, so that every year, hordes of Polish labourers crossed the frontiers to lift German potatoes and swedes often hundreds of miles from home. The *Junkers* paid them far less than they paid their own people, and yet they took home much more than they could under the Czar. The German railways ran special trains for these crowds with fourth class carriages, without bogies or compartments, only a few seats round the edges and overhead rods to which standing passengers, packed like cigars, clung. On long journeys everyone subsided onto the floor. A train composed of them would burst out at its destination a veritable swarm of such people in a few minutes, for travel by this means cost about ten miles for a penny.

Am I the only person who now remembers Fourth Class? It was still running in Germany when I was a child, still sucking in and pouring out its masses of humanity, in dark heavy clothes smelling of home grown tobacco, with their nondescript packages, massive boots, and fleas. Yet I find that merely to mention them causes surprise.

Next in order came the raven haired Nora (of her I shall try to say more later, for she turned out to be controversial but interesting). She had married Rudolf v. Lettow-Vorbeck of the *Garde zu Fuss*, without a brain in his head, whose uncle however was the brilliant later successful defender of German East Africa (now Tanganyika).

The guards' regiments took it in daily turns to do duty about the court. The officers who were not on parade were expected to do odd jobs in the palace and about the person of the Supreme Feldherr. They stood outside council chambers and audience rooms, carried messages between ministers, lined the walls of the throne room during presentations. This, of course, conduced to the militarised splendour which William II liked, but did not originate. It went back to the practical spirit of Frederick the Great, who thought that if he was to pay a lot of officers in peacetime, they might as well do something. Officers in peacetime, it was assumed, would develop bad habits. The German word for an officers' (or serjeants') mess is *Kasino*. Besides, one specially charged to protect the King, should know the King's habits, and naturally, the King should know him. Guards commissions were of course, much sought for their prestige and influence.

The officers in waiting had their own guardroom in the palace and from time to time, their Lord would come down graciously and without ceremony to pass the time of day. He enjoyed these personal familiarities very much: it is, however, less certain that they did. He combined bonhomie and the immense prestige of his imperial office with an erratic temperament and only a limited ability to relax. The soldiers, other, no doubt than the top brass like Leonhard or the Moltkes, were terrified of him because you never knew where you were. He might confer the privilege of his familiarities as much as he pleased: they still had to treat him with a hopelessly inhibiting ceremonial restraint. Court anecdotes are almost always banal, so I will shorten this one. The All Highest on one of these evenings, suddenly said to Nora's brainless husband 'I say, Rudi, what's happened to your hair?' Rudi, who was balding replied without thought (he was, after all, incapable of thought) 'Wegstudiert, Majestät' (Gone through study, Majesty). Such banter would have been acceptable at the court of William's cousin Edward VII. There was a horrified silence, while everybody watched the cloud. Was this the end of poor Rudi? As it happened the cloud passed. One was allowed to laugh.

Wolf-Werner, the fourth child, was the most level headed, the most like his father, of the five, and was to be groomed to take over the estates; and so, as was usual in landowning families, after his military service, and the university, he was sent to Wanzleben to serve as a farm apprentice (élève) under Erich Kühne. This was the link between the Blumenthals and Wilhelmine, for through him Irene was invited to Staffelde and, by way of friendship with Nora, the introduction between Wilhelmine and Albrecht was made. By 1912 Wolf-Werner was already Vally's right-hand man.

He had, in Prussian terms, the characteristics of the English country gentleman. He managed the estates profitably, was respected by his equals, and kind if firm, with his tenants, and he took part in local public affairs. Later he became the local *Landrat*. This office combined the functions of a local administrator and representative of the ministries in Berlin with some of those, such as licensing pubs, of the English bench of local JPs. Imagine the local work of an English county and district council being done for a district by a local and paid landowner.

Finally, here is Albrecht, my father, slim and dark, and feeling rather out of place at this roistering dinner table. I am not sure exactly how one roisters, but whatever one does, it was not for Albrecht. He would probably have preferred to be upstairs with his books, but here he was at a banquet to celebrate his homecoming, and he could not get out of it. Everyone in full dress and full of wine: he sipping slowly – perhaps too slowly. They had pulled out all the stops. Selli had even served up her famous *Kaneelganz* (Cinnamon goose), the secret of which died with her. Also, on such occasions Vally could entertain a hundred guests to a full-blown dinner, served from first to last on silver (hot food cannot have stayed hot for long) with wines drunk entirely from silver, save for himself. He used gold.

Wilhelmine was, in spite of all she said later, enjoying it very much. The noise of talk rose above the clatter of the dishes as proceedings rose to a climax, and then Vally was on his feet, rather tipsy, very amiable, exerting a public charm to toast his new daughter-in-law. On such occasions beautiful women in German households were seen, but not expected to make a reply – which was lucky, for Wilhelmine would probably have burst into tears and ruined the whole show. Then there was cheering and clapping, and that rumbling accolade, made by sliding one's foot backwards and forwards on a wooden floor, which German audiences still make at concerts.

Vally sat down, and then those in the know waited for a signal which he invariably gave at bean feasts, and which was peculiar to him. He knocked his goblet over, and the wine surged down the middle of the table, so that nobody who had made a gaffe need feel embarrassed about it. The ladies now withdrew to Cornelia's drawing room while the gentlemen crowded the head of the table and lit up cigars. Their session would end very soon, for the ball was waiting for the Herr Rittmeister and he was going to open with the bride. And the bride, let me remind you, was in her bridal dress, veil thrown back, train and all, revolving like a giddy-go-round with her hussar father-in-law, still agile on his feet at the age of 64 (so was I). They danced as I did later at Elmau waltzes and the open Reinländer besides figure dances and the Court Quadrille. Some of these proceedings began with a Polonaise, or might end with one which stumbled enthusiastically all over the house. In some establishments, individual couples still performed the minuet, and in West and East Prussia, that is, the more Polish areas, the Mazurka.

After a while the older people retired to wine or tea or cards or gossip: or Vally, with cronies, would go down into the cellar, fetch out special bottles from the bins and sit about on stools. Slowly the rest, exhausted, drunk or randy would collapse into bed, or not. One breakfast time, two elderly counts were espied from my mother's tower bedroom, in their night-shirts, sitting with their arms round each other's waists, on the terrace steps.

Albrecht was a studious Blumenthal, but unlike bishop George or Leonhard, he did not combine study with action. It came as no surprise to me to learn about his reclusive grandfather Herrmann, grieving amongst his books at Schlönwitz; but Herrmann had wasted the best years of his life in the hateful occupations of a peacetime subaltern. Albrecht was determined to be an academic success, and this meant making a name in the world of learning and research. He was now 23, having just taken his doctorate (the equivalent of the English BA) in what the Germans called philology. In fact he was a classical scholar. The difficulty was that he had to go up the ladder from the bottom, keeping his wife and any children who might come and finding enough time to do his research. So he became a *privatdozent* at Halle.

German universities still had the rather loose arrangements of mediaeval times. A *privatdozent* was a town crammer. He was paid by his pupils, not by the university, and in theory anyone could be a *privatdozent*. In real life, a man without qualifications or luck would attract no custom, but if he was successful, and success was easily ascertainable by the performance of his students, he would attract a following and in due course be offered a job, not necessarily where he was practising.

One of the features of German university life, distinguishing it sharply from the English was that students moved from one university to another; you might do a year each in Bonn, Jena and Giessen. This peripatetic habit resembled the ancient wanderings of the guild journeyman, celebrated in Mahler's *Lieder eines fahrenden Gesellen*, and just as the guilds had their welcoming guildhouses in most towns (identifiable to this day by their wrought-iron signs), so there were student corporations which tended to repeat themselves from one university to another. These had often begun, as was common in the middle ages, as Languages or Nations, and if you belonged, for example, to one at Greifswald, you could claim admission to its equivalent at your next stopping place. In recent times they had developed socially rather than territorially. The Borussia at Bonn and the Saxo-Borussia at Heidelberg no longer catered exclusively for Prussians or Saxons and Prussians, but were sought by the duelling aristocrats. They usually kept, and still keep reserved tables in restaurants or beerhouses.

This mobile habit would spread a teacher's reputation, for good or ill, throughout the German world. The nationwide unity which it gave to university life was the support of the private teacher. All the same it was not easy, because to rise in the academic world required original achievement as well as teaching success, and as the former represented pennies in heaven while the latter was bread and butter now, Albrecht and his peers were in a long drawn out dilemma at the start of their careers. He solved it in a way which is said again to have made him unpopular with his family, but for which he can scarcely be blamed. Bob had already had his share under Prussian family law. Now Albrecht claimed his. Perhaps (I do not know) it was the way he did it. It was not I understand the most tactful thing to do, but naturally Vally paid out. Wilhelmine says that she was against it and that she was blamed for it by other Blumenthals. I think that she exaggerated. She was always apt to take things personally, and Albrecht would probably have made his claim whoever he had married – unless his wife had been a tactful millionairess – for the case was strong. Why should he not use his rights to further an academic career, if Bob could use his in bezique, bottle and bed?

I would go a little further. If Wilhelmine was against the move, it seems likely that she was against it because she mistrusted his academic ambitions. She was brought up with men of business, who made 'brass' and no nonsense. She admired Vally and his like for the same reason. She was initially ignorant of the learned, and despised what she called Albrecht's namby-pamby friends. I do not want to overstress this. Despite the way she spoke of this time, this must have been the period when she got, presumably from him, her knowledge of Greek playwrights remarkable for a Yorkshire girl of her educational background.

So Albrecht made a wise decision. He found it convenient to do some research at the Laurenziana in Florence, well away from it all. They found lodgings with a Signora Daddi up at Fiesole, and spent a happy unhurried summer in each other's company, getting acquainted. It simplified matters that he spoke good Tuscan, and sometime about now he began to take an interest in Dante's *Divina Commedia*, of which he projected a complete German translation. As a poet himself, he was well equipped to do it, and it seems that he spent a lifetime on it, but at his death in 1945 the vast manuscript was nowhere to be found, and in 2002 it had still not seen the light of day. There is no doubt that it existed, for Werner saw it.

Harriet, as it happened, spoke Tuscan too. She had been a paying guest with the Marchesa Antinori. The Antinoris were very very grand. They were also rather poor, not having at that time achieved their present fortune as winegrowers. Still, they had to keep up appearances, which meant being driven in a landau to the evening *corso*, and bowing behind fans to other *aristos*. The coachman had a magnificent livery which he wore only during the 45 minutes, and the marchesa, splendidly caparisoned above, covered her legs with a rug to conceal the raggedness of her skirt. It was a household which surprised Harriet in more than one way. Dinner, until she became fluent, was not the sort of event to which a demurely educated English girl could get accustomed. The pitch, tempo and sound of the discussion mounted from *andante* to *allegro vivace*, to *prestissimo* and *con fuoco*. By the time that everybody was shouting at everybody else, it was not possible to attract anyone's attention vocally; so you flapped your napkin, and if this failed you threw something usually a piece of bread which might hit its target, or land in the soup, or knock over a candle. It took her a fortnight to discover that these prandial brawls were no more than conversational small change.

'Really well brought up Florentines' said the Marchesa 'who quarrel, poison each other without fuss'.

★ ★ ★

I have already described the principles of the modernised feudalism which Joachim Frederick (I) and the Great Elector thought out, but their arrangements were already breaking down by the end of the eighteenth century: we have seen Henry (VIII) commuting servile work at Horst in the 1790s.

The crash came when the army, which was supposed to be the object of the exercise, entirely failed in 1806; but the Bonaparte style legislation which abolished the jurisdictions really put the hat on it. It forced the Prussian state to raise an army on a new basis, and the landowners, to preserve their position, had to capture the state apparatus. Hence aristocratic Landraths like Wolf-Werner. They only partially succeeded, mainly because it was too big and they were too few but meanwhile the pre-revolutionary *douceur de vie* persisted, and something like the old order was re-established by a mental reaction, very widely sustained, against the French.

Probably the old life was reasonably *douce* for more people than merely the aristocracy. Vally made money from his estates but he had investments too, and his tenantry was willing to be ruled by him in most things because or as long as they were prosperous; and besides, he provided some of the rudiments of a welfare state. If someone in the village was ill, Vally sent his own doctor down. He saw to it that the parson, Lutheran of course, baptized, confirmed, married, buried and registered everyone without fee. This was important educationally and from the point of view of personal status, for in Protestant areas confirmation was a vastly significant moment in everybody's life.

You were confirmed when you were considered ready, at about sixteen. Readiness meant a fairly grown up outlook, some real knowledge and some understanding – or ability to pretend to an understanding – of Luther and his doctrines. It was not automatic or perfunctory, and it was signalised by two important marks: the lesser, in aristocratic families, was that you were given a signet ring. The other, infinitely more important and universal, was that you ceased to be addressed (apart from family and close friends) with the familiar, patronising or childish 'Du', and became 'Sie'. These things happened to me, though confirmed at Winchester. My godparents, who, of course, were invited, could not come because the new Nazi exchange control restricted travel to Party-sponsored travel in groups. But they, especially Tante Su, wrote me long serious letters of congratulation and advice, and sent me suitable presents, and my mother gave me a signet which had belonged to my father. So far, so good; but when I went to Germany a few weeks later, it came as a shock to be addressed with all the ceremony due to an adult. The English language does not possess this distinction which entails no mere substitution for it affects the grammar; it resembles passing a frontier: suddenly everything is said differently like 'tenez la gauche' instead of 'keep left'. Every German went through this major change in public attitudes to him at an impressionable time. I found that though confirmed in England, strangers in Germany seemed to know. It was much more important than an English coming of age.

There were problems. When may I address you as 'Du'? One-sided use of 'Du' is obviously patronising. So there has to be some kind of agreement, and since the original change was associated with the solemnity of confirmation, such agreements amounted to a good deal more than the English 'call me George'. Even now you find people drinking blood brotherhood. You put your glass nearly to your lips, I pass my glass and arm through the crook of your arm nearly to my lips. Then we both say 'Hoch' or 'Prosit', and drink the lot simultaneously. This is, socially speaking, like delivering a deed creating a kind of lien, which is publicly proclaimable. It carries risks too: it was common for newly pledged blood brothers and sisters to quarrel soon.

It was a feature of Prussian aristocratic family life that servants were entangled in it. People worked at manual occupations when they were physically fit for them: Prussian schools, for example, always adjourned for the 'Potato Holidays' so that everyone could help with the lifting. But service in the large households was a career requiring address, an excellent character, a variety of skills and a sense of responsibility. No doubt, odd jobs were done now and again by the very young, but people were taken on and trained with a long future in view only after confirmation. This type of household was a complicated organism and an important one, full of valuable and breakable objects. Honesty was essential where *die Herrschaften* ate off half a ton of assorted silver and left crystal perfume bottles and gold watches about in the bedrooms. A light and certain touch was necessary to wash the daily used Dresden coffee cups (I have some still) or dust the Meissen, or arrange flowers in the Worcester, or, now, in the Chinese vases from Tsing-Tao.

A whole complex of activities centred on the kitchen. Much was grown (and shot) on the estates. Somebody had to examine and grade it for the household – or butcher it. They made jam, of course, and bottled immense quantities of spring vegetables and fruit for winter use. There was a delicious thing called the *Rhumkompott*: a barrel with a loose lid stood in a cool larder, and as each kind of fruit was ready for the table, six pounds* of it was put into the barrel and a bottle of rum poured in too. This went on all the summer until the barrel was full.....

Then there was the pond, or some other stretch of still but clean water, refreshed, if possible by a slow stream. In the cold of winter, when it had frozen solid, the ice would be cut out in blocks and put in the ice-house, a deep well inside a thickly thatched construction in a shady spot. The ice remained fit for use all the summer through at about 26°F and was brought up to the House as needed. There was also a chamber beside the shaft where meat was hung. Meat was also preserved by smoke in a cone-shaped smoke-house, in the top of which the smokeables were hung from rows and rows of hooks, while sawdust and chippings smouldered below. You would not use proper wood: that would be wasteful.

Everything was used. The chief ground crops were roots: beets for sugar and cash, and potatoes. There were dozens of recipes for cooking potatoes, upon which all Prussians were experts. There was, by the way, a Prussian Eleventh Commandment: *Never cut potatoes with a knife*. Wilhelmine did not know about this at first, and provoked a good deal of astonishment and rather impolite comment. I myself always regret breaking it: there is, undoubtedly, something in it.

The creature that was the other part of the staple was the goose. Observe the economy of this. The goose would eat anything which might be thrown onto the kitchen middens. Great communal flocks could be managed by a single child, the legendary goose-girl of Slavonic story telling. The flocks were, as ancient Rome knew, better than watchdogs, especially when wolves penetrated from the wastes of Poland and the whole population turned out to hunt them down.

Then the geese scavenged the village and kept the lanes clean of refuse. The goose-girl's mother was entitled to an extra goose at Christmas, Easter and

---

* Half a kilogram was called pound = pfund.

Whitsun; and there was a residual survival of feudalism which gave the lord every seventh goose out of each tenant's share. Somehow, as Vally wrote, there never was a seventh goose.

Roasting a goose was thought wasteful and only to be done when you were in an extravagant mood. When you had cleaned the feathers you stuffed the pillows with them. The feet were boiled down for glue, the bones for jelly or aspic; the breasts were cut off, clapped together into a blunt package weighing about a pound, smoked and wrapped in skin. Known as *Speckganz* (Goose bacon); they were eaten in slices raw with bread, and were utterly delicious. Wolf-Werner faithfully sent us one for Christmas every year till the Second World War. Next Goose fat was widely used instead of butter, for the north German (roughly Friesian) cow produced masses of thin milk for cheese, but hardly any cream. A very well educated *au pair* girl whom we had in 1960 had never seen proper cream until she came to us.

Then the liver, with any other flesh still to be found, might go with pork, into a *terrine*, or be converted finally into a sausage filling for which – wait for it – the intestines would form the skin.

In this economy, the tenants had their share. We are, be it remembered, still at the end of the horse and buggy era, and the railway station at Tantow, was quite far off. It was an isolated life, and the Lord owned the horses and the buggies and the winter sleighs. In theory, any tenant was free to leave. In real life he had to be exceptionally independent or exceptionally unhappy to do so. Mental independence was not encouraged. Vally gave them the *Preussische Kreuzzeitung* to read, and nothing else. And the expense and the difficulty of organising a family move was very great. If no friend would help (and the Lord would see to that), you had to get in a removal man from Stettin. You had to find out his name and address, and the only telephone was in the *Schloss*. And how on earth would you support life when you reached town without much money and without the customary *leumund* or recommendation? Most tenants made the best of it, and the Vallys of this curious world saw to it that best was not too bad.

It was, to begin with, in their interest, for unwilling labour does not pay. The tenants were paid partly in kind, including free housing maintained at the Lord's expense. Even the most pot-bellied nobleman cannot eat and drink more than a very limited amount; it was, in a practical sense, impossible for anyone to spend more than a certain amount on himself. The larger the household, the greater the prestige, but also the more actually consumed by other people. In Staffelde, the family and its guests might amount to a continuing average of a dozen people, and there would also be five or six chief servants and about 24 others from carpenters to scullions (not all of whom lived in). Thus, measured in kilos, the gentry consumed only about a quarter of what went into the Schloss: and if the family got the first cut, the second, given an intelligent cook, might be as good.

Now the cook, Selli was at the very centre of the web. She was a raven haired genius, by now heavily built and wheezing: a tyrannical hypocrite who knew the weakness of human nature only too well, and if she took a dislike to somebody she invariably managed to goad them into some indiscretion. A handsome young footman, in his first proper job, was taunted so persistently with insinuations about his sexual habits, that he eventually shouted – at kitchen dinner down the table – 'halt dein Maul, du alte Sau' (shut your trap, you dirty old sow).[*] So there was Olweg saying quietly in the study 'mademoiselle wishes to speak with the *Herr Rittmeister*' and Vally heaving a sigh and saying to the demure lady, smoothing down her snowy apron, 'what is it now, Selli?'

And so, as Vally said afterwards 'she is a Satan and it is all grossly unjust, but one of them has to go, and Selli is necessary to me, while he is not'.

Cornelia had taken on Selli at the age of sixteen. Really good cooks were addressed as 'Mademoiselle' for which 'Selli' was short and she was the technical manageress of the provision business centred on the Schloss. But she and Cornelia had something very interesting in common, namely a high level understanding of food. All the great households had their culinary secrets. Somehow Staffelde penetrated the guard with ease. It was widely hinted that Cornelia bribed other people's retainers to betray their art. Not so: Cornelia had a perfect analytical palate and memory. When she ate something, she knew exactly what was in it. The morning after dining out, she would summon Selli and dictate a recipe. 'Selli, at Herr v. der Osten-Penkun's we had a *paté en croûte* of crayfish and cod, about six to four, with a tablespoon of parsley between twelve helpings and half a teaspoon of . . . .' And then it would be served up as a trial, and if it was not quite right, Cornelia's memory would adjust it for the next time.

In an England where cooks are not respected and food is swallowed regardless of anything but a lip service to hygiene, I can corroborate this independently. Until smoking and middle age made inroads, I had a very similar, presumably inherited faculty. If I were noticing properly what I was eating, I could go home and cook the same thing myself. I imagine that it depends on an arrangement of the taste-buds.

Here, while I am about it, is another story about cooking. Horcher and his wife started a little restaurant in Berlin at four marks (say 17p)[**] a meal. He served; she cooked. There was no menu. He simply asked you what you had last eaten and when. Wilhelmine and Albrecht often went there. The meal sent up was *always* exactly what you most wanted. Naturally the fairest in the land crowded in. He had to take on waiters, extend the premises, engage other cooks, raise the prices.

---

[*] It was ruder than the translation suggests. 'Maul' is an animal's mouth, 'Sau' of a woman was unspeakably filthy in a general way, and he used the disrespectful 'du'.
[**] 25 marks to the pound.

Alas, he had no head for business, and anyway the large catering establishment which had somehow grown up around him was unsuitable for his methods. People began to drift away, talking of nine-day wonders. He went bust.

He restarted somewhere else in Berlin. Of course it was an instant success. The business grew again, and in the same way with exactly the same results. He went bust a second time. So he began again..... and when I was at Oxford in 1938 it was rumoured that old Horcher was starting up yet another venture. No doubt he and Frau Horcher will be doing it in purgatory until the Last Trump (in German the Last Trombone) ensures that no pot will ever boil over again. Henry tells me that he has seen a restaurant called 'Horcher' in Madrid. I am glad to hear it.

So far, we are still below stairs, but now, with Selli panting ahead, we must climb into the zone of personal service. This required other sorts of skills, of an important and discerning kind: memory, tact, deftness and sympathy. It would never do to put milk in old Geheimrat* Ganz's coffee. His indigestion might upset some scheme of the Herr Rittmeister's. If, in the early morning, you came face to face with a Herr v. B emerging from the bedroom of the beautiful baroness H-B did you drop him a curtesy, or roll up the carpet? My lady catches her skirt on the iron step of the sleigh just as she is setting out for dinner. No time to change: it would spoil her coiffure. It has to be mended speedily and perfectly, not cobbled, and without lifting above the dictates of modesty.

Here we are back to confirmation. It was a common practice, especially for a daughter now leaving childhood, to find a village girl of about her age to become her personal maid. They would, in effect be brought up together, and the association often lasted a lifetime. When the young baroness married into another house, the maid came too. She was the fierce guardian of her property, convenience and reputation, and often the repository of her most intimate secrets. She was the model for the soubrette of the operettas. Such a relationship, not in Cornelia's case, was, obviously, sometimes tinged with lesbianism which, indeed, might be explicit if highly discrete. I have seen a picture of an Austrian countess whipping her smiling maid's backside: a fantasy picture, but I think that it refers to a reality: perhaps even in extreme cases a fact. The dovetailing of experience and adventure, the maid living through her mistress, especially if she were beautiful, often conduced to an attractive communion of affection and service. Conversely, the employer owed it to her maid that she should rise when she rose, and should not suffer for her loyalty if things turned out to be difficult. Such a maid wheeled Eva Maria v. Kameke 300 miles in her cripple's wheelchair during the Russian invasion and was raped twice before they reached Berlin.

* Privy Councillor.

At Staffelde Lila, as lady's maid, was in charge of the bedrooms and the staff of housemaids and boys who looked after them. She, like Selli, had been taken on at sixteen; and they hated each other; from 1895 to 1915 they never exchanged a spoken word or sat at the same table. Lila was one of two whom Selli could not destroy. Fortunately for everyone, the Staffelde household had been set up by Vally and Cornelia from scratch. If they had to come with Cornelia into an already established organisation the mind boggles at the probabilities. As it was Lila had the bedrooms on the upper floors swept and garnished by lunchtime, and had her staff hard at work in the sewing room, the boot room and the laundry, for the volume of work was vast, all the afternoon.

Selli directed scullions and kitchen-maids and porters, and bickered with gardeners in the basement. They were separated by Olweg's ground floor. German officers used their batmen as personal servants in their flats at garrison towns. Quite a number of head butlers had left the army with their officers. I have a feeling that Olweg was not such a case, unless he had already been in household service when he went into the army, for he seemed to be almost the caricature of the unflappable, perfectly turned out, tactful gentleman's gentleman. He knew the appearance and relationships of everyone in the world who might matter to the Herr Rittmeister. He could recognise an approaching visitor a mile away by the manner in which his horses were driven, or a newcomer by the arms on the door of his carriage. The parlour maids and footmen who worked on his floor were devoted to him. They served unnoticeably like the secret nocturnal cream-fed dwarves of the fairy tale. This was a great achievement for a chief servant who had no direct means of hiring or firing. Olweg might have echoed King Mongkut of Siam, if he had ever heard of him: 'I tell you, there are three thousand women in this house, and three thousand women is very much uproar'.

There were other head servants, but of a kind with whom a daughter-in-law's contacts would be only intermittent. There was a head gardener; a coachman who, with four grooms, lived in the village. He managed the extensive stables which were the main source of agricultured energy. There was the bailiff, who was the estate manager, and who was closeted most mornings with Vally in his study. All these people were recognisably of the House, almost of the Family. You might order them about, but they earned your respect by their efficiency and that honest seriousness which formed an attractive side to the Prussian character. And besides, the chances were that they had held you in their arms as a child.

In a kind of way, it was a club. But these households usually had an odd hanger-on (or two) who never fitted. These people were professionals or semi-professionals got in for some special reason. Some families, for example, had forbidding English or Scottish nannies who could see anyone off. There was too the Lutheran pastor who was given lunch, safely at the bottom of the table with somebody's tutor. There might be several tutors. My father was educated by them. Wilhelmine believed that he would have been a better man if he had gone to school. I doubt if there is much in this. There is no evidence that he was bad, and as I shall show, he may have been heroic. He in fact went to school later, and if he had been sent to an early school his career would have been different and I would presumably not be writing this.

Now tutors, doctors, vets, parsons, lawyers and suchlike tended to despise the servants (who were not impressed) and the gentry paid, fed and despised *them*. This had two deplorable results. They were generally lonely and rootless, and the tutors seldom had proper authority over their charges. A boyish prank might earn a horny-handed slap from a coachman: if you pushed the tutor into the pond everybody laughed. I suspect that the Prussian junkers have had a bad press because these sons of the pen took their excessive revenge later and in print. Wallenstein called Colonel Aldringer an inkswiller and got himself murdered. If they had stood up to the nobles as man to man and behaved properly to the servants they would have earned the respect due to any real person such as a head gardener.

Yet the schadenfreude of the *Herrschaften* was unlovely. It is related that Gutzke, one of my father's tutors, coming home from the village one night in the deep snow – drunk of course – met a person in the middle of the beaten path. 'After you', says Gutzke, taking off his hat politely. No reply, 'After you, Sir'. No reply. 'Well, perhaps I'll go on then'. No reply. 'In that case, would you kindly stand aside'. Still no reply. 'Well I – I shall have to get past you somehow'. No move. 'God damn it man, get out of the bloody way', and he punched him squarely on the jaw. It was the village pump. The attitude towards such people which this story exemplifies (for it cannot be true) coloured Wilhelmine's view of professionals then and later in life. It was with such people that Albrecht, as a *privatdozent*, seemed to be consorting. Perhaps the story is told really against Albrecht. One thing seems to emerge: Wilhelmine, subliminally or otherwise, was disenchanted, with her husband's friends and ambitions.

So they returned from Florence, and the personal contradiction became even more evident. There was, to begin with, Stefan George, Helmut von Krause and their circle. Albrecht seems to have been infatuated in that peculiar German way. If Wilhelmine is to be believed, he would stop in the street, raise a finger to his lips, look like a sheep and whisper with bated breath: 'There's the Master'.

Also, being quite unself conscious, he would appear in public in claret coloured gloves. Given half an endearing chance he would have:

> 'Walked down Piccadilly
> With a poppy or a lily
> In his medieval hand'.

He was a follower of the Yellow Book; Oscar Wilde was, if not a hero, at any rate a martyr in his hagiology. At Farsley the Oscar Wilde affair had been rigidly censored: indeed it is possible that she had never even heard of him, let alone had any idea what he was supposed to have done.

Albrecht's sexual sophistication, in comparison with hers was now becoming a positive disadvantage, especially as she was six years older than he. She was jealous. He had no business to know so much or give so much worship to anybody but his pedestalled wife. How different he was from the strong, practical – and rich – men of action in Yorkshire and Further Pomerania. Her account of what followed does not seem to me to be wholly reliable. According to her she thought that Stefan George was stealing Albrecht and decided to face him. He came, cloak, broad brimmed hat and all, while Albrecht was out. He was perfectly courteous, but made it clear that Albrecht was his own master. It was the only dealing with George to which she ever admitted. I think that she expurgated the story, probably to help justify her divorce.

I believe that his sophistication was mechanical only: he was emotionally over complicated, hopping in and out of bed with men and girls as the fancy took him, and he had little sense of humour or sense of proportion. My Uncle Gaunt was staggered when he lost a game of Tennis and his temper at Farsley; moreover, she had little idea of, or would not understand, what his work was or what it meant. She had to entertain academics, some of them distinguished in their field. Brought up in the English social tradition of general conversation only, her artless prattle must have made Albrecht turn inwardly purple; conversely, when they spoke of things which interested or concerned them, she was furious at their, in her opinion, lapses of manners. Careerwise, she was becoming a millstone round his neck. If the blame needs to be estimated, Albrecht never could have been a very good husband, and the two were victims of Abimelech's unfortunate intervention. But there was one thing which Albrecht could not have found out until it was too late. Wilhelmine was the kind of person who, as soon as she had got something, wanted something else. As long as she had not got Albrecht, he was the something else. When she had him, she started to look round. This was not promiscuity: it might have been better if it had been. It was a perverse restlessness.

However, things were, it must have seemed lucky for Albrecht – or well planned – that at Christmas 1913 she had become pregnant. She could be explained. Moreover something else was on the way. She could be distracted and relieved of her household duties at Halle. Soon she was enjoying life at Staffelde, while Lila and Selli fussed around with layettes and good nourishing food. Things would be alright. It was a golden summer.

Chapter 6

WORLD WAR I IN GERMANY

The warlike earthquake which overthrew the social fabric of Europe caught everybody by surprise. I find this odd, for the history of the whole generation had been violent. In 1900 the Boer War and the Western interventions in China were in progress, King Umberto I of Italy was assassinated and William II was talking at Bremerhaven about Huns; and in the years before 28th July 1914, fourteen major international figures were murdered, there were fourteen revolutions or insurrections (not all connected with these murders), the international arms race sucked in five great powers, and there were seven wars. Four revolts (Portugal, Catalonia, Ireland, and Russia) took place in Europe. The Balkan Wars disrupted the important German trade with the near East and stopped the Orient Express. The Herrero rising in South West Africa, was actually in a German colony and went on for years. The armaments race and the colonial wars had caused constitutional crises in Britain and Germany with opposite resolutions, and had been followed by the supremacy of the German sabre-rattlers after the Zabern (Saverne) incident of 1913.

Perhaps the fact that all these sensational affairs had been settled somehow, made people think that the murder of the Archduke Franz Ferdinand and the Duchess of Hohenberg at Sarajevo on 28th June 1914 could be played down too. If Prince Lichnowski is right, the factor which must have changed everything was the re-opening of the strategically widened Kiel Canal three days before, for according to him, the Kaiser and his advisers decided in 1912 to provoke a War when the canal was ready. But few could be expected to know that. The holiday season was approaching: the weather was gorgeous. Harriet was in Munich.

I have never understood Wilhelmine's connection with Munich. Certainly, she must have been there from time to time before she was married. She had some English acquaintances, including Margaret Tennent who became Margaret Grosvenor, and Kathleen Alexander, a rather peculiar red-haired creature who will in due course appear again. She was presented at the Bavarian court. The long triple aisled throne room in the *Residentz* had large statues on pedestals in the rows of arches separating the three aisles. The Regent and his Court were on the dais at the end of the central aisle. The pillars and statues and the officers of the *Chevaux Legers* narrowed the approach to the Throne. A portly Excellency started up the aisle behind, instead of beside his notoriously hot-tempered Irish wife. Half way up he trod on her train, and brought her up all standing. She turned, slapped his face, and marched on. The Bavarians, who in a previous generation had been used to another Irishwoman, Lola Montez, were not at all surprised. Lola, after all, had horsewhipped the editor of an Australian newspaper.

Despite her advanced pregnancy, Wilhelmine was at the Selliers in July. They had a beautiful house and garden off the von der Tannstrasse. I suppose that she had gone there partly to see Harriet, and I half suspect, to get away from the increasingly complicated Blumenthal situation. These Selliers were Cornelia's relatives and of Huguenot stock like her; but more importantly old father Sellier was a friend of Vally's. This connection was, at a considerable remove, to have a decisive impact on my life.

Up in Staffelde, Lila made tiny garments. Her lawn baby clothes, embroidered, of course with Bs and coronets, have been used by all Wilhelmine's descendents. The powers mobilised. Albrecht was called up as a trooper to the 2nd Heavy Cavalry in Cologne. The Austro-Hungarian ultimatum to Serbia was delivered on 23rd July. On 25th my mother heard the troops marching past the windows. My only brother, Werner Gaunt (later called Richard),[*] was born next day. There was confusion, not least in the hospitals whose staff and doctors were being called up too. Sweating physicians and harassed matrons were running the maternity wards like sausage machines. There was even a shortage of parsons, and a very hot Roman Catholic priest had to stand in for all. He baptised both Wilhelmine and Werner along with six others and rushed on. I sometimes wonder why he did not use a hose.

Wilhelmine was, by the way, quite a small person, but she had enough milk for two. There was somebody who did not have enough for one, so Wilhelmine fed the other baby along with Werner. Later the mother came to thank her. She was an enormous woman.

They must have left the hospital almost at once, for the next glimpse of Albrecht is at the Dom Hotel in Cologne. He was some kind of orderly, temporarily attached to the Headquarters of the military governor of the Rhineland, which, since many of the officers concerned were his relatives, must have been embarrassing for a mere trooper. Cologne swarmed with the military. They had lunch at the Dom. Every time an officer came into the room (and it was a fashionable place then) Albrecht had to leap to his feet and stand rigidly to attention until given permission to sit, which, no doubt for Wilhelmine's blue

---

[*] I shall call him Werner until the moment when he took the new first name, and Richard thereafter.

eyes, usually came quickly. All the same, it took over two hours to get through that meal.

A contemporary Count Alfred Keyserling was a wealthy unpopular Rhineland figure; unpopular enough for the local students once to have thrown him into the river. The other fashionable hotel in Cologne was the Disch, at which a very grand society reception was to be held. Everybody from the Metternichs to the Krupps had been invited – but not this Keyserling. They were a formidable lot, not likely to be insulted. He quietly bought the Hotel Disch, and on the great day stood at the head of the steps and, with the utmost urbanity, turned all the guests away. The splendid row which followed, reverberated for months. You could not challenge him, because he had already once refused a challenge for the sensible reason that, being an excellent shot, he could easily kill his man; but everybody who could think of an excuse, sued him or the Hotel Disch. All very Rhinelander and bourgeois.

By the declaration of the 1st August, Germany was already at war with Russia. In the west, operational movements began next day when the army entered Luxemburg. The Second Heavy Cavalry moved on the 3rd before dawn. My mother watched them ride away into the darkness. Werner was a week old.

At about the same time, too, the *Garde zu Fuss* detrained at Cologne and set off westwards. It was time to get back to Staffelde. Despite the requisitioning of the railways, this was not too hard, especially for a baroness with a baby and a nurse. Nor did Harriet have much trouble. The British declaration caught her and many other English holiday-makers in enemy territory and without passports, for only Russia harassed travellers for them. Nowadays the authorities would promptly have rounded them up – a custom instituted by Bonaparte – and variously maltreated them, but civilisation still prevailed in Germany, or at least Bavaria, and though they were all worried, they were entirely at large.

A curious feature of the second Reich was that the states maintained internal ambassadors to each other and some like Bavaria and Saxony maintained independent diplomatic relations with foreign countries. There was thus in Munich a British Minister who, of course was packing his bags. He made arrangements with his official friends and the Bavarian State railways: so after a day or two Harriet unconcernedly bought a ticket and caught a train to Switzerland. No trouble at all. But beyond Switzerland the French were in the grip of a black Teutophobic hysteria. Everybody coming from the East was a Spy. Moreover, *La Belle France* was again being penetrated by *les sales Boches*, Little Belgium having already been raped. At Basel, the guns of Belfort could be clearly heard. As a matter of fact, in that neighbourhood the only people who were doing any penetrating were the French;

the guns were the opening barrage for a French southern offensive. But there was an official and police panic, and all sorts of innocuous people were being put inside on childish pretexts. EF Cummings in *The Enormous Room* relates how a British officer arrived at Marseilles and was incarcerated for a year at la Fertaé Massé because his Pushtu inflected French sounded like a German accent to some garde mobile. After the war, the French government had to rehabilitate the memory of over 1,500 French citizens who had been wrongfully shot as traitors. Fortunately Harriet had a document signed by the Minister at Munich: but much more importantly (for, who knows? It might be a forgery), she spoke fluent French and had a genuine liking for French people. So she argued her way to the Channel and got across on a returning troopship. She found England in the grip of a similar outburst of unthinking hate.

Nobody has ever satisfactorily explained why the western belligerents were suddenly almost choked by a mutual loathing which was persistent, deep and dangerous, whereas in the Second World War, when we had to fight the loathsome Nazis, no such visceral feeling was discernible. I have mentioned some French symptoms. In England Jewish shops with names like Mandelbaum (not to mention Blumenthal) had their windows broken. They stopped playing Beethoven at the Proms; and all kinds of stories about German frightfulness were circulated. The Nurse Cavell controversy at least produced the finest stone statue of the twentieth century but what is one to make of the rumour, encouraged by *Punch*, that the Germans were using corpses in the manufacture of margarine? The faithful First Sea Lord, Prince Henry of Battenburg, was driven from office with insult because of his German background, yet he himself had suffered at Prussian hands. This kind of nonsense encouraged by commercial journalism invaded attitudes towards persons whom, only a few days ago, one had taken quite naturally or had hardly considered at all.

The same was happening in Prussia. I have indicated elsewhere that Bismarck's policy, though not expressly anti-British, had disadvantages for British trade; there was, too, a growing seed of Anglophobia in the ruling clique, beside the ever-present suspicion of the French. Colonial competition and its concommitant naval arms race, had made things worse. Now the *Entente*, the usual German term for the wartime alliance of their enemies, included vast hordes of Russian slavs, and from the East German point of view, a Russian invasion meant barbarism. This was precisely what was in progress now, and the Germans, egged on by the Kaiser, saw themselves as the champions of culture. This not unreasonable outlook led, however to outbursts as irrational as those manifested among the Allies. Berlin professors were engaged to rediscover or invent good Germanic words for the foreign expressions in normal use. *Sauce* (even though very Germanically pronounced as 'Zohs-e') was forbidden; you now lubricated your food with *Tunke*, which was ridiculous. *Telefon* became, rather agreeably, *Fernsprecher* ('Far Speaker'). Lists of forbidden words and their authorised substitutes were issued. One was hung up to satisfy public patriotism, behind the kitchen door at Staffelde. Vally sensibly kept it there. Wilhelmine suddenly became *Die Engländerin*, a word which, because of its phonetic lay-out, can be spoken as an insult. One odd feature of this linguistic campaign was that it was aimed mostly at English and French, with whom the Germans had most in common. Russian words like *Litevka* (a buttoned-up jacket), *Droschke* (cab) and *Bortsch* (beetroot soup) survived. Vally gave her the magnificent Staffelde tower suite for her own use. She and Werner could be almost as secluded as she wished, for it had a private sitting – and bathroom. There was, by the way, a back staircase as well, for a previous owner whose suite lay immediately underneath, had arranged it for his mistress. Then, when her English allowance suddenly ceased to come through, he placed his bank account at her disposal. Nobody had thought about the practical day-to-day consequences of a major war, and everyone thought that this one would be short.

Wilhelmine, emotionally attached to England, had wholeheartedly thrown in her lot with Germany. Quite a number of English-born wives of Germans had gone home while the opportunity still existed. They had, she learned later, been badly treated and made to report weekly to the police. She, however, rejected the opportunity, which was offered to her (in Munich perhaps), and I think that she was right. All the same, home-sickness set in, now that Farsley was unattainable, and Albrecht was not there to defend her against the increasingly hostile atmosphere. Vally did his best, but Vally was not Albrecht for whom she had come all this way in body and spirit.

There were two doors into Vally's study and an immense desk but he was always ready to be interrupted, and kept two chairs specially so that people could drop in for a comfortable chat. One of Wilhelmine's problems was that she had virtually nothing to do, and as a baroness was expected to do nothing. Even Werner involved her in very little, for Lila and Selli did most things. She was soon bored and restless. Vally had his worries. All the footmen, grooms, under-gardeners had been called up (which resembled undermanning a factory) and he was short of farm labour. Two sons were in the army, and another God knows where in the Pacific. And then there was Waleska at Damen. One day he answered the telephone in the hall. It was nice, he said, when he came back, to hear her voice, but they were having trouble. Staffelde was well inside Germany and protected by the Oder. Damen was nearer the battle zone.

The trouble of the sort which they were having at Damen soon spread. Olweg came into the study looking serious. There was a Polish riot in the village and they were all coming up to the Schloss. If the outbreak of war had caught many holiday-makers in the south, the embattled eastern fronts had trapped the Galician labourers in thousands on the Prussian estates. They wanted to go home. Why could they not? They had no idea of the practical difficulties, and besides, few of them understood German. This was a little known social episode in the early stage of the war. Depending on their precise origin, they might have been fighting each other. Instead they were stranded together in the Prussian countryside.

As about 500 burly Poles were surging up to the Schloss, Vally took a gun, and Olweg who always loaded for him at shoots, took another. Then they went out and stood on the steps. The mob halted uncertainly, shifting its feet. It was leaderless and short of ideas. Wilhelmine saw, but could not hear the proceedings through the window. It might have been simpler if Vally had had any idea of the military situation but nobody knew, for the good reason that the German Command was preparing one of the greatest strategic surprises of the war. Whatever it was that Vally said, however, seemed to make its mark. After a while they wandered away and he came in mopping his bald head.

By the end of August there was news that Rudi v. Lettow-Vorbeck was expected back at Cologne. Belgium had been overrun, the army was swinging into France driving the Entente before it. It really did look as if that war, at least, might be short. Nora went off to meet him. They were dimming the lights and the train from Brussels was expected very late. Nora was awakened on her station bench by a persistent boy's voice in the gloom. The words against the background of railway noises, were 'Telegram von Lettow-Vorbeck', 'Telegram von Lettow-Vorbeck'. It dawned on her at last that she was meant. The message read 'Regret Lieutenant Rudolf von Lettow-Vorbeck, *Garde zu Fuss*, died a hero's death before Cambrai fighting the English'. Then the train arrived.

The effect was shattering. Nora was very Prussian, and her Guards connection with the court had been a sort of conductor for Anglophobia. Also I believe that she loved her father and was jealous because he and Wilhelmine got on so well. She returned to Staffelde broken-hearted and furious. Here, however, is a conflict of evidence. According to Wilhelmine, *Die Engländerin* became the scapegoat of her misery. Nora blackened her character to Vally, to the servants, to relatives. She was rude to, or snide about her, and circulated disagreeable insinuations (which faithful friends reported) behind her back. Yet she was very ready to sympathise with Nora's loss; an unself-regarding capacity for such sympathy was an attractive facet of her character, and the loss itself like the lengthening list of casualties among her friends, served to deepen her anxieties. There was no news of Albrecht. How many Blumenthals had already died for their country? Was Vally to lose all his sons? What with the Russian steamroller crushing its way towards Waleska? And of course these worries and antipathies were felt as strongly among the servants and villagers. Would Anna so-and-so (three months gone) ever see her Peter (for in the villages nobody arranged a marriage till the girl was safely pregnant) again? What about Joachim, reputed to be a by-blow of Herr Robert's and an excellent groom too? And the mutual relationships of the *Herrschaften* were matters of animated interest and partisanship. In the general neurosis the intense heat did not help.

At this time the news of Hindenburg's brilliant victory over the Russians in the so-called Tannenberg battle exploded, like a firework display, over the eastern sky. The Russians have always alarmed the Prussians, and everybody east of Berlin had forebodings about war on two fronts. The hordes of Asiatic savages, Tartars, Cossacks, looters and rapists with their stock-whips and knouts, were eating the fair East Prussian land like locusts. Loose cattle and refugees were drifting back, spreading rumour: atrocious tales were being embroidered.

Actually the frontier population had been evacuated largely through official action. Not many were raped, even by Cossacks, because there was hardly anyone there. Nor was the land particularly fair; when it was not sandy waste, it was covered with pinewoods and lakes like Finland. No matter, the Russians were coming ponderously on. Anyone looking at a map would realise that Königsberg and Allenstein were bound to be lost. Graudenz? Thorn? Danzig might be a battlefield. Would the army be able to scramble back over the Vistula? There had been a great battle at Gumbinnen, which must have been lost because the Commander-in-Chief, General v. Pritwitz (a relative) has been dismissed.

I am trying to reconstruct how these events seemed to a group of slightly hysterical and only partly informed people in an isolated Prussian estate during an appallingly hot summer. It is no part of my purpose to say whether Hindenburg, Ludendorff, v .Francois or Hoffmann really won the battle; whether Samsonov, Rennenkampf, or Zhilinski lost it, or, come to that, whether it took place at Tannenberg. The victorious article of faith was that the aristocratic Hindenburg (another relative) had by a smashing victory, imposed a just retribution for the dreadful day of Tanenberg in 1410, when the Teutonic Knights had gone down before the chivalry of Poland. No German had ever forgotten that disaster. It was, after all, one of the cardinal events of European history. So now there was a shout of triumph from ten million throats.

According to Wilhelmine, like Deborah after Sisera's murder, Nora triumphed too. Look what has happened to Wilhelmine's Russian friends! *Aetsch*!

The isolation and the friction were not, however, uninterrupted. Otherwise life at the Schloss would have become unbearable sooner than it did. Nora was not always there, and besides she had her own small child to mind. Occasionally they went to Tantow, or Stettin, and at least once Wilhelmine went to Berlin. The great receptions had ceased: for lack of gentlemen, but there were visits and visitors. In the horse and buggy era there was no question of wasting valuable wartime petrol. The horses had to be fed whether you used them or not. The passage of time eased the pain in Nora's heart, and besides, the news came through that Albrecht had, like his father 49 years before, been commissioned on the field. This made everybody a little happier, and Vally actually proud of his youngest son. At least it seemed to spike some of Nora's guns.

Nora has appeared as something of a villain in this narrative so far. In 1982 I was discussing her (dead some years back) with some of my Blumenthal relations. They and in particular her daughter Heloise (born in 1912) thought that she and my mother were kindred spirits. When I explained that she did not like Nora, they showed considerable surprise. The dislike, they said, was certainly not reciprocated. Nora had a great respect for Wilhelmine. All I can make of this is that there was a furious mutual opposition engendered by the highly charged war atmosphere, which slowly simmered down, but left an enduring and typical resentment in Wilhelmine which Nora did not nurse. I hope to be able to relate some episodes which were very creditable to Nora and exhibit her as a sympathetic and unusually courageous personality.

After a while, a convalescent brother officer in Albrecht's unit appeared, having promised to seek Wilhelmine out. The Western Front had turned into a rat-ridden festering military swamp, where the ordinary subaltern's expectation of life was nineteen days. It seemed that Albrecht, having done all this as a trooper, was rather better at it than those who had gone into it direct with their new commissions. Moreover, he was philosophical, and able to shut the horrors out of his mind when he needed to relax. He was translating Aeschylus..... There were some little keepsakes. It was reassuring. The war, thus far, was not grinding Albrecht into a different shape.

Then Werner, having cut lots of lovely tushy-pegs on a big bone ring, started to crawl about and (with help) to walk. He was a fascinating and charming creature, and there was competition to play with him. One day Vally at breakfast said suddenly 'have you heard the latest'? Everybody looked up expectantly. 'Selli and Lila have spoken to each other' – Cries of disbelief. Curiosity, the German vice, nearly precipitated a stampede to the kitchen. But it was true. Selli and Lila both wanted to play with Werner. The one pulled funny faces, the other appeared in her best sparkling brooch. Somehow they were both on the kitchen floor without noticing it, while scullery maids looked on incredulously. Olweg tactfully nodded the others back to work and slipped out. When they got up off the floor, a twenty year feud had ended.

Thus by mid-1915 a relative tranquillity had descended, interrupted still by the odd outburst of temperament, or by one of those terrible telegrammes. The Russians had been driven away. The estate was working with a good deal of the Galician labour permanently replacing, at proper wages, the young men who had gone to the front. Some of the village women were sad, and of course, taxes were much higher: but this made, in mundane ways, little difference to Vally who paid most of them. What he suffered in additional taxes he now saved on the socially obligatory entertainments of peacetime. The standard of living in the village and at the Schloss hardly changed. And then one day there came another of those telegrammes. Olweg offered it gravely to Wilhelmine on the usual salver. Albrecht was missing.

Wilhelmine related that as her mother became more isolated from reality there were periods of weeks when she never opened her mouth or showed any sign of emotion. She had a theory that if only Elizabeth had been able to weep, it might have been alright. The grief and anxiety and the sickness of hope had much the same effect on Wilhelmine, at any rate outside her tower. She would not, at his age, have let it affect Werner very much, or at all. She was, I am sure, able to weep and probably did, but in public she maintained a stony and conspicuous self-control, which at least warded off insult and over-sympathy. She must have been very difficult, sitting silently at table, walking silently in the corridors, or travelling silently beside Vally in his carriage, but for a while she could do nothing else. If she had opened her mouth she would probably have burst into public tears, and that she was determined not to do. I do not think that she meant it unworthily, but possibly she was trying not to make the uproar which Nora had made, and which had probably caused Vally a good deal of worry. Of course, she overdid it: worse still, she soon added an empty boredom to her other distresses. If you will not talk to anyone, no one, in the end will say anything much to you. She tried doing some gardening, but this was utterly unheard of in such a family. Baronesses digging? Impossible! After many days of obstruction she had her way The whole village turned out to watch.

Chapter 7

MUNICH, SWITZERLAND AND ME

The worst of it lasted only a few months. Vally invariably read any postcards which came, regardless of the addressee. In fact postcards were his way of telling all the world about something. One morning Wilhelmine came down to breakfast and found one in Albrecht's hand from Corsica. 'Young Albrecht seems to be alright' Vally said. Then he returned to his newspaper.

But it was not as simple as that. It made the situation, she asserted, intolerable as between Nora and herself, so Wilhelmine decided to leave. 'You've nowhere to go', said Vally, but she said that she would make a home in Munich. She took a flat there, for which, like everything else, he paid, in the Schneckenburgerstrasse,* and the Selliers, prompted by Vally, were very nice to her and introduced her to all their friends. Pride made her take as little of his money as possible, so she and Werner lived a simple life. It sounds more than simple; there was a daily who did for her, and she and Werner habitually lunched out; but this was the custom of Munich in 1915. Even the maid was given a small daily sum for her midday sauerkraut and beer, which she had with cronies or boyfriends in a café. My mother found a cheap restaurant behind the Feldherrenhalle, where she became a habitué. There was nothing odd about this except the identity of another regular who usually came in with other, rather deferential men, or with his family. The face seemed familiar.

During World War II I had the following slightly embarrassing encounter. I was sitting in the Underground opposite a tall naval officer in a blue raincoat which concealed his exact rank. The scrambled eggs on his hat indicated great importance. I was in uniform myself. We both got off at Green Park Station, and I ventured to address him. I said that I believed that we had met somewhere. He was very agreeable, but said that he was not sure that we had. We parted: I saluting his presumed rank. Some days later I saw why I believed that I knew him. His face had been in the newspapers ever since the spring of 1940. He was King Haakon of Norway. Wilhelmine had much the same problem in her restaurant near the Preysingpalais. Her neighbour at table was the Bavarian Prince Regent.

---

* Schneckenburg – snail shell, but there had been a poet, so called.

In the recent history of the Wittelsbachs there had been the deposition and drowning of Ludwig II, alleged to be mad but actually only homosexual and mildly eccentric. His detractors could not have believed their own propaganda. They deposed him in favour of his brother, who really was insane. The reason, of course, was the ambitious uncle, who stopped short of murder, but fixed the sordid business to get his hands on the tiller and the property. It worked, more or less, in peacetime, though a good deal of the income had perforce to go in maintaining the mad Monarch. Then came the war. The whole resources of Bavaria had to be employed in waging it. The King had his secured maintenance, the Regent had not. All of a sudden he was (as regents go) poor – and anyhow most of the court servants and cooks, if not too old, were in the army. His Royal Highness took to popping across to the restaurant opposite for lunch.

This was a happy time. The war was not going too badly and Munich was far and safe from the trampling and thunder of the active fronts. The population, anyway calmer by nature than the semi-Slavonic Prussians, were less neurotic in the circumstances; and if there was no Albrecht, Wilhelmine was unknown, save to the Selliers who preserved her anonymity. She easily passed for a German, speaking and behaving exactly like one. She was and for the rest of her life, remained better educated in German than in English. Here in Munich, hostile nationalism had no hold over her. She was much with the Selliers, playing with Werner in the garden, or getting involved in the literary and artistic community of that Italianate city, with its Baroque and rococo, and its stuccoed classical streets where the spirit of the great Lenbach still presided, and the red twin towers of the *Liebfrauenkirche*[*] topped with onions, threw their shadow across steep ancient roofs.

Many German churches have their story about the Devil. In the *Liebfrauenkirche* near the west door is a hoof-shaped mark on a paving stone. The architect could not get the building up in time to honour his contract. He got the Devil to help, but had to agree that it should not be possible to see out of the windows. The church rose like magic. The Devil arrived at the west door to inspect his handiwork. From there it was indeed not possible to see out of the windows; they were and are, masked by the pillars all the way along the nave. 'Where does all the light come from?' he said suspiciously. 'You never stipulated that the windows should be blocked', came the smooth reply. Lucifer stamped with rage and disappeared in a puff of brimstone, leaving the Mark of the Beast.

The church, at this period, was a dark soaring place with its night-blue vault high above, spangled with golden stars. The darkness was caused by some pretty but rather opaque stained glass which effectively carried out the Devil's intention. There was a good deal of stained glass in Munich generally, and a school of glaziers

---

[*] This beautiful dedication means 'Church of the Beloved Lady'.

had developed and kept abreast of the times. A little later, in the '20s and '30s this school, dominated by the remarkable aesthetic personality of Sepp Frank, managed to be both modernist and decorative. When Wilhelmine and Percy built their house at Wentworth, they installed one of Sepp Frank's windows in it: a brilliant affair in reds and blues of a praying saint. It was only after a moment that it dawned on one that the saint had a green head. It sounds awful: it is, in fact, splendid.

In 1960 I revisited the Liebfrauenkirche. I found that the war had blown out the windows, so they had taken the opportunity to spring clean the light. Pale glass let it in. The pillars and vaulting were white. The improvement was staggering. The Devil really had been chased away and the Munich school of glaziers was going strong.

Outwitting the Devil was a widespread mediaeval German sport. The infernal gentleman was not a very clever fellow. There are, too, a good many surprisingly good-natured German jokes about fools. I imagine that they come from the same psychological source. There is the ancient legend of the Ship of Fools, and my father used to tell me stories about the foolish town of Schildburg. They cut down the trees in the nearby mountains, and dragged them to the gates to build a town hall. Then someone said 'if you'd lopped off the branches at the top of the hill you could have rolled them down'. 'What a good idea', cried the lumber gang – and, suiting the action to the word, dragged them all back to the top of the hill..... They got their town hall built in the end, and found that it was pitch dark inside. So in good weather, the corporation employed gangs of sunbeam catchers to trap sunlight in large leather sacks and empty it out in the council chamber. This method of illumination was simpler than that practiced with cucumbers by Gulliver's Lagadians.

In 1975, Henry and I stayed at Meersburg, a charming small mediaeval town on the north shore of Lake Constance; a modern fountain had been erected for the embellishment of the town by the Guild of Hundred and One Idiots. May they live forever!

One of the differences between the Bavarian and the Prussian was related to religion. The protestant Prussian tended to bottle things up inside and, if ever he said his innermost thoughts, he said them direct to his God. Naturally, he sometimes blew up. The Bavarian, with his rather lightly taken confessor, was more used to letting it all out. In this respect, the English Wilhelmine was more Prussian than Nora, but the moral climate of Munich, with its artistic intrigues, was more sociable and less oppressive than that of Pomerania or Berlin. It is hardly a coincidence that the least inhibited of the Scandinavians, the Danes, and the Bavarians each have a royal brewery and a penchant for amiable booze ups, and of course there is the annual Bavarian Saturnalia called *Fasching*, which so far as the boozing is concerned, has spread to most of Germany since World War II. At this period immediately before Lent, the rule was that any kiss offered by anyone must be returned. As the masked proceedings go on, day and night for ten days, many new relationships are formed. Some women even had fleeting affairs with their own husbands.

Sometime soon, a message came *via* the Swiss Red Cross that parcels could be sent to Albrecht through them. He was at Clermont Ferrand in the Massif Centrale. He needed boots and books. So there was great joy – and ingenuity. She bought maps of France, cut them up and sent them between the leaves of the books. This stratagem was so naif that it succeeded, where others, like inserting them in the bindings failed. A cobbler made a large hole for a compass in the heel of one of the boots. This got through too. We had it for years. Albrecht had had an adventurous captivity. The German U-boats had begun waging indiscriminate war or had initiated an under water blockade (it depends on the point of view) against shipping, and had sunk a French hospital ship. The French promptly locked German officer prisoners up below the waterline of their hospital ships, Albrecht among them. It was a boring business, but being brought up on deck blinking in to the noonday glare of Algiers or Oran by polite French naval officers was a compensation until it was time to weigh anchor and return to the oily smelly compartment where there was nothing to do. Then one morning he was discharged to a prison in the Corsican port of Ajaccio.

It was full of subalterns and short of guards; conditions were relaxed, and everybody indulged in escape dreams. Albrecht had been lucky so far: his Mediterranean cruises had at least given him changes of scene, while other prisoners were bored stiff. Of course the daydreams turned into plans. They would recut their uniforms into imitation civilian clothes, let themselves over the wall with ropes, inevitably made of old blankets, and walk. So far the plan seemed workable. There were plenty of loose window bars, but the seas about Corsica were dominated by the enemy navies. If the prisoners of Ajaccio had had any news the attempt would have seemed more forlorn than they thought. They would walk to the east coast across the island, steal a boat and sail to Italy which they believed to be friendly. They had no idea that the Italians, persuaded by a massive bribe, were about to desert their German alliance. They actually deserted in May 1915, in accordance with the secret treaty signed at London at the end of April. Albrecht's chances of getting home on reaching Italy without money were therefore not good.

The Great Night came. They swung down the prison wall and set off gaily into the countryside. By breakfast time, they were well away, and as far as they could tell, unobserved. They lay up in the maquis till sundown and went on. Eventually they were walking with the sea distantly ahead. A lorry load of *gardes mobiles* appeared from behind and simply picked them up and took them back to Ajaccio. They were hungry, and the *mobiles* gave them bread and onions and lots of red wine. It was all very matey and tiresome, but the prison governor bellowed at them in his office.

They had not reckoned with the poverty of Corsica. They had in the early mornings passed the odd peasant on the way to work. The police learned that four men *wearing rings* had been seen walking in an easterly direction. So, when the governor had stopped bellowing, they were hustled into solitary confinement, and after a few days were taken to the escape proof castle prison of Corte on a rock in the centre of the island.

Albrecht was in Corte for over eighteen months, and never managed a break, and it injured his health. Then he was suddenly moved to Ajaccio, put onto a steamer, disembarked at Marseilles and escorted, first to Clermont Ferrand and then to Mons-en-Pévèle, where the Swiss Red Cross caught up with him again.

Nothing shows the Swiss in a better light than their impartial and painstaking care for prisoners and wounded. They were extremely tough. Prison commandants were terrified of them, and prisoner-of-war administrations tried to hide their less desirable establishments from their gaze. No matter: sooner or later a foreign office would have an embarrassing visit from a Swiss minister and his esteemed colleague from Geneva. They soon found out about Mons-en-Pévèle, which was cold, overcrowded and insanitary; and since the Red Cross was still a well-knit international body, Albrecht's identity, brought him a visitor, none other than Harriet, who had got herself a job in the French Red Cross. She was alarmed at his appearance, though he assured her that he was well. In any case a Swiss medical inspection was due. Shortly after this, Wilhelmine had further news of him and they began to exchange letters.

Albrecht never had to use his compass because the scheduled inspection revealed that he was suffering from some form of tuberculosis, induced probably by bad diet, lack of fresh air and sun and the damp and nasty state of the prison cages.

At this point Wilhelmine tells a curious story. She determined to go to France to see him, and somehow got a Swiss safe-conduct. I suppose that she must have left Werner with friends (what friends?) while she passed over to enemy territory. Considering that she had been sending Albrecht maps and compasses, she was taking her life in her hands. She went to Mons-en-Pévèle. Rather hostile French guards ushered her into a room with a barrier across the middle. She was told that she must not speak. Albrecht was brought silently into the room. He did not speak either. They gazed at each other for a few long minutes. Then the presence was withdrawn and she returned the way she had come.

Was this story a romance? At first I thought that she was projecting onto herself an account of Harriet's visit, but the details do not fit, for Albrecht and Harriet certainly spoke to each other. What is more, she described in a disjointed fashion, a number of occurrences which may relate to this adventure. Once she was locked up at a Swiss frontier and then stripped naked. Another time she had bought 'real' chocolate in Switzerland intending to let Werner, who was with her, have some, but found after she crossed the frontier, that customs officials had pilfered it. This must refer to a very short time in Switzerland, for otherwise they would have been used to chocolate, and the story would have had no point. In addition, one of Albrecht's prison poems was written at Mons in November 1916.

His next places of call were Carcassonne in the spring of 1917 and Moulins in the summer. One of his prison companions throughout much of this pilgrimage was a graceful Rhinelander called Curt Haniel, for whom one of the poems was written. He and Albecht became close friends. It was an influential friendship.

There were Allied prisoners in German cages who, like Albrecht, were consumptive and the Swiss persuaded both sides to make exchanges. Switzerland, in that war, was one of the ready-made corridors for communication between enemies. The squads of exchanged prisoners were meticulously counted and receipted at the respective frontier posts, before being received into the luxurious atmosphere of a neutrality protected by the citizen army of the Swiss nation.

For many years tuberculosis had been treated mainly by putting the patient into high air, and Switzerland had, in the form of mountain sanatoria, a considerable industry which was really a medicated branch of their tourist trade, very profitable before the war. Now hotels and sanatoria alike stood empty, while the hospitals of the embattled nations were drowned with wounded from Ypres, the Somme and Verdun, Galicia, Italy, and the high seas. Neither side had facilities for dealing with exchanged tubercular prisoners, and the French, in particular, were terrified of the disease. Hence both alliances were only too glad to hire Swiss sanatoria, and the Swiss were glad to oblige. This merciful common sense created employment and reinforced their neutrality. The German government hired the hospitals at Davos in the Engadine. Wilhelmine learned that Albrecht would soon be sent there, and then began receiving letters from him direct. It might be feasible to see him there. Tremendous and joyful flurry! No more maps and compasses. Residential visas were the thing. Private travel regulations had been much barbarised since Harriet so nonchalantly left Munich in 1914. Now you had to have a visa obtained in Munich to get into Switzerland, and a permit obtained in Berlin to get out of Germany.

There was much rushing to and fro. Eventually all was signed and sealed and so they presented themselves before the Swiss bayonets and barbed wire at Schaffhausen, and re-entered the Promised Land.

War economies run down. Some changes for the worse occur abruptly on the outbreak: - you cannot get decent shoes because all the shoemakers are making army boots – but you get used to these and then resigned to the shallow downward steps of progressive deprivation. By this time, for example, sugar was tightly rationed in Germany, but everybody managed because, originally, they believed that it was needed for explosives, and then because they learned to do without.

Wilhelmine and Werner made that journey by night, and her first measure of the decline of German civilisation was the blinding illumination of this Swiss frontier city. There was no black-out in that war, but the dark was symbolic as well as real. German morale was on the decline, but here in Switzerland the old confident arts of peace flourished. There were shops full of chocolate, and there was nothing to stop you eating a Wiener Schnitzel as big as a dinner-plate every day! Cuckoo-clocks were cheap. So Muti really did buy Wernerli the first chocolate he ever had.

Schaffhausen to Zürich; change; Zürich to Arth-Goldau; change. 'Good God, there he is on the platform'. And that was where Albrecht set eyes on his elder son, who ran up and down the platform shouting 'it's my daddy; it's my daddy'. Then they caught the train to Chur and another one on the Rhaetien narrow gauge, up to Davos.

Albrecht was wearing a second class Iron Cross. As the Germans did not have our sensible plurality of decorations the various classes of the Iron Cross did duty for most things. The first World War began its devaluation. Second class Iron Crosses were not all that uncommon. According to my Winchester housemaster, a British infantry subaltern on the Sinai front was captured by the Turks. A shell had broken his leg. The Turks put him in a hospital, full of syphilitic Turkish soldiers. A German general arrived. Nobody told him. He marched round the wards dispensing Iron Crosses to all, including the British subaltern. The Turks were highly amused.

It was a second honeymoon but with responsibilities. Albrecht was acting as a sort of adjutant for the many German military in the Davos santoria. And besides the Germans had wives, children and other hangers-on who trickled through from Germany. They needed an adjutant too, and as Wilhelmine was energetic, strong minded, practical and the only baroness in the place, she took the job. It mostly involved dealing with the Swiss who knew about her English background, so she got on well with them to the advantage of the local Germans. Whatever good Davos did for the consumptives, it was certainly a healthy place for the healthy; they all throve, particularly Albrecht, for lots of milk and eggs soon put him right. Once they went up to St Moritz. They heard the guns on the Piave booming across the mountains, and there was an earthquake. The buildings shook. Cracks appeared in the plaster, and there was an extraordinary sound in the valley like the baying of gigantic hell-hounds. Albrecht restarted his scholarly pursuits; at Christmas 1917 he addressed some poems, written mostly in captivity to Wilhelmine, and embellished them for her in his attractive hand. I have them now.

There is another incident which deserves a mention. Wilhelmine paid a visit to friends of Vally's who lived at Oberhofen on Lake Thun. Lenin was living nearby and he regularly came to the von Arx's hotel where she and Werner stayed. Werner, standing on a stool behind the reception counter, used to talk to him. Apparently that evil man could be quite jovial when it didn't matter. He left shortly afterwards in his celebrated sealed train for St Petersburg. I am typing this on 7th December 1984, having just read with pleasure that the Chinese seem to have repudiated most of the doctrines of Marx, Engels, and Lenin himself.

For the belligerents, the winter was in most ways the worst part of the war, but for Herr and Frau v. Blumenthal, fortunate and relatively free in the Engadine, this was not so. They lived a happy rather ordinary peacetime family life, circumscribed only by Albrecht's parole. Werner became a very strong, but it seems, rather temperamental boy. Albrecht slowly recovered. He and Wilhelmine conceived me.

Wilhelmine's pregnancy at Davos posed a problem. Vally had kept up the odd Swiss connection since his days as attaché in Bern. Among these was a Herr Dumont, a distinguished Bernese lawyer, and she addressed herself to him on the difficult problem of Swiss nationality. If I were born in Switzerland I might be a Swiss citizen. This could have all sorts of consequences.

The ordinary insulated person of uncomplicated parentage never has to think much about nationality, citizenship or allegiance. His experience is confined to filling in passport applications, getting the occasional visa and passing oddly uniformed officials at capriciously sited frontiers. But a growing minority has problems which stem from the insane world of nation states which erected their sovereignties upon the ruins of a once united Christendom. Some attempt to describe this poisonous jungle seems worthwhile if only to draw attention to a heartless and disgraceful aspect of modern life. I hasten to add that it was considerably better and more intelligible in 1918 than it is in 2007.

In the first place, every sovereign state defines in its own way the nature, purpose, origins and incidents of an individuals' relationship with itself. In 1918, for example, there was no such thing as a British citizen but if, no matter how accidentally, you were born on British soil, you were by English or Scots law a British *subject*. But another state might hold a different view. Ruritanian law made you a Ruritanian subject if your father was a Ruritanian (a common state of affairs). Thus a baby born of Ruritanian parents in England would have both nationalities unless there was a treaty between Britain and Ruritania applying some different rule. There is, unfortunately, no such treaty. The practical consequences are inconvenient and intricate. Since you were a British subject, the British authorities will not allow the Ruritanian diplomatic representatives in Britain to act for you and, of course, the Ruritanians return the compliment. But what about third countries? Ruritania is at war with Boldavia. As a Ruritanian, you are called up into the Ruritanian army. As a British subject you commit a breach of the Foreign Enlistment Acts if you obey the call. Britain is in the EU, Ruritania is not. Are you entitled, as a British subject, to the trading advantages of other British subjects as against outsiders in the EU? Do you suffer from the disadvantages of such a status in other countries? Do you, by any chance have the disadvantages of a Ruritanian in the EU and those of a British subject outside it? And supposing that Britain and Ruritania go to war, you commit treason (for which you may be hanged) against one side or the other if you serve in either armed force and if you serve in neither you risk prosecution by both countries.

Besides all this, most countries have invented a thing called citizenship, which is not an act of providence but a privilege to be treasured and cared for like some delicate plant. If you do something considered to be inconsistent with your obligations and privileges as a citizen, then, in many states you lose your citizenship. Each country with this absurd and cruel concept defines the obligations and privileges differently and as losing citizenship in one country does not necessarily gain you rights in another you may end up stateless. It seems that at one time if an American citizen voted in a British election he forfeited his citizenship. Irish citizens could vote in British local government elections lawfully in Britain and without risk in their own country. So Paddy O'Murphy can go home to his shack in Connemara but poor Silas K Brickenbacker, the indiscrete American may not be able to return to his little old home in Massachusetts.

The problem of the unborn me dates back to one of the sixteenth century battles of Novara. Each side had hired a Swiss army. Both armies were poorly paid, and since 'pas d'argent, pas de Suisse', when the two forces came face to face, they saw no particular reason to kill each other. Unitedly they ditched their employers and imposed all sorts of disagreeable conditions on both and excited a thrill of moral revulsion in central Europe and even among the Swiss. They resolved that no citizen of any Swiss state should henceforth serve a foreign master militarily without the consent of his government. This rule still stands. In 1918 there was no dual nationality treaty between the German Reich and the Swiss Federation; hence those born of German parents were German and liable to German military service, whereas persons accepted into a Swiss *gemeinde* (civil parish community) were Swiss and liable to Swiss military obligations. This might put me to a disagreeable election when I reached my 'teens', and meanwhile my status would differ from that of the rest of my family. On the other hand there was, for example, the prestige of Swiss neutrality. It might be a useful holt-hole.

Entente and American propaganda spoke of a War to end War and of the world government which was to spring fully disarmed from the head of the League of Nations, but Germans (whether they had heard of President Wilson's Fourteen Points or not) entertained no such illusions. War was a calamity which, somehow, just happened. Ravening armies had trampled the German lands too long and too often to leave no impression on the national mind, and in particular the Thirty Years War, had happened since the invention of printing. People read *Simplicissimus* (I mean Grimmelshausen's, not the comic magazine) and Schillers *Wallenstein*, and I myself was impressed as a child by the horror prints of Urs Graf exhibited in picture dealers windows. Add the instability of frontiers, and it was natural for Albrecht and Wilhelmine to talk at length about some form of reinsurance, but in the end the complications seemed too great; she would have to stay behind if he was recalled to Germany, and, of course there was the tug of imperial and Prussian allegiance. Had they known that the Reich had only another eight months to run, I wonder what they would have done?

As Albrecht had now been pronounced fit to go home, there was no reason to delay, but it was a wrench to leave, early in 1918, their land of milk and honey. Berlin was cold, dark and badly fed. But everything went well: I gave my mother very little trouble, and emerged, composed and healthy into an increasingly bewildered world. The Kingdom of Prussia gave me a savings bank account with, oh joy! The sum of one mark in it. In 1998 I asked the German Embassy in London whether the sum was recoverable and what it was now worth. 'Yes' they said, and '55 marks'.

Then came a final glimpse of an older order just before the grand smash. I had to be shown to my relations and christened at Staffelde. Vally was certainly pleased to see Wilhelmine. I am not sure that he and Albrecht were quite as pleased to see each other. According to the Staffelde visitors book, which I saw in 1977, Irene Kühne, Tante Su and Wolf-Werner were my godparents. My name was inscribed on the silver portable font. Much Sekt was drunk, the family plate was extracted and Werner rushed about shouting 'I've got a brother; I've got a brother'. Albrecht had me named Wolfgang; custom demanded that I should also be called Werner; but Wilhelmine insisted on Charles as well, and in English. The Lutheran pastor made offensive noises about this; Vally said, 'why not? He's her child', and afterwards he got splendidly drunk. 'I shay – you know what? Wilhelmine knowsh whatsh what. The othersh can't make boysh – she can!'

Chapter 8

DEFEAT

My parents' private disaster coincided with the public catastrophe of Germany. During the four months between my birth and the collapse, Albrecht had an undemanding military job. His wartime experiences had heightened his need to move from hard realities into classical antiquities. A brother officer had told Wilhelmine that even in the trenches near Cambrai he translated Aeschylus. Some of his prison poems certainly reflect this escapism; so I believe that he was already fishing for a job in some university. The war was going badly, and things could not go on like this for long.

The October Revolution, followed by the Peace of Brest-Litovsk, had put Russia out of the war at the turn of the year, but the attrition of the fronts and the British blockade were making such inroads into German resources that a quick, desperate victory was necessary to prevent the sands running out. They were calling up boys of sixteen into the army. My v. Heydebreck relatives lost theirs.

The troops released from the Eastern Front were brought westwards, and a four-fold grand slam had been prepared. This began with the German offensive of 21st March 1918. Brilliantly planned on the model of Hindenburg's victory at Tarnow, and meticulously organised, it made a victorious start aided by a providential fog and a tactical surprise. Two literary figures, the novelist Rudolf Binding and the critic (Sir) Herbert Read fought as captains on opposite sides and within a few hundred yards of each other in that battle. Both published accounts of it and both, in due course, became friends of the family. Rudolf, a charmer, was a tower of strength during my mother's divorce; she taught Herbert German. Later she introduced them.

Read writes of sudden and alarming things looming up in the thunderous mirk; how the French to the right vanished into thin air. The storm of the German bombardment was unendurable. They retreated to the second line which, when reached, had mostly been obliterated already. Back to the third, tramping wearily through the uproar. At last the reserve line came in sight. They ran for it. The turf had been cut and placed in front. The trenches had not been dug.

Defeat stared the dejected British infantryman in the face, but scowled upon Binding. Everything went splendidly at first – better than anyone had hoped. Then something went wrong. What happened illustrates the danger and weakness of lies. Half-starved Germany was at its last gasp. Imperial propaganda convinced the people and army that the Entente must be in even worse case. One good heave and it would all be over. In this frame of mind the hungry German troops burst through into the wasted and despairing allied back areas. Waste and despair was not what they found. On the contrary they found riches and plenty. They simply would not go on until they had helped themselves to a good meal. Binding describes how he found a whole village full of Germans as drunk as owls. Discipline had cracked. They hunted pigs and chickens rather than their enemies. They never reached the Channel, for British reinforcements came up in time to fill the gaps while they were otherwise engaged.

The effects broke the credit of the imperial regime and its hold over the people. Once the military tide actually turned, ever so slightly, the Second Reich was doomed. It had sowed at least one other seed of its own destruction. By allowing Lenin to be imported into Russia it had unleashed something which nobody knew how to control. The wholesale mutinies of the Russian armies made the German offensive of 21st March possible. When it failed, they provided the example for the German mutinies of November 1918. It was the sailors of the Kronstadt base who consolidated the revolutionary hold on Petrograd. The Kiel mutiny of the German High Seas Fleet made the news in Berlin. The collapse was sudden, stupefying and total. On 1st November a wounded but still firm imperial administration maintained the dignities and apparatus of the state. Twelve days later, the dynasts, from the Countess of Waldeck to the All Highest himself had gone. As the westward train was about to leave Dresden, King Frederick Augustus of Saxony said to the assembled politicians on the platform (in broad Saxon, as usual) 'Nu mach'r Dreck aleene'.* A general staff had signed an armistice at Compiègne on behalf of an army which had already fallen to pieces. A million soldiers tramped home – or caught the first passing train. The officers had no recognised authority: their commissions had presumably lapsed with the departure of the monarchs who had signed them. In some places crowds of troops swarmed through the streets. Here and there were formed bodies shouldering their way under the personal magnetism of some respected commander. All that they wanted to do was to get home.

The new republicans had in theory taken over. In real life this was not so. Germany was, as I have tried to explain, an organism with a Prussian military soul which, in war, permeated everything. The military collapse destroyed the organism.

* Now you'll have to do your shitting on your own.

The government could not govern: there were no instruments to hand. And besides all this, it was simultaneously assailed from at least three directions. In the first place, the Armistice did not end the war: only the fighting. The Allied troops could go safely home: there was no armed enemy in the field, but they maintained the naval and economic blockade. This exacerbated the breakdowns in government and communications. Food supplies became erratic, especially in the big cities. Like everyone else, Wilhelmine found herself queuing at soup kitchens. During the war fuel had been rationed. Now the trains stopped running, the heat was off, the lights were out because the power stations could not keep going. Berlin is cold in winter.

Secondly, there were the extremists. Barricades began to rise. Agitators tampered with troops. There was a week long communist rising in January 1919 and a three week soviet in Bremen. One officer (a total stranger) took refuge in Wilhelmine's flat until she could find him civilian clothes. There were house to house searches for 'reactionary elements' and food hoarders. During one such, I apparently gurgled so winningly from my cot at a large official, that he decided to forget why he had come. It was difficult to get about, because rival armed groups ceaselessly examined papers. Everybody naïvely complained that nobody was in charge. In March the communists, led by the vixen Rosa Luxemburg tried again. She was killed. A public opinion against revolutionary excess was forming. It was as hostile to the republic as it was to the extremists. Its backbone was the dispossessed military and officialdom. With this, too, the new government had to contend.

The fabric of Germany wore very thin. Mints and government printers ceased operations leaving an extraordinary shortage of currency. Long distance communications were nearly at a standstill. Economic zones shrank to the environs of a town, and the local authorities began to strike their own coins and banknotes. I used to have square iron one-pfennig tokens of Berlin, and notes, with silhouette pictures and rhymes, issued by the small municipality of Naumburg. I know not why my mother travelled at this time, but it must have been hair raising. You got into the first train pointing in roughly the right direction. Often you climbed in through the broken windows. Travellers sat on each others' laps or piled up on the floor. The engines belched sulphurous filth. The trains rocked and clattered on the unmaintained permanent way. Accidents and robberies were common. Years later I remember expresses with an old empty carriage behind the engine to take the shock of a possible impact. This *Schützwagen* (protective coach) had a big white plate with red lines across it, to warn passengers to keep out.

In this trough Europe was attacked by the Spanish 'flu leaving, however, a worse trail of destruction among the defeated. Very many, mainly the cold and under-nourished died in the disaster which claimed more victims than the war. My mother had some trouble keeping me alive. She averred, and I have no reason to doubt it, that it permanently affected me. I have a strong basic constitution, but I catch things. So far at 64, when this passage was originally written, I have had to overcome whooping cough, measles, blood-poisoning, pneumonia, tuberculosis, two attacks of meningitis, pleurisy, five slipped discs and six miscellaneous operations, not to mention annual attacks of influenza and a nervous breakdown, and I have twice been knocked down by traffic in the street – but I survive.

The following represents an attempt to reconstruct events and to explain why, if life was so difficult in a big city, my parents did not move to Staffelde or Schlönwitz. They were perhaps too closely marooned in Berlin until after the suppression of the Berlin communist outbreaks and the Bavarian revolt of April and May 1919. They must, however, have visited Staffelde later in 1919, but Albrecht was fixing academic jobs. Wilhelmine stayed on in Berlin while he made his arrangements in Jena or Marburg. He had an affair with a very attractive woman and Wilhelmine became instinctively aware of it. The fact, however, was forced upon her by a foolish accident. Albrecht put letters in the wrong envelopes and she received one which was not intended for her. When he next appeared, she handed it silently to him. He turned as white as a sheet. Knowing Wilhelmine, I doubt if other encounters were as tranquil. I think it very likely that she had started to nag much earlier and as often happens, to neglect him emotionally in favour of her children. Hence this affair was in part a consolation.

I know little of medicine, but I have at one time in my life had the same sort of tuberculosis as Albrecht, and I was persistently randy while I had it. The difference, I am sure, was that Albrecht had a nagging wife, so his affairs were predisposed to turn into affairs of the heart. In any case, once discovered, he saw no reason to retreat. They drifted into a sort of unhappy opposition and separation. The so called feud with Nora must, I think, have had something to do with this. My mother had reached a state of neurotic suspicion where she could not believe anything good of her, and Nora's very presence at Staffelde seems, in her mind, to have polluted the place; hence, malice became a major element in my mother's attitude to the Blumenthals generally. Albrecht and Nora were fairly close, and my mother was probably jealous. Suspicion was a prominent characteristic of the female Hainsworths, and it worsened with age. As I have already written, my mother's belief in Nora's hostility was mistaken.

Vally probably restrained the family from joining in the fray, and in any case they had a nine-day distraction. The war had shelved the question of What To Do with Bob. Apart from writing to my uncle Gaunt for some cigars (which Gaunt faithfully sent), no word had come from the South Seas. The fact that he was alive had trickled in in 1919 via Gaunt to Wilhelmine, who duly passed it to Staffelde. Now Bob trickled through himself, having picked up a gorgeous girl called Elsa on the way. They had no money of course, but were otherwise none the worse. When war broke out, Australian warships landed troops at Rabaul. Bob and other planters had seized their rifles, dragged their uniforms out of mothballs, and jumped into the bush. It was quixotic and unwise. They had no hope in their isolation: The Australians simply waited till Bob and Co got bored and hungry, and emerged from the jungle to surrender. Being uniformed they were taken at their word and shipped off to an open and quite entertaining camp near Sydney, and their unsupervised plantations either went to rack and ruin, or were taken over by Australians. It might have been otherwise if they had not fought, and Bob might have had a different Elsa at Kuragakaul or Natava. As it was, having lost all *Für Kaiser und Reich*, they enjoyed a healthy if modest existence in New South Wales until shipped as disposable prisoners, back home, where neither Kaiser nor Reich existed any more. It was on the voyage that Bob and Elsa met. She was a Habsburg Italian, daughter of the city architect of Graz. She had married a Croat baron called Paul Rauch v. Nyek who had had a plantation in Samoa. He died there in March 1918.

Vally very properly refused to put Bob into Schlönwitz. He had had his portion, so he kept him living free at Staffelde. They were entertaining guests. Nora naturally was still there. The new Polish republic was demanding Danzig and other, as yet undefined, slices of the former Reich, and there were threats of renewed wars in the east. It was not certain what might happen to Damen, so Waleska and her children were at Staffelde too, and, of course, Wolf-Werner, as the local Landrat was permanently in residence. It was not an over-full house, but in that family Albrecht was the odd man out, and Wilhelmine could hardly go there without him.

She was being thrown increasingly on her own resources, and then she heard that Abimelech was dead and Elizabeth very ill. Abimelech's death severed her from her childhood; from playing under his office desk in the Mill when business colleagues talked impressively overhead, from pulling his beard when she sat on his knee, but by hook or by crook she would go to England; this however, was not easy. The country was still under armistice, that is to say, technically at war with the allies. There were therefore no British consuls in Germany to whom she might apply for a visa. Hence, she could only go to a neutral country, seek out a British consul there, and try her luck. Even this was difficult; the validity of German imperial passports was doubtful, and the republic had not yet issued new ones.

Wolf-Werner, as solid and common sensible as his father, solved the problem. As *Landrat* he could issue passports: he validated hers.

I do not know where Werner and I were left, but I assume at Staffelde while Wilhelmine had another of her hair-raising journeys: this time to the Dutch frontier. The *maréchaussée* were not hostile, but they took their time. After a long night, she was on her way to Rotterdam. Here she had a piece of luck. The British consul knew something about her. This was not the efficiency of the famous British Secret Service, but drawing room gossip. His family knew Margaret Grosvenor, and anyway he was sympathetic. He bent the rules, marked the passport 'British Subject by Birth' and eventually put her on a boat to Harwich. It took time, with her irregular status, to get ashore, but she managed it. The consul had lent her some money out of his own pocket. Eventually she caught the express at King's Cross for Leeds.

The cook who opened the door at Claremont thought that she had seen a ghost. More importantly, everyone was there because her mother was dead and the funeral had taken place two days before. On the other hand she was an object of great solicitude, and besides, she learned that she had inherited, one way and another, a good deal of property.

Abimelech had left everything equally between his children. The boys bought out the girls from the business at a valuation. The goods and chattels were another matter. Equality, there, was secured by a family conspiracy against Ethel. They divided up the things into six lots, and then sent Ethel in to choose 'because she was the greediest'. When she had chosen, they immediately divided everything up again and sent her in and so on. Eventually the moment came when she really was unable to state a preference. Justice!

Abimelech had died some while before, and much of Wilhelmine's share had gone into the hands of the Public Trustee, who, in that war acted as Custodian of Enemy Property, but not quite all. Some, substantial portion had been quietly salted away for her by her brothers, who, now that she was there to receive it, produced the rabbit out of the hat. It made all the difference, but the knowledge that there was more in official hands gave her a motive for returning to England. This time, however, her visit had to be short. As things turned out, it should have been shorter. Two days before she got back to Staffelde, Vally died while reading his newspaper at breakfast.

Chapter 9

REVOLUTION AND DIVORCE

Wolf-Werner now owned everything at Staffelde, even the pair of gloves on the hall table when Vally died. He had fetched himself a wife from Hamburg, the young and charming Trudel Govertz, whom he had married six weeks previously. Albrecht got Schlönwitz.

Vally's death cut a mooring rope and the balloon went up. Wolf-Werner, as universal heir (a sort of executor) had to get in the money owing to Vally and settle his outstanding debts. As Vally had been a good businessman, the debts were not excessive, but the cash had to be found. Nora, Bob and Wilhelmine all owed money to the universal heir. Nora dared Wolf-Werner to enforce his rights. He refused to be bluffed, and took her to the courts. Then of course, poor Bob could not pay. How could he? He cast around for some solution to help Wolf-Werner. Had he not managed a plantation? Two plantations, in fact? He would approach Albrecht about Schlönwitz. Albrecht, who was immersed in his classical learning and his girl-friend was only too ready to listen. He had no desire at all to farm a 600 acre estate. Wilhelmine would have liked to live there but Albrecht let Bob and Elsa in as his tenants. Wilhelmine had nothing against Bob at all but Albrecht's decision widened the gap between her and him. Save for talk and fairly frequent visits by my brother, Schlönwitz, though my father's property and later connected with the heroic Pastor Bonnhöffer, disappears, save once from this story. That occasion arose in 1994 when Henry, Nieves and I went there. It is now in Poland, where Stolp nearby had become Słupsk, it and some other nearby places had become Swonowice and the estate had become part of the large agricultural collective of Zitzewitz (Zitzewitz is as funny in German, as Great Snoring or Middle Wallop is in English). We found the stationmaster's wife in a signal box with chickens, and she told us how to proceed. We had first to embark on a track made of a double line of bricks across a bog which had once been an irrigated meadow. The sluices had all been wrecked. The bog stretched half a mile wide but over the horizon, and was wholly devoid of animals. We eventually reached the village. The parish church had been taken over by a Roman Catholic priest, and a Miserere on the wall behind the pulpit was in the form of a portrait of Bonhöffer. We also found an aged German cultivating beans – a sort of serf, I suppose. Otherwise the place was a disorderly shambles, and my father's house, accidentally burned during the war, was untraceable.

Wilhelmine now went back to Berlin, and was there during the Kapp *Putsch*, the abortive four-day right wing insurrection of March 1920. The republic, against expectation, was establishing a weak yet definite authority over the extremes. It had, however, already had its future stolen before its birth. In June 1919 the republicans had signed the Peace (or in German the Diktat) of Versailles, which came into effect in January. Apart from disarmament clauses, this deed had three main features, whose full character only dawned slowly on the German public. These were the formal admission of War Guilt, the territorial cessions, and the extraordinary reparations provisions.

The war had unleashed all kinds of suppressed or frustrated instincts. The so-called statesmen behaved like carrion crows. The Americans, having forced a spurious self determination on some of the peoples, refused to have any part in maintaining the stability of their handiwork. Lloyd George was interested only in a quick general election, yet destroyed the South Welsh economy by gifts of free German coal to the French. The French were determined to avenge the 1870 war. Only the Italians were predictable. They were ready to sell anything, and, as they were an unmilitary lot, they had to pitch their prices at a modest level. The Russian revolution had now reached its imperialist stage with Trotsky's westward invasion, and while ragged German troops evacuated the Baltic republics before him, the European victors suddenly had to fear that it was they who had somehow to uphold President Wilson's new nationalities. As Germany was falling apart and there was no reason to think that the Poles would keep Trotsky out of civilisation, it was not really surprising that the disarmed and psychologically insecure republicans should have signed anything for a quiet life, even for six months of a quiet life. Six months was about all they got.

The events of 1920 decided the history of the world. In the first place the territorial cessions were enforced. This meant Alsace and Lorraine to France, Eupen and Malmédy to Belgium, which was fair enough because they were victorious powers. Then came northern Schleswig to the Danes. What on earth had they to do with it? They had been neutral throughout the conflict; and then worse still, wide rural provinces and iron mines to a Polish republic which still existed mostly in the imagination, and whose pretensions grew as the Russian danger melted in the battles before Warsaw. There was even a bit (Lloyd George did not know where Teschen was) for something invented in New York called Czechoslovakia and another bit – Memel, now to be called Klaipeda – for Lithuania. Much worse, however, Danzig and the Polish corridor disrupted the eastern century-old economy; and the communications between Berlin, Stettin and East Prussia. The Poles organised their railway timetables so that north-south travel between the Baltic and Warsaw was easy, but east west traffic between the two separated parts of Germany never made connections. The newly created Free State of Danzig was cut off from the East Prussian population by a mountainous wall of tariffs and official obstruction. It had been their mart for centuries.

These manoeuvres were designed to drive the solidly German Free State into political as well as economic union with Poland. Presently these follies were extended. They began to build an alternative commercial port at Gdynia on Polish soil. This wasteful political construction was all based upon the absurd assumption that the boundaries of the Corridor were immutable. A child with a map could see the fallacy, for Poland was squeezed between the monstrous predatory power of Russia, which she had just narrowly repulsed, and a sulking Germany which she was determined to antagonise.

By 1922 the two outcast powers, separated only by the Poles, had come to an understanding which bore fruit in covert German rearmament. This was due, as much as anything else, to a common dislike. The Poles continued to strut as if they, not the French were the rock of their destiny. In this they were encouraged by the course of the Polono-Communist war. The French had sent the incompetent General Weygand to advise them. Marshal Pilsudski had ignored his advice and won his famous victory.

And so the Poles galloped through their dream world (with panache) to their own destruction only seventeen years later at the hands of another Russo-German alliance. When one pities, as one must, these gallant, charming people, it is as well to remember the appalling misjudgements of their leaders.

Yet while the Poles were again creating the Polish problem, the victors were creating a German one. There were several interlocking factors, of which the territorial cessions were the worst; but there was War Guilt, and there were the associated reparations. These were connected. The republicans had been forced to sign an admission of war guilt on behalf of the whole German nation. Now there is at least a case, perhaps a strong one, for fixing a guilty stigma upon the Kaiser's government. But the ordinary German felt differently, perhaps through the effects of propaganda and political immaturity, but differently all the same. He felt threatened in 1914 and marched to a war which was strategically aggressive, but in his belief politically defensive. When General Montgelas published *The Case for the Central Powers* he was arguing what most Germans, Austrians and Hungarians believed, namely that in their historically accidental central position, they were surrounded and threatened by the great Entente with its vast colonial resources and its disruptive hangers-on. The war was fought in *defence* of the Fatherland: How then could such defensive patriotism be condemned?

But supposing that there was a case against the German nation, it had never been tried. No investigation had ever been made. No court had considered the evidence. The accusers had simply met representatives of the accused, and bullied them into admissions: hence the German name *Diktat*. The scene at the Versailles signing ceremony was harrowing. When the Allied diplomats had assembled Clemenceau called to the ushers 'faites entrer les allemands'. Count Brockdorff-Rantzau, the leader of the German delegation, refused to stand when the document was presented to him and Harold Nicolson, who was there, said when asked how he took it: 'a gentleman does not look at a man in obvious distress'. But if there was any guilt, it was the guilt of the Kaiser's government which the republicans, by their nature, had repudiated. When they saddled the nation with the Kaiser's guilt, the nation naturally asked if they had not exceeded their brief. It is fair to say that there is an element of the disingenuous in this question. The republican power seizure was tolerated at least as much because the monarchs had lost the war as for any other reason.

None of this might have mattered much if there had not been the so-called Reparations. This was the morally emotive term for a war indemnity, a tidy way by which victors looted losers without rapine and rape. This was now imposed by the name of a punishment and assessed as at December 1920, and the sum was colossal.

Disorder and Depression thus surrounded my parents as the fortunes of their marriage declined. Albrecht worked at a book and they lived for a while at Freiburg-im-Breisgau. He was obsessed with his affair, she made other friends. The peace treaty made it possible to get some of her money out of England – just in time, now that Vally's support had dried up. Moreover her money was in sound pounds: his income as a don, and his rents from Schlönwitz were being eaten away by the times. She moved to Baden-Baden and made friends there with Willi Talker, another literary figure with Eva Konstein his girlfriend and their circle. Husband and wife were now irreconcilable, and divorce proceedings were set on foot in Freiburg. Despite Wilhelmine's later account it is pretty obvious that she was the aggressor, but was pushing at an open door. Yet it might never have happened if life had been easier and less fraught with psychological troubles for the Germans and particularly the Prussians. When the bottom falls out of the barrel (to borrow a Germanism), the things in it get damaged. The struggle over reparations played its part in all this. While it was in progress it was impossible to put the bottom back or repack the contents. The immense burden could not be discharged in gold because there was not enough gold. Nobody wanted Marks. The Entente especially the French, demanded payment in kind and at depreciated values. Atlantic liners, warships, coal, railway engines, rolled steel, machine tools were taken. It was this which began the slide towards inflation. The solid objects which the currency represented and which underpinned its value, were being removed, and anyhow nobody intended to earn surpluses which would be promptly and smugly carted off by the French. Productivity fell with a bang.

The reader may now experience a feeling of *déjà vu*. The republicans who signed the treaty at Versailles were obliged to try and carry it out, just as the Prussian King who surrendered to Bonaparte after Jena had to do the same for him. In each case the government found itself having to act as an agent for the French national enemy against its own people. The difference was that the Prussians all knew that their King had not repudiated the national tradition. The republicans, on the other hand, existed only by virtue of such a repudiation, and the public was by no means certain on whose side they were. Indeed, considering the terms to which they had committed the Germans, there was some emotional justification for the belief that they were really agents of the enemy.

It was, of course, grossly unjust, but there was worse to come. Since they really were on the right side they set about avoiding payment by every conceivable subterfuge; but precisely because they were subterfuges, they could not bid for public support by proclaiming them. Moreover, they were not in proper control of much of public life. There were the demilitarised Rhineland zones. The General Staff, officially abolished, functioned underground and covertly pursued policies designed to revive the imperial military glory. General v. Seekt's *Reichswehr* was not so much a small army, as the treaty prescribed as an elaborately trained cadre of officers and NCOs for the mass army of the future.

If one feature of republican Germany stood out more than another it was the conspiratorial atmosphere. Everybody was involved in some underhand dealing, speciously justified by the need to defy the Entente and their disgraceful *Diktat*. Foreign policy, to reverse Clausewitz's aphorism, was war carried on by peaceful means. Such a habit of mind destroyed the very basis of decent morality and fertilised the seed-bed in which the weeds and nettles of Hitlerism flourished.

But while this settled a long term trend, in the immediate present the government had to wrestle with a disastrous problem of economics. An inflation had already begun. Now the yield of taxes was insufficient to maintain the public institutions because of the shrinking economic base; and foreign trade had virtually disappeared. They took to printing money and raising and then re-raising expensive foreign loans. The inflation began in earnest.

On 1st April 1921 my parents were divorced. My mother said that the affair was bitter and that my father made all sorts of unfounded accusations which the judge rejected. Afterwards, she related with *Schadenfreude*, he asked his mistress to marry him and she 'would not have him'. I do not wholly believe this or much else of her version of the divorce. He certainly did not remarry at that time, but how did she know? And it is equally certain that his book *Griechische Vorbilder* (Greek Examples) was published at Freiburg at this very time, and that he sent my mother a copy inscribed in his beautiful hand: -

>To his wife
>Wilhelmine von Blumenthal
>In memory of the eight-year long period of marriage
>And love,
>   The Author

For I have it. I also have other works including a book on *Aeschylus*, published in 1924 inscribed: -

>Wilhelmine Baker in reflection upon many years
>Of love, trust and friendship,
>   The Author.

It was she not he who wanted the divorce and my later experience as a practising lawyer, suggests a man, advised by a lawyer to put in some kind of defence lest he lose everything by default, and then being unable to speak to the professional pleadings. In any case, my mother won hands down and cleaned him out. She took virtually everything he had, except Schlönwitz, down to the most personal possessions: his diagonally set signet (Werner got it), his books, his collections of stamps, seals and coins. He kept only his desk and I suppose his clothes.

This business must have lasted a few weeks after 1st April, and then Wilhelmine, as free as air, set off for Munich, just as the Erzberger government took office with Rathenau as Minister of Reparations. She established herself in the Theatinerstrasse, and I ascribe to this time a brilliantly lit mental picture of sitting among the summer trees by the Isar and watching timber rafts floating down. Each one had a lumberman who had a little hut on his raft and a steering sweep pivoting on a wooden block.

Wilhelmine immediately bought a bit of land and started to build herself a house. The inflation was now running fast, but her basic funds were in sterling. She had no thought of coming permanently to England, for she was advised – and it was obvious – that in an inflationary situation it was wise to have property, and that with widespread unemployment building would be cheap. Britain was in the grip of deflation and the Geddes Axe. She was converting English pounds into German property. The state of the exchanges was such that with a few pounds, a telephone and good timing, she could make profits daily which would be worth something real as long as they were spent at once. I originally wrote this on the 16th February 1977 when the newspapers announced the nominally disastrous inflation rate of 16½ %. No Anglo-Saxon, therefore, has any conception of what befell the ex-enemies in 1921-2. At one point you could not get the simplest meal for less than 100 million marks and you tipped the hat-check girl 60,000. The contractor building the house had to be paid quickly, daily, and in cash. The amount of money became, literally, a burden. A boy-friend had to help her with suitcases full of the millions. In Brussels in 1944 I came across a survival of this wheel-barrow inflation: 26 safes in the garage of an ex-Gestapo headquarters. They were all crammed from top to bottom with sealed packets of Austro-Hungarian one-million crown notes. Their face value must have been measurable in light years. They were dull rather pale greyish on one side and brownish on the other. I wonder if anyone knows how they got there, or why they remained so long unknown. Like an idiot, I failed to keep even one.

The house rose steadily throughout the rest of the year while the Germans writhed. Transport was in gross confusion. In Munich Wilhelmine was in the front row of a housewives bread riot when thousands of tigresses packed the Marienplatz and stormed the Town Hall waving their ration cards. Bread somehow appeared. In August somebody assassinated Erzberger. By the autumn Bavarians were talking seriously of secession. It looked as if the pattern of 1919, with variations, might be repeated. Trouble in Saxony was averted by the old King. He came to Dresden. A vast crowd shouted for him at his hotel. At last he was persuaded to show himself on the balcony. After the uproarious demand for a speech had subsided into a breathless silence the old man spoke: -

'Ihr seid schäner republikäner!'[*] Then he went inside. After a stunned moment the demonstration broke up in peals of laughter.

By the winter Wilhelmine had changed her mind about her and her children's future. I think that Albrecht must have decided to demand our custody; she paid a visit to England in January 1922, for she related hearing of Rathenau's assassination (on 31st) while waiting for a train to the Hook of Holland. Werner and I must have been left with some friend in Munich, and these combined features may have enabled Albrecht to allege plausibly that she was neglecting us and intending to alienate us from father and fatherland. He applied to the Court. I wish that I remembered the drama which followed. She packed herself and us onto a

---

[*] You're a fine lot of republicans. The words were spoken in broad dialect. Perhaps a translation should begin 'Ee, bah gum!'

train to Holland. Court bailiffs came in hot pursuit. There was a traumatic delay at the frontier. Uniformed men burst suddenly onto the platform with papers in their hands, and looked up and down the train. The train left them standing. Arrived at Rotterdam, police were on the platform. A Dutch inspector at headquarters faced an expostulating German consul. The Dutchman could see no reason in Dutch law why we should return to Germany. We left in triumph for the Hook.

Though I have no recollection of these events, and would not have understood them if I had, I do remember that crossing to Harwich. It was a fearful storm and I was uncomprehendingly seasick to the utmost point of misery. I was not quite four, but lest the reader disbelieve that I remember it, I also remember very clearly coming to Farsley and staying with Wilhelmine's brother Charles and his family. I could not speak or comprehend any English. I tried to make something by tying string to a door-knob. A huge alien grown-up stood over me shouting 'NO' in a manner so hostile that even I realised that he must have been trying to say 'Nein'. I could only repeat over and over again 'Ich möchte Etwas bauen'.*

---

* I want to build something.

Chapter 10

THE TRANSITION

Childhood is the time to learn languages. I remember a few incidents in the English-learning period, but little of the process itself. For one thing, I was ill a good deal. After Farsley we stayed with Harriet and her husband, John Mercer, who taught mathematics at Cheltenham College. I had ear trouble so that sounds like that of passing cars hurt my head, and other troubles too which kept me in bed. I was, of course, nursed by people who spoke no German but were universally kind: these illnesses taught me English very quickly.

Then my mother found a house at Hythe near Folkestone. It was called 'Wymondham' and half a dozen steps ran down to the gate on the Sandgate Road. I associate this entirely with Englishry. Werner, who was eight, and had been bullied in the *Volkschule* in Munich, went to school in Folkestone, and there was a governess called, believe it or not, Miss Grundy. Werner must have had school trouble as an 'enemy' foreigner who probably spoke the language with a marked accent. He used to come home sometimes looking very miserable. He also suffered a misfortune which still gives me the shivers. When fishing from Folkestone pier he pulled the line up quickly in a high wind; the hook blew into his face and became firmly embedded in his lip.

My mother still had hankerings. She and Albrecht corresponded and through her Munich friend Margaret Grosvenor she caught up with Kathleen Alexander. To get her blocked funds out of the hands of the Public Trustee she needed a reliable solicitor, and Kathleen suggested a long-established City firm called Baker & Nairne. It was a family firm whose members were distantly related to her. Wilhelmine sought an interview with Mr PRA Baker, now, the senior partner. They met, and he instantly fell in love.

As he was a shy small man who had never been in love before, she had not the least idea at first what was passing in his mind. He was simply a man who was rather energetically getting her money back. Percy was a competent and conscientious *homme d'affaires* and also had many friends in the right places. He had, as I have mentioned, a talent for friendship and he had been brought up at Winchester and

Oxford in the '90s. At that time, such institutions were small enough for most people to know each other, and yet to supply a considerable proportion of the few people who mattered. Percy was not distinguished or famous or ambitious or powerful, but he was liked by many people who were. He had known Carson and F E Smith, one strong, the other drunk. He did not like, but managed to tolerate Edward Marshall-Hall. Every year a small group used to dine together for old time's sake. They were Percy, Miles Lampson (later Lord Killearn and ambassador to Egypt), 'Robin' Dawson, the Editor of the *Times*, and Cosmo Gordon Lang, Archbishop of Canterbury. If you wanted to invest your money there were Schröders and Cazenoves. There was Alexander Nairne, simultaneously Professor of Divinity at Cambridge and a canon of Windsor. Did you want a seat at Lords for a Test Match? There was old Leveson-Gower. So, of course, there was somebody in the Public Trustee's office. This person was Cecil Hunt.

I would like to have been Cecil Hunt. Not, you will understand, in detail, for in later life he became sarcastic and embittered, but in general outline. He had three complete and unrelated careers. He began at the bar and became a very busy and well paid Chancery practitioner. I think that it was in this capacity that he and Percy remet after the university. He was unfit for war – something wrong with his leg – and he went into the Public Trustee's office where until about 1924 he managed the investments excellently and incidentally his own, so that he remained, despite the war and the abandonment of his law practice, well off. He and Phyllis, his entertaining and strong-minded wife built themselves a splendid house (by Lutyens) at the corner of Mallord Street in Chelsea, and he advised Percy about Wilhelmine's property. Then he decided to drop everything and become an artist. He made a comfortable living as a successful and under-estimated landscape painter, mostly in water- and body-colour. This side of his character appealed to Percy who had artistic abilities too. Meantime when Wilhelmine's money was at last extracted from the Public Trustee, there was much more of it than she expected.

While an affair of the heart was developing among the deed-boxes of Salter's Hall Court, Wilhelmine was still feeling the tug of her children's country. Now that she no longer had Albrecht, she wanted him again – and he wanted her. There was a passionate correspondence. If only she and the children could come and stay at Staffelde again, they could, as wiser and more experienced people take up a more mature relationship – perhaps not exactly from the point where it had broken down, but somewhere not too far off. Were Werner and Wolfgang, after all, not Germans? She too was still a German citizen. It would not be difficult..... He would meet her at Ostend. She decided to go, and went nearly half way to remarrying him, and I think, she estopped herself from complaining about his conduct – not that it made any difference! The bags were packed, the tickets bought and the taxi took us all down to Folkestone harbour. The steamer was not there: it was prevented from docking by one of the worst Channel tempests in living memory. We took a taxi back to 'Wymondham'.

Albrecht loved her and he loved us. His rage, however, ensured that the die which had been thus miscast, should not be recast. Wilhelmine thought it an omen: and besides, Werner and I caught measles and became for a while immobile, and Percy started visiting Hythe on business. There seemed to be a great deal of business requiring the attendance of Frau von Blumenthal's solicitor in Hythe. This had a comic effect. Miss Grundy gave in her notice because, she said, she was not used to working for ladies who entertained unmarried gentlemen.

The Munich house was standing, almost, but not quite finished. My mother went there to decide what should be done with it. It was an important link with Germany, even if she had reneged on Albrecht. With her sharp eye she noticed that the cellar was damp and might, perhaps suffer from the high water table of the nearby Isar. There was an eager buyer in the field. Quickly she accepted his offer – mortgage and all – before he might notice, and she found herself with a useful German income paid regularly into Martin's Bank in Munich. My mother was in some ways insensitive, or impudent or socially dumb; in 1927 I was with her in Munich when she decided to visit the house. There it was with its stucco façade and copper covered corner turret. We rang the bell. The owner ushered us into the sunlit sitting room. I paid, like a child, little attention to the conversation; I think I played with a toy motor car, but as we left I heard a pump start up in the basement.

Percy became more assiduous.

The Bakers had two houses in Cottesmore Gardens, behind Kensington High Street. They lived at No. 20 and let No. 22. They also had a country house called Flutter's Hill, at Longcross near Virginia Water. Owing to their extraordinarily conservative way of life, I had a direct experience, until old Mrs Baker died in 1929, of life in an Edwardian household. I must be one of the few living to have seen it.

Granny was a frail kind little thing in widow's weeds. She sat by the drawing room fire on a rocking chair, her feet on a hassock with a shawl fastened at the front by a large brooch consisting of some Scottish semi-precious stone set in a twisted gold frame. She smelt faintly of eau de cologne, and her grey hair was mostly hidden by one of those lace pancakes which you sometimes see in caricature. She seemed immemorial and treasured and breakable. She had, evidently, been bereaved long ago and had settled for the comforts of widowhood. As a matter of fact her late husband Frederick Arnold Baker, had died only about eighteen months before, but nobody ever mentioned him.

Her two daughters, Cathy and Agnes, were married: the one to a distinguished Scottish surgeon, reputed to listen to a roast chicken with his stethoscope before carving it, the other to a Suffolk solicitor. None of the four sons yet had wives. Arthur, a naval officer, came home occasionally when service life permitted, Percy, Freddy a barrister, and Edward (called Edard) lived at home with their mother. Percy as head of the family was 47, and he lived a quiet life being nice.

The routine seldom varied. The men came home from work and everybody changed for dinner. They had a glass of sherry in the drawing room at about 7.15. There might be a guest or two. Dinner comprised soup, fish, a bird or a joint, two or three vegetables, a sweet and cheese. They washed it down with Hock, and drank coffee and port while the ladies adjourned to the drawing room. Next came brandy. Then the men rejoined the ladies. Everybody drank strong black tea, and indulged in the old fashioned drawing room amusements which were already out of date: the piano, the banjo, Edwardian music hall songs such as *Tableaux Vivants*, or they read to each other dramatically or they got out games and puzzles. I remember a huge heap of Chinese ivory spillikens and an eight-piece gold puzzle ring. Percy owned a canary yellow tailcoat, which Arthur had had made for him at Shanghai as a joke, and his appearance in this usually heralded charades or even, occasionally a rehash of some otherwise forgotten nineties musical. There was, of course, Granny's scrapbook, and her jewel box crammed with jewellery of every kind, especially Indian gold, all higgledy-piggledy.

Finally, at about 10.00pm you were given a pint of milk and went to bed.

Such a nightly regimen might reasonably have been matched by a moderate breakfast. Not at all. Porridge was followed by kedgeree or a curled whiting; then there was bacon and eggs and usually devilled kidneys, a lamb chop and sausages, the whole being accompanied by gallons of coffee, toast and home-made marmalade. And in case you were still not satisfied – and usually they were not – you could carve yourself great slices off a ham which invariably stood on the sideboard. One might have imagined that these elderly and middle-aged people would be large or at least fat, but this was not so. They were all shorter than average and, except for Agnes who ate the least, spare.

The Bakers first noticed that something was up when the head of the family actually stayed out one evening. They were agog. Then he brought Mrs von Blumenthal to dinner and they were charmed. Arthur was more than charmed and Percy had to warn him off. This sort of thing went on for months. Wilhelmine, enured to treating social relationships as a game, found that her German affairs made it convenient to play hard to get. There was some sort of arrangement or court order which entitled Albrecht to see his children at intervals. I have already described a visit recorded in the Staffelde visitors book in the spring of 1923. Germany was still rather disturbed, for this was the year of the *Reichswehr* mutiny and Hitler's beer cellar insurrection in Munich, but these affairs seem to have had only local repercussions; Wilhelmine went to Munich sometime during the year; she paid (the only one) all her debts to Wolf-Werner. Also we all went to the Oeynhausen estate at Rossbach in Saxony.

This famous place comprised the battlefield near Naumburg where Frederick the Great won by a cavalry ambuscade one of his most remarkable victories. The Dutch style step-gabled house was on a low terrace in a splendid chestnut forest, which sloped gently away on one side and rose steeply behind the garden on the other. The drive swept up round the terrace to the front door. Apart from ourselves and Tante Su, and also her sister Tante Annette who came occasionally (they owned Rossbach jointly), there was Uncle Bob. He had managed to marry his Elsa at Martyanec, her home in Croatia, and had brought her back in triumph together with Cornelia their daughter and Ruthger, their baby son. Later he and I had an odd joint experience. As a subaltern in the 70th Buffs, I was exercising my platoon in the fields behind Dover Castle. There was much roaring of aircraft overhead in the low cloud. The 9.2 inch guns at Dover Castle began to fire, and then salvoes of shells landed in our fields. This was the action, though we did not know it, when the battle cruisers *Scharnhorst* and *Gneisenau* forced the Straits of Dover. When I met Ruthger after the war, he was blind. He had lost his sight as navigating officer of the *Bernd von Arnim* one of the *Scharnhorst's* escorting destroyers, named, incidentally, after another relative, when she was hit by a Dover gun. I believe that those who tried locally and failed to stop these ships were unjustly blamed. Visibility, even at the top of the cliffs, was down to 300 yards. I am one of the few independent witnesses to this.

Elsa was a well dressed vivacious Italian. Bob was charming, always equable, always willing to give some time to us children: he introduced me to the joys of chocolate cigars. He seemed rather bulky, and being lame, walked with a stick. One morning, early, I met him in the forest in his pyjamas with a rook rifle under his arm. 'Come and help me shoot squirrels. The chestnuts are valuable'. It was a lucky morning and he was a dead shot. They were all red squirrels but not agile enough for him. Albrecht, I am afraid, was not half as good. I remember another time when he peppered the tree-tops with growing exasperation, while the only squirrel in sight leaped gracefully from bough to bough into the distance.

Rossbach had one remarkable feature. It contained a number of pictures by the Cranachs. There was a tradition of some relationship. I do not remember these pictures as such, but years later on seeing some Cranachs for the first time consciously in the Munich Pinachotek, I had a very strong feeling of *déjà vu*. Later still Robert, the family genealogist, demonstrated that the tradition was correct. The Cranachs are ancestors of my grandmother Cornelia.

We enjoyed ourselves at that house. The garden was all bushes and glades with the noise of a waterfall somewhere, lots of gorgeous dragonflies darting in and out of the shadows, and a swing. I learned to use that swing until I could fling myself from end to end of the half circle – and higher – while the trees wheeled and plunged and my mother would cluck about calling 'be careful'. I thought that it was a technique, like bicycling, which one never forgot, but I tried a year or two ago, and could not make it work. Then there was a lovely way down past the pump from the garden into the kitchen, where people steamed and boiled, and baked bread and made little round biscuitty things the size of golf-balls. And of course one helped.

On the other hand, sometimes one was less helpful. Some child and I sat with long sticks of rose-bush on the top of the terrace wall and tapped passers by on the head. It was alright until the postman, who was on his bicycle came by. He did not like it at all; he dismounted and came charging up onto terrace, where he ran, full of sound and fury, straight into Elsa. She became very voluble too. My mother appeared and joined the furious counterpoint and really, we had no idea that we might be doing any harm. Luckily Bob appeared wanting to know what all the noise was about. Then the sun shone again.

I made up my mind that the world was round. Our bedroom was on the second floor looking back along the road; the flat orderly fields and ditches stretched away towards nothingness. In the other direction was Naumburg with its vaguely cathedral-like central building on the skyline. I used to wake before dawn and hear, far far away, the sound of a cock crowing. The cry would be taken up by another nearer at hand, and then another closer still and so on till the nearest cock was bellowing for all his worth. Then the sound would begin to recede as the call was answered by others towards and then past Naumburg. By that time the light would come from the direction of the first criers, and soon they would all be silent for the day. I imagined to myself that this call rang on round the world as the globe turned into the light, until 24 hours later it reached the point outside Rossbach where it had started, and so on round for ever.

Then it was time to go. One of those blue misty dawns; a long long train journey, another stormy seasick crossing from Boulogne. It was cold and my ears were giving trouble again, and generally it was horrible. Also the weather held up our entry into Folkestone. At long last we got in, and a nice little man smelling of tobacco came up the gangway and carried me ashore in my dressing gown, along the quay and into the Lord Warden. I knew who he was, of course, but this was the first close personal contact I had with Percy. He was calmer than Uncle Bob. I felt better in no time. One of the terrors of sickness with small children is incomprehension.

Percy had come down with a pocketful of assorted rings (Henry Searle, the King William Street jeweller was another friend) to pop the question. He took Wilhelmine out for a walk near Hurst Castle, and after she had said 'yes' he spread them out for her to choose. She came back wearing a curious bluish ruby surrounded by tiny brilliants, all set in platinum. Evidently he was pretty sure of his bird.

This was 1923. He was 48 and she was 40. The situation was reversed in more ways than one. Albrecht had been struggling. Percy had arrived. It was difficult for a divorcee to get married in the Church of England, but Geikie Cobb, the then controversial rector of St Ethelburger's Bishopsgate, agreed to do it for Percy. So they were married there, and for the second time, Gaunt gave her away. Percy made her sign her will in the vestry. Gaunt said 'You've got someone in charge now'.

St Ethelburger's was the tiny congested Gothic church which was utterly wiped out by an IRA terrorist lorry load of explosives in the 1990s. I saw the explosion from a window of our flat at 2 Paper Buildings in the Temple.

Percy celebrated the wedding by persuading William Russell Flint to paint her portrait. It had to be done two years later. I seem to be the only person who likes that half-length. It sets forth very clearly the spirit of her pale handsome rather imperious personality, with the dark shining hair and grey steady gaze. It is quite unlike the work which later made him famous. The light and liquid wash painter on this occasion used his water-colour as a Chinese artist might have done, on silk. The peculiarity of silk painting is that whatever you do, remains unalterable. It is a very deliberate technique, rather like the calculated social games which she used to play. *Le style, c'est la femme?*

Chapter 11

WHOOPING COUGH, MARGATE AND BEATENBERG

So here we are at the Boltons. It had a schoolroom where I played Punch and Judy – audience and all – from a corner behind its brown leather sofa. The lower conservatory, which had a potted palm, contained a gramophone with doors in the front. I played it rather well. I conducted the *Unfinished Symphony*, and strutted round and round to the *Torgauer March*. I had musical ideas and composed large scale works in my head when lying in my cot of a summer evening. Somebody else came in at the drumming climax of one of these *Meisterwerke*, and put me in a panic.

I distinguish this period by four enormous events. Firstly, I had whooping cough. Hardly anyone, thank God, nowadays has it in its developed form, but to a child of five before the invention of antibiotics and immunisers it was terrifying. You coughed and when you tried to draw breath to cough again some blockage made you strain so that you would only, and against your will, let out a sort of howl. You were desperately unable to keep food down even for a couple of minutes. I was already afraid of seasickness. This went on and on and on. I ran a high temperature and had hallucinations in a room flicker-lighted mostly (it was the depth of winter) by a coal fire; and a sort of medicated smoke lamp made the room foggy. I was conscious of concerned looking grown-ups in the gloom. There was a night-nurse, and more than one doctor appeared, sometimes in the dead of night. In truth they could only make the patient sufficiently comfortable to be able to fight the disease himself. This was all very well in theory, but how could it work in a child's world dominated by delirium, nausea, near-suffocation and the accompanying and cumulative weakness? I think this was done by a primitive psychotherapy: by calm and confidence so that the medicines (cloudy liquids in square large bottles) might do some good if one believed in them. The whole thing took six weeks in bed, and another month or so before I was allowed out in any shape less than that of a cocoon.

It was now spring. The Turnbull children had also caught something, so we all went to a Margate boarding house under Betty's care, slept eleven hours a night and played cards when we were not eating or building sandcastles. The weather was perfect and we, and Betty were all very happy. Never a cross word even when I smashed one of the landlady's choicest (or most hideous) mantelpiece ornaments: a veined puce coloured affair full of old bus tickets. 'One of a pair', she did not fail to point out. 'Them flar vawses is expensive', she said. Ten years later Percy was driving with me in the car at night in Wentworth, when a black shadow darted in front and there was a wheel thud. We had run over a poodle. We knew the owner and rang her bell. The cook answered the door.

'Them dawgs is expensive', she said.

After Margate we went to Switzerland so that Albrecht could see his children on neutral ground. The place, an undistinguished-looking roadside village, was sundered by a ravine with a wooden bridge, and it straggled along the mountainside above Lake Thun. It was Abimelech's Beatenberg, where he and my mother had got to know a very respectable Bernese family called Egli* who lived at Oberhofen on the lakeside. The only Miss Egli was said to have married beneath her, to wit to a Beatenberg peasant called Gaffner, and it was Röseligarten, their chalet, which we took for the summer.

Herr Gaffner was not much in evidence because of the seasonal movement of milch cattle. He was mostly on the *alm*.** She lived in, and combined the functions of landlady, cook, housekeeper, nurse, dogsbody and all.

This old-fashioned mountain log house, stood apart in the steep fields below the road, with a shingled roof held down against winter gales by large stones. Under the deep eves facing the valley was a veranda with arches, which acted as a balcony for the living room. Back to back with the latter was the kitchen, which therefore looked up hill. There was a huge kitchen oven built through the wall between, so that it projected eight feet into the living room, where it was a high flat tiled cube with a single step on either side. It provided the heating. You could sit, or lie on it, and in really freezing weather people slept on it.

The front door went in at this level, but the hillside was so abrupt that the back door went out at the basement where they kept chickens and cheeses. It stank splendidly. At intervals Herr Gaffner appeared with another cheese: a great cartwheel of it, weighing 44lbs, which could be brought down only on a sledge, because, as at St Ives in Cornwall, anything with wheels would run away. He was partial to cheese, was Herr Gaffner and so, he discovered was I. So he would surreptitiously pass me slices of this gorgeous new cheese, when nobody was looking. He had other uses. When a chicken had to be killed he would seize one and chop its head off on the chopping block. Then he would hold its legs while it violently flapped its wings. Once he let go accidentally and it flew headless down

---

* Egli = leech.
** The high summer pasture owned by the village in common.

the hill until it suddenly turned turtle, rolled in the hay and had to be retrieved. We children enjoyed this vastly, but my mother, who thought him plebeian, suddenly took against chicken slaughter and cheese, and forbade both. It worried nobody. We watched these scenes just the same, and he was more circumspect about the rest.

He was very strong.

He felled his annual tree in a minute or two. The branches and most of the bark were off in half an hour or so, and then he balanced it on his shoulder, and walked steadily the uphill mile home, where he trimmed the bark by lunch. He made his wife kitchen furniture of it. His only tools were an axe (using the back of the head as a hammer), a wooden mallet, a bit and brace, and a saw.

Earwigs swarmed at Röseligarten and we waged joyful campaigns with sticks and anti-earwig powder, tearing the loose bark off the fences to reveal teeming hordes underneath, but at night they would walk across the ceiling and drop off, so that you heard them go plop on the floor, the furniture or worst of all your bed. You lived in fear of one falling into your mouth and hid under that awful feather mountain (so beloved by the Swiss) until you boiled.

The bumpy mountainside fields, and the thickets, were a paradise of wildflowers and, in that pre-insecticidal world, teemed with butterflies, bees, wasps, ants, and everything else of the kind imaginable. If you sat down among the hummocks on a sunny day, you vanished among the grasses and heard no sound except that of insects. Brimstones, Blues, Fritillaries (quite apart from the usual Whites) swarmed. Red Admirals were not uncommon; White Admirals too. We were quite used to Peacocks and Camberwell Beauties (or something very like), but our great excitement in the open was chasing the immense, swift and agile Swallow Tails, or in the darker places, the Commas with their muscular flight. I was too young and small to take an extensive part in these hunts, but Werner became very expert with net and killing-bottle, and at mounting the specimens. He was soon exceedingly knowledgeable, even erudite, on butterflies. On one occasion he caught something, which he could not classify. He brought it to London and showed it to the authorities at the Natural History Museum, who had never seen it either. They made him, at the age of ten, their youngest official collector.

I became fascinated by ants, probably because I was nearer the ground than my big brother; and besides, one could just watch them instead of rushing about all over the landscape. I imagined them as organised armies (with words of command) subsisting in a world, which was essentially like our own. There they are, clambering through the primeval jungle of the hay meadow, struggling to the tree top view of the universe at the crest of a stem of grass, or helping each other to drag home a pine needle as big as a scaffolding-pole. I was right about the armies, for I witnessed a battle at the edge of a wood; with hindsight, I think that it was a slave raid. There was also the passionate determination with which they hurried their pupae into safety at the slightest sign of danger. I became, in a rather unformulated way, familiar with different types of these fascinating creatures, from the tiny pale sluggish breeds living mostly away from the light, to the big black-and-tan wood ants, as hard as nails and in perpetual movement, with their inquisitive and much used antennae. I thought then that they were probably near-sighted, a failing for which the sensitivity of their antennae would compensate. Later I read books about them, but I have never studied them scientifically.

Then one could look up from the engaging things at one's feet to the splendour of the finest view in the Alps. The blue lake filled the valley and was furroughed by the two or three paddle steamers plying from Thun, out of sight to the right, *via* the shore villages such as Gunten and especially Oberhofen where those two very proper von Arx spinsters kept a hotel and the grossest fattest basset hound called *Pluntschi*. Then to Interlaken, which was in dead ground and slightly to the left. Above Interlaken the great rock masses of the three famous mountains towered into the sky: the inappropriately named Jungfrau (Young Woman), the Mönch (Monk) and the Eiger (Old Man). Behind the wooded valley side opposite, the other giants of the Bernese Oberland reared up: the Blümlisalp, notorious in mountain gossip, the dangerous Finsteraarhorn, begetter of storms and the useful cone-shaped Niessen, by whose condition one could accurately foretell the day's weather.

Trägt der Niessen einen Hut	The Niessen, hatted, gives the sign
Dann wird das Wetter gut.	That now the weather will be fine.
Trägt er ein Kragen	Dressed in collar, grey or white
Dann soll man's wagen.	You'd better think about your plight.
Trägt er den Degen	His sword, however, makes it plain
Dann gibt's Regen.	That very soon there will be rain.

The hat was a morning shadow on his top; the collar a circlet of cloud a quarter of the way down; the sword a straight bar of cloud half way up.

At the foot of Beatenberg (the mountain of St Beatus, an alarming missionary hero) is Beatenbucht (his Bight) on the lakeside, and it is connected with Beatenberg by a steep funicular. The mountain was terrorised by a giant, whose name, Kindlifresser, (Baby Gobbler) adequately describes his reputation. He lived in a cave at Beatenbucht, and was at war with the local dwarves. St Beatus arrived on a floating cloak with missal and hoste to impose peace. It is not clear whether the object was to blast him with heavenly displeasure or merely to prescribe a change of diet, but old Kindlifresser went to sleep during the sermon, the dwarves swarmed about him and cut off his head, and they used it to block the entrance to the great cave, where, indeed, it may be seen to this day, and they all (except Kindlifresser) lived happily ever after. An old sculptured fountain in Bern portrays the giant fressing his way through a helping.

We stayed several months. My mother's Swiss and German friends Rudolf Binding, Dr Dumont, the vivacious Freda de Rüthi came and went, and so did my father. Werner went up and stayed on the *alm* during the *Kuhreihen*, when they round up the cattle, make the last cheeses and come down in triumph, cowbells suspended from yokes all booming and jangling. At this point my mother vanished into a hospital where she had a miscarriage, and Werner went off somewhere too. Frau Gaffner looked after me. Thus, for a period, which left a distinct impression, I was brought up like any little Swiss. I was given a large map of Switzerland mounted on wood and cut into squares, which I used, happily, to fit together, so that I learnt where Glarus and Olten were, long before I ever heard of Bristol or Birmingham. I know most of the 27 cantonal flags and Gessler, the wicked Sheriff of Uri, who made everybody bow to a fur hat on a pole and was so nasty to Wilhelm Tell, is the foremost figure in my demonology, while Tell himself (son, apple and all) was the pattern of courage, skill, plain speaking, helmsmanship, target-shooting – you name it. These stories linked the simple Swiss patriotism with a personal liberty quite different from the Prussian collective liberation. A Prussian was not a Frenchman. The Swiss was a man. It was natural for a Swiss to enter the citizen army as part of the contract of mutual support and comfort between himself and his peers, legendarily symbolised in the Oath of Rütli* so natural, in fact, that every trained Swiss – including Herr Gaffner – kept his uniform and rifle at home, and the entire serving nation could be mobilised in a day.

Then my mother and Werner returned, and we went shopping for fireworks in Thun. I was not clear what they were, and could make very little of the woman behind the counter who kept saying 'das ist sehr hübsch' ('that is very pretty'), when it so patently was not. At Hilterfingen we (except me – I had nothing to remember) got off the boat because we had forgotten the Chinese lanterns. More shapeless parcels. Altogether baffling. But a day or two later things became clearer. They were to celebrate the national festival – obviously something to do with William Tell – with bonfires on all the mountaintops, and with all these fireworks and things and it was going to be Great Fun. It was too. I was allowed to stay up late. Bonfires blazed everywhere, rockets shot into the air or down the hillsides into the water, and we each took a Chinese lantern on a stick and went to the Hotel Victoria. There were processions of noisy burghers walking the paths

---

* Actually they wanted to tax the newly opened trans-Alpine commercial traffic but it is most unwise to mention it.

with lamps on every hillside; the valley was alive with them and they were reflected in the untroubled lake.

We left in early October. The Niessen had worn his hat nearly every morning for months, so that the worst (or best) was a grandstand view of the occasional thunderstorm ('angels throwing boxes about') across the lake. Now he put on his collar, and Percy arrived to take us home. It was, especially across France, the coldest journey I ever remember. It was not officially winter in France and therefore the train-heating systems had not been turned on. We unpacked our bags and put on everything we could find. Wilhelmine even put on a pair of Percy's trousers, and he dozed in the next compartment wearing two hats.

The journey was notable for something else. The French had re-laid the track on its original bed through the old battlefields. The skeleton cathedral ruins at Rheims stood, in the red dawn, on a bluff above the destruction, and as far as the moving eye could see, the land was a mass of perfectly round holes: big, little, huge, middle-sized, deep, shallow holes all touching each other so that no ordinary ground lay between save the tattered sub-jungles of barbed wire and the zigzag or bastion traced trenches; and everything was filled with water covered with sheets of ice. I am glad that I saw what the conditions were like, before someone came and tidied them up, and before literary historians drained away the blood. I travelled that way several times before the mess was finally rolled flat. I think that the very last occasion was in 1928 when, as I neared Rheims I looked out as usual, and saw a single, if large, square crater field remaining to demonstrate the uselessness, and folly of the industrial approach to war. The Americans had not learned the lesson for World War II or Vietnam. The British did much better in Palestine, North Africa and above all in Malaya.

My next great event may seem curious for a child. It was the first public occurrence, which I ever remember, and it was, of all things, the post-war crash of the French Franc. It is not really so odd that I remember it. I had been used almost from birth, to changing money and variable exchange rates. Moreover coins are small glittering things which children like, and they become very observant of the details: the fact that English silver was then milled but German had a motto struck into the rim, or that English coins turn over horizontally but continental ones vertically – not to mention the differences of symbolism, name and subdivision. Moreover, coin, unless exceptionally light-metalled, seems solid and dependable. A move from coin to paper is disappointing. Economics without psychology is nonsense.

My last enormous event happened at Eastbourne. It became more and more oppressively hot until I woke to find alarmed faces about my bed. With recollections of whooping cough I thought at first that this was a return to illness. It was in fact the thunderstorm of the century. The rain poured in torrents, the heavens flashed and banged with fork and sheet lightning. All night long it raged, never getting any cooler. Then a torrid yellow steamy day; we dragged our tired limbs about after the sleepless night. With the evening, the storm returned. I cried, not exactly from fear, but from weariness and hatred of whatever it was that would not let me sleep. That night was as furious as, but longer than the first. The rain beat leaves off the trees; at times the lightening played like a kind of daylight; the thunder never stopped until dawn, and still it got no cooler. Again a steamy day with a brazen sky and a yellow burning sun. By now I was not alone in a state of jitters. I was being wheeled, towards evening in a sit-up push-chair when it started with a great roar out of the setting sun. I held onto the arms of the chair and tried not to scream. And then nothing more happened. It was over. The night was cool.

Chapter 12

EDWARDIANS AND MATRIMONIAL MUDDLE

We were soon off again. Wilhelmine had opted for the quiet bosom of London family respectability but apart from a natural restlessness, I think that the miscarriage was a central event. I learned of it only years later and from Werner. I gather that it would have been a girl. As she grew older she used, increasingly, to expatiate on the way in which girls grew ahead of boys, and on their greater sophistication. Thus a late miscarriage, in any event one of the worst experiences which can befall a woman, must have been especially frustrating and sad. Then her tendency to long for something, which she did not possess, must have come into it too, and she was on the threshold of her change of life. There were the occasional black family quarrels, but to Percy she was still the new wife with whom he was in love. He was kindness itself to Werner and me, but I think that he must have seen disquieting signs and wanted her to himself uncluttered. So Betty reappeared from Stafford and we went down to Flutter's Hill for the winter while Percy and Wilhelmine stayed in London.

Normally the Bakers lived there from the week before Ascot until early October. In the winter it stood in the care of local staff. It was, thrift-wise, obviously a good idea to make more use of it. So we went into occupation, and the odd Turnbull child came and stayed, rather less permanently, to make the place, in effect, into a country nursery.

Only twenty miles from London, at Longcross in Surrey, Flutter's Hill still possessed neither gas nor electricity. The brown, agreeable, drinking water was pumped up daily from a well under the kitchen by an irregularly exploding petrol engine. The only telephone had a hand crank which you wound to activate a bell at the stables, solely to summon the carriages. There was rabbity land with Guernsey cows producing lovely cream, and a splendid avenue, half a mile long, of limes, which curved up to the slight eminence upon which the house stood. It was a slate-roofed heavily ivied, single storey Victorian house, probably built for a retiring colonial. Its veranda roof was supported on green painted timber uprights. Open coal fires provided the heating, oil lamps and candles the lighting. I doubt if it had been redecorated since 1890, and lamp and candle vapour (only badly trimmed wicks smoked) had darkened the ground floor ceilings. There was a carved pine staircase, and at the half-landing hung a spectacular row of large pot-bellied brass jugs. These were filled early every morning, left on the kitchen range until they nearly boiled, and were then brought up to the bedrooms. The only bath had to be filled in this way, till Wilhelmine suggested putting in a boiler. You did not just have a bath, you ordered one.

Longcross was a straggle of well-to-do Victorian houses with their land and lodges. It had a hideous little church. The Baker graves are in the churchyard, since vandalised. The village ended with Dick Turpin's Cottage on the edge of the Common. The ascription to Turpin may be a mistake, but the association with highwaymen is probably correct, for this was the beginning of the notorious Chobham Heath where they had been rife. Nowadays gypsies concentrated there for Ascot and also to settle their mutual debts. Their encampments covered hundreds of acres with scattered caravans, tethered horses, ponies and *animals* (by which they meant donkies), and their solid, almost cubist shelters built of grey felt. These measured about 10 x 3 x 3 feet with the entrance at one end, and at the other a conical chimney thinly trickling smoke. They seldom held more than a lonely man and his dog, and when the tribes drifted away there were usually one or two souls left to while away the winter doing odd jobs.

Gypsies were regarded with suspicion. It was said that if you refused anything, your ricks caught fire. Certainly they behave and looked differently from English people, and spoke a language of their own, but I remember no single case of trouble with them at that time or later, and such gypsies as I have met have been uniformly courteous and ingenious. My wartime Gypsy batman told me that they only got upset if you refused them water. So would I.

At Flutter's Hill many birds built their nests in the old ivy, and as the spring came they would wake us with their dawn chorus, and on bright and playful mornings would chase each other through the bedrooms, skimming familiarly in and out from window to window. Then we would all start to talk or have pillow fights until Betty came chattering in, or Mrs Harding the housekeeper and cook arrived with admonitions and hot water. She was the wife of Young Harding. She was certainly 55 by then, he well over 60, but still known as Young Harding because he had been taken on as gardener's boy to Crittenden, the gardener and church bell ringer. James Crittenden was by then in his 80s but still very expert with vegetables – we always had new potatoes perfect at Christmas – but, as nobody was ever really in charge there, he sold most of the produce. I doubt if it worried the Bakers; it saved them the trouble of paying him properly, and his wife was a nice old body whom they did not want to throw into the street.

But the nights were different. The house stood at the top of an open lawn unprotected from the prevailing southwesterly. The winter winds howled in the chimneys, rattled the panes and thundered in the trees. The candle flames shook and threw shadows behind the furniture. Lamps in brackets lit the passage ceilings and made deep pools of black inhabited by unformulated horrors. Unfortunately there were Yellow and Mauve fairy books, from which somebody would read alarming tales of bow legged hobgoblins who might people the hostile night. I dared not venture alone to the lavatory because of the shadows on the way. One evening we had to go down to the lodge at the end of the avenue. There was a cold strong wind, and Betty carried the lantern. I got left behind somehow among the roaring trees. The lantern disappeared round the curve leaving me alone and panic-stricken. I rushed blindly screaming after it... This was the sort of thing which my mother understood, and years later I discovered that Fanny had exactly the same problems too.

We were also, of course, going abroad. I remember picnicking at Vitznau (Lake Lucerne) on the beach under a fig with my uncle Charles and his children, and also a trip to Lindau on Lake Constance. I have a soft spot for this lake. Lindau was an ancient southward facing island Free City, a staging point on the pack-route between central Germany and Italy, and the people provided a safe harbour and passage across the lake, and armed guides far into Switzerland. It became rich, and much of the beauty in which its merchant patricians invested has survived. Westwards along the coast is Friedrichshafen, where the Zeppelins and Dornier aircraft were built. Once, in about 1930, I saw from a lake steamer, the extraordinary DO-X moored there. She was an experimental and unique twelve engined flying boat. A winter earlier we travelled from Munich to Basel by the lake Constance route. It had frozen solid to the bottom for a quarter of a mile out from the shore, and one could see the vestiges of a sunken Neolithic pile village; this had caused great excitement among the learned. They certainly investigated it thoroughly, for there is now a reconstruction standing on piles off the beach, and an excellent museum.

Two other things have endeared the lake to me. One is the good, mostly white, table wine grown all along the northern shore by the Margraves of Baden. The other is the decorative ironwork: ornamental grills, elaborate gates, guild signs, ingenious or odd weather vanes, balustrades, and iron screens or communion rails in the churches. It is an early Baroque period craft and has kept pretty close to the same style ever since. Sometimes you cannot tell if something was made 200 years ago or last week.

We got back to London. Werner was sent off, miserable; to a preparatory school called 'Pilgrims', because it was on the Pilgrims Way, above Westerham in Kent. I was put into a girls' school called 'Glendower' then opposite the Natural History Museum. I could read, but learning to write was apparently difficult. It was a problem of muscular or nervous co-ordination, perhaps (I do not know) related to Dupuytren's Contracture, from whose effects I began to suffer 30 years later. Capitals I managed. Then came those beastly small letters. I thought that I had mastered them, but one day I was mildly surprised when they gave me capitals again. The ways of teachers like Tolkien's wizards are, in any case, incomprehensible and not to be meddled with. The headmistress appeared: an impressive iron grey lady in rustling silks and a walking stick. She seemed, quite kindly, to want to know why I had gone 'back' to capitals. Since nobody had explained the direction in which I had gone, I found the question unintelligible. Best not to argue. So they put me up in a small hot upstairs classroom (to practice pot-hooks and copybook lettering) with some immense girls who were supposed to keep an eye on me and do their prep. They gossiped all the time; but apparently I did enough pot-hooks to satisfy the authorities, and as I was seven at the end of that term I was moved to Wagner's, a well known school (now unfortunately defunct) just around the corner at 92 Queen's Gate.

Meanwhile, we had exchanged the house at the Bolton's for a three-storey maisonette at 42 Queen's Gate Gardens. This represented a slight decline in the family fortunes. Percy's practice had struck a bad patch, due probably to the post-war slump. It was in the drawing room there that William Russell Flint painted that portrait of my mother. We lived there from 1925 to 1930 and it was a time from which I never recovered. I will attempt to explain this, but the story is complicated, trivial and obscure.

I was not unhappy, but, as will be seen, I had progressively to find my happiness myself. I had to achieve it in a world of my own, cut off from most of real life including my family, which formed the largest part of it. The reason, I saw later, was that some things went wrong with that family life. For some of those things there were important compensations, but they were compensations only. I have seen and envied conventionally happy families, but theirs' is a kind of life beyond my experience. One of its features is long residence in one place. I had hardly ever experienced this, and this was a predominating state of affairs until I could run my life in my own way. 'Home' was not a beloved and familiar place. It was somewhere where one slept. One got up in the morning, went to school, returned, had tea, played a little and went to bed. Percy, I think divined this. He often came up and read to me in bed, and that was a joy: *The Wind In The Willows*, or *The Jungle Book* or later, Kipling's other stories of service and Indian life, but as soon as the holidays broke out, we would rush off somewhere, usually leaving him behind. These 'somewheres' we enjoyed vastly, so that we regarded the return 'home' with gloom, and this did even more to prevent a proper family atmosphere from developing. The need to abide by the bargain with Albrecht institutionalised our broken home, but I have come to the conclusion, already adumbrated, that from some early stage in her second marriage Wilhelmine was no more loyal than she had been to the first. She told me once, that Percy made love in a horrid way – whatever that meant. She compared him unfavourably with Albrecht in all sorts of ways and she began to tease and taunt Percy: to create deliberate disturbances in his settled habits and to complain to all and sundry about the stuffiness (as she thought) of his relatives. She took a dislike, which she did not hide, to his friends and then complained that he would not let her into his professional secrets or have dealings with his clients. She was thoroughly mixed up. Instead of 'forsaking all other' she never got Albrecht out of her system. She was also jealous of the friendliness between Percy and ourselves. She became sharp-tongued and domineering at home. She interfered and hectored so that one heaved a sigh of relief when she went out shopping.

There was one occasion which, though the worst of its kind and so atypical, marked a watershed. It happened shortly after I had been staying with my father, and I was prattling away (I was eight) about it, in the way that little boys do to their mothers. Suddenly the weather, so to speak, changed. I had said something, which I do not now remember, about what we talked about. She began to cross-examine me in that Gloucester Road teashop. What had I said? What was it exactly? Why didn't I remember? I had said that I had said so-and-so? Why was I changing it? But I was changing it? How could I change it if I didn't remember? It went on and on and on; not only in the teashop; not only on the way home; but when I got home and day after day. It reduced me to a sort of wreck, destroying the benignity of my environment. For the first time it dawned that my mother was not to be trusted and that where her interests were concerned, no confidence was ever respected. I suppose that in a new bout of litigation, something which I had said conflicted with some affidavit which she had sworn; but she never ever explained this and I have inferred it simply from her savage persistence. It is possible, I suppose, that my father might have taken advantage of whatever it was, but I doubt it, because he always refused to discuss her with me.

There began, too, a campaign of vilification against him. We were forbidden to call him our Father and had to refer to him as 'AvB'. In this Werner, apparently joyfully, joined. He would leave for Germany complaining loudly, and return with complaints or funny stories at AvB's expense. I was young, but not as gullible as that. I had never seen my father in a temper, nor had he ever treated me with anything but courtesy and kindness. He, like Percy, was very different from my mother, as she had now become. I could not help making comparisons. The propaganda simply did not fit.

I began to have the first of the nightmares which recurred until I was about fifteen. I was walking across a dried up landscape under a burning sun. I came to a field-gate in a hedge. Beside the gate were some tin shacks and written in the dried mud at the foot of the gate was, in huge figures, the number 800. Immediately I saw this I was projected helplessly into the air towards the sun. Then I would wake up.

My doubts were sustained by a particular incident. It had never, with so exacting a mistress, been easy to keep servants. It now became downright impossible. But there was Anna a neat little woman who stood it for about a year, left, and then came back for a time. One summer's morning in about 1926, at getting-up time, I had a quarrel with Werner. My mother came storming in; there followed a general altercation in the course of which I told a lie. Breakfast was silent, my mother as often thunder faced. As soon as Percy had left for the office, she said that she was going to beat me. I was to sit alone in the study with a book, until the time came. I was thought not to like books (I adored reading, but it was part of my secret world). Eventually, Anna came in to say that I was to go upstairs. She then went up ahead of me, along the landing to the door. She stood aside for me to go in, and as I put my hand on the doorknob she squeezed my elbow and whispered 'good luck'. I had to open that door, and my mother was standing at the end of the room. I had to cross that room to her.

It is important not to mistake my meaning. This beating, which was the last at home, was probably just, and it was far less cruel than the many days of inquisition, which I had lately experienced. I do not remember the pain. But it seemed that there was another, perfectly reasonable person in my world, who was not impressed. As soon as the coast was clear, Anna (who made no direct comment) gave me a cup of proper tea – which I was not allowed.

That was a convenient biomp. In the summer of 1925 a compensatory event occurred but this one had separate roots in the past, and has affected my life profoundly ever since. I went, for the first of many times to Elmau. We flew in a fourteen-seater Handley Page from Croydon to Cologne, with a stop at Brussels. It was then a prodigious thing to do, and as there were only eleven people in the aircraft, one of the empty seats had to be balanced with a weight. We travelled at a dial airspeed of about 90 miles an hour and I was very sick. But I could boast to all my little friends.

Chapter 13

ELMAU AND CONFUSED EDUCATION

Johannes Müller, of Saxon peasant stock, was born in about 1890. He had a university degree, Lutheran ordination and a way with girls. Indeed, he obviously had a very large weapon, which he did not hesitate to use. A cynic may plausibly say that this affected his theology, but, as I will hope to show, this would have mattered little. He thought that many people's unhappiness might be assuaged by living in a tolerant community where, for a while, they might forget their real or fancied obligations and, with others, do as they pleased. He got to know the Countess Waldersee, Curt Haniel's sister or cousin. The Haniels had built most of the Rhine bridges and were fabulously rich. She had married the Field-Marshal almost in nominal charge of the international force at Peking during the Boxer troubles.* Müller persuaded her to lend him the Rhineland château of Mayenberg to try out his ideas. To what extent they were his or hers, I do not know. His numerous writings are not of equal quality, and sometimes they fall off into the banal or preposterous. Her portrait suggests a very intelligent woman.

Naturally Müller made influential acquaintances. Women would confide in him, and the sort of woman who knew the Haniels and the Waldersees were, at any rate outside the bedroom, to be reckoned with. I have no doubt that his sort of group therapy was sometimes intimate and the size of the group limited. But, besides this, he had liberal and sensible ideas in the buttoned-up atmosphere of Wilhelminian Germany – and he attracted the attention of Prince Max of Baden.

It is confusing, if conventional, to name the prince in this way. Actually, he was the sovereign Grand Duke of Baden, a state about half the size of England which formed an 'L' along the German side of the Rhine from Lake Constance almost to Mainz – Haniel country. A prominent imperial politician, he was the last Chancellor of the Second Reich. His 1915 Speech from the Throne to the Estates of Baden is printed in Müller's collected works, published long before Prince Max died. I knew him quite well in a childish kind of way.

Müller had several acknowledged children before he married Irene Sattler, the sculptress daughter of a Munich architect. She was one of the last of Hildebrand's

---

* He arrived when it was all over.

pupils and so in the artistic succession from the great Lenbach. She made a bronze plaque of me at the age of eleven and a marvellous head of Hildebrand himself. She and her father must have contributed to the Elmau pool of ideas. She was in the ordinary sense fecund: eleven children and the nickname 'Mother Earth' after her bulky Nordic blondness and kind patience in that vociferous household. They conceived (*mots justes*) Elmau.* They acquired a huge property comprising foothills, woodland and meadow just below the Wetterstein range, which forms, at Mittenwald north of Innsbruck, the 2,000 year old boundary between Austria and Bavaria. The place was approachable only by carriage or sleigh, or on foot. No cars. Professor Sattler designed a large building with a green copper spire (now somewhat mottled) vaguely reminiscent of a south German monastery but with the internal economy of a 200-bedroom hotel, together with a large house 300 yards away for the Müllers. The Prince's association made the enterprise possible even at the height of World War I, when it was constructed. I assume that the money came from him and the Countess.

The Elmau system neatly fitted pleasure, psychological relief and profit together. The building (called the Schloss = château) has the usual drinking facilities. There was a place called the library which had virtually no books. There are still very few, but when I remarked on this recently to a Müller, I was greeted with indignation. There was a Great Hall ceiled with high wooden arches, with a stage at one end and a gallery at the other. Underneath was the dining hall. The wide arcaded passages and the entrance hall are floored with marble, and nowadays there are indoor and outdoor swimming pools.

The amenities were maintained for residents only. The terms were always *en pension*, and everything casual like drinks at the bar and cups of tea was paid for, not with money but signed chits called *bons*, which were put on a weekly bill. This effectively shut out strangers.

Only slightly unusual so far, other things set it quite apart. The first was the breath taking beauty of its woods and mountains, in which no other human habitation was visible. It had been the talented King Ludwig II's favourite country. The second is a derivative of the isolation. It is so *quiet* that you could almost hear the music of Heaven. But thirdly, the service was performed by semi-volunteers called *Helferinnen* (girl helpers) of good family (I recall an Oldenburg and a Zitzewitz) who, work permitting, took as much part in the social life as anyone else. Müller being Müller, most of them were pretty. The practical reason for this arrangement, was that nobody had to feel inhibited 'in front of the servants': therefore there were no servants. This was a sort of adaptation of the training of aristocratic girls which I have already mentioned. Possibly these *Helferinnen* were

---

* I have lately gathered that it was burned down in 2005.

the origin of Elmau's somewhat *louche* reputation in the outside world, but if so, this was a mistake for the girls were well supervised. Elmau was certainly a House of Assignation, but it was by no means a brothel.

Fourthly, and this was vital, you ate at common tables of ten, and it was an inflexible rule that you sat according to table plans, which changed daily. In my childhood, a separate children's table kept parents unbothered and it was normal to separate spouses. You might spend a couple of meals with a furrier, a publisher (there were several of them), a Swedish diplomat, a Dutch lady professor, a conductor, a novelist. It was a seedbed and cross fertiliser and started many new friendships.

In addition, there were the regular events. There was dancing in the Great Hall after dinner two or three times a week. Müller wrote and talked a lot of high flown bosh about dancing, but he was an accomplished dancer himself, and he rightly insisted that you kept quiet when actually dancing. This was a matter of manners, for the music was played on a grand piano, and the dances were mostly waltzes (Chopin, Strauss), Rheinländers, and twice every evening, the Quadrille. Since few at first knew the steps of the Rheinländer (a very vigorous dance) or the mathematics of the Quadrille, there were hilarious afternoon lessons where losing your Rheinländer partner or clubbing your Quadrille made everyone happy. Some never danced: others danced like mad. There were, after all, gorgeous *helferinnen* for the asking. Nobody worried either way. There was, several summers running, a lady with a white-fringed shawl who always danced by herself.

On other evenings there was chamber-music. Musicians like Elmau, and come up for their keep. Many of them were very distinguished. This is still true: Benjamin Britten regularly came. Müller's daughter Bobby (officially Sieglinde) continued the tradition. I went to all the concerts from the earliest time, and acquired a passion for that sort of music. Nobody thought this odd in a child of seven. So I was hearing Beethoven quartets, and Brahms recitals, Reger and Marcello, singers, 'cellists, what you will.

Lastly there was Johannes Müller and his moralisings. A movable pulpit was erected on the stage, and we, or some of us, sat in solemn rows. He would appear in a black tail-coat and a white stock, looking solemnly ill at ease, enter his pulpit, spread his arms and utter the opening 'My dear friends'. Somebody, eventually a very shapely blonde called Fraulein Ihm-Diepken, the equivalent of the Adjutant-General at the court of Catherine the Great, would take the whole lot down in shorthand, and in due course it would appear in Müller's private periodical *Die Grüne Blätter* (Green Leaves). She also had to appear at the Thursday Questions and Answers in the Tearoom. Dr Müller replied orally to written questions. Some of these would be humorous, if not frivolous, and probably planted: and the good Doctor would be in a genial mood, and wearing a pair of leather shorts and ornamental Bavarian braces. It cannot really be said that they suited him: it is hard to imagine a less attractive physique. He was short, fat, nearly bald, and his prematurely white-haired bullet head was equipped with a grey handle-bar moustache. He resembled a perspiring cottage loaf.

Yet he gave his wife eleven children, and could sort out all sorts of psychological hang-ups, run a vast business and lay a woman or two (besides his Adjutant-General) every day. In the German fashion, he had disciples, but the difference was that he despised them. No sheeps' eyes for him – especially from a woman. A witty mien, intellectual frankness, a straight mature gaze and – pants off. The Müller House had a double-bedded recessed balcony suitable for nocturnal athletics even in winter, and perfectly visible to anyone who cared to watch.

Some people however were not impressed. I never watched the balcony and would never have taken my troubles to him, though in the eleven years that I knew him we got on well enough; and, at the top of the scale, I do not think that, for all his frequent visits, Prince Max was much impressed either. To him the Doctor was a useful adviser among many – and anyhow Elmau was fun.

Wilhelmine got to hear of Elmau through the Selliers. Being distant relatives, I suppose the rumour of it reached them by way of Albrecht's friendship with Curt Haniel. In the summer of 1925 they and we arranged to go together. Albrecht, so far as I know, never went there. We, two Blumenthal and three Sellier children soon got to know the Müllers of our age. We formed a sort of permanent gang which reformed at every visit, but Werner seldom came, whereas I went for most of the summer holidays from 1925 to 1936, and in some years twice.

My education at this period was a theoretical model of disorganisation. Theoretical, I say, because the object of contemporary preparatory school education was to acquire enough information to pass into a Good School; but mine enabled me to do that, and to do it rather well. Perhaps standards were low even at the best schools, so that it was relatively easy to pass anyway. Or more probably, it matters less than teachers think to miss even large parts of a precisely timed curriculum. Between 1927 and 1932 when I went to Winchester, I attended three different schools, and as I spent each spring term away altogether, I invariably missed the geography of Ireland and the Wars of the Roses.

Before I go to Pilgrims my first preparatory school, I must go back a year and say something about Wagner's school. The name was pronounced as an English word, and Orlando Wagner, the father of Sir Anthony Wagner, the distinguished herald, was impressive and businesslike. He occasionally wore that most elegant of garments, a frock coat. I could already read and write, so I went into the second form. Among boys the atmosphere of 1925 was intensely hostile to 'the enemy'. So when I arrived with my knowledge of German and peculiar name I was instantly set upon during break, and ended up with a bloody nose. The thing came as a total surprise. It had never occurred to me to feel in that sort of way as a member of one nation, to another. I was always called Charles in England and Wolfgang in Germany. Why not? So the fist which landed on my face arrived out of the blue. I picked myself up off the floor and yelled blue murder, and the authorities tidied up the mess and saw to it that this particular trend did not become trendy.

My first ally was a boy call Arrowsmith. We were drawn to each other because we still found it hard to spell our own names. Then there was an Indian boy (turban and all) who had only one conversational gambit. 'Have you ever been from India to England on a battleship?' One summer morning I was delivered as usual by my mother to school. Lounging on the front door steps of the school was an utterly charming man dressed in white court breeches and an off-black tail coat with golden cuff embroideries. He had a sword and one of those interesting white feathered hats which only the British can invent. He chattered happily with me and every other boy. Eventually our Indian battleship boy appeared in a slightly smarter turban and said:

'Hello, where are we going?'

'Durbar', said the man.

'And will I be carried on the shoulders of two – idars?' (I didn't quite catch the word).

'No, Highness, we both walk, but we go there by carriage first.'

He uncoiled himself, beat the dust off his breeches, took His Highness by the hand, and they got into a brougham which was waiting about 60 yards up the road. It set off sedately up Queen's Gate, turned right at the top and stopped. I saw them get out.

The battleship never reappeared.

It was about then that I was introduced to something called 'cricket'. I do not think that my parents had quite realised the consequences of commencing a half German boy's education at an English girls' school. My mother had played cricket as a child (at Aunt Hannah's?). She presumably thought that they would at Glendower.

Anyhow we set off for Battersea Park where this thing happened. I had a cricket bat, but no idea what it did. We went in a double-decker horse-bus: it must have been the last in London, and I was disappointed to discover years later that Orlando Wagner owned it. It was a hot day. We debussed and found this place. There was a great deal of unintelligible talk, and somebody said 'you go over there', so I went clutching my bat. They said 'No; leave your bat here', so I left it and went again. There was an iron railing with lots of bushes behind, and in front of this I stood and admired the landscape in which figures rushed about. After a while, I noticed that a ball was lolloping in my direction; there were loud, rather technical yells, so I seized this ball (which I had stopped with my foot) and hurled it towards my party. Everybody within sight now burst into a chorus of incoherent rage. Practically everything stopped, and a furious unknown master appeared and wanted to know what I thought I was doing. As I had not the least idea, I could not help him. I see it now. There must have been two games going on side by side. I must have stopped a perfectly good boundary shot from another game. I had then appropriated their ball and hurled it into the middle of my own, which therefore suddenly had two.

They sorted this out and we restarted. After a while another ball appeared. More technical yells. So I decided to leave it strictly to itself. It went through the railings and disappeared into the bushes. After a slight pause it dawned on me that I was supposed to fetch it. So I squeezed through the railings and started to beat the bushes. There were agreeable little trails in them, and butterflies which I rather liked. My search was not successful. Everybody came pouring through the railings. After a while they found the ball and started again. Then, believe it or not, the ultimate; *two* balls entered my life. Actually, one came to rest against my heel, while I was picking up the other. I held it up in a questioning manner; half the field yelled one thing, half another. Somebody with a bat was running hither and thither, and somebody else at the place where there was only one stump was jumping up and down. So I decided to throw the missile at him since he seemed keen to have it. I missed of course. There was the usual roar of indignation while somebody retrieved it.

At the end of this hot and toilsome day everybody in the 'bus said loudly and repetitiously that I had Spoiled the Whole Thing.

This was not my only Cricketing disaster. After we had played in Battersea Park for a bit, it was decided to play the kind of cricket which had three stumps at each end. After the ball had been bowled six times at one end, you all walked over to the opposite side and they bowled it from the other end. I was quite good at this walking business, though not sure why one did it. I think that they must have written me off, for balls seldom seemed to come my way, but I sometimes failed to notice the change-over, and would suddenly find somebody standing next to me, apparently taking my place. Once in conscientious panic, I rushed across regardless and woke up under a tree with a bruise on the side of my head. We all got home half an hour early, and I became a sort of mad mascot. This sort of accident also happened to me elsewhere.

My efforts at football were not much more distinguished. We played this game on a field, which was not level, belonging to Kensington Palace. It was fairly obvious what one had to do, and as I was large for my age I played 'back'. When the other side came near my goal, I would rush at the boy with the ball; he would lose it; kick me on the shin, and then I would hop about in an agonized manner. Spectators did not admire this. Indeed, I must admit that football is not my thing. Backs seldom score goals at the best of times, but I did at least score one, years later at Winchester against my own side.

But lessons were different. We learnt rithmatic (especially twystimes), and what a noun was; Mr Wagner took us with dramatic panache through the Gospels; and there was a terribly nice, no nonsense woman called Miss Cornwell who lived in Cornwall Gardens and never got boys into trouble. I once went to her flat, where she gave me lemonade and little iced cakes.

The great feature of Wagner's was that we learned in a logical fashion. I must have been quite an apt pupil, for I went up each term. It is mainly due to Wagner's mathematics that I still do not usually need a calculator. I would have reached the top in my fifth term if I had not been suddenly sent to 'Pilgrims'.

The contrast could hardly have been greater. It was a rambling cluster of school-like attachments to a small mid-nineteenth Century house facing south, halfway up the North Downs above Westerham, and I was overnight a border. Mr Nettle, the headmaster, looked like Hergé's Professor Calculus. He was an easy going old boy who kept little control of his staff. Food (mostly toad-in-the-hole, tapioca and stewed rhubarb) was discouraging. There was a general feeling, championed by a self important matron, that if you had not been to India, you were of no account. I met this particular attitude again later. The teaching was confused and incompetent. I was expected to unlearn my simple and logical arithmetic in favour of a farrago of ham-handed nonsense called 'practice', I suppose derived from the habits of illiterate nineteenth Century accountants. The ways of teachers, as I have said once already, are incomprehensible and not to be meddled with. I stuck privately to what I knew, and did 'practice' to keep the peace.

Someone else in my dormitory was less lucky or less tactful. He was weedy, bespectacled and in another class. One day Mr Nettle came into our form with him. He said something to the form-master. Then he told the boy to bend over the window-sill and gave him six with a cane. This was usually done over his drawing room sofa, but there were workmen there. We were told not to look, but of course we all did. At bedtime somebody said to the boy 'Come on, show us your bot'. He knelt on his bed and dropped his pyjamas as if it had nothing to do with him. The welts were quite black, and boys from other dormitories crowded in. The matron came and looked as well. She said nothing.

This singular episode is connected in my mind with the endemic violence and collective bullying. A year or two earlier, Werner had been stabbed in the shoulder-blade with a chisel. There was a nasty habit of mobbing. In theory, if a boy got above himself, a mob might be organised to set upon him and put him in his place; so that in principle no boy, however big and strong could get away with it. The *matron* once threatened me with a mobbing. In practice an unpopular boy was shamefully bated and bullied, and a bullying demagogue could rely on a mob to terrorise some wretched child, defenceless because of the rule against 'sneaking'. How on earth Werner got through that place without serious injury to his psyche I cannot imagine. Perhaps he did not. Half a term was enough for me, and I was not bashed about much.

Wilhelmine and Percy evidently thought so too. They found me a seaside school which, because of the lottery of libel I will call Nameless. The headmaster must have been a friend of a friend; I will call him Inkhorn. I shall disguise all the other names connected with this school.

It was one of those brick and pebble-dash buildings which you find on the south coast. It looked towards the sea half a mile away, and it had a large field bounded by a six foot ash grey fence; there was a dark little pavilion in one corner. There was a big school-room divisible by a moving partition, and a small schoolroom round the passage corner. As there were four classes, the lowest had to be taught in the dining room. A diminutive indoor swimming pool was floored over in winter for use as a carpentry shop. The pride and good fortune of Nameless, however, was the excellent gymnasium, splendidly equipped with ropes, wall-bars, and horses. It was also used as an assembly hall and chapel. The playing field became a swamp in winter and rock hard in summer, so that there were long periods when athletics and gymnastics were the main forms of exercise, and Mr Inkhorn insisted on everybody learning to swim. He was an excellent instructor at this, and everyone learned the knack very quickly.

He devised ways of engendering term spirit. The most conventional was to get everybody to join the Boy Scouts at eleven. Again, he was good at this. He understood the ways of nature, with which good scouting is so intimately connected. He took endless trouble teaching boys how to tie useful knots in the dark, and lay and kindle fires (with two matches) in a wind. There was even something, though not much, in the joke about rubbing two sticks together. Most of us used the bow-actuated fire-drill.

The most successful begetter of co-operation was however, the indirect result of the inadequacy of the playing-field. The under-scout age boys went either to the beach, which was a stony one seamed with groynes, or to a large oakwood. We picked teams, and threw stones, or, as the case might be acorns at each other in prolonged and sometimes tactically well organised battles. People often got hurt. Usually it came to handstrokes – occasionally to lost tempers and general fury. On the other hand, there were moments, especially in the wood, when these minor wars broke up into wandering gangs which avoided each other, and at some periods there were no acorns.

As always in schools, the quality of the teaching was variable. Inkhorn taught geography and French admirably. His wife, who acted as the school secretary, taught art successfully to the talented, but was, perhaps, less successful with the clumsy ones like me. She was a dark handsome woman who could talk to children with sympathy and sophistication. We all liked her. Then there were Professor Blanc's fascinating evening science lectures with practical demonstrations on chemistry, botany and optics. The only science I ever learnt came from him. There were Sunday film shows, and rather splendid occasional events when we all sang popular songs, or put on plays. Bearing in mind that this was in 1927 Nameless was remarkably inventive and modern. And, besides, the food was excellent. I can remember the legs of mutton, the acres of treacle tart, the gorgeous bread and dripping. We were remarkably healthy and happy and our education, if rather lopsided, was not too bad.

All the same the school was liable to criticism. I think that the Inkhorns must have been working too close to the margin. They hoped, I can only suppose, by their brilliance and enlightenment to attract backing. None of us could otherwise explain the special position of Crumplington and Poop. Their parents were very rich. Mr Poop, in particular was a sallow joke, who appeared in a chauffeur-driven Rolls Royce with a costly cigar between his thick lips. I was in the Second form. Crumplington and Poop were neither at the top nor at the bottom of the Third. For reasons, to which I will return, there were no prizes at that school. All of a sudden there was a special school assembly decorated with odd parents. Mr Inkhorn made a long speech and then, to the school's bewilderment, presented a prize each to the smirking Crumplington, and the fat and unlovely Poop.

Nameless had a system of recurrent, fortnightly, sticks and carrots. This was quite logical and sensible if simply described and applied without second thoughts. If you reached a fairly good, above-average standard (where a standard was measurable) you got a reward, usually in the form of time off. If you fell a long way below the average you were punished. There was, in athletics as well as, say, mathematics, a small elite at the top, a large ruck in the middle and a few below who were in trouble.

Here the doubts spring up, for the punishment was to have your naked behind beaten with a shoe. If a boy made too many mistakes in class or at some game it was – shorts down and over the table.

This curious regime might not have been suspect if it had not been for the dormitory events. On my fourth day I woke in the morning to a sound which I could not identify. I sat up and said 'what's that' and somebody said 'Sh-h'. It turned out to be the sound of somebody being beaten in the next dormitory. If Inkhorn caught anyone talking in bed, he had them out and beat them, sometimes very hard. I should say, at once, that the pain, even if intense, was, on the whole not important; but it was another Crumplington and Poop situation. Many worse things than talking in bed habitually went unpunished. So what on earth was this about? Presumably the Head did it for some reason which had nothing to do with school rules, just as he gave Cruplington and Poop prizes for no reason connected with their achievements.

We talked about these frequent happenings a great deal, of course. It should hardly be otherwise for when we all bathed in the summer, there were usually a few pairs of bruised buttocks on show. We were not sophisticated nor had we heard of Sigmund Freud or the Marquis de Sade, but none of us had much doubt that old Inkhorn did it because he enjoyed it.

If Inkhorn, why not we? The staff were out of earshot during a half hour before dormitory lights-out, when we were supposed to be reading. Somebody suggested that we might whack each others' bums. Everybody egged everybody else on. Somehow the lot fell on me. Someone kept *cave* while the others took it in turns to give me four each on the bare with a leather soled slipper. It was fairly painful, but my chief sensation was an extraordinary sense of pride, and next evening, when the subject of course came up again, the six of us settled a rota for the six weekdays, leaving out the Sundays, which were unsafe. My turn came on Thursdays for four terms. The system was the light of our lives with its risks, secrets and special intimacy.

Chapter 14

THE REAL DIVORCE

I had two terms away from school at Lugano when I was allowed to get to know my father. The idea was that he would teach me German, which was supposed to have grown rusty, but he soon found out that there was nothing in it, and read me the fascinating boys' novels by Karl May, who was, rather inaccurately, called the German Henty. Karl May is more full-blooded, much more detailed and much longer. Mostly it happens in the sands of Arabia, the Syrian cities and the Sudan, where one's dragoman addresses one as 'effendi', the Druses or someone threaten one with knives for professing the wrong number of sacraments, and one is captured several times by slave traders, or stripped of one's property by rascally pashas.

I was becoming estranged from my possessive mother who wanted me to remain the baby. She belittled me whenever she could, so that Werner now became the pattern of everything practical, solid, splendid and ingenious, while I had to be the failure. I think that this was the origin of this nonsensical German rustiness. Of course, it made me jealous of Werner, but it mainly made me hate her and gravitate towards others who treated me with repect.

Now I was with my father and enjoying it hugely. We stayed at the *Weisses Kreuz* (White Cross) at the top of Lugano, opposite the railway station. Our two side rooms had balconies over the staired street, and when the cathedral bell next door tolled enormously at seven in the morning, the view across the roofs down to the lake and over to the Monte Generoso, sparkled. There was everything which a boy might want. Great international expresses picturesque with their different coloured carriages stopped in the station. You could post a letter in one and know that it would be in Calais by the morning: or you could get into one the other way to the frontier at Chiasso. There were excursions. We would walk up the Monte Bré, the sugar loaf mountain to the left of the town's lake-bay or go up in a swinging funicular. There was a splendid network of tramways in the countryside – to Luino, Ponte Tresa or whatever. The eastward side of the lake had not yet been desecrated by the road, so you got to the lovely lakeside village of Gandria or beyond it to

Porlezza in Italy, by steamer or you got somebody to take you in his motor-boat, and persuaded him to let you steer.

Lugano was a prosperous but comfortably small place, very Italianate, with dark grocers' shops smelling of garlic where you bought olive oil by weight. In the steep street of steps running past the Weisses Kreuz there was a little place where a man ceaselessly turned out macaroni: he had a hand machine which he put out into the shady street as soon as the sun was up. There he was, turning and turning his handle all day, stopping only for crowding customers: large women with wicker baskets, cooks from neighbouring establishments, with trays on their heads, and nondescript fat little men who looked as if they had put on two pairs of trousers.

The town was, as I have hinted, an up and down sort of place. You went east and west along the quay, or northwards up a slope so steep in places that the main way up was a vertiginous funicular. It operated by gravity, one carriage with a full water tank came down, dragging the other empty-tanked vehicle up to the top. The one at the bottom emptied, while the one at the top filled, and the roles were reversed. The fare was one Rappen, about one tenth of a penny.

Nearby was the not very noticeable Church of the Angels which contained, under several layers of Zwinglian white-wash, a large fresco of the crucifixion which had just been detected and was being restored. The church was crammed with scaffolding and hostile notices, but my father, with his Latin appearance and fluent Tuscan made short work of them and we spent happy mornings high in the light, watching the restorers at elbow distance. They had to work on tiny areas of the huge painting at a time, and it eventually took eleven years. In the year 2000 I went back to look. It really is a staggering affair by the Milanese Bernado Luini, and I do not understand why it is not famous. To my eye it compares well with the celebrated Tintoretto *Crucifixion* in the Scuola di San Rocco in Venice, and it is certainly easier to see.

So what with sight seeing, boating, Carl May, tramways and general chatter we entertained ourselves hugely, even, I think Albrecht did, but there was one thing which he never did. Try as I might, I never got him to talk about Wilhelmine.

He was an odd looking figure. He was slim, with steeply sloping shoulders, and he habitually wore a bottle green riding coat and breeches, with his thin legs encased in green-khaki puttees; on his head he wore a green-khaki felt hat with a wide flat brim. This had a circular dent in the top, which Werner and I called the duck-pond. It cast his dark narrow face with its thoughtful brown eyes into an ever deeper shade. It he had been a larger man he would have been the villain of every melodrama from the *Silver King* onwards, but he was not tall and he was very lightly built. A sort of German *bersagliero*.[*]

---

[*] Light Infantryman.

THE REAL DIVORCE

When the time came to leave Lugano, and be delivered to my mother in Paris, he took me there a week early and showed me round. It was overwhelming. It was an exceptionally lovely spring with the trees in their first flourish. We put ourselves into an open *fiacre* at the Gare de l'Est, and the coachman let the horses amble gently across the town; Albrecht gossiped with him, and occasionally told me where we were. I, for my part, was staggered during those first 40 minutes by three things: dirt, noise and confusion.

Soft coal stoves for house-heating had, over the years cast a deep layer of bluish-grey filth upon everything. White stone was everywhere black; white paint, dark grey. The Louvre was coal black: the Rue de Rivoli was coal black. No windows seemed ever to have been washed. In contrast with tidy Switzerland there was an extraordinary quantity of mess in the streets: rags, dung, dead flowers, tattered advertisements, old newspapers. It was like the end of a market day all the time. A later experience confirmed all this. My mother, Werner and I dined at a hotel near the Gare du Nord. A fat rat was nosing about in the pot of a large potted palm at the end of our table. We showed it to the waiter. He lackadaisically flapped his napkin at the rat, which seemed surprised. After a few moments it jumped down and trotted away across the floor.

The noise and confusion in the streets continued from dawn till the small hours. The boulevards had been built to accommodate a heavy but slow moving traffic. To this had been added a double tramway with unimaginably long and unwieldy trams coupled in pairs. These monsters blocked the roadway every time they turned a corner, and they had a strident bell which the driver operated by stamping on a pedal. It was very necessary, for everybody who could make a noise, made it. The First World War had multiplied the traffic a thousandfold – had not Galliéni's taxis saved the Battle of the Marne? – and every vehicle possessed a horn. Motor engines were noisier and smellier than they are now. Traffic control was minimal and there was no speed limit save that imposed by the mutual antagonisms. Whenever anybody got in a driver's way, the latter hooted, or if a coachman, bellowed obscenities, and of course, everybody was in fact and sound in everybody else's way. In many places the traffic hardly moved, in others it hurtled, and the police added their complications by standing on pedestals ceremonially waving white batons. Sometimes, however, a whistle screamed above the din. This meant that a policeman wanted to cross the road – and woe betide anyone who knocked a policeman down! His whistle was the signal for yet another traffic jam.

It was rather fun sitting in this uproarious ocean in an open carriage in the sunlight under the trees, and it was not all cacophonous. Music came from the many pavement cafés. This feature of Paris has vanished since World War II. Every café had a small band, or a man playing an accordion or piano, and their music was the background of many of the side-streets. It all made Paris, despite the din, a much more inviting city than it is now.

We stayed at the Hotel MacMahon near the Etoile, and Albrecht showed me round with croissants and enormous bowls of coffee in the mornings, and sailing boats in the fountains of the Tuileries gardens. I found the Eiffel Tower quite natural, and since I had heard a great deal of talk about the *Mona Lisa*, I was surprised how small and brown she was. I was impressed then as now, by the enormous extent of the Louvre, with its great wings reaching predatorily towards you, on either side of the gardens. Curiously enough – for we must have walked along them many times, I took no impression of the Champs Elysées at all, and it was only some years later that I discovered with real surprise, where they were.

At this point there was a change of plan. I was not to be handed over in Paris, after all, but taken to Calais and put on the boat care of the Purser. I was delighted. My father, as a matter of fact, was less enthusiastic because it disorganised his travelling arrangements; but eventually we reached Calais and a nice kind fat Chief steward. I stood on the upper deck, and there was Albrecht on the quay, waving as I had once seen him wave on the quay at Lindau. Sadly waving, waving, waving…

I never saw him again.

I was, naturally, cast down by leaving him, and I assumed that, like Werner, being with him would become a matter of routine. I was pleased but not demonstratively pleased to see my mother at Dover. She expected contrasting shrieks and peals of happiness and joy. She was furious when she did not get them, and, having no sense, she showed it. We had a taciturn journey to London; she was ostentatiously grieved for days, with a curdled face looking as if she had eaten something. I think that it was shortly after this that the incident in the Gloucester Road teashop occurred. It is now obvious, that she thought that Albrecht had deliberately (one of her favourite words) tried to turn me against her. This was Oedipus – or rather, Jocasta. There was something incestuous about it, and the fact that Albrecht had done nothing which she suspected, made not the slightest difference.

I do not think that I am exaggerating when I speak of Jocasta. Some time, perhaps a year later, we were, for example, staying at Hawksworth for Christmas. To my fury, I found that I was expected to share a bed with her, which meant that I could not read after bed-time. I complained about this to my cousins. She overheard us talking, and the result was another three days of sulks and grieving. I was almost glad to get back to school, but not actually overjoyed because my parents had, I think rightly, decided to take me away from Nameless. Whether the stick-and-carrot system or our private amusements had come to their ears, or whether, as I think they doubted the school's ability to get me into Winchester, I do not know.

Percy, being a Wykhamist, had set his heart on Winchester for me; but, more I think, to the point, Werner was having a wretched time at Sherborne. Twelve-and-a-quarter is too young to go to a public school anyhow, and Sherborne had the bad arrangement of a headmaster's house, where Werner was. I do not know exactly what happened; but it seems that the over-busy headmaster neglected his house, save for occasional and erratic incursions; these were apt to be disastrous because he was an eccentric, and later, it seems, an unhappy and drunken man. Meanwhile the older public school abuses flourished – the bullying, the domination of the flannelled philistine, the false loyalties. Werner developed a carapace and chameleon qualities. He actually managed to look like a proud, narrow rugger-playing tough.

For the fifth time, then, I became a new boy but this nearly coincided with other changes. Granny Baker died. The Baker patrimony (which included the best central site in Wellington, New Zealand) was shared out. The Cottesmore Gardens – Flutters Hill complex was wound up. Percy now had money, and he and Wilhelmine found a fine three acre site in Wentworth, an estate near Virginia Water, not far from Longcross, and started to build a house.

Wentworth had then two, instead of four golf courses, a lot of fine building sites (some already built) and much untouched woodland. It represented an amalgamation of two estates. The larger had centred on a mansion which had become the club house, and which had belonged to Count Morello, a Spanish field marshal after whom the bitter black cherries are named. They grew on scarlet flowered splendour in north walls and we made delicious jam from them. His daughters sold the property just as the smaller part came onto the market. This belonged to the Anglo-Swiss de Salis or von Salis family and centred in the other, more impressive mansion later converted into the dormy house. The de Salis, neighbours of the Swiss Blumenthals were one of the two great families of the Engadine, and for centuries lived, and still own, a palace at Soglio above the Maloja Pass between St Moritz and Chiavenna. Their rivals, the von Plantas of Zuoz, also developed English connections: two of them, father and son, were the first keepers of the Library of the British Museum, now known as the British Library. So Percy took the conveyance of this unfenced sloping site, and we all went down with an architect. A tramp-like figure with a battered hat, was sitting on a mackintosh square among the hummocks. Even Percy did not at first recognise his one-legged brother Edard, a life-long birdwatcher, who had no idea that this site belonged to us; it was simply a good place to observe the pipits. So we called it Pipits Hill.

My new school was Allen House at Hook Heath, a suburb of Woking only a few miles off, and the new house at Pipits Hill went up as I settled in at that school. It was a fine spring and a hot summer. My mother had an inspiration. A tile-roofed summer house for eventual use with a tennis court was built before anything else, and we used to camp in it at weekends while the house was being built. Up with the lark, primus stoves and the house developing from marker pegs, to trenches, to foundations, to bare walls and so forth. Wilhelmine made the architect include all sorts of practical features then little known in England. These were often small (like tiled window sills), but made a difference to management and had to be planned beforehand. The resulting habitation was well ahead of its time, with an insulated roof and glass wool between the joists. The attic play room covered the whole of the house, and it had a carpenter's bench. We built a model railway on a great shelf running round it. Werner at Sherborne had become a good carpenter. He might have made a sculptor if encouraged. I helped by holding things up or finding screws; I was the carpenter's ham-handed mate. All the family joined in. We put in stations and signals with their mechanical and electrical apparatus. Wilhelmine made curtains to hang from shelf to floor and Percy painted a scenery scroll as background three feet high and all of 40 foot long, with houses and roads, advertisements and fields, birds, sheep, cattle, shops, clouds – the whole of life, and all to the right scale.

In 1960 after the house had long been sold, my daughter Katharine and I visited Pipits Hill. There were builders in. We found Percy's painting still intact in its place. In 1976 Henry and I called, and found some slummy occupants, with furniture against the windows and flashy cars lying about in the drive. They alleged that there had been a fire up there and that the painting had gone.

I do not remember Pipits Hill with much pleasure or Allen House with much inspiration. My mother's bullying possessiveness was, at least, turned upon improving the property. It needs a lot of work to lay out three acres of garden on virgin soil. The trouble was that Wilhelmine and Percy really liked gardening. Werner and I, unfortunately, did not like it at all, and we were bored stiff with the whole business. Too much of the holidays seemed to be taken with digging and trenching, banking up, laying paving, cutting turf and planting shrubs. If we flagged, we were lectured on gratitude.

So, on the whole, Allen House, though pedestrian, was a welcome refuge. It had two headmasters. Herbert Lyon was a lame elderly bookish bachelor with interests in the theatre. Charles Dewé was practical, energetic, logical and married. Though, as time went on, I got to dislike Lyon, because he was apt to put the blame for his mistakes on others, they made an excellent team and I never lost admiration for

Dewé. He was always clear sighted, willing to listen and unpretentious. According to him, the school's only purpose was to get you through Common Entrance. He would be delighted to do better for cleverer boys, but he would sacrifice nothing of his main objective for them, nor would he take much credit for their success.

The principle was admirable but its application was unavoidably uninspiring. We did Latin, Mathematics, English Subjects and French six mornings a week – in that order; one each of these on four afternoons and the one in which the school was thought, at any given time to be weak, also on four afternoons. There were two half hour periods of preparation separated by chapel, every evening: there was a chapel every morning. We played cricket in the summer, football in the winter, and rugger with athletics and hockey in the spring. There were six classes in each subject and promotion up one ladder of classes had nothing to do with promotion up another. The whole of one's life was utterly predictable, but there were prizes in profusion. Only the extremely wicked or the very lazy were caned, but a good many more had to do those tiresome impositions, in which you had to write out 50 times phrases such as 'I must not stick my tongue out at the matron unless she tells me to do so.'

Human nature had, however, introduced its deviations. Charles Dewé was an inspired French teacher, but rather impatient at Latin. Herbert Lyon took English subjects more than competently. Claud Douglas, who later became an osteopath in America, taught mathematics brilliantly: in fact, his mathematics, learned at the age of twelve, got me through School Certificate with (I believe) record marks at sixteen. There were, however, less fortunate choices. In the stillness of the afternoon one could hear Old Red Hair, as usual bellowing at Third Form Latin. He also screamed his way through every game of rugger – the slightest thing seemed to set off the bomb. Everybody quailed; you felt that at any moment he might attack you. How on earth can you concentrate on the pluperfect subjunctive when you are sitting on a volcano?

Then there was Hair Oil, a rather vain young man who was in charge of cricket, in which, as you know, I did not shine. His remedy was to make me field in the slips, at silly point or at silly mid-wicket. Balls shot between my feet, whistled about my ears, while floods of abuse followed every dropped catch. At Old Hair Oil's French and English classes, he was volatile too but the practice was more direct: he threw things. Dusters, rulers, chalk, books hurtled about the room. A near miss cracked a window; a hymn book flew into the rose garden. Never a dull moment, but he was likeable in a way that the Red Haired Master was not. Also, he had his inspired moments. One Sunday he read us the whole of the Book of Esther with a thundering dramatic sense which, I believe, none of us ever forgot.

If Gessler is the first in my demonology, Haman the son of Hamedatha the Aggagite is a close second.

I was in the chapel choir, which meant practices in our spare time. In return we had an annual choir treat, in the form of a visit to the daylight full dress rehearsal of the Aldershot Tattoo. Tattoos were beautiful and fascinating performances in the presence of enormous audiences. The Rushworth Arena at Aldershot accommodated 20,000. The profits went to military charities. There were also annual ones at Tidworth.

I saw them both in their glory: the Tidworth Tattoo at night, as it is meant to be seen, the Aldershot one twice in daylight, which is, if anything even more interesting, because one could see the back stage and the mechanics as well. The Aldershot Tattoo was the great one because it was nearest to the centres of large population. Usually about 5,000 troops took part.

Certain incidents stand out in my mind. Once, at Rushworth, sixteen regimental bands performed not merely as a musical but as a drill unit; the whole parade – playing fit to bust – wheeled as one, on a front which must have been at least 200 yards long. Stop and think of the practical problems.

Then, when the bands had marched off bottom left, suddenly a mediaeval town grew up out of the ground top right, and an army of mediaeval infantry with siege towers and trebuchets and battering rams appeared. You were moved to the Hundred Years War – and there was a queen interceding for some bedraggled burghers before a portable throne. Once, they performed the battle of Dettingen – the last in which an English king was in command – and you witnessed that curious, I believe unique, tactic, when the infantry marched upon the enemy in line, volley-firing and reloading as they came. Another time, at Tidworth I beheld a display of drill by the Rifle Brigade which, I think, was never equalled for speed and precision.

As military and patriotic shows, ministering to a sense of national self respect without militarism, I think that the tattoos were a true form of Art. They cost the nation nothing, for the troops were there anyway, and as a form of training in organisation and staff work, they were valuable exercises in their own right. It is high time that they were revived.

Also I am hostile to those who despise patriotism. You might as well despise your family or your elephant.

Chapter 15

HITHER AND THITHER

Being mostly at boarding school, Werner and I were seeing too little of Pater. His idea of fun was field sports or golf. Wilhelmine's miscarriage had put an end to his dream of children of his own, and so he adopted us unofficially but deliberately. This was not easy with Albrecht just across the water and Wilhelmine's wandering habits, but he could take moral advantage of the recent quarrel between his wife and Albrecht, for she was now less keen to send Werner to Schlönwitz.

The first result was a compromise. Pater did not like going abroad. The food was funny, the climate unpredictable, the place full of jabbering foreigners but he was prepared to try, if he could fish. So we found Bignasco on the Maggia, which runs into Lake Maggiore at Locarno, from which something between a tram and a light railway went up the valley. It was a fun railway: if you asked the time of the next train, the man was quite likely to say 'will after lunch be convenient?' and it habitually stopped at nowhere in particular, so that the driver could deliver his Aunt Ottolina's shopping. At Bignasco we stayed at Franzoni's, in an ancient tumbledown village, where children and hens wandered about in the only street. The shallow tinkling summer river meandered from blue pool to blue pool among the rocks in a wide winter bed. There were some good trout, and also greyling, which are bad for trout but delicious to eat. The scenery was lovely, in its mountain cleft.

Pater ran out of flies. Franzoni said 'yes; there were flies at the shop' – in Italian. So we went to the shop, which obliged us with bluebottles in fours on little skewers. Franzoni was amiable and clearly thought that this English family was mad. He was used to Cecil and Phyllis Hunt, but they were artists and comprehensible. But these? Fishing? And what was wrong with bluebottles? He always used them himself when he could not hoik fish out of the river with a net, or tickle them. Why on earth did not the mad *signore* use a net like everyone else? So Pater tried bluebottles, but could not get the hang of it somehow, and as netting trout was beneath his dignity, he went off to Locarno in the tram and bought coloured silk. With this and a few strands from chicken feathers he tied very passable Alexanders under the trees in Franzoni's café garden. Franzoni was fascinated. This man might be mad, but he was deft!

So now Pater went out in the cool of sunrise and came back with trout for *breakfast*. Who ever heard of fish for breakfast? And there was old Fanzoni frying trout at eight in the morning, vigorously and, to Pater's disgust, in olive oil with GARLIC. Pater's Scottish ancestors spun rapidly in their graves, but he ate the trout and did it again next day. Franzoni warmed to him: there was something in these Alessandros after all, and Pater meanwhile worked upon the old man as a cook. He drew pictures of a trout on a grill. Ah, the *Signore* was an artist, too? Why did he not say so? Out came Pater's holiday sketch book. But this is my *Signora*! Anna! *Anna*! ANNA! And here is the village church. Anna!

And so my stepfather was promoted from lunatic to artist, and Franzoni *grilled* his trout for these eccentric breakfasts. Werner helped because he took to fishing too, and he and Pater were as happy as sandboys.* I tried to fish as well. Somebody had given me a split cane fishing rod, with which I caught a miller's thumb; Pater sensibly lost it on the way home.

We sometimes went to Locarno to lunch and sat about on the beach while Pater macaronically helped fishermen to their nets, while boats drifted about in the calm blue water. These were quiet days.

Though I prefer the scenery of Lake Lugano, Lake Maggiore is beautiful, especially at its southern end which is embedded far into Italy at Baveno and Stresa with their tiny Borromean Isles, entirely covered with buildings. Isola Bella has a church, a palace, gardens including a cultivated garden of poisonous plants and some almost Babylonian terraces. Isola Madre is an island hamlet. In 1970 an American parson escaped from a package coach tour because they always arrived at their destinations of an evening and left next morning, allowing no time to see the holy places which he had saved up to visit. 'The list of places which I had *not* seen was growing too long, so I left the party and got onto this train at Milano. I meet them in Paris, France, in three days' time.' At this moment the train slowed for the stop at Stresa. I pointed out the islands and told him that they were the birth-place of that redoubtable nobleman, St Charles Borromeus.

'Gee, is that so? He's my patron saint. Can I get off here?' I offered to throw his bags out of the window to him. The last I saw of him, he was trotting off, beaming in all directions.

Eventually we decided to go home via the Simplon. This involved taking a train through the mountain to Domo d'Ossola to catch the Orient Express. So Franzoni and Signora Franzoni all the little Franzonis and their friends and relations pushed us and our luggage into a carriage, and off we went. At the frontier a half company

---

* What is a sandboy? A relative of the Lillywhite boys of the song?

of *carabinieri* in full fig got on. They were very impressive with their blue uniforms faced with red and silver, their white, silver buckled accoutrements, the whole thing crowned with a Napoleonic hat and a tall red and blue plume. Little did we know that this was the day of all days for all good Domodossolites, the feast of Sts Something and Something Else. The town was crammed with people, troops, *carabinieri*, fairs, booths, side shows, ice-cream, and decorated from every lamppost with yellow wooden arches holding electric bulbs. Also bands wheezed excitedly, and thousands of umbrellas impeded the movements and obscured the vision of people trying to watch the bedraggled processions; for it was pelting with rain, so that the gutters flooded in torrents, and the priests in the processions slopped wetly swinging their censors and chanting quaveringly against the elements. And it was cold.

We fought our way to the hotel through this disaster, for we had to stay the night. We could have overseen the processional route, which looked like a battlefield, from our useless balcony. There was kitchen trouble, and the macaroni was lukewarm. The bedroom ceiling sprang a leak. All in all, it was a quick end to an idyllic holiday.

The next three years were an alternation of Pipits Hill quarrels, visits to Elmau, English and Scottish holidays with Pater, and the treadmill at Allen House.

I have written, so far, perhaps slightingly of Allen House, but its very dullness and solidity made it dependable. I was usually glad to get away at the monthly week-end off; and the food was the worst I ever encountered at a school. I have, however, good reason to be grateful, and so, I think, had others. The hard slog kept up term after term, really did force us to educate ourselves, and prepared us for the hard boring slogs of real life.

Boredom, I think with hindsight, should be part of education. I do not mean, obviously, that teaching should never be interesting, but I deprecate the vogue for pleasing, fascinating and flattering the modern school-child at all costs. It unhelpfully separates school life from the realities of life. Some things have to be learned by tiresome processes: to avoid such processes is to empty out the baby with the bathwater. Dewé and Lyon knew this, and during one summer holiday, they had a library built and crammed it with books. It was like opening a door suddenly on a sunlit landscape. It also puts me in mind that of my four previous schools, the first three had no library or book collection at all, and at Nameless there were about ten shelves of stuff so ancient that Inkhorn once urged us to read Maeterlinck. Meanwhile their modest and clearly defined objective somehow acted as a magnet, attracting boys to greater efforts than they believed that they could achieve. Not only did nobody ever fail Common Entrance:

exhibitions, scholarships and special awards kept coming in. A mood of sober confidence developed.

We were less successful at sports and games. A school of only 60 boys can seldom be distinguished even though the playing fields were better and larger than at Nameless. But there were other schools of similar size in the district, and they mostly defeated us at everything except hockey. It was at a Homeric hockey battle that I first met Henry Brandon (later Lord Brandon of Oakbrook), who was at a school called Ripley Court. We made an instant mutual impression as we smote the ball and each other with those dangerous but exhilarating wooden clubs. I have often wondered about the temperament of sport. Why are the English addicted to football, but the Welsh to Rugger? Hurling attracts passionate Irish partisanship but is virtually unknown elsewhere. And how does it happen that an Indian champion Olympic hockey team was subsequently defeated by every reputable home club? At Allen House we played far less hockey than anything else, but played it better. Perhaps we tried too hard at the others.

Games should, I think, be played for enjoyment. If you play badly you play badly. It is obviously a good idea to improve, if you can, but I have never believed that the matter is a serious one. Here I found myself at odds with most of my environment. I never went to a school which did not take games in dead earnest, so that one was constantly under pressure. There was hardly any free time, for when one was not in class or preparation or eating or in bed, one was involved in some compulsory and competitive game to which the authorities attached an excessive and moral importance. Of course exercise is essential to growing boys: that is not in dispute. The question is how the exercise taken should be regarded. This was not the product of sour grapes, for after eleven I was large for my age, and formidable in team games except cricket: and I could sprint very quickly indeed. At seventeen I could run 100 yards in 10.1 seconds on grass and I was urged to enter for the Olympics.

The elder products of the public schools such as my stepfather all thought like this too. There was never any escape worth having. Of course occasionally one might get away with reading a book, but when Pater was at the office, my mother's main object was to get us out of the house. Werner *wanted* to play golf. He had to have somebody to play against. That was me, and if I did not want to play, my mother curdled. Looking back, I think that I was not unjustified. There is no greater bore than having to play regularly some game which one does not enjoy and in which the odds are always loaded against one. When I was twelve, he was sixteen. The distance between us was too great; but as a matter of fact I did not do too badly, for, at golf I did win sometimes and in my own right, for Werner always played to win. The proceedings cannot have been very interesting for him: but he was remarkably patient.

The ceaseless pressure upon my time or freedom may have been responsible for another recurrent nightmare. I had a version of it as lately as August 1980. I am being pursued by a powerful person. I am trapped against a bare wall with a high window. I try to scrabble up the wall to reach the window-sill but fail. My pursuer is upon me. I wake up howling: or more often Fanny rescues me by waking me up.

Increasingly as time went by, I used to escape simply by going for a walk on my own. I enjoyed these very much. I like walking. I like being alone, and I could talk to myself. This I did, often at the top of my voice, like the Punch and Judy show at the Boltons. Only a few years ago, I was chattering away like this to myself on the Embankment when I came face to face with a girl who was doing the same thing. We laughed but preferred our own company.

Thus at this earlier Pipits Hill period we only really enjoyed the time when we were somewhere else, for we were not yet sufficiently emancipated to take our own measures. Fortunately we were, fairly often, somewhere else – Elmau, for example. I remember visits there as halcyon, except in winter when they tried to teach me to ski.

Otherwise, Elmau was always fun. There were the Selliers and the Müllers, and I was beginning to dance. In the summer there were the gorgeous walks: along the ridge behind the Schloss to the Grasseck, where the graveyard round the tiny church records one Martin Grassegger and several hundred years of his descendents, some of whom, in that name, were still farming its steep pastures. Or we might start at dawn and go up to the Schachen where King Ludwig II had a mountain shooting lodge on the edge of a cliff. It faced the *massif* of the 9,000 foot Zugspitze across an enlarged chasm so barren and stony (though with a stream) that it is called the Vale of Hell. The lodge was a tall timber chalet for the King, an equerry or two, and three or four servants. But when you went up the narrow spiral staircase you suddenly burst into an astonishing oriental saloon, which filled the whole of the upper floor with stained glass windows, scarlet, blue and gold brocade sofas, Samarkand rugs, a vast golden chandelier, and, of all things a fountain. It is a blinding place designed to shut the world out. In it, you have not the faintest inkling that you are in the high Alps. Notwithstanding that everything in it is Bavarian-made, even the hookah, you might as well be in Sarajevo or Beirut.

Or if you are feeling energetic you can go on another 2½ hours (they reckon distance by hours in the mountains) to the Meilerhütte, a permanently manned Alpine hut on the highest pass into Austria. This makes 6½ hours and 4,000 feet uphill so far. Easy going, beautiful and calm. If you leave at half-past-three, downhill all the way, you can just scrape into dinner at the Schloss at seven. A girlfriend and I did it in 1976, but we dallied at the Schachen, started late from the Meilerhütte, and had to beg our supper at 8.15. Everybody tittered.

Once, when Werner was sixteen, and I twelve, we made the Schachen at 9.30 in the morning. It seemed silly to walk back for lunch when we had packed lunches with us. We resolved to go down via, first, a hut called the Knorrhütte, and then via another called the Angerhütte. It was very very hot in the Vale of Hell – nothing but stones and the sun at its height, but we found one tree, under which we had lunch. There was still plenty of time and the Zugspitze towered above us. On its shoulder we could descry the Schneefernerhaus, a very large mountain establishment connected with Garmisch-Partenkirchen by a railway, tunnelled right through the mountain. Could we not go there, take the train, catch another round to Klais and so get back to Elmau by late evening?

We decided to do it. The Vale of Hell became eponymously stifling, stony and hot. At the end of it, we were faced with a steep zig-zag path rising perhaps 1,500 feet up the scree. We ought to have taken it steadily, but Werner's feet were troubling him and he wanted short cuts. We made the Schneefernerhaus at nine in the evening. The light had set behind the mountains so that our Hellish valley was in total darkness, but the sun's rays still illuminated the sky. I did not appreciate the magnificence of that nightfall: too tired and also the Schneefernerhaus was what it is – a mixture of a hotel and an echoing railway station carved into the rock. All the same there was still a train to catch, but no connection at the other end. We decided to catch it and see what happened. We arrived in Obergrainau at about eleven. There was a celebration in progress and the whole village was drunk; we were too far gone to care. I walked as in a dream; Werner's blisters forced him to walk bare-footed. We found someone who let rooms and was willing to take us. The name helped. Werner rang Elmau. I slept in the bed; he kindly, on the sofa. It cost us four marks* with breakfast. I was none the worse, when I woke up; he, poor chap, was. His feet were killing him.

Elmau is a whispering – or rather, a bellowing – gallery and what Wilhelmine said or did had the habit of being embroidered public property three minutes later. She had, of course, put on her distracted Mother act by teatime. By dinner we had fallen over a precipice, been drowned in a mountain pool, frozen to death *and* eaten by wolves. I do not blame her for being worried, for mountains are not to be trifled with, and it is best to worry too soon than too late Werner's telephone call should have set minds at rest. Crowds listen only perfunctorily to good tidings. A couple of Elmauer whom we chanced to meet at Klais looked as if they had seen ghosts.

* 17p.

Mother was a picture of ostentatiously controlled anxiety. The Schloss, we noticed, consisted of two factions: most thought that it was rather a lark, and admired the distance which we had achieved. The other very reasonably thought that we should have planned it; but everyone agreed that Wilhelmine should not make a fuss. She didn't.

The kaleidoscopic Elmau life pattern was relieved by intrigues (in and out of bed), odd events and personality changes. Apart from Prince Max there was Adolf v. Harnack, the Lutheran theologian, an amiable old codger with a bald pate surrounded with a nimbus of white hair. He was very courteous and ancient; perhaps too old for his years. Very occasionally Müller would let or make him speak on moral or theological subjects, but he spoke with effort and flatly, as if he was digging it up out of a long lost mental hoard. I thought him quite witty at the time, despite the delivery. He gave me a Bible which I still have.

Then there was Alexander Sturdza, a Roumanian prince. According to his cousin, the statesman historian Neculai Iorga, a Michael Sturdza had been a hospodar of Moldavia and one of the politicians who managed to intrigue Roumania out of the Ottoman frying pan without being burned to a frazzle by the Russian. Alexander was his grandson, and had been a politician himself. He was, I think through some quarrel with Titulescu, at odds with the ruling faction at the rather steamy court of Bucharest. Oil was making the very important very rich, but the standard of education even at the highest levels was not remarkable. The Hohenzollern-Sigmaringens shored up their throne with an opera-house, but even in the short annual season, audiences could be drummed up only with difficulty. The leaders of society went, as was commonly the case elsewhere, in order to look at each other and tumble the singers. They habitually took two boxes: one for themselves and 'one for their coats'. The King's red-haired mistress Magda Lupescu, was rumoured to share her favours with, amongst others, Titulescu. I cannot help thinking that Alexander had had disappointed hopes in that direction himself. He was exiled, and spoke and wrote of the Roumanian court (at which his wife and sons were still living) with a biting fury which was at once sad and entertaining. I have already mentioned the Blumenthal connection with Sigmaringen. Magda ended up near my brother, where he lived at Estoril for some years after World War II.

> Magda Lupescu, on one of her bunks
> Reached Estoril with ninety-two trunks.
> No one else travelled with quite so much luggage.
> But ninety-two trunks was the least of the baggage. –
>
> Quacks and Quotes.

Sturdza, though a Roumanian, was exceptionally sophisticated. He spoke faultless German and French, and later taught my brother the history of the Thirty Years War. He claimed to be a hereditary knight of Malta; I can explain this intrusion into a celibate order only as a divagation of the mad Czar Paul who was a sort of schismatic Grand Master after Bonaparte captured the island. Long after we got to know Alexander, on an occasion when he met Pater, it turned out that he spoke very accomplished English. He had no passport but apparently relied on his famous name and an Alpine Club membership card. I say 'apparently' because so much about him was apocryphal, and in 2001 Oliver Turnbull, a real member of the Club searched its records for him and found no trace.

He was a crooked little figure, always with a twinkle in his eye, and he used a butterfly as his initial. He gave my mother some lovely Nymphenburg pieces – plates and ashtrays – with butterflies on them. He was reputed to hate Prince Max, but, having played *Boccia** with Harnack and the two princes many summer evenings running, I do not believe it.

Then, of course there was Fasching.

Since Lent is tied to a variable Easter and Fasching to Lent, you cannot without a mathematical and theological training – or the aid of diary printers – be quite sure when this annual fuck-up is to be. At Elmau they filled the ballroom with a labyrinth of drinking booths where, and elsewhere, the uproar went on into the small hours. We all played silly jokes, like rechalking all the numbers on the soles of boots left outside doors for cleaning: old Harnack got a pair of ladies high heels. Another night, we rolled up a corridor carpet and played bowls with skiboots up and down the marble. So nobody was particularly surprised when it was announced that the Devil would be delivering a homily in the Ballroom.

It was known that Alexander Sturdza was coming at the end of Fasching, so everyone was disappointed to hear that he had been detained. He would have enjoyed the Devil. Came the evening. Everybody crowded for the front seats, and lots of people who never came to hear Johannes Müller, added to the congestion. The Devil was, of course, late. Slowly conversation brightened up and became noisy. People moved their chairs for better comfort or prominence. Where the Hell was he? Then all the lights went out. Expectant hush. Everybody strained their attention upon the stage and its portable pulpit, thoughtfully contributed by old Müller. There was nothing there. The silence seemed to go on for ever.

Give the Devil his due. There suddenly came, but from behind, a deafening metallic clatter. Everybody spun round like a top, and there was the Demon King, illuminated nose and all, standing at the back of the hall on a soapbox waving a huge cow-bell.

---

* French *boule* or *pétanque*.

'My dear friends…' he began blandly, '…there is no reason to be surprised. Is it not written that the first shall be last?'

Chapter 16

MORE ANGLICISED

Pater decided to engineer English and Scots family holidays which, in theory, indulged his passion for fishing. At Queens Gate Gardens we had acquired a motor-car. My mother gathered a certain amount of plant-life during her drives, but in those days you did not have to report such things to the police, and of course Wasp, the Flutter's Hill coachman was no longer available to talk to the car while he groomed its mudguards. It had to be kept in Mr Varndell's garage in Queens Gate Mews. We were rather envious of an Indian rajah who owned an impressively named Hispano-Suiza: it had a bonnet about a mile long behind a tiny driving-cabin upholstered in blue and gold. One day it caught fire... which, I am afraid, made us all feel better.

By Pipits Hill we had acquired a boxed in affair capable of carrying us all unfrozen with our baggage. So we went to all sorts of places. There was a cottage at Lustleigh in North Devon which we hired from a Colonel Dunlop. Werner wallowed in Devonshire Cream (made in the Colonel's farm). The Colonel had a library full of books about battles. I read about Nelson's victories, and Navarino and Lissa, with those stylised Victorian diagrams. We also went a great deal onto Dartmoor and Exmoor, or to see Cecil and Phyllis Hunt at Manaton. It was there that I first learned of the fury of the Reformation, for the little ancient church has a beautiful fifteenth Century painted screen, from which some puritan vandal has roughly gouged out all the faces.

Another time we lived on porridge and haddock in a boarding house at Findhorn on the Scottish North-East coast, near Forres. We fished the landlocked sea-bay from a boat. The lines were baited with mussels, three hooks on a T-bar. You lowered till you felt the bottom and then pulled up a foot. You very soon caught herring, and sometimes two or three at a time, with the occasional crab. Sometimes the fish took the bait so strongly that we were all hauling up and letting down as fast as we could, and the boat was carpeted with struggling fish... On other days we crossed the bay to the burrowed sand-dunes on the north side, where Pater and Werner shot the peculiar black rabbits of Pater's boyhood in the '90s, or plover on the beach. The weather was bright and windy and cold, so that one had to be energetic or heavily wrapped – or in a nice sheltered spot with a good big dune to one's north-east and the sun unveiled at midday. Then, with luck, one could picnic.

Not far off, we once took the Manse at Aberlour on the Spey. The ground floor consisted of two huge rooms. One was the kitchen-cum-laundry-cum-larder-cum dining room. The other was a bedroom with beds at one end and a bath, free-standing in the splendour of its brass taps, at the other. Wild rabbits had got in through a broken ventilator. We hung a wire noose over this ventilator to ensnare them, and one night we were woken by screams. A rabbit, struggling with the noose round its waist, had smashed a leg, the bones of which protruded from the fur. We had never meant to inflict a cruelty and the scream haunted us. In February 2001 Henry and Nieves' greyhound injured her shoulder and screamed and screamed. The agony of an inarticulate animal is a terrible thing, and Nieves had to decide on poor Rosie's life in the sitting room then and there.

There were, modern people may be surprised to know, overnight railcar sleepers, which we used in the 1920s. It was easy and cheap. You could have an end-opening box-wagon attached to any overnight express on 48 hours' notice. Your car was driven across the concourse at King's Cross or St Pancreas into it. The end was shut down. We got into our sleepers, and – heigh-presto – we were slowly bowling through the Highlands towards Crianlarich (what a lovely language is the Gaelic) or Fort William. Restaurant cars were civilised, with napery, silver and liveried stewards who brought you the most splendiferous four-course breakfast, all for 3s 6d.* Then out into the morning dew on the platform, the box-car unhitched, away went your friendly train, a steam shunter pushed the box-car to the ramp, and in half an hour you were on the road.

We were now going to the west coast sea-lochs and heather-clad stag-shoots of Argyll, besides the Isle of Skye, with its weather and midges. It rained and rained until it cleared – to a fine drizzle, and you scratched and scratched. If the midges danced at ankle-level it would rain: if at head-level it would drizzle. Only Pater, whose skin was made of leather, did not scratch.

Then suddenly, with an east wind everything turned to magic. Comfortable clouds sailed along in the sunlight throwing dark blue shadows, which chased each other across the hillsides in the crystalline air and one had the pleasure of being drunk without the blurring of sensibilities. You could see details miles away; you felt no need to speak, as if you were already understood. I felt it easy to see why these Atlantic coasts have supported many hermits. Like the flashing revelations of Judea, this is a country which God used to visit. Otterburne, below the Border is in some ways similar – though the vistas over the land are longer and the cloud and

---

* 18p.

shadow effects capable of being even more impressive. Otterburne is Chevy Chase, the scene of forays and feuds governed by strange loyalties and honourable codes long since vanished from western society, but perfectly understood till the British left, on the Indian North-West Frontier. The Scottish west was murderous and turbulent, acquisitive and brutal because the pressure on the land was greater. Yet the spirit of the West Coast seems finer – more elegant, perhaps. Atmosphere is a curious thing. You doubt its existence because it exhibits nothing measurable or capable of description yet you think that you feel its effect upon you. I suspect that it is like the machine by which one detects good and bad temper in someone without having him say a word.

Cathedral building seems to be connected with the same complex of instincts. I suppose that you invite God to visit a particular place and provide a house in which his natural spirit can manifest itself. But as nations differ, one would expect variations in the wavelengths upon which they approach their godhead. This would account, engineering and artistic considerations apart, for the marked distinctions in building styles between, say, Norman and Italian Romanesque, or between English and French Gothic. I have looked at many churches, from Justinian's astounding Santa Sophia westwards, and if the inspiration purports to be a common one, the execution seems to disclose fundamental variances. My suspicions are reinforced by the buildings designed for other religions. The great Siamese temples are all monastic but though they house mysteries, they welcome popular interest. There is plenty of room for visitors who troop in and out continually, but you are there as a person not as one of a mass, and they arrange for your sacred contacts accordingly. The vast Wat Po has a recumbent Buddha whose feet are as big as three men *and* you can get hours of massage or music lessons. In Isfahan the Friday Mosque is, with its out buildings more like a village than a place of worship. In the summer the faithful use an open courtyard as big as Trafalgar Square, but in the cold highland winter they adjourn to an arcaded construction so oppressively dark, low, and interrupted by pillars that it feels like the vault of some apocryphal mediaeval bank.

If the great Teheran mosque reminds one of a bank the vaults of the National Bank in Teheran are quite another thing. The Persian crown jewels were kept there, it is said, as security for the national debt. Imagine a darkened room about half the size of a tennis court, dotted with illuminated show-cabinets. The much coveted Peacock Throne, a straight-backed high-standing armchair studded with rubies and emeralds, is fragile in spots; you can see the light through parts of it, which appear to be made only of stiffened linen. It has been manhandled a good deal between Delhi, Afghanistan and Persia, and shows it. I gather that various bits of it have been lost. I was puzzled by 24 round golden hats, also studded with rubies, each surmounted by a large nob. They seemed like ceremonial headdresses for odalisques at an Empress's purification. My English catalogue was silent, but the French one made all clear. Their function was culinary. There is a Persian dish of rice, butter and herbs which is placed already on its plate with a cover, before each guest. This *pilao* is then violently shaken and the cover instantly removed. These were the covers – valued in 1970 at £125,000 each. I wonder who washed them up.

Other showcases disclosed golden dishes piled, apparently, with illuminated cherries and greengages, which were in fact uncut rubies and emeralds: heaps and heaps of them. There was, too, the Shah's disastrously vulgar modern crown, complete with plume on top, and an extraordinary pearl tiara resembling an embroidered plum cake, made for a Khajar prince in about 1820. It might, perhaps, have suited a seven foot man standing on a footstool, and I could not imagine a man with a head big enough to wear it.

This profusion apparently represented only a quarter of the known original collection. It also contained some splendid arms and brocades but the rest – the more easily lootable remainder – left me quite cold. It was a display of riches without taste or sense of design and though, no doubt, it was more valuable than the English Crown Jewels, it was in every other respect far inferior. I reacted in much the same way to the Ottoman collection in Topkapi. The brocades and cloth of gold and the swords and other arms, and some of the caskets were beautiful, but much of the rest was expensive rubbish.

This blomp has taken me several thousand miles away.

This was a time when my mother came to my rescue. She began to realize that Pater's efforts, however kindly proposed, would never illuminate me. So she took some trouble to provide me with other mental stimuli. She liked the design of architecture herself, perhaps through Albrecht's inspiration, so we looked at a great many ruins besides living buildings.

Fountains Abbey is the largest and most complete of the British monastic ruins, but Rievaulx attracted me more. There is Kirkstall, then blackened by industrial smoke, and the still impressive remains of Byland and Jervaulx in their rural solitudes. The Wolf of Badenoch slighted the cathedral at Forres because its bishop denounced his carnal appetites; the English sacked Jedburgh, and sectarian savagery has caused the large chapel at Holyroodhouse to remain roofless. The Scottish ruthlessness in theology and politics caused most of the Scottish casualties. The English were more practical. Monastry buildings formed convenient reserves of quarried stone and carpentered timber. Some of the pre reformation monasteries had been immense. The one at Chertsey was a monkish town, yet its ruin was so complete that its plan is unknown and its exact location a matter of reasoned guesswork. English cathedrals have their beautiful and characteristic closes because, unlike their continental counterparts, they were monasteries with extensive buildings. The local townspeople cleared the materials but the ground continued to belong to the cathedrals and was turfed over.

It is time to return to Allen House, for Woking is not far from Chertsey. In a previous chapter I have said something about corporal punishment, and the reason for this is that it represented, for good or ill, the form in which sex first entered our lives. We were absurdly innocent and had no idea that this was happening, even when at Nameless we practised flagellation for fun. This may be hard to believe but there is no doubt about it. Our parents and teachers took great care that we should have no truck with sex. In this respect the teaming masses of the urban slums were more healthily and sensibly brought up. Our ignorance was quite startling. Even at fourteen, I had no idea why I was born. Like the lady called Todd, I thought that a child came from God, and I surmised that He arranged some form of spontaneous combustion.

At the opening of the Spring Term of 1931, Lyon delivered a harangue. 'Dirty Talk', he thundered, 'is the beginning of all the big rows at public schools, and a boy who is expelled from his public school is FINISHED.' The utmost purity was now to be observed, and any boy who fell below the highest standards would be in serious trouble. I doubt if there was a single boy present who really understood what he was driving at. It seemed, however, that swearing and lavatory humour were out.

This regime was not oppressive because we could not complain of losing something (whatever it was) which we had never had; but the trouble is that these natural urges develop in the subconscious whatever anyone may do, and they find their way out in forms which we recognise now but did not at the time. Once more, I got involved in a flagellation game. It was in fact a homosexual, but again innocent affair. A friend of my age and I were wandering covertly in the rose garden. He picked up something lying in a bed. It was a cane. He made it whistle through the air and then we looked at each other and said 'shall we try it?' Without another word, we trotted to the one place of concealment in the whole complex, behind the carpentry shop. Here I bent over and he gave me six; then he took his turn. We hid the cane under the shop, which was supported on concrete blocks.

Next morning it was 'shall we try it again?' And it became a habit, for every morning for the remaining eight weeks of that term. Multiply that out, and imagine the accumulation of welts. It would have been impossible in the summer when we all bathed... The term ended. He left, and I saw him again only once – by accident on the Embankment during an air raid. He came up and had supper at my flat in the Temple, and we never alluded to the subject.

By the winter I was all set for the run up to Winchester and had become, to my surprise, Head Boy. This probably had something to do with my size – I grew 1½ inches in one term and could knock anyone else down. Some 50 years later an Ear, Nose and Throat specialist spotted that I had a broken nose – which I must have contracted while boxing at Allen House. I had, in any case, an unfair advantage from greater reach and length of stride in most of the athletics. It was customary for the Head Boy's mother to give away the silver cups at the School Sports. She never had managed to overcome her fear of public appearances, but silently handed pot after pot to me, while Lyon did the announcing. It was not quite a clean sweep.

The special Winchester entrance examination was much feared, and though Lyon was a Wykehamist,* nobody from Allen House had ever taken it. So I was made to do scholarship papers. One mathematical question remains graven not only in my mind but on Claud Douglas's. *If George is x years old, how old will he be in the year x^2?*** I muffed it; it took Claud a fortnight. We cheered ourselves up with the thought that boys like me seeking bare admission to this threatening place, would need to be made of commoner clay. I thought that I could manage adequately in most subjects except Latin, to which I had never taken. This gave some cause for additional disquiet because Winchester was supposed to be the classical school *par excellence*, where perpetrators of false quantities were cast into outer darkness, or worse still, relegated to Eton. I sat for that examination in a state of alarmed determination, which is not a bad frame of mind for such a purpose. I passed, as it turned out, as high as a non-scholar could, and as I had been put down for Percy's old house (Culverlea how Serjeants) I was told to present myself there at the commencement of Short Half 1932. He was as pleased as punch.

Now Werner had gone to Sherborne very young, whereas I went to Winchester relatively old; he had already done five years hard and got all his School and Higher Certificates before I left Allen House. At barely seventeen he was not likely to get much more out of Sherborne. It was resolved to take him away, but the problem was what to do with him. This was where Elmau came in, for my mother had become acquainted with the remarkable Kurt Hahn.

Hahn was Prince Max's private secretary at Salem, the Windsor of the rulers of Baden. In the new republican Germany, the prince was faced with the need to find a new sort of education for Bertold, his only son. He was not, however, anxious to put him into the state school system: in the abrupt change of political outlooks Bertold might have been much more unhappy than he deserved. So he told Kurt Hahn, his clever secretary, to solve the problem and in doing so Hahn found his

---

* After William of Wykenham, who founded the school. The word also means a large spider.
** 48. An exercise in reading the question.

vocation and made himself famous. He was, indeed, a good publicist, but he would never have got anywhere without Prince Max and Bertold, with their support, money, prestige and above all the use of their country properties.

To Hahn the English Public School seemed to be the most successful existing institution for breeding reasonable leaders of men. They had apparently conquered or, at least, settled half the world; they had defeated the German Reich, and yet had contrived a free constitutionalism which everybody wanted to copy. All the same, he noticed that these schools, which subsisted in a monarchy, were somewhat isolated from their surrounding communities and that this would be a disadvantage in a republic if the object was to educate a prince, and Hahn doubted the wisdom of the enclosed monosexual school, not for the conventional reasons, but because it would be so unlike real life as to mark the school off from its surroundings. Thus he designed a boarding institution which was to be embedded in the local population. Apart from academic work, the pupils were to do things which were locally useful or learnable outside the school, and it was to be co-educational. Moreover, since it would not be feasible simultaneously to go out into the local villages to help or learn and to copy the public school emphasis on games, useful physical work was largely (but not wholly) to supersede the games. Reality, in other words, was to be substituted for make-believe.

It is over 80 years since this rational scheme was launched, yet its principles have attracted little but lip service in the outside world. Such is human cussedness. I would have given my eyes to have gone there, had I really known what it was like. Unfortunately I was committed to Winchester before my fortunate brother got to Spetzgart, its Lake Constance branch, but his testimony seems conclusive. He was happy where he had been miserable. His physical development was much in advance of anything which mere games-playing could have achieved. The class and preparation hours were shorter than at Sherborne, yet they easily learned more. He became generally well educated and if actions speak louder than words, he sent his sons to Gordonstoun which was supposed to be based on similar principles. Incidentally he acquired a life-long passion for sailing.

One factor which decided my mother to send him there (for I doubt if Percy had much to do with it) was that my cousins Alexandra and Marion v. Blumenthal were at Spetzgart at this time. A wheel had come almost full circle. They were the daughters of that Gerda v. Rheinbaben whom I have already mentioned. Marion ended up, after marrying and divorcing another Blumenthal, as – headmistress of Salem!

Life at Pipits Hill was difficult. Werner and I got on better as we grew up, but I could never take much interest in his crazes (motor cars at this time), and he was still too old for me. But the real problem was our mother. As soon as we settled in after an absence, the quarrels began. These mounted in bitterness as we grew older and developed the courage of our views. It mattered very little what was discussed: I can remember screaming, hysteria, tears and flouncings about the way to carry a ladder, the relative talents of the sexes, the value of experience, ribbon development, whether to take the car to the station or to go on a bicycle. Werner and I would make ourselves scarce – I even preferred golf to hanging around. We would then return at lunchtime to a whey-faced fury and the whole thing would start again. I assiduously developed my solitary walks.

And so I did not face being a new boy (or rather, new man) for the sixth time with quite such trepidation as otherwise I might have done: and anyway, Pater was helpful. Had I realized the nature of the change through with I was to pass, I would have been more troubled than I was. My trunk had been delivered. I wore the complete suit which was required, and a straw hat with the broad blue and yellow riband of my house. I said good-bye to my parents at King's Gate, that curious chapel over the street near the Cathedral Close. I walked back to the house and settled down in my toyes* which had been allotted to me in the hall, to wait for the next event. There were a lot of people about and after a time somebody called a roll, and the housemaster said prayers.

What next?

After a few minutes somebody rushed into the hall and shouted something unintelligible. Everyone stampeded for the door. It seemed sensible to do the same. The whole crowd hurled itself pell-mell out into the yard up some steps, through a door into a large room at the side of the house. There was an old man with a torch sitting at the end, and boys in a queue were successively dropping their trousers and apparently showing him their genitals. I was choked with disgust and baffled. I asked a bystander what was going on. His reply was more baffling still: - 'Haven't you got a T-J?'

I tried someone else.

'Haven't you got a T-J?'

People were taking off their shoes, I noticed. So the only thing was to observe carefully and do the same as everybody else.

The story is that in 1916 Winchester College was briefly occupied by some Indian troops who left behind a particular strain of *Tinea Cruris* (Athlete's Foot) which had never been eliminated. This was the routine examination, which usually landed a few people in treatment. It was never eradicated in my time, though I never caught it myself. But the whole thing was new to me, and puzzling too. Another man who came to the house a year later, decided that the object was to

---

* A carrel allotted to each man for his own exclusive use.

ensure that no girl got in. My worry, however, was different. What on earth was this T-J that I apparently had not got? We pulled up our trousers, put on our shoes and returned to this hall. I asked a neighbour what a T-J was. He looked a bit surprised and said:

'Good God. Haven't you got one?'

He vanished through the door and returned with a very large man who said:

'Haven't you got one?'

I said: 'No'. It seemed the right thing to say. Then everyone started trooping up to bed and so did I. I was standing in my cubicle untying my tie when a boy with curly fairish hair in the next one said over the partition:

'I'm your T-J'.

'Oh' I said.

'I have to show you everything'.

'Oh'.

I undressed and washed and got into my pyjamas.

'My name's Johnson'.

Then he intoned an extraordinary sound, which was something between a chant and an extended bellow:

'Were. Weer. Weem!'

'That means twenty-five past', he said. 'You'll have to do it tomorrow'.

He was actually shouting 'Worthy's been', a reference to a long dead butler who used to come up to the lowest dormitory and tell its junior that it was 9.25. The news was passed upwards by yelling, and the custom continued long after everybody had a wrist watch, to disturb the peace of the neighbouring houses.

Chapter 17

WINCHESTER

The French word *protége* had been mangled and transferred from the protected new man (every male was a man)* to his protector. Johnson told me this while everyone was on an early morning walk to St Catherine's Hill next day. It is a steep hump with an Iron Age earthwork (known at Trench), and a clump of trees atop. When William of Wykeham was looking for land for his educational experiment, he lit upon a half moribund hospital under Papal protection whose property included the hill. There was a, now vanished, chapel in the clump, and the Pope let him have it on condition that the school prayed there twice a year.

'Now don't forget anything I tell you', he said, pointing out Lavender Meads and New Field, across which we were walking. I had heard of the Notions Examination new men underwent at the end of their first fortnight, but not its size and scope. He gave me a 200-page dictionary and said 'learn that. I'll test you next week'.

The word 'notion' meant any word, habit or custom peculiar to the school. Commoners (I was a commoner) lifted their hats to dons, but scholars wrapped their black gowns round themselves. This was a notion. Something which was forbidden was said to be non-licet;** something which was contrary to custom, such as walking alone when another member of your own house was in sight, was a Bad Notion. The difference was that the perpetrators of bad notions were frowned on; breach of a non-licet led to a caning.

'Notions' in the plural meant the school language. Of course, many of the words were merely place names, such as Moab (the old conduit in College) and Edom (the boot room) because 'Moab is my washpot: over Edom will I cast out my shoe',*** and some were whimsical like Goodgodster (a brown bowler hat), but there was an ancient residue, some explicable, some not. We said cud for beautiful. This came from 'couth', the opposite of 'uncouth'. There was no special word for 'girl', but a duck was a face, and so a cud duck was a pretty girl, like my cousin Phoebe Gaunt. Parents were pitch-up. A lavatory was a foricas. If you were ill, you went continent; when you got well you came abroad. A matron, save in my house,

---

* A baby was a very small man in arms.
** Pronounced Lie-Sit.
*** Psalm 60 v 8.

was a <u>hag</u>, and the chief matron at the school sanatorium proudly used the title <u>Sick House Hag</u>. And so on for 200 pages.

We climbed to the top, took off our 470 hats, and the Headmaster, a clergyman, read prayers. Then the roll was called by the Praefect of Hall (a very august person), and as you answered with the Latin <u>adsum</u> (I am here), you started back to your house: not, however, some people. There is a prehistoric labyrinth marked in the turf up there, and the new men of certain other houses were required to <u>toll</u> (run) the entire length of its convolutions. I left with the impression of small boys weaving an elaborate dance on the horizon.

After breakfast we set off for the class (or <u>Div</u>) rooms, which were beside College, five minutes away. This was known as <u>going up to books</u>. This expression arose because the whole school was once taught in a single large room (now called <u>Seventh Chamber</u>), with six benches, each used by a different class, and their names were entered in a book. The benches themselves came to be called <u>books</u>. Then, for unexplained reasons, three of the six books disappeared, so that in my time, the school was divided into <u>Second</u>, <u>Fifth</u>, and <u>Sixth</u>. Second Book was the Choir School, sixteen treble-voiced boys called <u>Quiristers</u>, who wore a special livery, and did not count. Sixth Book was the equivalent of the Sixth Form. Everyone else was in Fifth Book. In a school now swollen to 470 men, this simple system had to be refined, and so Fifth Book was divided into <u>Parts</u>, of which the <u>Senior</u>, and <u>Middle</u> had three <u>Divisions</u> (<u>Divs</u>) and the Junior two. I entered the school at the third from the bottom, namely <u>Middle Part Three</u>. To complete this disquisition on <u>books</u>, the evening preparation period was called <u>toyetime</u>, but a daytime one was a <u>books-chambers</u>.

Now work, though visibly harder, (except for mathematics) than at Allen House (sorry, <u>tother</u>), was not my difficulty. The real trouble in the first fortnight was that as soon as one came out of one's div, or lunch, or a game, there was one's <u>tegé</u> (not T-J) waiting to hustle you off to see this or that, to cross-examine you on progress, to give you new lists of things such as house senior praefects, to learn. I am bad at learning by rote, but the quantity got greater every day. In particular there is an endless school song called <u>Dulce Domum</u> in bad Latin which turns out to be a paean in praise of the holidays. I used to take my Notions Book and lengthening notes to bed and mutter under the bed-clothes, for if I failed my <u>notions examina</u>, my tégé and I would be yoked together for weekly examination until I passed. So he did his best. Life meant learning uninterruptedly (save for food) from the seven o'clock morning bell till lights out at 9.40pm. Try it yourself.

Four things determined one's school status. Achievement was respected. I won a school prize at the early age of sixteen. Thereafter my position was secure.

Secondly there was physical prowess, at games or whatever. These paladins were ornamental in their panoply and everyone made the correct noises at matches: indeed at certain matches everybody yelled their bloomin' 'eads orf (or, backed up), and unfortunate juniors (fags) had to learn their names. Thirdly advancement to a place of authority made a considerable difference. Lastly you were classified by the year. During your first two years you were a junior, and in my house the senior junior was called the nailer, and was in charge of the others. When I was nailer, I had to manage the logistics of the house play – Molière's *Fourberies de Scapin* – from lighting and curtains to programmes and seating for a three-day presentation in the old school.

And so the awful evening came. All the juniors stood in a semi-circle in Hall facing the Senior Praefect, who pointed at the junior junior (not me) with a cane and said

'First verse of Domum'.

To fill out the atmosphere the housemaster, the Rev, W.D. Monroe (or Munner) was a stocky, learned figure especially in Sanskrit which he was fond of quoting. He had been a missionary in Bombay. His ringing hellfire sermons were much appreciated by one and all. He had married twice. The reigning Munneress was a blousy formidable figure whom everybody, after the mindless fashion of crowds disliked. I did not dislike her, but I think that the House opinion reflected a subconscious disapproval of her husband's policy, which in 1932 was to have as little to do with the house as possible. The logistics such as food, laundry, servants, he left entirely to his wife. Discipline he left to the Senior Praefect. Health to the matron; Games to the various house captains; Academic standards to the men themselves. He appeared only to preside at lunch and to read preces in the evening. He was utterly inhibited. When he retired, he made a brief speech in which he urged us 'not to indulge in smutty limericks which can do so much harm' and that was almost all he said. It is fair to say that since I wrote this I have heard stories of his kindness in earlier years, but Culverlea was bound to be dominated by the Senior Praefect, who reigned unsupervised over all. In the year before I came up, the Senior Praefect had been a brutal foul-mouthed terrorist, whose name was still whispered.

The house was thus in a subdued, over-disciplined mood and as it happened, the new Senior Praefect, Toby Low, was quite as strong (without bullying) besides being a paragon. A record breaking long distance runner; the finest serjeant-major that the O.T.C had ever had; a leading classical scholar; but above all, as Senior Commoner Praefect, he was the other 'head boy'. He was determined to make his house the 'best' house, which really meant the house which won the most cups.

Under his leadership we achieved this easily. Toby Low, of course, went far. The youngest brigadier in World War II, he became a member of parliament, a minister, took a peerage as Lord Aldington, became chairman of the Port of London Authority, and ultimately – supreme distinction – Warden of Winchester College.

This was the figure which confronted us at my first Notions Examiná. We were all frightened. I was tongue tied, utterly and absolutely purple faced. I forebear to describe those three terrible hours. Next morning my tégé greeted me with resigned fury. What the Hell was I playing at?

Things were now really difficult. My fortnight's grace being up, I was, as the expressive notion has it, <u>in sweat</u>. I had to wake up my <u>gallery</u> (dormitory) every morning, then tell each man the time every five minutes. I was Toby Low's <u>jun:man</u> (personal fag) and had to run his errands, housemaid his study and clean his daily and military leather. And besides, juniors had time consuming chores such as <u>watching out</u> (retrieving balls) at Winchester football practice games and preparing the praefects Sunday teas. So where could one find the time to learn one's notions? An endless corridor of weekly examination stretched ahead in my mind.

Oddly enough, Toby Low came to my rescue. He had me into his tiny study and gave me a rocket. He thought that I was insufficiently conformist and that I would never get on if I did not accept the situation and swim with the tide. If, however, I did swim with the tide, he thought that I might swim faster than most. I told him that that was what I thought I was doing, but that everything was so new, with my partly foreign background; and try as I might, I simply could not learn things by rote. He said that everyone else could, so why not me? He asked, unexpectedly, what I had in mind to do when I left school. No one had ever asked me such a question seriously. I said that I had thought of trying to become a lawyer. He said 'you'll need to remember things there.' I said that I could remember things by way of their logic. He said, 'Alright, but you'll have to get through your notions examiná, you know'. I said that I would try very hard. He sent me back to my toyes, but ten minutes later he came round with a book and said 'would you be interested in this?' It was Marjoribanks' biography of Marshall Hall.

I scraped through next time.

The average size of a house was 40, College 70. Each house had a <u>Mugging Hall</u> where you lived and worked, a <u>Grubbing Hall</u> where you ate, and galleries which were dormitories. The college organisation and terminology was slightly different. Our Mugging Hall had 34 compact and well designed oaken toyes built solidly by the walls. They were a modernised version of the mediaeval monks carrel, about four feet wide, enclosed, with a bench, a desk-slab and shelf. The left or hall side was open; on the right there was a cupboard. The whole thing stood as high as a man, and you put your hat on top of the cupboard. In the middle of the hall was a large table, and people could sit round this on stools to read newspapers, and there was a gramophone which, in free times, blared jazz incessantly. During toyetime the praefect in course sat at the big table to keep order. At the near end a small, slightly higher table was permanently screwed to the floor. From it, names were called (roll call), preces were read and over it you had to bend when you were beaten.

This communal life bred a peculiar custom which has always surprised my non-Wykehamist friends. We did each others' work. At toyetime, especially, you took your books and sat in his toyes, and between you, you worked the allotted task out. A third man might join in, by bringing a stool and sitting beside the toyes. There was a constant, though restrained buzz of conversation. The authorities encouraged this mutual self-help; in College they even paid the senior men to tutor the most junior. As you became more senior, you naturally acquired a specialist reputation. There was usually a Latinist. We had a brilliant mathematician (prematurely killed in a car smash) called Bill Bruce, and so on. It was a notion that you could, if stuck, ask the praefect in course. I was once asked in that capacity by two very baffled juniors to construe 'timeo danaos et dona ferentes'* – one of the only two Virgilian lines which I know that I can manage. By this admirable system we learned hugely, and became accustomed to mutual helpfulness which no preaching about team spirit could possibly inculcate.

If work-sharing showed the Wiccamical spirit at its best, games, I think showed it at its worst. Everything at Winchester has its history, some good, some disastrous. In 1394 the founder had provided for 70 scholars and ten commoners, but the shortage of schools after the Reformation brought a demand for places, and commoners multiplied.

By 1650 over 100 of them were housed in a large building near College, later known as Old Commoners. The school had always played communal games on St Catherine's Hill. This is the origin of the belief that Winchester is the oldest public school: it is not the oldest school by a long chalk, but the combination of work and organised games, now the distinctive feature of Anglo-Saxon education, did, I believe originate at Winchester. The Hill ought to be a place of pilgrimage for Olympic winners, who owe much more to it than to Philippides or Zeus.

The home-made games grew into the peculiar institution called Winchester Football, and the first two sides were College and Commoners. It was played on a field called a canvass measuring 81 yards by 27 – about a third of the area of a soccer field – with nine foot netting along the long sides, with inside, a row of posts supporting a rope stretched tight, to prevent players cannoning into the netting. We used a small soccer ball, and the whole of the end of the canvass was

---

* Aeneid. I fear the Greeks particularly when they bring gifts.

the goal. Dribbling was not allowed: the ball had to be kicked as hard as possible, but you might, if you could, catch up with it and kick it again. You could handle the ball if it came from an opponent, but only to drop-kick it. To score a goal the ball had to go over the end untouched by any defender.

A match began with a scrum call a <u>hot</u>. The rugby scrum must be derived from the Winchester hot, for Winchester Football is much older than Rugby, and Arnold was a Wykehamist, but heeling was not allowed: you had to push the other side off the ball. When the ball was free, a <u>hot-watcher</u> would kick it towards the ropes, the hot would break and the battle opened up. Hotwatchers were light fast runners. Lurking behind all the rest were the stars of the game, called <u>Kicks</u>. Bearing in mind that a goal was no goal if touched before it went over the line, kicks developed great skill in propelling the ball high as well as far.

Originally, I believe, the hot was simply a ball-less 'push of war' between the neighbouring communities of College and Commoners. The peculiar rules about kicking and handling the ball had, possibly, a separate origin, for in our paved yards we played a game called <u>Kicking up in Yard</u> which had all the kicking features but no hot: it could even be played one-a-side. Someone, sometime must have suggested combining the two.

The game became institutionalised in two forms: twenty-two a side and six a side, but the twenty-two were reduced to fifteen, the remaining seven standing as reserves. <u>Fifteens</u> were then played at the beginning, <u>Sixes</u> at the end of a Short Half. It is obvious that the big version was more like a push-of-war, the smaller like Kicking up in Yard. Moreover there is still a horseplay custom at Wykehamist dinners, that you all form a hot after grace according to the part of the school in which you had been. It is written that two Wykehamists met in Tibet, and on finding that they were both Commoners, formed a hot against the table (having drunk <u>stet res Wiccamica</u>* in Eno's), drove it through the wall of the hut and stampeded all the yaks.

Meanwhile the demand for a Winchester education grew, and tutors began taking boys into their houses because Old Commoners was full. The membership of the five tutor's houses soon equalled that of Commoners, and they were making a third side in the football. By the 1850s the school had reached 300. Teaching had moved from Seventh Chamber to a new large hall called <u>School</u> in the seventeenth century, but how to teach 300 men of varying ages in the same room, even if you did use William of Wykeham's beautiful cloister in the summer? The attractive notion for the Summer Term is <u>Cloister Time</u>. Old Commoners had been rebuilt, because it had become uninhabitable, in the 1830s. In the 1860s they built four Commoner houses (of which mine was one) and converted New Commoners into

---

* Untranslatable. 'May Wiccamicalism always exist.'

a block of classrooms. Thus the school developed its modern form. Thus also the tripartite division for football into College, Commoners and Houses (short for Old Tutors Houses and abbreviated O.T.H) survives.

Now the dispersal into houses of similar size facilitated the playing of small-team competitive games, and in an evil hour somebody gave a cup for soccer. Somebody else followed with a cup for something else, and by 1900 there were 24 cups, mostly an under- and over-sixteen cup for each game. These were organised as single league tables; hence, for example, in <u>Common Time</u>* it was necessary to get through 242 soccer matches (2 x 11 x 11) in ten weeks, every house having to field two teams on most playing days. It was supposed to be creditable for a house to do well in these competitions, therefore you showed your loyalty by playing keenly. Some housemasters took this very seriously. This was admirable for those who liked it, but for those with less skill or other interests (between them a majority) it was a boring waste of time.

But it was worse than that. The whole concept was essentially false; here were nearly 500 boys taking something which was meant to be recreational and enjoyed, far too seriously in the interests of a trivial ideal to which they had to pay lip service. A boarding school is, physically, something of a prison anyway. This made the house into a prison of the spirit, founded upon a hypocrisy which, like all hypocrisies, had to be maintained by force. A housemaster ordered all his men to watch a particular match. Four of them were absent. He had them caned. It was a sign of changing times that if everyone agreed that it was proper to cane for the disobedience yet the order should not have been given. This constricted atmosphere jolted me like a sudden whiff of coke fumes. I had seen foreign countries, spoke a second language, played with princes and heard the political, artistic and court gossip of half a dozen lands. But this house horizon was limited to its walls, and the exaggerated respect by juniors for senior, made it impossible to find friends outside of one's own year; and besides, believe it or not, it was a bad notion to make friends outside the house. Consequently I was entitled to make friends with only three other people in the whole school.

I began to compensate. The horizon was wider in one direction – Up to Books. I began to work like a demon to hide from the bleakness of existence, exacerbated by the fact that in the rare moments when one had some time to oneself there was absolutely nowhere to go. Sunday praefect's tea, for example, was held at the table in Mugging Hall, and everybody was cleared out of their toyes during those two hours. Those who did not have pitch-up could only go for a walk or sit in a huddle on the concrete gallery stairs trying to write letters home on their knees. It is a mark of the housemaster's isolation that after over twenty years he had no idea that

---

* The Spring Term.

this sort of thing was happening. One Sunday I was walking down the road and overtook the Munneress. She asked me where I was going, and I said that I was simply wandering because I was fed up with sitting on the stairs. I assumed that she would have known. She was horrified. It was a cold day. She turned straight back, made the matron open up a spare room on the sickbay side of the house, and then went to the gallery stairs herself, with a plate of cakes, and invited everybody in.

I did, however, make a discovery some time in that first term. The school library, then over the class-rooms, was open (my tegé did not know) on a Sunday, and it was warm, quiet, and had a few comfortable chairs. Hardly anyone came there. Rummaging the shelves I found and in due course read a copy of Engels' edition of <u>Das Kapital</u>. It had been there at least since 1905. I found it remarkably dull.

I have so far tried to convey the flavour by describing the men, and so, activities and places. Now for some personalities.* I begin with the Test Cricketer Harry Altham who was also a well read classical scholar with a feeling for the drama of words. It was from him that we heard the good Wiccamical story of Gloriana's arrival in the Armada year to inspect the school. She was received <u>Ad Portas</u> ceremonially at the gates with Latin speeches, to which she, of course, replied in kind. Then she went round the school poking into corners and asking questions. At one point she abruptly asked a small boy:

'When were you last beaten, child?'

Without hesitation he replied:

'Infandum, Regina, jubes renovare dolorem.'**

She gave him gold.

Henry says that the same thing happened at Westminster. I am not surprised: she probably staged it.

Then – hurrah: – the Munner with his Sanskrit retired in favour of Jack Parr, a bachelor with a rolling walk, a military moustache and a twinkling eye. He partly rebuilt the house and refurnished it. The ghastly old beds disappeared. He took to wandering in <u>toyetime</u> gossiping with men of all ages. He instituted fortnightly play readings in his drawing room with sandwiches and Hock, and though quite unmusical himself, he provided a splendid gramophone and room to build up a library of classical records. I ran this aspect of the house for several years.

In the wider school he wrestled with the lowest division by unorthodox methods. He thought that <u>up to books</u>, men were mostly bored or in opposition, and glad of any diversion. Leading the master astray is the oldest school-boy sport.

---

* An extraodinarily beautiful Illustrated Stroll Through the City and College by Rupert Hill with over 80 watercolours by Dennis Page, published in 2005, vividly reflects the atmosphere both now and 70 years ago. I think that this tour de force is obtainable through the Wykehamist Society in College Street Winchester. It is well worth its £20.

** Aeneid Book II Line 3: 'Unspeakable, Oh Queen, the grief thou biddest me renew'.

As he taught almost all subjects to his rather thick charges, he could capitalise on this. Latin periods were side tracked into Pythagoras. Tudor history somehow developed into French verbs, and Transubstantiation moved into the punctuation of the English sentence. By the end of term his victims were astonished to discover that all unbeknownst, they had gone through the syllabus. He had, of course, a first in Greats. He had also been decorated for gallantry. He was also the finest after-dinner speaker I ever heard, my later work causing me to hear a great many. I do not say that Jack Parr was an incomparable housemaster, but I do say that I cannot imagine a better. Under him things mostly seemed to go right. 35 years later, when he was an old man in retirement, a contemporary of mine proposed that we might all subscribe for a present for him. The response – parents of old boys including my mother joined in with a will – surprised the proposer of the idea and apparently astounded him.

Now I must turn to other Winchester Worthies. The Headmaster, Dr Alwyn Williams was tall handsome, hawk faced and had the rare distinction of a triple First. As an Oxford Doctor of Divinity he was a tremendous spectacle in his black and scarlet robes, but we first met him at a sensible institution called the Headmaster's Monthly. Once a term the Headmaster took over each division for a whole day. It gave us some real contact with a figure who is apt to be magisterially remote. Williams was slow spoken and intellectually courteous. If you said something which might be off the beam, he helped you, however young, to take your idea to its origin in one direction and its conclusion in the other. One could surprise oneself, thus, into feeling a fool without anyone else noticing. He was a historian. I first specialised in history under him and, as he became Dean of Christchurch shortly afterwards, I was his last pupil. He ended up as Bishop of Durham.

Spencer Leeson (unlike Williams, a Wykehamist), his successor had been a barrister and a civil servant and, I believe that he was a little unsure of himself. He had a slight speaking impediment, and his learning was less impressive than Williams'. He had ideas, such as the Importance of Fitting Oneself for Life, which he somehow never managed to convey to us. Equally, he had good teaching ideas, yet somehow did not carry conviction as a teacher. This sounds like the description of a budding hypocrite, but he acted as my tutor for two terms and I got to know him quite well. He was a charming and human man. He soon got himself ordained because religion was the mainspring of his life, yet his highly declamatory sermons were faintly embarrassing in a school full of connoisseurs of sermons. We marked them animatedly out of ten. I have told friends that I liked him very much yet disagreed with nearly everything he did. I cannot for the life of me remember why.

Two incidents however symbolise the relationship between him and the school. I record the first in a spirit of affectionate malice. Some industrious devil discovered just before an O.T.C camp that between Spencer and Leeson there had been two regrettable Christian names which he had suppressed. So platoons were heard singing to the tune of *Frère Jacques* as they marched: -

> 'Spencer Leeson
> Spencer Leeson
> Dormez-vous?
> Dormez-vous?
> Stottesbury Gwatkin
> Stottesbury Gwatkin
> Ding dong dou! Ding dong dou!'

The second incident arose when I edited The Wykehamist, a fortnightly school journal. I wrote a leading article in the style of his only too parodiable orations. When I was about to leave, it fell to me to recommend my successor. Leeson said:

'Are you sure that he will not parody the Headmaster's sermons?' I said 'No Sir'. He laughed.

No school is complete without its butt. We had two. At class rooms you would hear the gentle drone or the trumpet-like rhetoric of the various teaching styles through the many open windows. There would also be two windows from which uproar not to mention bits of paper or more solid objects issued while above the riot the master's high pitched voice rang out like the bell of the Inchcape Rock in a hurricane. One such window concealed C.H.O'D Alexander, world chess champion, attempting to teach mathematics; he was a charming man who ought never to have got involved with a pack of young demons such as ourselves. The other was Raoul Liétard, the French French-master. No French master can keep order in an English school class, and apparently the English have the same difficulty in France. It is not always a matter of language: and anyway Liétard spoke English excellently.

But we did not always exploit weakness. One of the nicest and most beloved of dons was Rockley Wilson, once Test Captain for England, who had no particular function in that society save to teach a little French for the sake of having him there. We much enjoyed leading Old Rockley astray but the curious thing was that we all seemed to know quite a lot more French after a term with him than we did before. I cannot imagine how this happened, for I have no recollection of *ever* doing any French during his French lessons. He had a capacity for gentle repartee: once a small man ran round a corner straight into Rockley's stomach, looked up and said:

'My God'.

'Strickly incognito, young man'.

I first noticed the influence of accidents on my life at the Aldershot O.T.C camp of 1934. I was a recruit that year. We arrived boiled like lobsters, off our train. There was a call for volunteers to wash up after supper. Like an idiot, I volunteered, and with others was fetched out of the ranks and paraded separately. After a long wait an officer appeared with a serjeant and four corporals, and said:

'Are you the demonstration platoon?'

As bemused recruits, we said nothing. I think that some of us thought that this was some military notion for a washing up party. We marched off into the heather where, instead of washing anything up, we practised some kind of platoon tactic. We got back to a very late supper, and were told to parade early next day. This we did. We practised something else until the rest of our army came steaming out to us. We demonstrated what we had done the night before for their benefit, and went back to camp. From about 10.30 we had the rest of each day off. The other hundreds all turned up angry and hungry in the late afternoon. This was our daily routine. We were, by accident, privileged persons.

That year I went to Vienna at Easter with my mother and saw a ritual Good Friday performance of *Parsifal*. This is a somnolent opera which producers have to trick out with eye-catching effects to distract the audience from its inadequacies. In a Venice performance in 1983 Klingsor had a scarlet plastic mantle which covered two thirds of the stage and was manipulated by eight entirely naked young women. This 1934 performance at the old State Opera was ornately produced in the style of a series of blue and *terra cotta* plates. The faded imperial decorations were still in use, and there were elderly officers in Habsburg uniforms standing in the pit. Vienna was a head without a body, and depression lay heavily upon everything. Some of the theatre's machinery was not too good either. When Klingsor leapt up and launched the Magic Spear at Parsifal, it was supported on strings which in turn hung from trucks somewhere in the empyrean. The trucks squeaked right across the music, and the spear swept past Our Hero who was supposed to catch it. It vanished into the wings and then reappeared behind him swinging backwards. Parsifal, who was singing fit to bust, was groping in the air, but missed it again. It was now within his line of vision, gathering itself for a return swing while Klingor remained in his ceremonial posture of baffled evil. Parsifal had already sung his triumphant note when the spear reversed past him. He hurled himself after it and seized it with might and main, letting out a great shout.

I have seen two splendid operatic accidents at Covent Garden. During the peasant rioting against *Boris Godunov* at Kromy, there were thunderous noises off.

These were not the False Dimitri's artillery, but the False Dimitri's horse, which eventually crashed its way onto the stage, Dimitri in the saddle, with crowds of peasants clinging to it for dear life. Dimitri sang bravely but brokenly on top, while underneath, his fiery steed heaved and stamped its way slowly across the stage and finally trotted off in a shower of rebels and <u>oprishchniki</u> (or <u>muzhiks</u>?). The audience cheered.

The other occurred when the love sick Chinese swains were serenading *Turandot's* window. The lady appears behind the bars. She grasps them firmly, for the gracious opening. They are stuck. The lady struggles. She is a strong lady and the walls of the palace shake and rattle. Meanwhile the orchestra, with presence of mind improvises. Suddenly, the sash goes up with a bang and a scarlet faced virago appears, wig slightly awry and puffing visibly at the embarrassed suitors.

I took school certificate and in the spring of 1935 entered for the Vere Herbert history prize. This was valuable; the £20 worth of books was worth £250 in 2001. You wrote four essays in the holidays and did an unprepared (<u>ex-trumps</u>) examination at the opening of Cloister Time. I took a bag of books to Elmau. The examination was on the first Saturday of term.

I had to read a routine essay to the first of my two tutors the following Thursday. The second one was usually for English: you read him essays about anything which came into his head. At that time my second tutor was Professor Gleadowe, the senior art master, a man of learned and wide-ranging artistic attainments. I first met him when he was teaching some people to make stained glass. We shared an interest in heraldry. On one occasion I had to write an essay for him on the question 'Discuss functionalism in architecture with special reference to Corbusier and the American aircraft carrier *Saratoga*'. His reticent line drawings were so delicate as to be almost invisible. With his help, I abandoned my appalling handwriting and taught myself anew. Our civilisation wastes such people. In World War II he languished in the Admiralty, investigating recommendations for honours, and after a while quietly killed himself.

But my primary tutor that Thursday was Harold Walker, the Senior History Master. I read him my <u>task</u>, and then over the coffee he said: 'Have you seen the Vere Herbert results yet?' I said no. He said: 'You'll find something there for you'.

I did indeed. I won the jackpot. I had become Somebody over night. I was never more surprised in my life.

Harold Walker taught me for two years. Many people have an enduring gratitude for the fire and scope of his learning. My contemporary Professor Christopher Brooke, for example, dedicated, under the initials H.E.W, his book on the <u>Saxon and Norman Kings</u> to him. He managed to engage our curiosity though by no means an incisive lecturer. His classroom method was that of the university. His voice rasped like a loud file and we took notes. Some of it was above our heads, but most of it was fascinatingly illustrated. He was the sort of man who captured the loyalty of a class, but could never have done the same for a house. But there was one thing which I did not find out until some 25 years later, at a dinner in his honour. He had spent part of his boyhood at Stolp and had known the Blumenthals.

And so, to end this movement, a trio: H.A. Jackson (called the Jacker), Budge Firth and Ronald Hamilton. They could hardly have been more unlike. The Jacker was a twisted apparently ancient, skinny furious and ambitious housemaster. Firth a fat, sybarite clergyman. Hamilton the slimmest and most handsome young man, newly arrived from Cambridge.

Everybody warned me that the Jacker was dangerous. In World War I the Germans had dragged him as a prisoner along a road in a sack behind a cart, and he loudly proclaimed his anti-Germanism. People commiserated with me. In fact, he could not have been kinder or more courteous, and this was particularly noticeable because I was having trouble with his main subject – Latin. He went to endless trouble. He had been a regular soldier, and like so many officers and gentlemen had found time for other interests. I dined with him once or twice in his house, where he had a collection of Chinese, mostly Sung, celadons, on which he was very knowledgeable. On the other hand, his House sometimes found him trying. On finding two of his men in a pub, he was upset to a point of hysteria, and at the annual <u>House Supper</u>, a function to which <u>pitch-up</u> were invited, he embarrassed everyone with an angry speech about the evil spirit abroad among their offspring.

Ronald Hamilton was a brilliant <u>div:don</u> whose main interests were French and German; and his attractive new wife was, I think, a relative of the Marschall v. Biebersteins. He had a second string in history and in mediaeval art and architecture. In later life he wrote some admirable <u>Holiday Histories</u> in which he matched the history of a period with its architecture, thereby giving the traveller a good deal of entertaining background on the things which he might see. He was a magnificent figure of a man with a striking pair of sunlit eyes and a flair for acting. In World War II he had a distinguished career in India and was, for a while, a lecturer in military history at the Staff College at Quetta. When my thirteen-year old son was preparing a project on *Frederick the Great* for his entrance battle into Westminster in 1974, I sought Ronald's advice. Back by return came a bibliography and his lecture notes from Quetta. At one of the few Wykehamist dinners which I have ever attended, I mentioned this to a group of people, who unanimously agreed that this was typical.

And so, finally, to Budge Firth. He got married in later life, so he could hardly have been a eunuch, but he seemed like one. Fat, shiny of skin with a high-pitched voice, this clergyman was the son of J.B. Firth the well-known Edwardian journalist, and a grandson of Jesse Boot the commercial pharmacist. He was so rich that he never needed to work. In fact he worked like a slave. I never knew a man who knew so much about so many things, or who absorbed the pleasures of this world with so much contentment. He took in learning and swallowed roast duck in much the same spirit. He was my Sixth Book div:don for two years, and my tutor for a while. Later, when I was living in the Temple, he became Master there, but died within a year. He could and did start arguments about everything under the sun. Should professorships of Divinity he abolished? This set the Marxists and the Christians at each others' throats. What was wrong with Jung? What indeed? He advised us all to read Spinoza. Sometimes we got a little out of hand in the pursuit of controversy and shouted the merits of the Monophysites or the evils of bimetallism, and once George Jellicoe cross-examined him (admittedly it was before breakfast) so persistently that he lost his temper and flounced out.

I ought not to finish this chapter without mentioning books. One might have thought that in so over-taught a historian as I was becoming, a great historical work would have figured importantly in my landscape. Not so! Budge Firth said that his life had been changed by Butler's *Way of All Flesh*, and it made a great impact on mine, too, but the book which fascinated and uprooted most people was Aldous Huxley's *Brave New World*, then the centre of outraged controversy. We were brought up in the distantly Victorian ideals of our muddle-headed post-Victorian parents. Brave New World slammed the door on all that. It took years for some of us to recover – if we ever did.

It is important not to stress the hardships of Winchester, mainly because boys mind physical hardships very little, but a civilising factor was the abilities and geniality of the dons. All the same we undoubtedly lived hard. Save in Common Time we rose at 7.00am, went up to books at 7.30am, chapel at 8.15am, then breakfast. Between 9.30am and 1.00pm there were four class periods. Games after lunch. Two class periods between 4.00pm and 6.00pm. From 7.00pm to 8.45pm was toyetime (prep). Preces at 9.00pm. Lights out at 9.40pm, but most senior men finished at 10.30pm or 11.00pm. Chapel was compulsory. Discipline was enforced (not very often) with the cane which praefects could but dons could not use.

Wiccamical ingenuity was considerable. The timetable, laid out by that distinguished composer and explosives expert, Sir George Dyson, was a miracle of flexibility, and great trouble was taken, especially for the seniors, to adapt it to each man. Hardly any had the same timetable. The opportunities available to us were, if not limitless, astoundingly wide. By way of examples: you could – 80 years ago, remember – learn Russian as well as Spanish and the others; there was a magnificent workshop; a quarter of the school played some musical instrument or other; and among the many societies, the archeological one managed to excavate a bronze age village, and organise holiday tours of French cathedrals, when we were, as a bonus, shown over those legendary miles of the Pommery champagne cellars at Rheims, used as feeders to the defences in the First World War. I also learned fencing (to improve my slow-wittedness) and the clarinet (to expand my lungs). The choices were entirely mine.

Chapter 18

HITLER

I became Senior Praefect, caught pneumonia at Christmas 1936 and, penicillin not having been invented, spent two months in bed, missed the scholarship examinations, recuperated in Capri and Rome and, finally, was accepted for Magdalen College, Oxford where Percy and Werner had already been. I also won another school prize not surprisingly, for a German oration. There was a ceremony called <u>Medal Speaking</u> at the end of Cloister Time, to which parents were invited. My speech was *Faust's* opening soliloquy, and I got a standing ovation from an audience in which only 5% perhaps knew any German. My mother was there. When I asked her about it, she said 'I don't know. I didn't listen. I thought you would make a mess of it'.

The great wide world, meanwhile, was heading for catastrophe whose trail passed even my door. Hitler came to power in 1933 when Werner was at Spetzgart. On that night all the boys and girls of Jewish origin took a steamer across the lake to Switzerland. How wise they were! Nobody at that time had any conception of the horror which Hitler was preparing, yet what was expected seemed bad enough. Communist propaganda had concealed or lied about the Siberian labour camps which, with trimmings, the Nazis now imitated.

The wave of sentiment which carried the Nazis to power was so strong that, despite some violence, the takeover was achieved by means which, however you look at them, were mostly legal. This is not always remembered. Hitler's dictatorial power was founded upon an act of the Reichstag passed in due form after a general election.

Moreover the Germans long supported his policies, which liberated them from the shackles of Versailles, and seemed to restore employment and prosperity. They cannot plead the illegitimacy of his government in extenuation of later events. They elected it, even if they did not all fully understand what they were doing. Thus the question of German national guilt depends upon whether they ratified Hitler's acts later, when they certainly knew; whether by that time, the ability to withdraw their confidence still existed and whether they would have withdrawn it if they had had the opportunity. I have no doubt that the Germans, by 1937, knew or were wilfully shutting their eyes. Concentration camps (usually referred to as *KZ*) were often mentioned in my hearing. It could hardly be otherwise. The disappearance of old friends had to be explained somehow, and besides, nobody thought that a KZ was a pleasant place, despite the propaganda. Some were close to big cities: Dachau, for example, is an out-suburb of Munich. I do not know if at this period the inmates were herded at a run through the streets to their daily labour, as they were later on: probably not, because there were too many foreign journalists about. The extermination camps, though they existed, were kept carefully secret. But if ordinary folk knew about KZ, the intelligent and well-informed must have understood where all this was leading. The Nazis played on the 'I'm alright, Jack' feeling.

So one comes to the question of ratification. I am afraid that they have to be condemned on that score too. They had adopted an abomination which promised them benefits in return for the destruction of law, democracy and certain scapegoats. These benefits went far beyond the tearing up of the Treaty of Versailles (a not unreasonable aspiration). They would re-establish the frontiers (roughly speaking – what's a few million Slavs between friends?) of the ancient Reich – meaning something golden, glorious and predatory. The German word *Krieg* (war) is connected with *kriegen* meaning to 'get or take', and *Reich* (according to the dictionary 'empire') means adjectivally 'rich'. The Nazis appealed to the myth of the tribal horde with its roistering chieftains ready to fill your hat with gold. Hermann Goering typified the idea and later Vidkun Quisling built himself a semi-palace in Oslo. I went over it. It had a special roistering hall on the ground floor. The gold, of course, was torn from their victims who had better be quickly forgotten. Most Germans accepted the benefits without too many qualms, and entered into the necessary military action with, if not enthusiasm, at any rate without resignation. When Memel, Austria and Danzig had been settled to everybody's satisfaction, what about the *Volksdeutschen* of the Czech Sudetenland and the Polish Corridor? By now they were undeniably cheerful about their ill gotten prosperity.

It can be argued with some show of plausibility that in this second phase the opportunity to withdraw their confidence no longer existed. Though there is something in this, I am not sure that it stands up. My own observation is that they mostly helped themselves to the loot without many second thoughts; but the fact which knocks the bottom out of the excuse is that many bravely refused to countenance the direction in which policy was moving, and suffered fearful martyrdom. I knew Elizabeth v. Thadden, for example. She ran a girls school and taught them to be truthful and upright and to look facts in the face. She was hanged on a tree in her own playing field. This complex of predatory prosperity and the persecution to death of anyone who questioned its origin, casts doubt on the theory that the Germans would have changed their minds if they could. They flocked into the S.A (Brown Shirts), and if mothers rightly feared for their daughters chastity when they entered the *Bund der Deutschen Mädels* (League of German Girls), the Hitler Youth took in the boys and used them on a vast scale,* for example to collect for the fraudulent winter relief of December 1935 in Munich. These boys, mostly nine or ten years old, with their favours and collecting boxes, were everywhere. They had the moral authority of the state behind them and they knew it. They simply followed you about clashing their boxes and uttering opprobrious remarks until a little crowd began to collect and you paid up. Millions were screwed out of the patient citizenry. The seduction and abuse of these children were thought out and organised by Baldur v. Schirach, a major Nazi villain.

Observant foreigners soon cottoned on. A devouring monster was growing up in Germany. As early as 1932 Pater's friends were predicting war, and advising him to protect Werner and myself. On the 8th January in that year we were persuaded to take a fundamental step. We were naturalised British subjects. We signed the papers in Pater's office in Salters Hall Court in the City. A little commissioner for oaths from the basement accepted our Oaths of Allegiance. It was, I must say, a wrench. We took a train to Pipits Hill and wrote to Schlönwitz. A few days later came a letter repudiating the naturalisation as effected without his authority and summoning us formally back to Germany. I reckoned that it was written for the benefit of the censor, for by the decrees of the German courts he had no authority over us at all. It was a pity that this, the last communication which I ever had with my father should have been in this vein: but who could blame him?

If war was foreseen so early with enough assurance for responsible people to take action in private matters, the government of Baldwin and Chamberlain behaved in exactly the opposite fashion. Their actions are intelligible only upon the assumption that war would be prevented. They must have held this view for at least three, perhaps four more years after well informed individuals outside politics had abandoned it. Ministers have civil servants, diplomats and spies to keep them abreast of affairs. I find it incredible that that they entirely failed to notice what was happening.** I can, however, believe that the information was filtered before it reached the cabinet, or that it was so monstrous that people could

---

* The BBC film *Hitler's Children* (2005) admirably describes the process by which the youth were indoctrinated.
** Written in 1977. In 2004 it emerged that Colonel Hans Oster's group had organised a coup and warned London by at least six respected emisaries, who were not taken seriously, save by Churchill who was not in the government. The action was stopped by Chamberlain's Munich adventure. After Stauffenberg's attempt on Hitler in 1945, the SS accidentally discovered some relevant papers of Oster's as a result of which, amongst others, my cousin Count Hans Jörg von Blumenthal was hanged.

not believe it; much as I abhor Neville Chamberlain I cannot believe that he had a sense of self-interest so limited that he would risk it in the destruction of the country. An unscrupulous, small town self seeker he may have been, but he was not silly.

On the other hand the incredulity with which some of the horrors were greeted is a matter of record. It is a disease of comfort and security to look too much on the bright side: to avert the eye from oppression and tyranny. This had been the norm of life in Russia since 1917, but the Russians might be expected to do anything, while the Germans were still quixotically believed to be within the pale of the decencies. It is remarkable how much it took to overcome this attitude. The peacetime Nazi treacheries, the War, even the more credible reportage failed to get this home. It was the discovery of Belsen, by my old friend Sir Bryan Urquhart when the conflict was almost over, which opened eyes.

We had the same problem in 1977. In the Diamond Jubilee Year of the October Revolution, a vast and aggressive military power stood armoured to prevent any understanding of the murder, cruelty and starvation practised at its cold heart.

And so I took my new nationality and as I thought sloughed off the old; but not for long. The treaty by which British naturalisation extinguished German nationality was the Treaty of Versailles. Within a few months, Hitler denounced it, I was now British in most parts of the world but German in an expanding Germany again. It was dangerous to go there, and after January 1936 I did not go again until the end of the war. Henry, investigating the nationality matter in the year 2000 concluded, with the aid of the German embassy, that despite the German State Treaty after World War II, I am still a German in Germany because my renunciation of German nationality under the Treaty of Versailles was made when I was still a minor, and that the consent of my legal guardian (my mother) could not cure the defect. I think that this must be right but it seems to have the odd result that Fanny and our descendants have dual nationality too, and can, in common with me claim German citizen rights.

We took to other countries for our holidays. In contrast with our present third rate condition Britain was deeply respected. A British passport was seldom inspected: so potent it was. The buying power of the pound was incredible by modern standards. We stayed a night at the *Truffe Noire* at Brive-la-Gaillarde. We had three bedrooms with bathrooms, a splendid four course dinner with two sorts of wine, brandies and coffee afterwards and breakfast next day. The *total* triple bill was just £5. In other fields British prestige was still vast. After the German seizure of Austria, Austrians came to Britain in composure. Britain would, of course, put these wrongs right. An Englishman's word and his cheques were accepted.

On one of these forays we went to Budapest, and stayed at the Szent Gellert Hotel. We could afford this magnificent place because we had sterling, and the Hungarian capital had depended on a large German traffic which Nazi policy had cut off. It, like Vienna, was a head without a body but, despite mutual dislikes, the combined areas of Austria and Hungary were still significant, even if only a shadow of the old Habsburg economic bailiwick. When Hitler seized Austria this area was sundered. Vienna, now part of the Greater German Reich began to revive. Budapest fell on evil days, cut off from its twin by an eastward-facing Iron Curtain. The blundering and unjust American anti-Habsburg doctrine, enshrined in the Versailles-Trianon-St Germain settlement, by creating the weak successor states, destroyed East European temperamental affinities, the economic union based upon planned communications, and institutionalised the artificial hatreds of the local nationalities which the Habsburgs had, if imperfectly, held in check. These, individually, could not maintain their independence against the predators and would not combine to do so. This was foreseeable at the time, but the Americans, having saddled the Europeans with this nonsense, backed out of the correlative obligation to maintain it. Hence the system collapsed with only a small German push (with great subsequent brutality) during World War II. It was artificially recreated (also with great brutality) behind the Iron Curtain for Russian thieveries, and collapsed again amid civil wars and massacres after the Russian withdrawals in the 1990s. The sufferings of tens of millions of East Europeans can thus be traced to smug American incomprehension. They constitute a case for keeping Americans out of other people's business.

Buda was a compact city on a hill; Pesth sprawled on the plain. They face each other across the wide Danube, and until Count Batthyany built a suspension bridge in the 1850s, they were connected only by ferries and an unreliable floating bridge, which I saw. The five bridges of the 1930s were all destroyed during the World War fighting.

The two cities were sharply contrasted. Buda was small. You could walk into the countryside (now garden city) in twenty minutes. It had always been the residence of the executive rulers, whoever they might be. The Ottoman governor of Hungary was called the Pasha of Buda. The Habsburgs drove them out, in operations in which, as I have said, a Blumenthal took part, and naturally rebuilt Buda in their own image as an eighteenth century capital associated with the curious Coronation (or Matthias) church.

In 1938, Hungary was still in theory a Kingdom, but since the native, Arpad, dynasty had died out and the Habsburgs had acquired their rights, the Apostolic Kings had mostly been absentees preoccupied with imperial problems in Western

Europe. The Magyars were proud of the Crown of St Stephen as a symbol of their nation and Christian virility. The grandfather of a Hungarian friend had, in childhood, known old guerrilla troopers of the anti-Turkish frontier cavalry. Till 1849 Latin was the educated language, and as late as 1936 it was still taught as a spoken language at schools such as Gödöllö.

In the fighting of 1945 the Russians almost flattened Buda, especially the palace, and an American stole the Crown, but later governments decided to restore the skyline. As there was no monarch to accommodate, the new palace was designed internally as a very good Hungarian art gallery. I am not sure if anyone has recovered the Crown, but it has now reappeared in the insignia of the modern Hungarian state. The same fighting is said to have severely damaged Pesth, but conditions were far better than in Buda. Pesth was not destroyed and the population mostly took refuge under ground, whence it in due course emerged dishevelled and hungry but alive, after a new oppressor had replaced the old. They had three advantages: their cunning (a Hungarian, it is said, can enter a revolving door behind you and come out in front); the fact that it was not their quarrel, and finally that nobody can understand their language. Now that the Russians have gone, they have got ahead with their own business. The atmosphere of Pesth in the year 2000 resembled that of pre-1939 Paris with its great boulevards, cafés and music.

To return to between-the-wars: when the Habsburgs collapsed, the Crown of St Stephen remained, and after communist convulsions, the remarkable Admiral Horthy, Prince of Nagybanya, became Regent in its name. Horthy's naval rank arose out of a series of exploits in the Adriatic in World War I including a destroyer raid up the Ravenna canal to bombard the Italian East Coast trunk railway.

This Hungary, a kingdom without a King ruled by an Admiral without a fleet, retained some of the trappings. They had their own sort of Beefeaters: splendid armoured men with conical winged hats, shields and partisans who marched, or rather clashed, across the palace square in very slow slow time.

From the Fischerbastei of Germanised Buda, you look across the Danube, which makes a gently convex curve, to popular almost uproarious Pesth. The plain is quite flat eastwards towards Hatvan, and Pesth straggled across it, becoming more and more spasmodic until it gave up in allotments and shacks which housed some of the poorest people in Europe. Whole families crouched beside garden walls in excavations protected by lean-to sheets of corrugated iron. The area was for three months annually under snow.

I have always been worried by extreme poverty. Once we were huddling into the car in Leeds station yard when I caught sight of a gang of children; they were ragged in those loose grey garments which one sees in Edwardian prints, and running about on the cold cobbles, without shoes. The picture haunts me, and when idealisms were discussed at school (or later), the doctrines, whether Christian, Marxist, Liberal, or whatever, seemed unreal unless accompanied by action. I still believe (though I can hardly claim to live up to the standard) that the best tests of such theories are contained in two questions: -

'Do I mind if it is applied to me?'

'Am I willing to do something about it?'

So when I was idealistic and seventeen, I asked to go and work for a fortnight in a boys' club camp, instead of going for a week with the O.T.C to Tidworth. Both took a chunk out of the summer holidays. The boys' (Crown) club was maintained at Hoxton by Wiccamical subscriptions. At that time a child in the East End of London never saw a field or the sea unless he was helped, and he had to be helped because even if he ever got there, he would not have known what to do. With scheming and goodwill these children could be given a fortnight's camping holiday for £1. Harold Llewellyn-Smith, who ran the club, had a farming friend near Freshwater in the Isle of Wight, who lent the camping field. The tents, blankets and other equipment were ex-army, scrounged or bought long ago. Contracts for bulk supplies were placed with the local shops. Harold did not believe in free gifts. He made his boys save up for their holiday and ran a bank for them. He knew all about them and could tell whether they were saving properly. Some could not – really could not – save more than a penny* a week. Somehow they were not disappointed.

There was an enormous heap of stuff at Waterloo. We filled up the luggage van and two passenger compartments. The Southern Railway Company Ltd did not bat an eyelid. At Brockenhurst they held the train for twenty minutes while we cross-loaded. At Lymington they held the steamer for another half hour on top of that. At length, in the gloaming, to Yarmouth, a lorry, a field, a tent pitched, a fire lit. Tea. Porridge, sausages, stewed apples and tinned milk. And so, in a miscellaneous heap to sleep. Ten of us.

It took us two days to set up that camp. Then the cooks, hefty 50 year old ladies, turned up. We went to Yarmouth, dangled our legs over the jetty and waited in the calm of the evening for the boat. It arrived with cheers and yells which might have been heard in Portsmouth. There were 140 of them. Harold had decided to let in the Double Six club of the incredibly poor from Petticoat Lane. I had always assumed that only barons (like me), or Wykehamists (like me) or whatever (like me) were snobs, but I found that the same displacement of values occurred among the poor, or that they were inclined to a furious parochialism, beside which the Wiccamical outlook seemed as wide as the sea. Our problem was to protect the Double Sixers from our own much more numerous Crown Club boys. The ragged

---

* In 1984 about one tenth of a penny. A pint of beer cost 4d.

Double Sixers were *visibly* poorer and less well nourished, and punier. You could tell them at a glance, even naked. If there were Crown boys who could afford only a penny a week, how on earth could some of these come at all? Harold, for once, looked uncomfortable and changed the subject. In a moment of madness, I had agreed to run the bank. You had to have one because if a penny – let alone a tanner[*] was missing, there was a fight. I discovered that I was bad at accounts; and every day there was the endless queue, followed by the casting up which never balanced. This queue was my introduction into a new sort of notion – the East End rhyming slang which is now under self-conscious revival. It was the ordinary material of speech then but survives genuinely only in odd expressions such as *titfor*.[**] It was a conceptual labyrinth. "Ave yer come for the Duke?"[***] I never understood the background of *Sproalsie*[+] though apples and pears (stairs) was easy enough.

I have already said that our sort of upbringing rigidly excluded sex. Theirs did not. There was I, supposed to be helping to take charge of that mob, everyone of whom knew more about real life than I did. In about two hours these children of nature reached back to their vivacious lives, their girlfriends and their cynicism. The girlfriends having been left behind in Hoxton, they started to look round. The local girls were used to this sort of thing – in one sense; but there were London girls on the beach too. The boys came straight to the point. It took a little time to sort out whose slip belonged to whom. After that we kept a rather closer guard, for those were, outside the East End, more shockable days. It was, altogether, illuminating and strenuous: and then we all had the business of striking camp and carting the whole lot back to Waterloo at the end of the fortnight, but I wanted to do it again.

But Budapest had another sort of poor besides, and these were the gypsies. We have Bartok's word for it that the gypsies of Galanta were musical. I am afraid that their bands, for which Pesth was famous, did not impress me that way. They were dextrous. I saw a man play a piece on his violin, then play it behind his back, then *pizzicato* with two violins and finally using one violin as the bow for the other. The musical sense, however, seemed to me to be lacking. These were journeymen playing difficult but largely worthless pieces to show off. The Spanish gypsies sometimes show a similar trait. I heard Fritz Kreisler, in old age, doing the same thing at Oxford. A breathtaking skill put to tawdry and uninteresting ends. The cafés of the Hatvany Utca (renamed piecemeal) were, musically, a bore. Fanny gave me a record of some early Hungarian music in 1984. This type of music obviously antedated the gypsies'. I doubt Bartok's dicta even more. I am, however, cheered by the modern (non gypsy) musical revival. In 2000 there were orchestras, opera, choirs and chamber music all over the place – some inspired by English conductors.

---

[*] 6d.
[**] Tit for tat = hat.
[***] Duke of Kent = rent.
[+] Sproalsionna Rhymes with tanner.

Chapter 19

VENICE AND OXFORD

We caught a slow sleeper to Venice. A middle-aged Hungarian tried to teach me how to pronounce Siofok (a town on Lake Balaton). To a stranger who had never thought about it, the place names made it obvious that Hungary is different; we had entered it at Esztergom. I left it near Nagykanisza. I had a hankering to go to Szekesferhervar simply because of its name; and the place called Fünfkirchen (Five Churches) in German is Pecs in Magyar. The full extent of the difference, however, appeared when I wanted a public loo. Did I use NÖK or FERFIAK? I had to wait till I saw a woman emerge from FERFIAK. In fact no western or Slav language gives the slightest clue to understanding. It shares 200 distant words with Estonian and Finnish. No wonder the Magyars feel different. They even write their names backwards, like the Japanese: I found a statue inscribed 'Byron Alfred'.

We crossed into Yugoslavia, and woke up in the misty dawn at the other end of the boggy forests of Rakek. Soon we entered Italy, chugged round the head of the Adriatic and came to rest in Sta Lucia, the Venetian terminus. We lugged our bags out, found a porter and straggled through the dark overcrowded hall of the old station building.

Then somebody opened a door into the world. Is it permissible to describe the light and movement as a fanfare of trumpets? The stimulus was overwhelming, as if I wanted to leap and shout. The brilliant light, the people crowding the beautiful new Scalzi bridge, a wedding party on the steps of the little domed church opposite, the *Vapporetti* nosing through the crowd, and discharging swarms at the landing stages.

It would be a mistake to describe the most described city in the world, so I will try to confine myself to some of the intervening changes – the gondolas no longer have canopies, for example, – and the great mainland industrial complex at the edge of the Lagoon hardly existed. The daily surge of commuters was much smaller and the Venetians found most of their work in the Lagoon or the city itself. The power boat was, save exceptionally, forbidden, and other boats, being hand-propelled, were smaller and slower. If vegetables, tourists, or bricks had to be transported, the job was done in smaller lots and at a much lower speed. To produce the same rate of delivery four or five times as many more boats had to be used: the waterways were alive with them. The weight of traffic too was greater than it is now, because the resident population was larger. There were few empty houses. In March 1977 I saw the inconceivable in 1937: the Grand Canal above the Rialto empty of boats on a Sunday afternoon. Hence the city areas near the main canals sounded quite different because of the absence, save for vaporetti, of engines. Splashes, voices and gondoliers' warning shouts were almost the only sounds. The island city was not given over to the tourist industry to anything like its present extent. There were, of course, hotels and boarding houses, but they were fewer and smaller. Tourists accounted for a lesser proportion of the economic product. The local attitude to them was less commercialised. Nowadays the gondoliers organise a *serenata* with electrically illuminated barges and professional (or at any rate paid) musicians according to a timetable every summer night, starting at the Molo and ending at Malcanton, with tickets. Then, three families put chairs on their coal barge, got me to collect wine from a shop and pushed off. Someone played the mandolin; we all sang and passed food and drink around. Other boats joined us out in the Bacino* in a jolly nocturnal water picnic with perhaps four other boatloads, without arrangement under the moon.

The smaller numbers of tourists were, for the most part wealthier and stayed longer. Coach-mobs did not surge along predictable routes, making sure that they had seen what the folks back home expected. The famous cafés at St Mark's were crowded by people who had time to get acquainted. There was besides, a noticeable and old foreign colony. Eccentric English ladies still owned *Palazzi*,** the Jews still lived in the eponymous Ghetto,*** and the congregation at St George of the Greeks had not dwindled to the few charladies who go there now.

Mosquitoes (now, alas, returning) were another feature, Everybody slept under nets. You crawled in and lay sweatily dozing until the dawn. Moreover Venice was nocturnally busy and noisy too. The last revellers went home at 2.00am: the earliest workers were on their way at 4.00am and there were plenty by 4.30. In 1985 the streets were deserted by 11.00pm and revived only at 7.00am. What with mosquitoes and animation, you slept little at night. The siesta was important.

Fascism, on the whole, did as much good as harm. In Venice it did no more that the dictatorial eighteenth Century government of the Republic. The phrase 'black market' meant a market cornered by a black-shirt, and in Venice there was a flourishing undercover business mainly in currency and coffee. Everybody joined

---

* The Basin of St Mark. It is a wide expanse of water opposite the Doge's palace.
** The Venetian word is Ca' = house. Only the Doge had a palace.
*** This word means a bakery. It has come into prominence for political and propagandist reasons. It was the policy of the old Republic to segregate colonies of foreigners. The most impressive cases were the Germans and the Turks on the Grand Canal.

in, for the long lived Venetian Republic was first and foremost a business, and the habit of turning an honest penny is ingrained in the people. By contrast the Fascists were good at public works. Many of the recent bridges were built by them, and they alone of governments since 1797 improved the sea defences known as the Murazzi, which, through subsequent neglect, were breached in the great Tempest of 1966.

Museums and arts were, however, neglected. The 1975 panic about destruction through air pollution is, of course, justified; it is the consequence of industrialisation at Mestre and Marghera; but in 1935 St Mark's was heavily shored up inside, so that baulks of timber everywhere obstructed vision. In the Querini-Stampalia, the pictures were so badly hung that it was difficult to see them. The Accademia was not much better. There was little music. For artistic satisfaction everybody seemed to rely upon the sempiternal buildings – which were falling down – and the literary coteries which had for the most part dispersed. Learning was neglected too. It is to the eternal credit of the old Republic that the university of Padua, alone in Italy, maintained essentially modern and scientific schools, but the consequence of a university at Padua was no university in Venice, where the archives of the Republic are an inexhaustible quarry of historical, economic, commercial and judicial material on everything under the sun. The huge collections in the Procuratie, the State Archives and the Zecca mouldered and few seemed to know what was there. The museums were shamefully run. The Arsenal museum, representing the mightiest naval and industrial power of the Middle Ages, ought to have been worth a visit. Not so: the few dusty exhibits were broken and nobody had troubled with a spot of glue.

Modern Italy is entitled, despite its corruption, to take some credit for the improvements. Venetian studies are reviving, encouraged by the Americans and the University of Warwick. Unfortunately in the new branch of Padua university housed in the great Ca' Foscari, the students of 1977 had been running wild and the beautiful house was degraded with tattered political handbills, party banners, slogans and graffiti. All the same, the museums, particularly the Naval Museum, and the galleries are intelligibly and decently run. An international effort is restoring the churches with their wonderful pictures. Going into St Marks is now like entering a casket of jewels. Under papal inspiration San Giorgio Maggiore, the famous island monastery across the Bacino from the Palace, has been rescued from imminent ruin. The Victoria and Albert Museum has restored the Logetta and, with technical hiccups, the Porta della Carta.

Most of the real work is being done by unobtrusive craftsmen, many of whom, nowadays, are women or foreigners; their pay is not spectacular but they do not skimp. This combination of craftsmanship and international money and learning is reviving the mediaeval attitude that such work, if no longer AMDG, is at any rate worth doing for the greater glory of itself.

In these years the city has, in parts, sunk, as a result of the industrial abstraction of water from below the layer of clay upon which it is built. An early eighteenth Century print shows the city at a higher level than it is now. Two things however, are new: the greater rate of abstraction and the pretence that much research is needed into its effects. When I first went there you usually stepped down into a gondola at the Molo,* whereas, like as not nowadays you step up. Allowing for the very slight tides, I believe that the difference is real.

I have often been ecstatically happy in Venice. I experienced this only in one other place – Oxford. If Venice is nearly all water, Oxford has its canals and watercourses. Both, too, have packed masses of ancient buildings many enjoying much the same uses as when they were built. Industrialised Mestre matches industrialised Cowley. Each city is partly protected by a bottleneck: Venice by its four-mile causeway, Oxford by Magdalen Bridge. Oxford had managed without a Rialto, Venice without a Carfax, but both maintain a vivid sensation of living continuity with a long past.

In 2001 Magdalen College decided, under the inspiration of President Smith, to write a history of itself. No such project had been attempted for 150 years or so. I offered to record my 1937 to 1940 experiences for them and the following is roughly what I gave them in a recorded interview. The ultimate work awaits (2007) publication. The College is an interesting body with an unusual past. It has, amongst other things, twice defied the government.

The university which I entered in 1937 was a different sort of place from that which it has since become. In 1977 there were 34 such institutions, in 1937 only thirteen and each was much smaller. Oxford had 2,200 undergraduates compared with the modern 10,000. Most men living in college had two rooms. I had a gorgeous eighteenth Century pair overlooking Magdalen deer park. My sitting room was high and panelled and big enough to hold a party of 50 as long as one removed the sofa into the bedroom. For this I paid £11 a term.

Everybody had a right of entry to a university partly at the taxpayers' expense provided until 2005 that one satisfies the increasingly exacting intellectual obsessions of the senior members. Now civil servants can come into it too. The public, represented by the politicians thought that the recipients of its money should take their position seriously; they were thought, in some way, to be privileged; and this the pressurised young were only too glad to do. The sense of their own importance was enhanced by the rise of the quasi-political National

---

* The quay of the Piazzetta.

Union of Students and the development of an academic jargon, especially among the sociologists which, like the Winchester notions, set them – or at any rate the left-hand half of them – apart as a peculiar people. There was much talk about responsibility, and other relationships with society in general. Indeed the 1977 undergraduate was obsessed with his position in society, to the extent that he seemed to fear that people might not think that he was grown up. This was idealism run to seed, and it emerged, unfortunately, in much squalor. Undergraduate riots and sit-ins, the daubing, as in Venice, of slogans and the persecution of unpopular opinions were nasty features of that student scene, which also contained misfits, as the sad statistics of suicides showed.

I must not give the impression that the universities have necessarily changed for the worse. It is obviously a great gain that many more people can use them, and that the curricula are more varied. But these gains were achieved at avoidable expense, and it would be wrong not to mention the cost. From 1960 to 1982 I taught law and architecture at the City University. In the earlier years, up to about 1970, it was obvious that about 15% of the students should never, as being unable to write a sentence or marshal an argument, have been at the university at all. Some of these had first degrees. Money spent on their so-called right to a university education was wasted.

Then, secondly, we were at once more arrogant and more modest. This is not a paradox; we had a different view of life. We did not think that the university was a very important place. It was just another stage in one's life. We were consequently not concerned with our position in society. I was surprised when my tutor, John Morris said that it was a privilege to be here. The earnest political undergraduates were unpopular because they claimed an importance which nobody else claimed.

This relative modesty was matched by a relative arrogance towards academics. Since the university was not a very important place, those who worked in it professionally were not very important people. An undergraduate who made friends on any noticeable social scale with dons, was thought to be setting his sights rather low. My tutors were men of the highest distinction or notoriety – John Morris the international lawyer, A.J.P Taylor the left wing historian, C.S. Lewis the Christian philosopher, but I noticed the fact only after I went down. I do not think that I was unduly insensitive: we breathed a different atmosphere, and dons, then, were seldom news.

Undoubtedly a contributing factor to this difference was money. 60% of the undergraduates, even then, received support from some outside source, though often the support was small; but the man who paid for himself set the tone. The morally weak dons could not so easily insist upon their own standards if their charges lost nothing by being sent down. The situation was very different in 1977. The student on a grant faced boredom and unemployment on dismissal, and he protected himself by joining a union. Hence a sharper and less tolerant relationship. In my time the don worried very little if his pupils learnt or not. In most schools (now significantly called 'disciplines') it was common – if disapproved – to miss a tutorial and you went to lectures only if you wished. I seldom did. If you ploughed an examination you were sent down – but otherwise nobody worried much about you. You were, after all, an adult.

On the other hand there were controls upon pubs and gates. Everybody flouted them. The Proctor with his bodyguard of bowler-hatted ex-police-men known as bulldogs, went the nightly rounds, taking names and fining people, so that the rule was nothing but a scandalous source of university revenue. Women had to be out of Magdalen by 7.00pm and you had to be back in college by midnight (or 12.20 at Christchurch) save at Balliol where, it used to be insinuated, the young gentlemen were expected to stay out all night. At Magdalen the rule was no hardship because it was easy to climb in – or for girls to climb out. I did it, I suppose, on average twice a week. The college sensibly made no effort to block the routes, because the harder the more dangerous to irrepressible youth. The college porters who patrolled the precincts, were tactful. Sometimes the young gentlemen were less so: one of them climbed through a bedroom window, trod on the face of a sleeping don and had to run for it.

Magdalen was peculiarly favoured, for it is the only riverside college, and had its own fleet of directly accessible punts. The water played a great part in our happiness. Unlike the Venetian water it was tranquil, and the River Cherwell was deeply embowered so that in places you pushed your punt through a green tunnel. I knew what I would touch as the pole went down and I could steer a punt to a tenth of an inch. I was happy to push friends for miles on a sunny afternoon, with picnic baskets and bottles and talk. There were other pleasures at other times of day. One could move so silently that one heard nothing but nature. In the early mornings I have met cats and snakes swimming unconcernedly. At night, with a girl, there was peaceful understanding in the moonlight.

The Cherwell flows into the Thames, which at Oxford is called the Isis. It is wide, almost treeless and at certain times busy with practising crews. When the bumping races are on, mobs of bicycled supporters waving rattles, blowing whistles and firing pistols bellowed their way along the towpath, and near the winning-posts on the Christchurch side were the college barges gay with flags and parasols. Formerly the Lord Mayor's show was water-born, because he had to be sworn in at Westminster Hall. When the new Law Courts were built in the Strand, the procession went by land, and the City Livery companies sold their barges to the Oxford colleges, who used them as clubhouses. They were all – 21 of them – still there when I came up in 1937, but the rot, in the form of a new seriousness was beginning. Christchurch already had a boathouse.

I have, like everyone else, a few blushmaking things on my conscience. There was controversy in Magdalen Junior Common Room (J.C.R) about the way in which a substantial surplus should be spent. The barge sinkers wanted to share a boathouse with Trinity. The civilised favoured restocking the excellent cellar. I swore to attend a J.C.R meeting. I got drunk the night before, and when I woke up the meeting was over. There had been a tie, and the president had used his casting vote the wrong way.

The barges have gone.

But, besides the rivers, Oxford had another sort of water. The narrow boats came down the Oxford Canal with coal from the midlands, and I used to watch those calm rather alarming men talking and smoking on the wharf. They were inclined to corpulence and wore khaki brown dingey suits with wide-brimmed felt hats to match, and their speech was incomprehensible. Their women were loud; babies sometimes shrieked, and there were wiry little boys playing determined games with stick and stone on the towpath. They reminded me of the Hungarian poor or the peasant labourers in the German fourth-class carriages. Years later it dawned on me that they were gypsies – very like the gypsies of Chobham Heath.

The unscrupulous anti-canal activities of the railways had nearly destroyed the commerce of the Oxford Canal, and in due course they filled in the old terminal basin – almost certainly illegally – and ruined the canal for ever as a coal carrier; it seems, however, to be slowly reviving as a fun waterway, while the wharf was sold to Lord Nuffield so that he could endow his college, and build it on the site after World War II. I have no right to complain about this, for his college gave me a sort of fellowship which I vastly enjoyed.

I hesitate to relate my academic career.

Bursting out of Winchester, let alone Pipits Hill gave me, by reaction, an almost hysterical passion for *laissez-faire*. I went to Magdalen to enjoy myself and, by jingo, that is what I did. I always went up well before term began and came down well after it ended. You cannot do that now. I did the minimum of work – or rather less: in particular none at all for Pass Moderations, because by a happy fluke, I had read all the set books at school. On Werner's advice I started to read PPE[*] but I found it objectionably Marxist, and changed, against Pater's advice, to Law. He thought that it was unwise to read a subject which is going to engage one's attention for the rest of one's life. He, a solicitor, had read law at Oxford; his view deserved more

---

[*] Philosophy, Politics and Economics.

consideration than it got from me, but when I see the boring specialists of modern life, I am sure that he was right.

I necessarily worked hard at my studious frivolity. I caught breakfast by its nine o'clock deadline: sent notes in verse to other colleges. Coffee houses at eleven, then drove out to Clifton Hampden or the *Swan* at Minster Lovell in a battered third hand car. I have known as many as ten men and girls find space in a car made for four. The police were tolerant for we seldom endangered anybody.

Pubs, unmolested by VAT, were incredibly cheap. Bread, butter, pickles and a huge chunk of Cheddar cost a shilling (5p), a pint of Oxford Bitter 4d (not quite 2p). Such prices reigned well into 1940. This, of course, was provincial and accommodation charges were comparable. Werner and I had bed and a tremendous breakfast at Blandford in Dorset for 4s (20p) each.

In the summer when the pubs closed, it was time to take to the water until Party Time from 5.00pm until college dinners at 7.00pm. One was supposed to eat, or at least pay for four dinners a week. Sherry parties occurred in somebody's sitting room. I gave many because I accidentally discovered a source of cheap sherry (17½p) in London. In Magdalen you needed leave to throw a party for more than ten with an upper limit of 25. I never invited less than 50. The legal limit, however, had an exhilarating origin. Franzi Hohenlohe[*] solemnly got leave for more than ten. On the day, contractors appeared and set up tables, umbrellas, chairs, bars on every available lawn. Waiters assembled. There was oodles of drink. The college, too late, shut the gates against people without invitations. But the place was full of them already, and anyway Franzi had invited a thousand. The rumour had now spread. Everybody brought all their friends. Crowds besieged gates or arrived by punt or just climbed in by the known night routes. Hundreds were already at it by 5.00pm. By dinner the thousands were ready to continue. At midnight exhausted or cheerful porters were pursuing illegal young women.

The temperature and backbone of the College were its servants. Dons forget this, but the servants were essential and permanent, dons and undergraduates were not. Also they were an interesting lot. The Head Cook, confusingly called Butler, was one of the most learned of men, and if you paid attention to his art (and he became a friend), he showed it to you. *Hamburger Aalsuppe*, with stewed pears of course; a *mousse de foie* with the College arms in truffles under the transparency; the most wonderful Kashmiri curried duck. Such things appeared at my private dinner parties, and the charge was minimal. My highest was 7s6d (37½p) a head for a seven course meal. Oh yes! Too, there were picnic hard-boiled eggs disguised as ducklings swimming in aspic. He kept a multilingual culinary library in his office, and it was something of an honour to be invited in.

---

[*] Prince Franz of Hohenlohe-Scillingsfürst-Ingolfingen. In the 1990s he wrote a brilliant and unusually organised autobiography called *The G.I. Prince*.

Head Porters were respected or feared at most colleges, because they headed the disciplinary establishment, and sitting at the gate, they knew and were known by everybody. Ours', Mr Kirkby, was one such solid figure and I think an over-average one. The staircase servants were called scouts, and besides waiting in Hall, each had his pantry. It was a strenuous life for Betnay, my scout because my rooms in New Buildings, were nearly a quarter of a mile from the kitchens. Each scout had about eight young gentlemen to look after. Your scout cleaned and cleared up for you, advised you about everything, told you the news and – helped you out of scrapes or let you sink. Your fate was in his hands. Betnay had survived as an A.B. from a minelayer, which blew up in the Irish Sea in 1917 when he came to Magdalen. He left only shortly before he died in 1972. He was a small wizened cheerful person with a protruding chin and quick deft movements. He was never out of temper and never obtrusive, but he understood all the – now lost – arts of domestic service of which he was proud. According to him the scouts preferred demon undergraduates to the studious or holy because, though they made more work, they were more fun. I do not regret keeping him busy, and after I went down I made a point of keeping in touch. Fanny became a friend of his too.

Obviously, then, I had little time for work in term-time. If I did three hours a week I felt that I was overdoing things. My law tutor, John Morris, did not approve of this. He would be satisfied, he said, with *five hours a day*. This was altogether too demanding. My legal essays were not good. We drifted into a smouldering opposition, exacerbated by a difference of outlook. He thought, as I have indicated, that I should feel serious-minded and privileged. We were bound to part, but, since I must have been an exasperating pupil for so formidable and clever a man I still wonder at the friendly fashion in which the parting came to be made. I think that he was much more tolerant and tactful then he was reputed to be.

And so I changed my school yet again and read history, with A.J.P. Taylor, C.S. Lewis and Bruce Macfarlane.

These figures have had, to requote Frederick the Great, their ears written off, so I will be brief. Taylor, I thought and think, was, for all his brilliance as a broadcaster and learning as a writer, something of a charlatan. His tutorials degenerated into Marxist and Slav propaganda, and when he tried to argue with me, a v. Blumenthal, that Russian policy, whether Czarist or Communist, had never been aggressive, I could only laugh behind my hand. No one, at that time, had heard of Burgess, Maclean and Philby.

Macfarlane, a mediaeval historian, was a very nice person with a well furnished mind whom it was impossible to dislike, but with an outlook which seemed to be limited by the fences of Academe. One could learn about the Albigensians from him but make little of their dualism or, indeed, practical applications generally. I enjoyed and respected him very much, but working for him was a beatific vision in which grubby present realities were invisible. Perhaps I can go a little further. Perhaps they were both touched by the same unreality, but Taylor was more of a social engineer than Macfarlane.

Compared with this, my frivolity at least involved circumstances.

C.S. Lewis was altogether more realistic. His studies were rooted in literature but never submerged by it. Indeed, nothing submerged that buoyant intelligence, and since reality held him, he conveyed his ideas to mass audiences in terms which they enjoyed and which, without a microphone, they all heard. His Christianity had something to do with this: a religious person, knowing his own insignificance, can be genial. An atheist sneers.

Chapter 20

ST TROPEZ AND FRENCH DEGRADATION

St Tropez of 1938 was a crumbling coastal village with a sleepy port, a single heavy policeman who slopped about in sandals, half a dozen artists, a photographer and a couple of unknown authors. Just outside the town an impressive new hotel was busy failing, for nothing ever succeeded at St Tropez. The Hotel Sube maintained a thin trade; the restaurants, of course, were called L'Escale and La Rascasse and served Bouillabaisse, the Provençal abomination of stewed fish lightly flavoured with carbolic. Every country, Norway, Ruritania, Morocco has its tradeeshional peasant dish: Vair good? Yes? NO. You throw the principal local meat and vegetables (or in Provence fish and vegetables) into a pot full of water and vaguely stew them. Of these boring but doubtless nutritious concoctions, Irish stew and Bouillabaisse are easily the worst, but propaganda and French prose stylists have elevated Bouillabaisse to something only slightly less sacred than a cow. There was, however a hot mayonnaise powerfully laced with cayenne, which you put into a fish soup, which then exploded in your nose and heated your eyeballs. I used this *rouille* to the horror of the local high priests, to take away the nasty taste. Indeed taste ceased altogether.

I was broke but I had had a bit of luck. Wilhelmine, Werner and I had gone to the Golf Hotel at Beauvallon opposite, and then they had abandoned me with money to go on staying there. When they were out of sight, I crossed the gulf and found a nice place which cost no more per week than the Golf Hotel was costing for a night. And besides, the Golf Hotel collected golfing bores, for it had a nine-hole golf course unique, I believe, on the Riviera. I took my revenge on one of the bores just before I left. He had been complaining about the golf course all the week. I extolled the virtues of the Venice course. I was used, I said, to the New Course at Wentworth – already to be conjured with. Venice, I said, had the advantages of the seaside, like St Andrews's. A fortnight later I met him on the quay at St Tropez. 'Oh', he said, 'I thought I'd take your advice. Off to Venice tomorrow'.

I found quarters over L'Amiral, a nightclub and house of assignation where the band roared and thumped the South American rhythms, which had stormed Europe.

It played beside a *piste* in the garden immediately under my window until three or four in the morning. Sometimes, for the door could not be locked, people would come purposefully into my room... Me-egh! On particularly festive nights the establishment... megh-megh... would raffle a goat, me-egh... This animal was kept in a shed but one night somebody let it out and it climbed the household stairs bleating indignantly. Everybody opened their bedroom doors and yelled instructions up and down the stairwell. It was far noisier than the band.

King George VI, – recently crowned after the traumas of Edward VIII, paid a state visit to France. The French took the whole thing with organised light-heartedness. At St Tropez there was, of course, a *fête Brittanique*; this was not a *bravade* (of which more later) but *sui generis*. They decorated everything with those odd-looking continental Union Jacks. The *maire* made a splendid speech from a tribune below the statue of the Baillie de Suffren, an admiral native of the town who had distinguished himself against the British; the band of the *sapeurs-pompiers* burst into the Marseillaise, and then began on a remarkable version of God Save the King. When it reached the end, the band started it again and set off along the quay pursued by the whole population. It went on playing this God Save tune all over St Tropez. It is the only time that I ever danced to it. We got very drunk in honour of an alliance of which much was hoped and little expected.

For France at that time was abject. Nobody cared a hoot for anything. The army, whose wine ration had just been trebled to subsidise the Algerian vineyards, was badly equipped and ill-disciplined. The Minister for the Interior, ultimately responsible for the *Police des Moeurs*, owned the biggest chain of brothels. Ministers were paid half a year's non-returnable salary in advance on taking up office, and made a nice little bonus by reshuffling every two months, under a constitution with a virtually indissoluble parliament. I met a high civil servant who had served under 40 ministers of Agriculture.

The symbol of life was the *petit apéritif*, which people drank from 11.00am onwards. The nation lived in a golden slightly alcoholic haze. It used to be said that you never saw a Frenchman drunk; it would have been truer to say that you never saw one wholly sober. The dreadful slaughter of the First World War had torn the fibre out of them and there was a determination not to fight another war.

The tendency to shield oneself from reality by alcohol was repeated at the political level by the use of concrete. The Maginot Line was to be the nice cheap way of isolating France from the nasty Germans. Life could go on, happy and carefree while a few well paid engineers and gunners with lots of lovely machinery kept the Boche out on one side while the Royal Navy did it on the other. Meanwhile strikes held up trains, postal services, production. The franc fell to a newer low every day. Even the vaunted *routes nationales* were mostly dust and pot-holes, while the Germans and Italians were building systematic motorways.

The odd thing about this was that the nation was emotionally very involved with a war on the doorstep of the *midi*. The Spanish Civil War was reaching its confused and tragic conclusion; and demonstrating again the moral paralysis of the French. France's only Spanish friends, the starving Basques and Catalans, were struggling across the passes to be maltreated by the *gardes mobiles*, yet the left wing south was raising funds for the ideologically bankrupt republicans, who preferred to fight each other rather than their enemy. In the summer of 1938 elderly bullfighters were touring the cities to raise money for their compatriots in the Languedoc refugee cages. There was tremendous enthusiasm. The ancient Roman amphitheatres were pressed into service and everybody went. We all went to the *corrida* at Fréjus.

I have no idea how much money they raised, but my introduction to bull fighting was hardly impressive. I refuse to be drawn into the interminable arguments about the cruelties of blood sports in general and bull fighting in particular. Some people are sickened or not by such sights, or by the road accident figures.

This corrida at Fréjus was so badly conducted that I, totally new to the sport, could see how bad it was. The maire presided with his lady, a very large person in an enormous hat. I had an urchin-perch on top of a ruined buttress, from which I could see the trumpeter: a thin, tobacco-stained little man with a boater on the back of his head. He stayed well behind the tribune, and it was his function by well directed tootles on his cornet, to signal the different parts of the performance. The place was packed: perhaps 5,000 people, sitting on benches and steps. A man said to me: – 'If the bull is any use, he'll come out on his own. If not, they drop the trap on his arse'.

Mounting heat and excitement. Tootle, tootle, tootle. Up went the trap. Loud yells from somewhere in the darkness inside. Then the bull shot out like a rocket, straight at the matador, his *quadrilla* and the *banderillero* who were there because the ceremonial procession had not quite ended. Alarms, excursions! Confusion! They all got out of the way somehow and the bull, unable to stop, ran smack into one of the wooden refuges, demolished it and knocked itself out. Everybody laughed like a drain. The trumpeter, it was said, had mistaken the mayor's lady's signal. I thought that he was merely practising.

After much recrimination the real corrida got under way. They dropped the trap on the second bull, who charged the *picador's* heavily padded carthorse and pressed it against the palisade. The crowd was shouting at the picador, a Frenchman, who naturally shouted back. He was a heap of a man, all twenty stone of him, and he held the bull's second charge off with his blunted lance until the quadrilla distracted it. There was, fortunately, a wind presaging a *mistral*. It kept us cool in the general excitement. It also blew the mayoress's hat into the arena, where it gradually engrossed popular attention. Everybody yelled advice about the hat.

The great feature of a corrida is the crowd. They are witnessing a scene of blood and danger in which they become passionately involved. They are not, as at a football match, betting on one side or the other. The bull is always killed unless he happens to lay out every man jack in the arena. It is the performance and the risk taken in killing him which counts: the virile grace, skill and courage which every male wants to show to his girl and which every girl wants shown to her. The clumsy, the ugly, the cowardly let down everyone in the audience. A really good bullfighter would, regardless of the pawing bull, have picked up that hat and given it back with courtly formality in the dust, and the Lady, no doubt, would have given him a rose for it. Actually a policeman vaulted the palisade and collected it. He was the hero of the minute.

I will not detail the remainder of that day of hilarious disaster; the *mariposa* which went wrong, the horse which bucked its *picador*, and, finally, the *matador* who turned out to be deaf and blind in one eye. He made four passes at the fifth bull, and missed each time. The killing pass is very difficult. You have to wait six feet in front of the bull till he has lowered his head to charge, and then go in with the point of the sword between the two highest vertebrae of his neck. If you get home, he crumples. If not, there is hell to pay. This matador was chased all over the ring. At the fifth pass he lost his sword in the side of the wretched animal's neck, and it had to be hooked out. Meanwhile the crowd passed from amiable barracking to abuse of a full-throated and surprisingly Hispanic kind. Even my friend John Orbach, not a Spanish expert, was bawling Spanish obscenities. Then they began to throw things. First, paper, then banana peel, then fruit and eggs. Half a melon landed in the arena with a squunch. Finally, in a fury they began hurling bits of the Roman ruins. One half tile sailed over and knocked a spectator cold. As the ambulances arrived, the maire and his lady left in suitable dudgeon.

In 1988 I broadcast this description of a *corrida* on Radio 4. I had a letter from a lady in Loughborough. She said that the gusto with which I described it showed that I was the lowest of the low. I replied that I described it as it seemed at the time, and that in my experience people who take her line are more interested in class warfare than animal welfare.

The contrast between these divided, disloyal, and egocentric Latins and the still confident and united British had lately been resoundingly confirmed by a series of popular royal occasions. There was the wedding of the Duke of Kent with the beautiful Princess Marina. Then came the Silver Jubilee of King George V followed, a few months later by his death, and then after Edward VIII's interlude, the coronation of George VI. I was remarkably well placed to witness these brilliant events: through Pater's talents I saw the three celebrations from inside the forecourt of Buckingham Palace, and the funeral from the steps of St George's Chapel at Windsor. Whatever the unease of politics or the troubles of economics (Ernie Bevin tried to organise a bus strike during the coronation holidays) the millions were at one in this: it was their country, their crown, their family and they belonged to each other. This, too, was the prevailing spirit at Elizabeth II's jubilee in 1977. Without it, we could not have survived 1940. It is, of course, an important target of Marxist disruption, left wing jealousy and Murdoch profiteering.

After a time even *L'Amiral* was too expensive. Mussels were the cheapest food. I got to hate the sight of them. So we went up to Ramatuelle. The houses of this mediaeval hill village were built as a pirate-resistant circular outer wall with the much higher Maison du Seigneur in the middle. Above it is a heather-clad ridge called, after the ruins of windmills, the Moulins de Paillasse. Africa reaches the hills behind which are called the Mountains of the Moors. I have seen scorpions, Mama Scorpion and her little ones in the goat tracks up there, and locusts and Praying Mantises too. Looking downhill from the embattled village, the vineyards with their farmhouses and cork trees filled the landscape to the glistening seven mile sands of Pampelonne and the sea. *Le bon Dieu*, I supposed, ordained that docks and nettles should grow together and corks and vines in the same soil. The sands (now called Tahiti) were accessible only from one end, along a narrow cart-track from St Tropez, which was so rough that few people visited them. There was a primitive bar, and if you walked a mile along the open beach everyone bathed naked, in spite of the byelaws.

I had a hot small cheap room in the annex to Madame Battini's hotel. The mattress was stuffed with hay and small insects. These used to bite my feet until I bought flee-powder. It mattered little. It was so hot that I seldom slept more than three hours at a time. I had brought a basket full of Roman Law books: Gaius, Justinian and so forth in an idealistic effort to make up in vacation what I neglected in Oxford. My studies were desultory because of the heat, and would not, I am sure, have stood up to the test of a degree examination, but they must have sunk into my subconscious. When I was very young I noticed that knowledge sank into the subconscious and then popped up again. Bad, as I have said, at learning by rote, I learned to repeat things to myself before I went to sleep and found them fixed in my memory next day, as if they had always been there. Most people have the elusive experience of disregarding, to their misfortune, a 'first instinct'. I think that this is probably subconscious knowledge which will not rise to the surface readily enough. There is a defect in communications between the depth and the surface which may be due to, or perhaps actually represents, a shortage of confidence. I am trying very hard to write these memoirs from these largely buried recollections, without trying to rationalise them too much or to trace them too precisely to their origins. It follows that some of these will have suffered distortions because one's mental machinery, being organically not mechanically based, is not a static contrivance. Imagine a television set whose quality of image and sound depended on what it had last eaten, or whether it had a cold or had had a row with its maker.

We were not fixed in our hillside fastness. We walked or cadged lifts to Gassin or Grimaud – hill villages both; to Cogolin round the Gulf, where they make the best briar pipes in the world; and once to Garde Freinet, high in the heather, where for a few years in the tenth Century the Arabs established a military colony. The landscape has changed a good deal since this time. Brigitte Bardot has attracted the swarms. The villages have expanded. There are yachting marinas and fashionable villas. Above all, the innumerable and enormous umbrella pines had gone, felled by German troops to make fields of fire.

One thing, however, has not gone. The *Bravade*. This word means a triumph or defiance. In about 1629 a Spanish armada appeared off St Tropez and, after a desperate battle, was driven off by the gallant people of the town. The anniversary is still celebrated. About a fortnight before, the maire issues a grand proclamation extolling the bravery of his people and recounting the stirring events of that day, which all are bidden to celebrate with music, dancing, fireworks – and water jousting. The booze-up begins after breakfast at the harbour. Each jousting boat has a stage like a mediaeval forecastle on which its mighty champion, armed with a scaffolding pole, stands. The boats, then rowing boats, charge past each other, and the champions try to throw their opponent off his swaying castle as they pass. If they miss, as they often do, they go round and charge again. It is a slow sport, but everybody gets very excited; and a champion may easily unhorse himself by his own efforts. Nowadays they have dieselised the *bravade*, which is a pity, for there is nothing like a crew of pastis-fuelled oarsmen for churning things up.

Ultimately the armada was driven back to the Iles d'Hyères, where much of it was wrecked. Old Spanish custom. Of these beautiful islands one, the Ile du Levant, was a nudist colony. It was a measure of the good side of the French that nobody then regarded this island as in any way odd or made it the object of prurient curiosity. I was on the way to the neighbouring island of Port Cros in a steamer which stopped to discharge some cargo. The girl clerks at a table on the quayside checking off the bills of lading were as naked as the day they were born. In truth Ile du Levant was not a colony but a refuge from the inhibitions of the town rat race. Now that the French have recovered from their depressed state, under the leadership of Charles de Gaulle and his puritanical wife, they have become less tolerant. The government has stepped in and every year takes over a little more of the island, allegedly in the interests of national defence. Slowly the visitors – for anyone could go – are being driven away.

Chapter 21

LOVE

Conflicting private experiences now began to coincide with the political madness of the nations. It was agreed that war was inevitable. The German airship *Graf Zeppelin* sailed, one day, over Pipits Hill and was suspiciously greeted by our friends. If Werner and I did not return to Germany we would be hanged for treason if we fell into German hands. We had not the slightest intention of going back, and therefore we would have to fight for our adopted country and increase the risk of capture. It seemed foolhardy to advertise our origin by keeping our very distinctive name, and besides, people remembered how loyal citizens with German names had been treated in Britain last time. A little camouflage might help. We converted Arnold Baker into a double barrelled surname with the aid of a hyphen and trooped, if two can troop, down to Pater's office to execute the deed poll. English law is funny about this. You can change your surname twice a week without any formality, but a baptised Christian name can be legally changed as Fanny did only at confirmation. A deed poll did not change your name, it merely recorded what you had decided to do already. It was convenient to have one, because bankers and other important persons thought that it was official. Werner hushed up his 'Werner', and called himself 'Richard', law or no law. He was logical and sensible. I was not. I was called Charles in England anyway and I stuck to the Wolfgang and the Werner, and still keep them. Why? The reason is, I hope, already plain as a pikestaff. I did not want to repudiate my tribe. It is the one decision in my life which I still regard as hateful. My son Henry reverted to the old name when he came of age. He did not, as it happens, bother with a deed poll.

While all this was going on, I slid into love. Some people fall flat. A neighbour at Chobham met a girl at a dance, proposed to her over supper and was accepted before Auld Lang Syne. Not a bit like me. I had been brought up to be suspicious of girls. I was seventeen when Richard's friend Christopher Rhodes brought his gorgeous Mary Kesteven to Pipits Hill. She was the first woman who ever treated me as someone to be respected, and I still feel grateful to her. At Oxford I knew dozens of girls in a cheerful unsophisticated way, but these were flirtations. I was sufficiently aware of my ignorance of sex to go out of my way to find out. I had no one except myself to trust; so in Paris I picked up a sympathetic looking little whore, and she carted me off to a tatty hotel near the Boulevard Bonne Nouvelle. I explained that I was a virgin. She was enchanted. She had, she said, a fetish about it. She certainly had. She was poor; her scent was cheap; and her voice rattled with *argot*; but she could not have been nicer or have taken more trouble, and I dare say that she enjoyed it too. I spent hours and hours with her and the fee was minimal.

Amongst my many Oxford friends it was natural for groups and combinations in clubs, boating parties and so forth, to shift and re-form all the time, but sometimes by the operation of chance, odd individuals tended to recur. I do not remember when I met Fanny for the first time, but I do remember an early occasion when I remarked, naively, that she was looking matronly that evening. I was in fact commenting on her rather full and handsome evening dress. Her swain asked her, apparently, whether he should knock my block off. But somehow we were often together, and after a while I found that she filled my mind when we were separated. Other people noticed this very soon, and began to ask us to parties together; my mother, naturally, observed it too. There was a moment in a hotel in Bourg-en-Bresse when I was writing a letter, and she sat down opposite me and put on a well organised show of understanding misery. She had behaved in exactly the same way to Richard.

In fact Richard kept himself to himself only by living an elaborate cover story. He coaxed a car out of my parents, and he also played a great deal of tennis. What more natural, then, than to go off for days and especially nights playing in tennis tournaments, of whose real existence I have never been quite convinced. My mother certainly had her suspicions, for she took to opening his letters and eventually came upon something which led to a flaming family row. He was in a weak position because he had no job and no money, but at this point he set about getting work with a will, and managed to hook for himself the perfect appointment, - no mean achievement because jobs were very scarce. It was well paid: it was respected: it was far from home. After some training he was sent to the British Consulate in Zürich.

For some considerable time, he had taken up with Mary Norris. Quietly spoken, she was a person of curious and sudden mental habits. She seldom reacted to anything conventionally. On one occasion she announced a dish of Arroz Cubana as 'buggered eggs'; on another she sent me, out of the blue, an excellent novel *Ma Wei Slope* about the Chinese courtesan Yang Kwei-fei; but she was not spectacularly beautiful, and Richard once described her whimsically as 'cross-eyed with legs like soda-water bottles'. Actually she resembled the actresses in Japanese acting prints. They carried on this surprising liaison in a flat in the Edgware Road.

I do not know what Pater thought about Mary but my mother was very nasty, and when it came to my 21st birthday party in the summer of 1939 she refused to invite her. On the other hand she could not very well refuse to invite my own nominees; if only because I had taken a great deal of trouble not to tell her anything much about anyone. Indeed the family upbraided me so much with never bringing my friends home, that I once invited a surprised numismatist about whom I cared nothing to stay for a whole week. It shut them up for a bit. At that 21st birthday, however, I hoisted my colours, by putting Fanny at my right, so my mother sang the praises of some other girl for weeks. She also invited mutual girl-friends of Fanny's and mine and discussed her with them. Loyalty and social decency meant nothing to her. Also it never occurred to her that these conversations would be faithfully and amusedly reported.

I had, at that time, a Magdalen acquaintance who was equally capable of occupying people's conversational time. This was Anthony de Hoghton of Hoghton Towers, Hoghton, Lancs. He looked like a sort of pig with very fair hair and a large fair jowly moustache, white eyelashes and that pink complexion which turns purple in later life. He was bulky and his walk was an energetic strut. When he got drunk, which happened often enough, he would become unpredictable. Years later he entered without warning the children's play room at Joan Conquest's, took the table by the edges, turned it upside down with one mighty heave and marched out glowering, leaving the two boys to pick up flowers, crockery, and wrecked railway trains from the flooded carpet. He always invited himself to other people's parties, though he was no sponger, and I, who rather liked him, found it convenient to invite him to mine. He and I used to discuss Thomism, in which he was learned, over breakfast in hall. He was extravagant in a lordly but unaffected way. He climbed into the commemoration ball at the nearby women's college of St Hilda, because he thought that someone there might like some Champagne and he happened to have a magnum handy. So up and over he went, and tumbled head first into the Dons' Common Room. He was received with courtesy by the learned ladies, who gravely conducted him to the front gate, not forgetting to restore the bottle which had rolled under a sofa. His extravagance led him into trouble with his father, Sir Cuthbert, who indited *grandis epistola a Capreis*, where he had been enjoying himself with his latest mistress. His menacing arrival being imminent, Anthony invited me to lunch in his rooms in the Cloister.

It was a thunderous lunch. Anthony had borrowed money, put it all on a horse which came in at eleven to one, paid all his debts and was showing a balance. The Baronet, who was hoping to enjoy a splendid triumph with his mistress, a slight, handsome and not very fashionable French girl, was balked and furious. Father and son were separated by the dining table: I sat opposite the girl. Sir Cuthbert looked exactly like his son only larger, redder, more porcine. They talked in the same way: that is to say that between long intervals of silent fury, one of them would deliver some darkly complicated allusion directed at the other but said to her or to me.

'You are, of course, familiar with the subjects favoured by Stubbs?' rumbled Papa at me.

'The bishop?' I said, as innocently as I could. Pause.

'I think that Bassanio was a calculating character', rumbled Anthony to the girl.

'Moi... je préfère le lac Majeur'. Pause.

I do not know how much crosser these ponderous cross-purposes might have become, but Sir Cuthbert was restless by the sweet and barely looked at the cheese. We drank the coffee after they went. The boarders had been repelled.

Back to love.

Fanny, though slightly younger, had come up to the university a year earlier than I. She was a Home Student, that is to say, a member of the oldest women's college now renamed St Anne's. So she was due to go down a year before me and took her Schools (finals) in 1939. We decided to celebrate her departure with an illicit night in Magdalen. This was exactly a week before my 21st.

I spent the Long Vacation partly abroad with my mother, very bored and lovesick. We said a ceremonial farewell at Mulhouse to Richard, who might be isolated for years by war. Then several of us, including Fanny, stayed first with friends in Somerset; and then a fortnight at Low Park in Cumberland. I was late, and brought my books in a borrowed wheelbarrow, but it was idyllic despite approaching war clouds, and in spite, also of my mother sending telegrams followed by the police demanding my instant return home. Naturally I returned with all the others when the fortnight was over, thinking that the end of the world was at hand. We all did. Fanny and I bade tearful farewells on the footbridge over Crewe station. And so home to another furious row but I had discovered that, as a last year undergraduate, I was entitled to have my call-up deferred.

So, back I went to Magdalen, or rather to 'digs' in Longwall, kept by a dried out spinster called Miss Smith. Fanny appeared and, with a girlfriend, took a flat in Park Town, a nice Regency crescent on the edge of North Oxford. She was over the quarters of an old and tolerant county court judge. We actually heard about the outbreak of war in a pub in Henley, where we listened to Neville Chamberlain on the radio. Brought up, as we all were, on *The Shape of Things to Come* and other horrendous anti-war propaganda, we expected that Armageddon would begin London-wards within the hour. So we all piled into our jalopy and drove like mad for Oxford. Apart from a general air-alarm, which seemed momentarily to corroborate our nightmare, absolutely nothing, as history records, happened.

Nothing, indeed, went on happening at our end of Europe, while the Poles were smashed and betrayed. The Russians had a walkover. Half the Poles thought that they were coming to help, and were surprised and disarmed and rounded up in thousands. The Russians had it all worked out: the class war was imposed to the final cartridge. They sorted out 15,000 officers and senior N.C.Os, caged them at Katyn and murdered the lot. Then they planted a birchwood over the death pits and hoped that no one would find out. For some months the Polish government in exile made innocent inquiries about their whereabouts, especially after Hitler turned on his ally. Innocence turned to suspicion and then to horrible certainty in London, before the invading Germans stumbled upon the evidence and published it. The Russians, of course, said that the Germans had done it. It was all of a piece with Auschwitz, they said. It was all of a piece with the Russian revolutionary practice of the time; and I read the evidence later in the war. Anyone who believed that the Russians did not perpetrate this massacre, would believe anything.

But we, in the West had the same lotus-eater's disease as the French, if in a less virulent form. If the Maginot Line would somehow make war hygienic for France, the Channel plus a little propaganda might do the same for us. It was thought that there was a real Germany ready to burst its Nazi bonds and stop this disatrous nonsense; so the R.A.F. was employed, believe it or not, for weeks showering propaganda leaflets in German upon the earth beneath. A realistic pilot who tipped his load out without bothering to untie the parcel was met with: -

'Good God, man. You might have hurt somebody.'

So the autumn wore into winter, and apart from odd minor shortages life, in a general way, was exactly as before. I now worked even harder at enjoying myself. When we were not talking, eating or drinking Fanny and I were in bed – usually till twenty minutes before midnight, when I would hurl on my clothes and bicycle back to my digs for the statutory midnight closure. What Miss Smith surmised about it all became very clear when my mother called, and she spoke to her about Miss Woods.

Like the winter of 1938-9, there was a great frost in that first winter of the war. The Thames froze across, and the Cherwell was frozen solid. I skated for miles up it, and even ventured out onto the Thames as far as Iffley. The university, meanwhile, began to take notice of the war. It invented something called a war degree, for which you could take pass examinations immediately, and these would mature into a degree in three years from matriculation, if you were called up prematurely. I took these examinations as a precaution. I have no idea now, in what subjects I took them. Anyway, I passed. In the summer of 1940 I took my proper honours degree in History, so that I finished with two degrees, but there was some kind of hitch. I was called up in the late summer and asked the college to get me my degree *in absentia*. Something went wrong, for I am listed under the year 1944, not 1940. I once asked to have this mistake rectified, but nothing happened. Perhaps nothing can. Is a degree indelible like baptism or knighthood? Supposing that you passed your examinations for a degree in Botany, but at the degree ceremony you strayed into the wrong batch and got dubbed a Doctor of Music by accident, are you for ever a D.Mus (Bot)?

Years later I went to Buckingham Palace to receive an O.B.E. (Other Buggers Efforts). There were all these people being put in pens and ushered along corridors and galleries to the State Ballroom and Her Majesty. At various checkpoints somebody marked one off on a list. I asked one of the equerries what would happen if somebody got the wrong gong. He said simply: -

'It hasn't happened yet, but we all get nightmares about it.'

Frieda Hostrup took this brilliant picture in Munich in June 1922. Kätzchen ("Little Cat") fell from the fourth floor balcony onto the pavement of the Theatinerstrasse, and recovered sitting in the sun on the balcony wall. I used to talk to her and we became friends. In the 1960s in the Temple, Wooter, our cat there had toothache and I soothed it away by massaging his jaw. Thereafter he regularly visited me. I am frightened of dogs, but, embarrassingly, they seem to like me...

My German grand-parents Vally von Blumenthal and his wife Cornelia née Kayser. He had earned his Iron Cross in the 1866 war. He had money but she was rich. This picture does not show that he was short and she diminutive.

The Hainsworths. Large persons L to R. Charles, Abimelech, Ethel, Elizabeth, Gaunt.
Small persons L to R. Wilhelmine, Helena, Harriet.
Taken in about 1888. By the year 2000 Abimelech had 400 descendents.

The ten Rhodes scholars at Oxford in 1908, taken in New College cloister. Albrecht is seated cross-legged on the ground at the left.

My parents at Grünewald near Berlin in 1912. They seem straight out of vaudeville, but Albrecht had hardly any sense of humour and Wilhelmine little more.

My stepfather, Percy, taken very
soon after the cat.

Subaltern in the Buffs, taken at
Torquay in 1941.

My father at his Bonchurch wedding in
1912. I can see why Wilhelmine fancied
him.

Me between Percy and my brother Richard. Goodbye to Richard on his way to his job in Zürich.

Katharine emerging from the Giudecca Canal.

Wilhelmine at 90 and her family. L-R Hilary (James' wife) seated. Me with Katie nearly invisible just behind me. Fanny. James, Patrick, Thuc-Nghi, Henry. On the steps Sophie, Antonia, William.

Henry and Nieves leaving the Church of San Vicente at San Sebastian after their Basque wedding. This was the occasion when the priest's acolyte wore a raincoat throughout. Virgin wreaths for the bride to sinister, swords for the groom to dexter and then they all danced in the porch.

Henry Brandon, alias Lord Brandon of Oakbrook. The ablest brain of the generation.

The author's nose at San Sebastion in 1981.

L-R. My blind cousin Ruthger wearing Croatian naval decorations, my brother Richard with American ones, Col. Wulf-Werner with a bevy of German gallantry medals, and myself OBE first, King Haakon VII last. 1988 at Hochhausen on the Neckar.

Finnish printworks. We were on a red carpet tour.

L-R Fr Symeon, Author, The Archimandrite Kyrill at the Stavropegic Monastery of St John the Baptist at Tolleshunt Knights in Essex 2. March 1994.

Blumenthal dinner. Facing L-R Leonore, Wulf-Werner standing, Sieglinde, Marion (her Rheinbaben blood showing through). Backs L-R Rosemarie, Ruthger.

Garden Party in the Inner Temple. L-R (Half off) Peter Inchbald, Fanny, Fanny's elder sister Mabel, The Principal Guest (just christened), Author.

A double illustration of the Nairne artistic penchant. A picture by Percy of his cousin Sylvester Nairne painting a landscape at Compton near Winchester in 1935.

This celebrated off-beat version of Venus wearing a hat and Cupid by my ancestor Lucas Cranach the Elder (1472–1553), is in the Royal Art Gallery in Brussels. He was a close friend of Martin Luther's and witnessed his marriage to Catherine Bora. Was she the model?

Victoria Fontaine-Wolf drew this in pastel in February 2007.
Fanny and our Ibo friend Caleb Durueke (aged six) agree that the likeness is good.

Robert Kayser = Elise Sellier

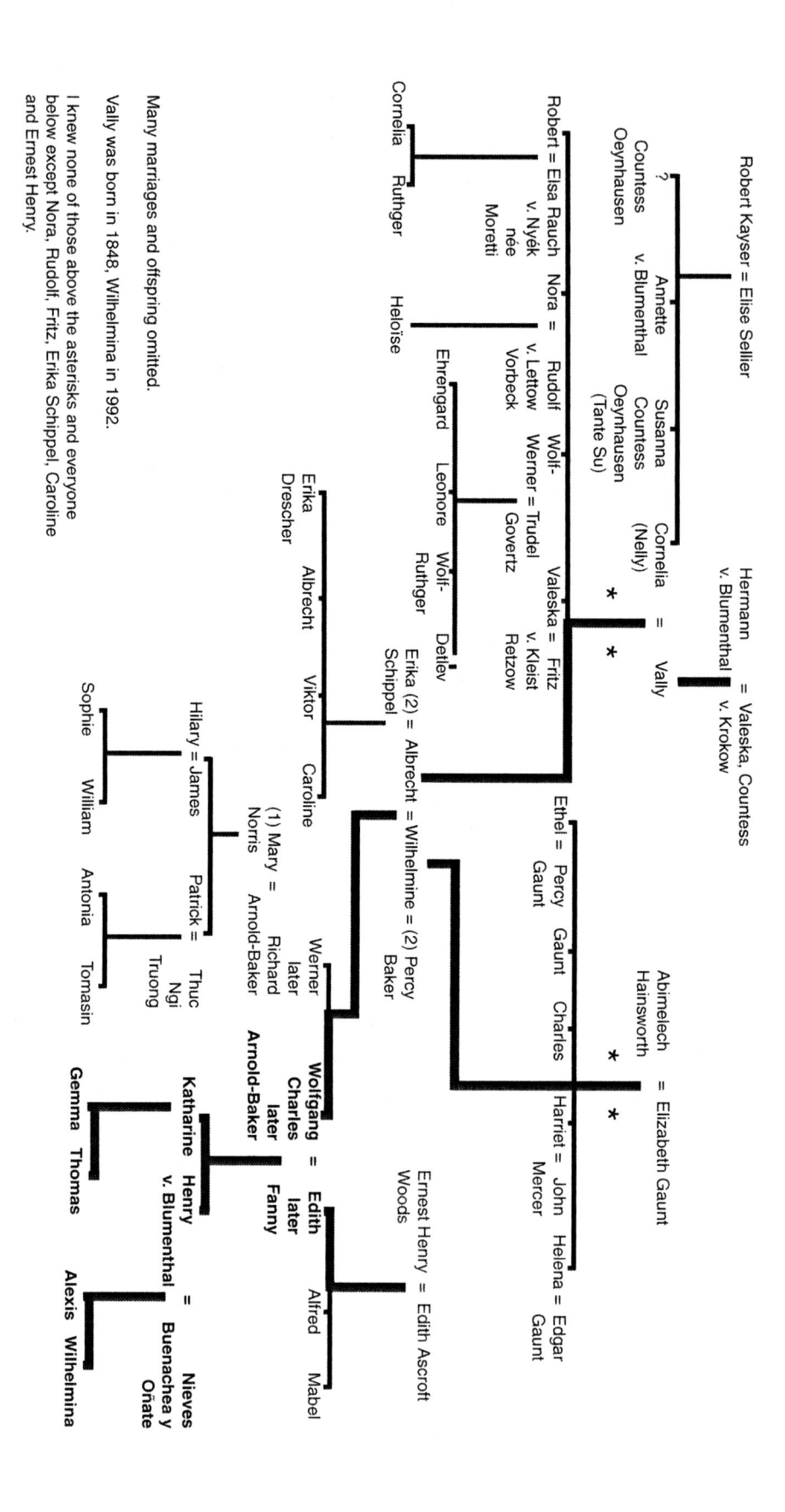

```
                                    |
    ┌───────────────────────────────┼──────────────────────┐
Countess                        Annette                Susanna           Cornelia
Oeynhausen                   v. Blumenthal            Countess            (Nelly)
                                                     Oeynhausen
                                                      (Tante Su)
    |
┌───┴────┐
Cornelia  Ruthger
```

```
Robert = Elsa Rauch     Nora =    Rudolf       Wolf-         Valeska = Fritz
         née           Heloïse  v. Lettow    Werner = Trudel          v. Kleist
         Nyék                   Vorbeck      Govertz                   Retzow
         Moretti
                                   |                |
                           ┌───────┼───────┐    ┌───┴────┐
                       Ehrengard Leonore Wolf- Erika  Albrecht
                                        Ruthger- Drescher
                                         Detlev
```

Hermann   =   Vally, Countess
v. Blumenthal   Valeska, Countess
                 v. Krokow

* *

Erika (2) = Albrecht = Wilhelmine = (2) Percy Baker
              | (1) Mary = Richard
              | Norris Arnold-Baker
        ┌─────┴──────┐ |
     Viktor   Caroline   ┌────┴────┐
                                Hilary = James   Patrick = Thuc Ngi Truong
                                  | |
                              ┌───┴───┐   ┌───┴────┐
                           Sophie William   Antonia Tomasin

Ethel = Percy Gaunt   Abimelech = Elizabeth Gaunt
         | |
    ┌────┴────┐   ┌──────┼──────┐
Werner   Charles   Harriet = John Helena = Edgar
later   Mercer   Gaunt
Wolfgang Charles   *   *
later
Arnold-Baker

         Ernest Henry = Edith Ascroft   Woods
                |
         ┌──────┴──────┐
   **Katharine   Henry = Edith   Alfred Mabel
   v. Blumenthal** later
                  Fanny
         |
    ┌────┴────┐
Gemma Thomas   **Alexis Wilhelmina**
                     Nieves
                     Buenachea y
                     Oñate
```

Many marriages and offspring omitted.

Vally was born in 1848, Wilhelmina in 1992.

I knew none of those above the asterisks and everyone below except Nora, Rudolf, Fritz, Erika Schippel, Caroline and Ernest Henry.
```

Brigantine Anna Maria von Blumenthal built near Vegesack in 1829. The White Horse in the centre of the Union Jack shows that she is Hanoverian not British. Like most continentals the artist was unable to get the Union Jack right.

A version of the usual Blumenthal arms. The Counts in the family add naked wild men armed with clubs as supporters. This Baroque one dates from about 1730, but is not the oldest; the one on the back cover is from 1882. The crest, blazoned as "a fully grown woman holding up a virgin wreath", is the same as that of the city of Magdeburg, which, however adds the motto "Who will take it?" Family mottos are uncommon in Germany and the Blumenthals do not have one. I have proposed for my own "All improvements make things worse" and "When in doubt, eat it".

Staffelde, where Albrecht was born and brought up. It remained in the family until they fled before the Russians in 1945, leaving it in flames behind them.

Magdalen in 1805. It is much the same in 2007 save that the roadway is now cluttered with vehicles.

Schlönwitz, my father's house, was originally brought into the family by the Countess Krokow. It was accidentally burnt down during World War II.

Bignasco in 1925, by Percy.

Schloss Elmau where I was more than half brought up until I was sixteen. The Wetterstein mountains, where King Ludwig II had his Schachen hunting lodge, form the background.

Abimelech's picture of Claremont, his house at Farsley between Leeds and Bradford, where he brought up his family.

Old Salters Hall Court, destroyed in the Blitz. Percy's office was just off to the right.

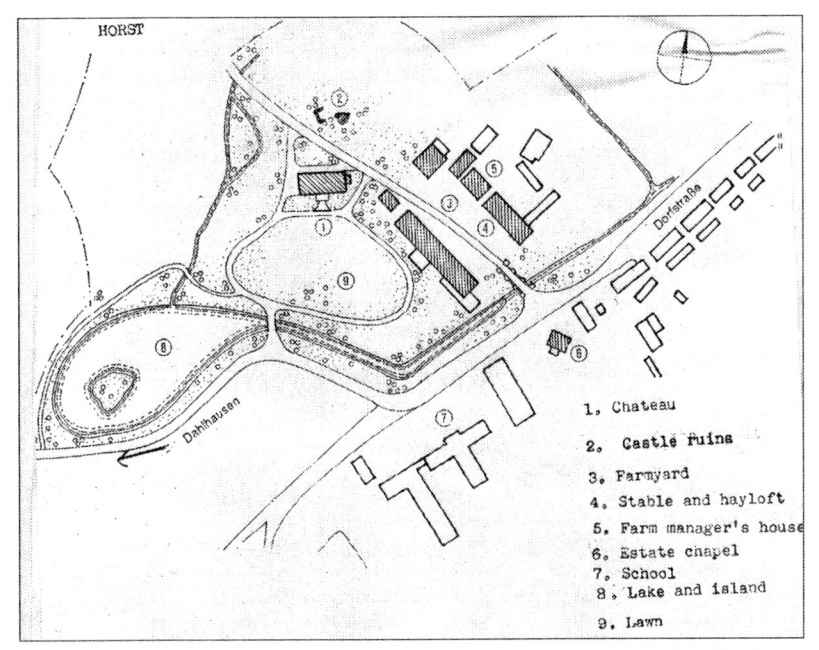

1. Chateau
2. Castle ruins
3. Farmyard
4. Stable and hayloft
5. Farm manager's house
6. Estate chapel
7. School
8. Lake and island
9. Lawn

A 1991 plan of Horst, the Blumenthal centre in the Prignitz north-west of Berlin for 600 years until they sold it to the Möllendorfs in 1824. In 1995 items 1-7 were much as when we gave it up. 8 and 9 are weedy swamps.

HORST in 1994. The estate was sold after 600 years to the von Möllendorffs in 1824. The ground floor existed then as it is. They rebuilt the upper floor as it is now. The ruins of the Castle are in the trees on the right. It was a refugee home from 1945 but deliberately neglected by the Communist government: for example the tree in the middle is self-sown and less than six feet from the nearest window, and plaster is falling off everywhere. Some floors are unsafe.

The Warden's Garden at Winchester College was flooded in 2000 and Fiona Smith took this virtually upsidedownable picture of the Chapel and belltower with Fromond's Chantry to the left behind the tree. The chantry is in the middle of the 14th century cloister and has a beautiful lierne vaulted upper room which Professor Gleadowe used as an art room.

Chapter 22

ODD MILITARY SCENES

The summons to die for my country was a pencilled flimsy so ill-written that it was hard to see if I was supposed to go to Chelsea or to Cholsey. It came while I was working at the Seamens' Hospital at Greenwich. My step-uncle Freddy was chairman of the hospital, and I lived in the Secretary's, Hugh Lyon's nice Georgian house in the hospital complex. He was a charming man who recited Lewis Carroll flawlessly, and Pater's partner Cyril Nairne was a frequent visitor. I got my keep and 10s (50p) a week. The hospital had always, since seamen came from all parts of the globe, specialised in outlandish, especially tropical diseases. The war too, was warming up; the place was over full and the offices had been cleared to make way for beds. Waist-high stacks of files and papers had been dumped higgledy-piggledy in box-rooms and attics. My job was to sort them out. This was not very easy because I could not understand their medical jargon; but it was not very arduous because nobody supervised me. I had never had any experience of files, records or offices, and anyway there was only one piece of furniture, a semi-collapsed ping-pong table. I began by borrowing a hammer and knocking nails into it.

After six weeks of dust and muddle, I had at least classified the files into groups by size of file, but what to do with the six-inch swamp of loose papers, letters, envelopes, deeds, receipts, prescriptions and God knows what besides? Downstairs Lyon was preoccupied with an enormous legacy from one Caleb Diplock, which subsequently became a *cause celèbre*. He had no suggestions to offer. A day or two later a large cheerful bustling cockney barmaid burst into the office. She produced a crumple of brown printed papers and said: -

'You was always kind to my 'ubby an' I thought you might like to 'ave these.'

Before Lyon could open his mouth, she had given a loud laugh and vanished. When we smoothed the papers, they turned out to be £3,000 worth of bearer bonds with coupons. That was the old East End.

Then I had to go to Cholsey. Pater gave me the poems of Keats for my pocket, and I set off. Fanny saw me to the back of the truck. The camp was near a requisitioned mansion at Crowmarsh Gifford, on the Thames opposite

Wallingford. The unit was the 10th Battalion of the Buffs, commanded by Brevet Colonel Lamont, a territorial. Except for the Adjutant, all the officers were territorials and a pretty scratch lot they were.

Dunkirk had just happened, and the armed forces of the Crown were, to put it mildly, in disarray. The War Office was summoning conscripts in tens of thousands to units which they could not arm, shelter or organize. This Kentish unit had Seaforth Highlander and Ulster Rifleman officers, N.C.Os partly from the Cheshire Regiment and partly from the Durham Light Infantry, and a Buffs colonel. They spoke various, sometimes mutually incomprehensible dialects, had been trained in different backgrounds with different systems of drill and had been taught to march at different speeds. There were hardly any weapons. I was in the first draft – 40 strong – and I was the last man to get a complete set of equipment and a rifle. For months afterwards there were men walking about partly dressed in civilian clothes. Worst of all, however, the N.C.Os had been through Dunkirk: some were lately promoted private soldiers without the right abilities. Many were still demoralised.

Colonel. Lamont had a Herculean task almost without support. For example: since this was a line unit, but most of the N.C.Os were riflemen, it was necessary to retrain the N.C.Os in simple drill, because rifle drill is different. Now the first thing you do with recruits is to drill them – an N.C.O's job. So how do you drill the recruits when you have to drill the N.C.Os?

If only I had not been miserable by the separation of love, it would have been a pleasant life. Military descipline was child's play compared with Winchester, and the four years in the OTC meant that, with a brushing up, I knew enough to be almost a trained soldier. The others had never in their lives done what they were told, or experienced discomfort. They found the food horrible. As it was better than OTC, I had no complaints. They moaned incessantly about crowded tents, and cold dewy nights and had to be pushed, pulled and persuaded into not fouling each other's nests. It was like living in a nursery for 600 spoilt children: yet I was supposed to be the one who had had an easy life. It was the same when we went marching. Three miles was enough for most of them – though of course they improved. I did not have these difficulties.

After about a week, I applied for a stripe. I was summoned to the presence and promoted Acting Unpaid Lance-Corporal. The very next day something happened which showed in what confusion this unit – and no doubt others – really was. There was to be a late morning P.T. session, under a P.T. colour serjeant. I discovered from daily orders, that *all* the officers and NCOs were to be away that day on a course except myself. In other words the entire battalion was in the charge of a one day old

Lance-Corporal. I had to get them to a large meadow on the map about a mile away. For this, I had to haul them all out of their tents (a job usually done by five orderly corporals). I had to parade them by companies (five serjeant-majors). I had to give them their marching orders (one adjutant). I had to march each company off in the right direction and the others without entanglement (five company commanders). And these stumbling recruits hardly knew what the words of command meant. When we reached the meadow I was greeted with: -

'Corporal, you are two minutes late.'

I don't tell this story often because it is greeted with incredulous astonishment.

An infantry assault bridge floated inexplicably to us: presumably as part of the flotsam of Dunkirk. Col. Lamont seized on this. Without weapons, we could not learn a lot of drill, nor could we learn to fight; but by God, we could learn to bridge a river. We all hugely enjoyed this. You calculated the width by sighting and reversed triangles. You divided the result by the length of the duck-boards. You laid out the mattress-like kapok floats at duck-board intervals, joined them together and then masses of men picked up the whole lot and fed it across the current. I could bridge the Thames at Crowmarsh Gifford now.

Fanny used to come down at weekends. She stayed at the *George* or the *Four Feathers*, and would wait until I got my pass. Often others would give her a drink until I turned up. This was pure good nature. There was no question of trying to steal the corporal's girl or to curry favour with him. They simply knew that all waits are long waits for lovers. Wallingford in those days was a smiling, rather beautiful country town with a life and soul whose distinct character the traffic, redevelopment and local authority housing have since killed. Migration and materialism have turned such places from human communities with internal bonds, into groups of housing units where people sleep, eat and sometimes fuck, between a more or less unwilling pursuit of wages mostly somewhere else. The lack of personal attachment to the local scene destroys the will to care for it, and the authorities, infected by a purely statistical approach, knock the national heritage about the ears of the inhabitants without much thought. It is significant that amenity and preservation movements are now arising to defend what is left. Previously they were unnecessary.

After a couple of months of that brilliant summer, the battalion was remarkably naif. Many thought of the officers as their employers: on pay days there were ructions if pay was not exact. The army habit of paying out in units of half a crown meant uneven weekly payments, for we were being paid two shillings a day. People seriously thought that the officers kept the change. Then because I 'spoke funny', I was thought to have special influence with the colonel or somebody, and odd characters tried to commission me to seek favours. It is not easy to turn a crowd of civilians into a force of soldiers.

These times were emphatically not the best, but at least, by now, everybody had a rifle of some sort. I was lucky; I had an SMLE which I knew, from Winchester days, how to handle. I was a good shot. Most, however, were stuck with P 14s or even older, and these not only kicked like a mule, but were hard to clean and being vulnerable to grit, could become suddenly unworkable, and had then to be taken to pieces. I could manage; and I was very busy helping uncomprehending unfortunates out of trouble.

By now the Germans had occupied the French coast, and were mounting the great cross-Channel enterprise which would sweep the British away and set the seal on their New Order. So the 10th Buffs and its only Bren gun was brigaded with the 7th and 8th for coast defence. I had been appointed a *paid* acting Lance-Corporal to do the job of the Battalion intelligence serjeant. The battalion HQ went to Brixton (Devon) and our function was to dig ourselves in on the coast and fill up every accessible place with obstacles and booby traps. As we had no transport worthy of the name, we would have to do or die on the beaches and hope that someone else would counter attack.

The whole of the population was in this. The spirit of that time was one of sober determination. We dug trenches and erected sand-bagged redoubts, while civilian contractors covered the beaches with tank-traps of concrete or steel scaffolding. Whatever else there was, there was plenty of barbed wire, both the ordinary and the Dannert, with which we festooned the landscape. The local authorities removed all the signposts and they painted out all the names on the railway station name boards. Farmers arranged to make their gates blockable. Brick and concrete pill boxes from that era still decorate the fields.

The air raids strengthened morale. In our neighbourhood Plymouth was attacked night after night. It made us feel that we were all in it together against this indiscriminate violence. The making of war directly on civilians was still a novelty which provoked a moral reaction. Lots of civilians armed themselves unofficially and made up their minds to 'take at least one with them'. The Local Defence Volunteers (later the Home Guard) were issued with pikes. Fanny joined the part time Women's Home Defence in order to learn to shoot. Gamekeepers mixed their buckshot with candlewax. An elderly lady of my acquaintance in Plymstock bought herself a cheesecutter. She had it all worked out. She removed three uprights from her landing banisters, so that she could drop the wire over the head of the first German who came up. London was having a rough time. Fanny, a housing manager, was stuck there. Her war was much worse than mine. Londoners went to work by day as usual and then had to endure the uproar and variegated dangers and discomforts of the Blitz by night. It went on for months, and people were haggard for shortage of sleep, and if not injured themselves, distraught for others. And meantime the destruction went on and the unpredictable mess in the streets disorganised life. Pater went one day to the office at Salters Hall Court and found that it had vanished. He was less ill-placed than many other similar businesses. On my brother's advice he had had all his vital records photographed before the outbreak, and could now extract them from his bank in Sunningdale. One sees pictures of cheerful grubby people making V-signs, but the aspect which is not so often mentioned is the quiet matter-of-factness of diurnal and nocturnal life, and the way in which people helped each other without thinking much about it. A semi-crippled night watchman is making tea on an old coal stove. A bomb falls at the end of the street. Amid the falling bricks and timber, everybody turns out to help the rescue squad. Somehow the old man has become the tea dispenser for 50 dusty throats. Nobody asked him, but somebody may owe his life to him.

Travel was extraordinary. Bombing might delay or divert trains which, like everything else, were blacked out. The window-glass was covered with glued stockinette to minimise splintering, and you could not see through it. The names of the darkened stations were almost indecipherably tiny, and far more were on the move than the trains were meant to hold. People took turns to sit down. The corridors might be jammed with luggage, impedimenta and snoring soldiers. Travellers were injured by getting out of the wrong side of a train, because they could not see where they were, or fighting their way to the door, and carried past their destinations. A night journey from London to Plymouth might take eight or ten hours. There was not, then, an alternative system of transport. You went by train, or you did not go.

Fanny managed to come down to South Devon most weekends. The journeys might be intimidating, but, as she said they were worth it even if, as sometimes happened, we were unable to meet. The deliverance from the pressure of London life into the peace of the Devonshire countryside (even with two appalling journeys as the price) made things bearable until the next time. In comparison with this, my only alleged hardship was to live in a bell tent with five others for those six cold months. I enjoyed it enormously, and was very indignant when, on grounds of health, we were flung out into a smelly concrete-floored tin boiler house from whose roof the condensation dripped onto our beds. The military medical authorities have strange ideas.

In November 1940 I was seconded to the Brigade HQ at Totnes as Brigade Intelligence Corporal. This involved no promotion, but was more interesting.

My main job was to know the brigade area (The South Hamms) thoroughly, and this I did by bicycle or by thumbing lifts. I visited every village, town, cove – and pub. The purpose was to mark up the rather incomplete brigade maps, for maps were in short supply, and military features such as newly dug trench systems were appearing daily. The Brigadier needed to know what places had completed their defences and what not. Progress reports were supposed to come in from outlying detachments – which might consist of no more than a few isolated men. Such reports, not being always reliable, or even intelligible, somebody had to go and look, and the brigade staff was too small to spare an officer for this, for more than 5% of the time. So a lance-corporal and his boss, a serjeant, did it.

This serjeant told me one of those bomb stories which ought to be true. He had been on the Tower Guard during part of the blitz, and they made it a point of honour to parade the Keys with full ceremony every evening as it had always been done for 600 years. One evening, when there was a particularly noisy air-raid, he was in charge of the Escort, and in due form was challenged by the sentry: -

'Halt! Who goes there?'

'The Keys'.

'Whose Keys?'

'King George's Keys'.

At that moment there was an almighty explosion and everyone fell down except the right hand of the guard. There was a small pause and much scrambling. And then the right hand of the guard said firmly:

'Pass King George's Keys. All's well'.

Now for the Great Totnes Bathing Hut Event. I had found a disused landing strip on the top of Bolt Head. It was just the place, at the entrance to the Kingsbridge Estuary, for a German parachute landing, and I told Brigadier Hewitt. He promptly sent a company up there. There was no shelter in the bitter gales on that table top above the roaring sea, and when I went up again I found the troops huddled in open trenches. The brigade Q staff started the rigmarole for doing something about it, but the company commander beat them to it. At Paignton vast wire entanglements cut off the esplanade from the beach huts, now unusable, for the duration. He borrowed them with the help of some friendly tank-transporters. As the bathing huts rounded the sharp turn at the top of Totnes main street, one of them knocked a corner off a house. It made it easier to get the others up to Bolt Head. The huts were now set up in a neat row on top of the headland, and the troops, like Caesar's, went into winter quarters. Everything would have been fine if the Town Fathers of Totnes had not complained. Then the council at Paignton woke up too and said: -

'Where the hell are our bathing huts?'

Nobody seemed to know. The Brigadier made soothing noises, but suddenly there was talk of compensation. The matter was a mystery till Paignton and Totnes put their heads together. Then the Brigadier saw behind the hill. I verified his wild surmise,

'Very enterprising of him,' he said to Liddell Hart, who happened to be there, 'Have I, by any chance, signed a requisition order?'

This was January. In February they were so short of officers that they offered me an immediate commission, thus by-passing the fearsome OCTUs.[*] I could hardly believe my luck. I returned to the 10th Buffs, put up my pips and was given a drink by Col. Lamont. Then I went on leave, bought the necessary camp bed and finery (beautifully cut by Adamsons in Oxford) and joined the 8th Battalion at Paignton.

This battalion was properly armed, so my platoon had its three Bren guns, its anti-tank rifle and its two-inch mortar, besides rifles, bayonets, pistols and things, all of which had to be carried by individuals. I lament the passing of the old bayonet. This admirable eighteen-inch hard steel instrument looked splendid on parade; you could reach a long way with it if you had to stick it into a German, and properly sharpened it was admirable for chopping up fire wood, cutting a loaf or a joint, or punching holes for the condensed milk. I doubt if those who devised the absurd little skewer which superseded it, ever had to live the rough and tumble army life, very little of which has much to do with an enemy.

The battalion, though as usual short of transport, had to make itself more mobile than the tenth, and so I had to make my people go on long route marches. I remember a gorgeous three day march in May, all alone with my blokes, strung out along the roads to ensure that we did not all get murdered by a single burst. We swung along the Devonshire lanes from Paignton to Ashburton singing.

At Ashburton I asked for quarters, and the local Bobby suggested asking the Portreeve, which I did. He said: -

'You can have the Guildhall after the concert; why not bring your chaps to it?'

They made speeches about us and gave us tea, and then we slept happily on the floor. Next day we marched through Buckfastleigh, where the monks fed us and showed us round, and so back to Paignton, 75 miles in three days and everyone as happy as larks. One reason for this was that my batman could cook. There is something humanly satisfying in such simple things. I would stand about seeing that everyone really had been fed. Then, one day, one of my corporals suddenly saw to it that I was. I felt that I was, at last, earning my commission.

That platoon became very self respecting. One of the activities of that period was the raising of war funds. The best remembered is probably 'Dig for Victory',

---

[*] Officer Cadet Training Unit.

where bits of land were acquired by parish councils and everyone grew food on them to reduce the pressure on the Atlantic convoys. Paignton organised a fund-raising event and we were asked to take part in the great patriotic parade. I inspected my blokes before the procession and thought that they looked good. Then we marched stolidly from Brixham to Torquay in the sunlight, and the crowds clapped and cheered us all the way. I do not know how much money we raised, but they were certainly very good for our morale.

Of course it was all too good to be true. I was suddenly posted to the 70th Buffs at Shorncliffe in Kent. 70th or Young Soldiers battalions were so numbered to make them obviously different. Indeed they were. They had been another panicky aberration of the War Office. The age of conscription was 18½, but somebody suggested that boys of 16½ should be allowed to volunteer for these specially formed 70ths. It had never occurred to those who dreamed up this beautiful idea that in a world where you could earn £20 a week (2000 equivalent, about £190) on demolition in the bombed cities, anybody who volunteered for the military fourteen shillings must have something wrong with him. Apart from a few eccentrics who really wanted to be in the army, the best we had were Borstal boys: but most were drop-outs and unconvicted bad hats. This might not have mattered much if these units had not been formed when every officer and NCO worth anything was otherwise engaged. The officers were elderly and lethargic, the N.C.Os corpulent. In 1941 it dawned on those in high places that all was not well. Certainly the discipline in my own regimental 70th surpassed belief. A subaltern who arrived before me had been urged by an outgoing colleague not to turn out the guard after 11.00pm because 'they might not like it'. Ordinary disobediences were condoned. Violence to NCOs was common. Equipment and clothing were being sold. At my first company parade 60% of the so called soldiers were absent.

To deal with this mess, practically everyone from the commanding officer to the corporals was replaced, and a ruthless but scrupulously just regime instituted. The new colonel was a phenomenon. Some army Wilsons are called 'Tug', some 'Jumbo'. This one was a Tug. Furiously red in the face he had a black but greying moustache, and a formidable muscular physique. The latent violence of his personality was such that one seldom noticed the most obvious feature: that he had lost his right arm. He saluted and did everything left-handed, and wore all his equipment the wrong way round for accessibility. When he entered a room, conversation died. The very trees wilted when he passed, and nothing escaped his eye – though sometimes, as I found out, he averted his gaze.

This was the holy terror who ruled my life for the next year, and revolutionised the unit. The method was a rigid application of rule plus sensible welfare. When a deserter was picked up by the police, he was remanded for court martial every time. In that year – a year of steady improvement – we had 104 courts martial. Every man convicted of desertion or absence without leave was automatically put at the bottom of the leave roster, because others had had to do his work meanwhile. Every man short of kit at the Saturday inspection was placed on a charge, and made to pay for it by stoppages. The routine was burdensome; reveille at 6.00am, PT, breakfast at 7.00am, barrack-room inspections at 8.30am; first parade at 9.00am and then exercises and weapon training, apart from an hour for lunch, till 6.00pm. Thereafter unsupervised clean-up for the troops, while officers were expected to dine in mess at 7.00pm. Then, after dinner, one did one's administrative paper work, read the next day's orders and studied the endless Army Training Memoranda and Army Council Instructions. You fell into bed at 9.30pm or 10.00pm, unless, of course you were an orderly officer up all night, or there were night exercises. On top of this the bugles might scream you out of bed on practice alarms at any time between 1.00am and 4.30am, and then everybody had to be at their emergency posts fully armed and accoutred in seven minutes. This routine occupied six days of the week. Sunday began at 7.00am. A church parade with a Commanding Officer's inspection filled up the morning. You got half a day off a week if you were lucky.

This, of course, was policy: Satan hath..... The other half of the policy was inclined to welfare, and here Tug Wilson had real understanding and sympathy, though he did his best not to show it. A man who kept himself clean and followed the rules; who did his training and was generally workmanlike had prospects. As the cadre of NCOs was eroded by the usual postings of military life, men were promoted to the vacancies from within the unit. In nine months we had young soldier corporals, serjeants and even officer cadets. There were sometimes imaginative rewards. An Italian corporal cook always kept a loaded rifle in the cookhouse. Looking out of the window he saw a Messerschmidt 110 gliding silently out of the eye of the sun. He calmly picked up his rifle, shot the pilot through the head and went on cooking. He got a fortnight.

The welfare problem was that many of these young people were, in truth, worried children who went astray for reasons which, in civilian but not military terms, were perfectly defensible. The main source of worry was the bombing of London. A boy who heard that his home had been wrecked and that his mum and dad were in with the neighbours was apt to go absent and get a job on demolitions to help his parents. Who was to blame him? For such cases various things could be done. The army developed a procedure for giving compassionate leave on a certificate from the local police. There was an excellent organisation, called

SSAFA* consisting of tough young women who would investigate problems, write letters, move heaven and earth. And besides, Tug Wilson could recognise distress like the next man, and when a deserter in real trouble was brought back, he was apt to remand him to court martial on a lesser charge rather than lose him for months in the Glasshouse.

As courts martial were sitting twice a week, they were more familiar for us than for most; Henry Brandon never saw one throughout his service. These were called Field General Courts Martial. There was a permanent President, a major who went the rounds holding the courts, and he sat with two officers from some unit other than the one involved. It was not a bad system, for the permanent president got to know the backgrounds and human problems, and he took great care that the trials were fair. There were quite a few acquittals, and though there were some stiff sentences, most were light. It should be remembered that a period in the Glasshouse** was much harder than the same period in a civilian prison: perhaps three times as hard. The prisoners were kept at spit, polish, PT and pack drill eleven hours a day, and came out as fit as fiddles. Short sentences were therefore useful and much used.

Around the turn of the millennium an ambitious solicitor mounted an attack on our court martial system in a series of appeals ending up in the European Court of Civil Rights. His client had few merits, but his appeal was upheld on the barrack-room lawyers ground that the general responsible for convening the Court-martial was the same as the one who confirmed the findings. The civilian judges of the European Court plainly had no idea what the purpose of an army (namely to win a war) is. I defended and sometimes prosecuted before over a hundred courts martial and was a member of half a dozen. They fell over backwards to be fair, and never did anything to please a convening officer.

My court martial activities might sound as if I sought popularity with the troops. I did not. My concern was to try and train them so that they would kill, not be killed. It is physically unpleasant for the trainee, but it need not oppress the spirit. When we had inter-platoon parade-and-drill competitions, I expected my people to be faultlessly turned out because that was something which any fool could do. I never had to bawl at them about this like other platoon commanders and they always came in first or second. On the other hand, if they broke cover too soon on a field exercise, or failed to oil a rifle, or to wash their feet, they got hell. They joined in the spirit. Once, at a target practice, they spontaneously put up a shilling each for prizes, and asked me to join in.

The proper equipment was now coming off the assembly lines and being distributed to the active units, who, in their turn disposed of obsolete stuff to

---

* Soldiers, Sailors and Air Force Association.
** Military detention centre particularly the one at Shepton Mallet.

troops like us. Weapon training in the 70th Buffs was versatile as a result. We learned how to operate not only the standard army weapons of the period, but others which might have been less expected. It was fortunate that some sensible person had laid up some of the last wars' weapons. They might not be very good, but at least they made the nation feel less naked. We, in the 70th Buffs were now the heirs of Haig and Kitchener. We learned to use Lewis guns and Vickers machine guns. We went further. In comparison with other units: -

> 'Whatever happens we have got
> The Maxim gun, and they have not'.

We never had a Nordenfeldt or a Gatling, but we did have flirtations with modernity. We had a smooth-bore quadrupedal gun for firing ginger-beer bottles full of petrol and rubber at German tanks. It was hoped that the stink would be drawn into their ventilation systems, leading to precipitate abandonment. It contributed to the lamentable disappearance of those china ginger beer bottles which had been such a feature of school life.

After a while the battalion was partly dispersed. One company garrisoned Lympne airfield; two others went to Manston, the most exposed of all the fighter bases, where the corporal cook shot the Messerschmidt; HQ and the training companies went to Hothfield Place, a Palladian mansion near Charing. You know Hothfield better than you think. It has that sweeping carriage approach; that pillared pedimented portico, and that vast echoing marble chequer-floored entrance hall specially designed for silent KGB agents disguised as sinister butlers. Old Lord Hothfield lived up at Appleby Castle in Westmorland, but his son Peter still had a room at Hothfield; the whole of the rest and the large estate being requisitioned except for one enormous double mattress on an upstairs floor. I appropriated it.

Hothfield laid a prophetic and trivial dream that I had had since I went to Winchester. I was going down a dark avenue with great trees over-arching the lane. There was always a loud rumbling sound, and I was never alone. At the bottom was a little bridge, which I never reached, with rickety white painted wooden railings bright in the moonlight. Beyond the bridge, the avenue went up a slope. In a crisis we had to man the Ashford defences, and we had emergency exercises to do it. With the pre-OCTU platoon, I was detailed to pretend that I was a German force probing these defences. I had 28 men on bicycles and a Bren gun carrier, which was a sort of open topped light tank. The moon was due to set at 2.30am. I brought my face-blackened force to the head of a lane which I had chosen, at about 2.00am. The carrier rumbled into cover, and by way of reconnaissance I stole, with my section commanders down the dark avenue over-arched with great trees, almost to the little bridge with its rickety white wooden railings bright in the moonlight. The defences were obviously at the top of the slope opposite, and we would be seen if we went to the bridge. So we turned back and waited for moonset.

I have carefully checked this episode, and I am certain that I had never corporeally been there before. I chose it by the map and had no idea that it was like that till I reached it and found it perfectly familiar.

So far, I seem to have represented Tug Wilson as a paragon. After all, he, more or less helped by us, reduced the absentee rate from 60% to seven per thousand in a year, and was sending men forward for commissions before that. In his gruff and impossible way, he was kind to me, and he was unexpectedly learned. He knew about my personal background because I thought it wise to tell him; but he knew, too, about my military ancestry and once quoted Leonhard to me. All the same he could be monstrously unfair, especially to officers, and I think that he must have been, very slightly, a snob and more than slightly anti-Semitic. All the same I personally had no real cause for complaint. After a time, he put me in charge of all the recruit drafts, which meant, in effect, that I had a company command though still only a second-lieutenant. Then I had charge of the potential officer cadets, and in the interval I had a spell as assistant Adjutant. Not many conscript subalterns were vouchsafed such opportunities. My only regret is that I never had any time on mechanical transport, of which I remained – and remain – quite ignorant.

The orders for one of our several moves in Kent during those thirteen months, said fishily that we were going to Grove Camp. It turned out to be Chartwell, Winston Churchill's house at Westerham. The great man was convalescing there. It was known that there was a particularly desperate unit of SS paratroops near Cherbourg, and we, with a battery of Bofors guns belonging to the Rough Riders were to sell our lives in his defence. The chaps were tickled pink. We had to go through the house and grounds every morning and night, even marching into His bedroom and loo with our Tommy guns. As I have recorded in *The Companion to British History* he worked a great deal in bed, with assistants feeding him papers from one side, and secretaries taking down replies or inspirations on the other. If he went out for a walk, a platoon crawled the ditches on either side. If he went for a drive two Bofors guns and three truck-loads of our people had to rush off in pursuit, with motor-cycle wireless men signalling his whereabouts (in code, of course), in case he tried to get lost. We never let him.

In the evenings the duty officers dined with him, unless, which was not usual, he was doing high international business over the dinner table. These dinners were quiet affairs. The Hero of the Hour sat with a book propped against a water jug –

he was reading Hardy's *Dynasts* – and pushed food silently into his big baby face. We, two or three of us plus a secretary or two and perhaps a guest, would talk shyly. Sometimes he would throw out an odd observation, quite at large. Once a message from Stalin about the Murmansk convoys made a stage-managed arrival and he handed it round. It was unbelievable. Once also he cross-examined us about our needs, and we told him about our shortages of up to date equipment. That stirred him. We were re-armed in 24 hours. This is recorded in his war memoirs: he took particular care to prevent any disciplinary action against us for short-circuiting the usual channels. He visited the troops in their tents in the hillside wood behind the house. He had not been a soldier himself for nothing. He sent the troops a barrel of beer every week.

I have three particular recollections of him. Even in his convalescent state he drank more than I could safely manage at a third of his age. A bottle of Brandy appeared at every dinner. We and the others would drink about half of it (it was very good), and he invariably drank the rest. Secondly, despite the famous cigars, at that period he did not smoke. True, he always had a cigar in his mouth, but it was a half burnt one which he would drop into his pocket and bring out again when he pressingly wanted something in his mouth. He kept it in his mouth sometimes at meals, extracting it, like a stopper, to insert food and then putting it back.

He had a mixed staff in which women predominated, yet with the exception of Mrs Harriman, no woman, even his wife, ever visited the house.[*]

After three months we resumed our usual work – at Shorncliffe, and then at twelve hours' notice, I was posted as an instructor to the pre-OCTU at Wrotham.

Wrotham Camp in June 1942 was disgruntled. An infantry brigade had been trained up to a very high pitch. It had been moved to these Nissen huts scattered in the muddy woods of the North Downs escarpment, and had, without notice, been told to get rid of all its other ranks, receive additional officers from elsewhere and turn itself into a training school. Of its three battalions, I joined the Royal Berkshires. I was very much one of the officers from elsewhere. I arrived on a Sunday. Luckily the first drafts of cadets were arriving next morning. It was a shambles. Nobody knew where anything was, not even the parade ground, a mass of soft ash when we found it, stretching away like an airstrip into the woods. So we set up tables and processed the cadets – which meant finding out where they came from, what they knew, who their mother's maiden aunt was, whether they spoke Pushtu and writing it all down on forms.

I went back to Square One. The brigade had pioneered the new battle drill, an excellent expedient for getting along in war. The main purpose of Wrotham was to

---

[*] Modern writers seem to believe that Churchill never went to Chartwell during the war. The above quoted minute shows that he did, but oddly enough it reads as if he were there only for a weekend. My recollection is that he was there as long as we were and that Attlee stood in for him at Downing Street.

ensure that every future officer, regardless of his service origin or eventual destination would know in a tight corner how to fight as an infantryman. So we had cavalrymen and gunners, pay clerks, engineers, school masters, military police and Heaven knows who, all for once, in it together. The intensive courses ranged from six weeks for those who knew nothing, to a fortnight for infantrymen. Each one ended with an astounding assault consisting of nine platoon attacks delivered over a distance of eleven miles scattered with hazards (you had at one point to jump off the roof of a house), and it ended up in a deep north Kent quarry. Here the end cliff had to be stormed, while live ammunition was fired overhead and flares, thunderflashes and smoke-bombs went off underfoot. The deafened and exhausted cadets eventually struggled to the top and consolidated their position. After five minutes, and without warning: -

'Right. On parade. Double home,'
and double home we did, four and a half miles, the officer instructors carrying the heaviest weights.

I did this every other Friday. Our course work was so hard, and for the instructors so monotonous that our services were not, uniquely, required once parades finished. So I would catch the next train to London and spend most of the night with Fanny, by then living in Courtfield Gardens. At 4.00am we would walk to Victoria where I would catch a train to Gravesend. If I ran the ten miles from Gravesend to camp I could get there just in time for the 7.00am parade. I did this two or three times a week, and was never late – more by luck than anything else, for air raids, through which we sometimes walked in showers of shrapnel, might have held me up. What things we do for love!

Others dissipated the strains in other ways. A dance in a local public hall led to a curious incident. We were all woken up at 2.00am by a tremendous distant explosion. For a moment we thought that the Boche had found us after all, but then silence. What had happened was this. The commanding officer of one of the other battalions, a young man, had been to a dance. Somebody had gone off with his girl, and on the way home a military policeman asked him for his work ticket. He was in a bad temper and full of drink when he reached his mess. He disliked that particular mess anyway, and decided to alter it. His method was to push four stickey bombs up the chimney, pull out the pin and retire.

BANG!!

Then he went to bed.

In the morning his parade ground was found to be covered with rubble and scattered window-frames. The colonel remembered that an administrative inspection was due to start at 11.00am. The War Office general with his bevy of quartermasters, accountants and armourers must be on the way already. Agitated telephone calls. Everybody lent a hand. Working parties cleaned up the parade ground; scaffolding went up round the mess 'for rebuilding'. The nearest gate was closed so that the general would have to enter at the more distant end. Signposts were changed. A wireless picket watched for the cortège, so that our cadet road-blocking exercise could irretrievably divert it through remote villages. The general, over an hour late, arrived in an apologetic mood.

Chapter 23

M I 6

In November 1942 Fanny and I decided to get married. We advertised the engagement and told our parents. Her mother, widowed almost since Fanny was born, was nice. Both my lot wrote expostulations. Pater, I think was influenced by Wilhelmine, but he was restrained and confined himself to urging me to make sure that I was marrying the right girl. If he were alive now, we could have set his mind at rest. We have been married for over 60 years. My mother, on the other hand, was grossly offensive. She had known all along that I had been seduced by an adventuress, and so forth. Oddly enough Fanny came to like her, in the end.

This was all predictable, for much the same had happened to Richard. When it became obvious that Switzerland would be lapped about by the German military tide, he was given a diplomatic bag and told to drive hell for leather for home. After encountering a corpse in the lavatory of a restaurant in the Dordogne, he reached Bordeaux, ditched his Morris Minor and got onto one of the last ships. Another of them blew up next door, but he was unscathed. Marine explosions seem to have become a feature of his life. There was one, I think, at Salerno and the eleven ammunition ships at Bari are said to have made the biggest bang in history.

So all of a sudden, here he was. He was called up, put into an OCTU, commissioned and posted to MI 6, and while I was in the 10th Buffs, he decided to marry his Mary. There was great maternal indignation, and I had flights of letters. Naturally I got special leave to go to his wedding at Nottingham. The two mothers were there and Ursula Wood the poet who later married Ralph Vaughan-Williams the composer. At the register office next morning the mothers were distant but Mrs Norris grew increasingly morose. She sat miserably on a chair wearing a plum-cake hat, and when the registrar asked what her husband's occupation was replied violently:

'I don't know. He's never done *anything*', and blew her nose.

In the train back to London my mother said:

'Now that Richard's gone, you'll have to look after me'. She seemed to have forgotten that she had a husband.

My mother took a flat in Park Lane, but Pater, who was a country mouse, stayed on at Wentworth. They saw each other fairly regularly: it was not exactly a separation, they simply lived in different places. Later on, he moved to a small hotel (almost opposite the astonishing edifice which houses Egham College), and she took a flat at Baron's Court, and would decreasingly stay with him. Of course she became increasingly possessive of me. Letters full of gush, self pity and impertinent questions arrived wherever I was, about twice a week. Often I could not bear to open them. If only she could have been friendly and nice! Then Fanny and I would have seen more of her and she would have got what she professed to want, with pleasure to all. Instead, I dreaded the hours which might have to be wasted for her sake.

So our marriage was meant, amongst other things, to put an end to this half-lit problem and put us on a straight and acceptable footing with the elder generation. For four years all our friends had known the position anyhow.

Fanny, meanwhile, discovered that it was more, not less convenient to be married in church than before a registrar. A register office marriage involved a rigid timetable, like marrying by banns. But military life being unpredictable, we wanted to be able to get married at short notice. Accordingly, she enquired after an archbishop's licence, and had a stroke of luck. The vicar of St Jude's, Courtfield Gardens, where she was living, turned out to be one of those ecclesiastical officials called surrogates, and could get us a licence easily. She was soon, on payment of £3.5s.10d in possession of a grand document beginning 'William, by Divine Permission.....' and ending with a dangling seal. So now we could do it whenever we liked. We did it on 2nd January 1943, at St Jude's and held the party at the Royal Court Hotel in Sloane Square.

Fanny's mother and mine met. Mine, no doubt for tactical reasons, had decided to bury the hatchet. So she was sweet and illuminated. Fanny's mother, on the other hand, could not resist the opportunity methodically to give Wilhelmine a piece of her mind. I do not blame her – but there is a time and a place for everything. The situation was saved by Arthur Barnes[*] who breezed in and put everyone in a good temper.

Then we went on our honeymoon to Oxford and most of the wedding party came too. We filled up two compartments in the train, and stayed at twelve Ship Street with Mary Stanley Smith, and there we threw a second party. Quite a lot of guests came to both. It was a very public honeymoon. We had, after all, shacked up together for long enough to want to see our friends.

Almost at once, a happy inspiration solved our problem of home-making. I had joined the Inner Temple as a student in 1938, and it occurred to me to ask if there

---

[*] The Rev. A P A Barnes, Rector of Winslow, an Oxford friend who later baptised our children.

was a flat available there. The Sub-Treasurer, Roy Robinson, looked at me as if nothing would surprise him and offered me a choice of 22. With the bombing there had been a hurried exodus, and I felt like a war profiteer. So, in a way, I was. Until 1953 I paid £100 a year for that two-roomed flat with all moderately mod cons in one of the best areas of London. As it was in a Regency building, the rooms were spacious and beautiful. I never made a better investment, and being tired of the rootless life we settled there permanently, and, apart from moves within the Temple in 1959 and 2000, we have stayed put.

These early months of 1943 saw a great change in my life. There was marriage with its pleasures and there was also physique. My military life had been hyperactive; the last chapter might be the story of a brawny subaltern. In fact my body was designed for other things, and instead of Richard's temporary muscular over-development, I remained rather light. I now did something to my back during one of the assault courses. The Commanding Officer promptly sent me off on two intelligence courses in succession, one at Matlock and another at Christ's College, Cambridge. The first was arduous because of an immense amount of memorisation. The second, and much longer one, meant happily sitting about in a lovely University City talking and reading German. I felt rather a fraud moving from hard physical work to a life of luxury and ease, and one might well wonder why I needed a course in German. The answer is that I am not a natural linguist. I had spoken little German between 1936 and 1939 (a period when I was learning French), and none since. You can become pretty rusty in seven years.

I spent six months in Cambridge in two stretches, and even learnt to punt from the wrong end. In the intervals, I had odd spells of not very hard work at Wrotham. During one of these I achieved a heart's desire. Every Englishman has a secret longing to run a pub. The soap operas are full of them. Not, I suppose being wholly English, my ambition was to run a museum. I was ordered to gratify myself. I threw myself and the battalion carpenter into this with a will. He rigged up desks, screens,and showcases while I cannibalised German illustrated periodicals and wrote to friends for material. I even assembled a collection of not entirely decent German jokes into an album with translations. My Nissen Hut Museum made an impression. The Brigadier, after looking round for an hour and laughing uproariously at the joke book, ordered the other battalions to re-organise their museums on my lines. I was very unpopular.

I was next posted to the 7th Buffs, then stationed at that improbably named place, Hassocks, and was promptly sent off on *leave* because technically some was due to me. The fact that I had been living it up at Cambridge for months was irrelevant. That was work. I then rejoined the battalion at Portland. The HQ was in The Verne, a mid-Victorian fort designed to withstand shell-fire, but based largely on the principles of Vauban. Within its ditches, its low profile counterscarps and ravelins there was a vast yard surrounded by the blank but loop-holed backs of the casemates. We had our orderly room in a hut at one side and the whole battalion with all its impedimenta could easily parade there.

The Buffs, with their Tudor dragon badge, had a continuous history since Henry VIII, but more recently Prince George of Denmark, Queen Anne's beloved if not clever husband and Lord High Admiral became Colonel-in-Chief. The Danish connection continued and it became the practice for Danish kings to become Colonel-in-Chief. The regimental grandees invariably received some degree of the *Dannebrog*; it was customary to salute a Danish flag, and at mess dinners we drank the health of the King of Denmark and Iceland – now a prisoner, and we always celebrated his birthday with pomp. Or rather, we did sometimes. The Buffs, like Wykehamists, tended to get such things a bit wrong. At The Verne somebody suddenly remembered that this was The Birthday, and that there was no Danish flag flying. Someone fetched a scaffolding pole. A hole was dug and the pole was up-ended into it. In the absence of halyards it had to be nailed to the mast, but the mast was already up, so the smallest corporal shinned up it with a hammer and nails. His exertions left the pole flagless and slightly off-centre. He tried again while a small crowd came and admired him. The tallest serjeant now appeared and held his feet. The flag was secured. They pushed and filled until the pole was upright. At last! The Guard could turn out and present arms.

This, in its way, symbolises the regime of Lieut-Col Floater,[*] who was a charming old fool. He had been a company commander but he clubbed his company so often that there was nothing but to promote him to the harmless post of battalion second-in-command. But no commanding officer could endure him for very long, and as seconds-in-command were promoted, Floater went the round of the battalions, filling in the vacancies. When he had done them all, with appalling irresponsibility somebody recommended him for a command. The 7th Battalion got him.

It had been quite a good unit, certainly better than the 10th Battalion, probably better than the 8th, and Floater was a man of such unimpressive character that for a while the unit, having seen him before, ran itself in spite of him. But even the weakest commander will get the strongest battalion down in the end, because in the absence of central direction, everybody becomes involved in intrigue. Moreover, outside authorities cease to have proper respect for the unit. This was very obvious when we began our move to Northern Ireland. A Railway Transport Officer (RTO) is a sort of military stationmaster but has despotic authority over anything which

---

[*] I have invented this name to avoid pain to his relatives. He must be long since dead.

goes on in a train. We took advice about entraining, from RTO Weymouth. Eight compartments per carriage: six men per compartment. So we squadded the battalion into 48s each with its carriage number, halted each squad opposite its carriage, and on the command 'entrain' in they got, heavy packs, rifles, tin hats, kitbags, rations, and spread themselves over the seats for their 24 hour journey. 'No', said the RTO ten minutes later; 'eight per compartment', so we hauled them all out, resquadded them by 64s, shuffled them about and re-entrained. There were now several empty carriages. We pointed this out to the RTO. 'Oh', he said, 'six per compartment it is; but', looking at his watch '.....you're off in three minutes. You'll have to reorganise en route'. Have hundreds of you ever tried dragging yourself, clobber and all down the corridor of a swaying train? A respected CO would have told the RTO to stuff himself in the first place.

I enjoyed Portland. You could go down to Weymouth in your off moments, which were fairly frequent; it had been a civilised little town ever since the band used to play George III into the water from his bathing machine. Fanny used to come down too, and once she brought a gorgeous auburn haired mutual friend, who had got herself commissioned into the WRAF. We enjoyed that nocturnal threesome very much. When one is under 35 and fit, sex plays an immense part in one's life, and I was very well armed. I held, and hold that sex, regarded as a form of entertainment is separable from love, and that a spouse has no right to regard the partner's body as exclusively his or her property. I loved Fanny passionately and still do, but, in the recurrent separations of war it was unreasonable to demand total continence from either of us. We both slept around before we were married, Fanny rather less than I. In fact, for the first two years of our bedfellowship, she was otherwise chaste. But we had conditions. We would not have children otherwise than by each other, and we would be frank about what we did. This worked well and our numerous letters were full of our sexual adventures. We managed to avoid jealousy, because the central citadel, which was love, was held against all the world.

We were depressed at the prospect of Ireland, where visitors were not allowed. Ulster served two purposes. Intensive war training in a European countryside could go ahead, but the forces could intervene if the Germans made an attempt on the undefended Irish republic which nevertheless permitted a German legation in Dublin throughout the war. I was particularly downcast at the prospect of active service in a unit which was so ill-managed, and so I enquired of Richard whether there might be a place for me in the War Office or some other staff. I was, after all, a well qualified military intelligence officer wasting my time as a second-in-command of an infantry company. It happened that the War Office *was* recruiting people, and I was summoned to an interview forthwith. Three august characters sat on one side of a table and I on the other. What on earth was said I have no recollection at all.

On one of the five days after we arrived at Muckamore, a muddy, suitably named camp outside Antrim, I was in the lounge of the Great Central Hotel contemplating my pint at five minutes to eight o'clock closing time when a man approached and invited me to dinner. I was, of course, suspicious. This, after all, was Ireland – or was he, perhaps, wanting to assault my modesty? Next moment all became clear. The All Ireland Bowls Association was holding its committee dinner upstairs, and were faced with sitting down thirteen at the table. Would I bring them luck? I was delighted. Upstairs I was received with applause, seated at the chairman's right hand, and a bottle of whiskey – Irish – was placed in front of me. Whisky was as rare as gold. I believe Scotch and Irish are spelled differently but as I can never remember which is which, I have used both. They assured me that it would embarrass them to do less, and this group of distinguished businessmen treated me with a sustained and utterly perfect courtesy. All the speeches were made in my direction. One might have been Charlie Chaplin. In the end I felt bound to reply. I was rather drunk, but not as drunk as all that. I told them that their speeches made me feel as a jack must feel in a match of champions, when the woods come curving gently towards it – but never touch, as in the finest tradition of Irish after-dinner speaking. They, on the other hand, were as drunk as that, and thought that this was rather good. They insisted that I should take my bottle in my hand away with me as a memento. I thanked them and said that as it was now mine, would they do me the honour of having a drink with me?

Eventually we all tumbled out with handshakes at one in the morning, and I went off to telephone. The cold air made me drunk in the telephone box, but I said that I had been posted back to London.

So I went to MI 6 and lived at home. The advantage, apart from being at home, was financial. One's basic pay was taxed, and war taxes were very high. Allowances were not taxed. I drew allowances in lieu of accommodation and rations which far exceeded my *gross* pay.* I even had a shilling a day extra for living with my own wife. Suddenly we were about three times as well off as before. After some months I became due for automatic promotion to full lieutenant. When nothing happened I wrote in. There was a sort of hiccough, and a note came back to say that as a matter of fact I had been promoted to Captain five months ago, and would I kindly collect what was owing to me?

This part of MI 6 was in the Charity Commission's building at fourteen Ryder Street, St James's. We had a safe so large that we ran a canteen in it, and the first floor corner room was furnished in the most oppressive Biedermeyer I ever saw,

---

* A second Lieutenant's daily taxable pay was 11s. I was drawing 16/6d in untaxed allowances. A Captain's basic pay was 25s.

even in Germany. I saw it again in 1971 when I went to meet the Chief Charity Commissioner. It was the same save that Colonel Felix Cowgill, had made it the centre of a beehive but now every thing was dusty, and the Commissioner did not understand his own job.

This section waged secret counter-intelligence outside the United Kingdom, and as the execrable Kim Philby (of whom more later) was there at the time, I can see little point in reticence. It received reports about German intelligence and its methods, personnel and agencies from sources as varied as life – bystanders, journalists, friendly powers, agents and spies of unequal dependability, bills of lading, wireless intercepts in huge numbers, dead airmen's map cases, the proverbial contents of waste paper baskets. We had to read these, which might vary from half a book to a few lines scribbled on cheap paper, and evaluate them, and see if they revealed a pattern which would give us clues as to enemy intentions.

The German intelligence system was less efficient and less well organised than ours. Their original service intelligence was called the Counter-intelligence (Abwehr) because the Treaty of Versailles had whimsically forbidden them to have a secret service. It was organised like a defensive system with a branch (Ast, alternatively short for *Abwehrstelle*) in each major German city, but Ast 10 at Hamburg, because of the port's overseas connections, developed a foreign intelligence network. One or two of the others did as well, but on a much smaller scale, Ast 10 and the Abwehr HQ under Admiral Canaris between them managing most of the active, as opposed to the defensive, work. We got to know their people pretty well because we had early succeeded in getting in on their system, so that we knew where they were, what they meant to do, and even what they knew.

Side by side with the Abwehr was the *Sicherheitsdienst* (SD = Security Service) which was an SS offshoot concerned with putting down treason, assumed everywhere to be rampant. It, too, developed a foreign intelligence service; in a one-party state the substitute for politics is technical intrigue, and the SS, headed by Himmler, hoped, by tapping separate sources, to discredit it, or even prove that it was treasonably supplying misinformation.[*] The SD chased and catalogued the Abwehr's agents, which was convenient for us because we had access to much of the catalogue. Conversely they did not tell the Abwehr what they were doing about anything else, so that the latter, which, after all was a counter-intelligence body and took an interest in anything suspicious, developed a card-index of the rather amateurish SD people too.

Besides this, there was the Gestapo (*Geheime Staatspolizei*: Secret State Police), originally a branch of the Prussian State Police which, by Goering's influence, had spread all over the German New Order, and supplemented and often rivalled the SD.

---

[*] Admiral Canaris was hanged in 1945 and some historians believe that the Abwehr had become a gigantic conspiracy against Hitler. I am not so sure.

The word was used, but inaccurately, to signify German secret police activity generally. If you add to this the German service police forces, and the diplomatic missions abroad, most of which carried unavowed Abwehr or SD people but reported to the Wilhelmstrasse, the result was a muddle which we enjoyed very much, but it created technical problems once one reached the higher flights.

The higher flights arose from the contacts which a counter-intelligence has with its opponents. We sometimes captured or converted their agents; there were, too, professionals who worked for both sides, and the people in neutral countries who had friends or commercial or even merely social relationships amongst the businesses, diplomatic missions and consulates of the hostile allegiances. Neutral capitals, especially but not only the well placed ones such as the Hague in World War I and Lisbon, Ankara and Stockholm in World War II naturally attracted undercover activity, sometimes thinly disguised. This could have risible results. An American colleague was sent, as it happened to Asunción in charge of a bogus engineering company. He knew nothing about engineering, let alone the bridges in which the company allegedly specialised. It had not occurred to his masters that somebody might actually want a bridge. So when an imposing gentleman with lots of money appeared wanting to negotiate a contract, there was panic. Much whisky seemed to be the only quick refuge. Dinner in a restaurant was proposed, while the backroom girl desperately telegraphed Washington. A night club, perhaps? A brothel? At four in the morning, they were blood brothers ascending a high-rise building in a rickety lift. The cable broke and they hit the bottom with a bang. 'We were so drunk, we thought we had hit the top, and, gee, when they got us out, we were in the wrong building anyhow..... I guess I was the vaguest engineer that guy ever met'.

Whatever the position, it could be used for feeding misinformation or political dynamite to the enemy. At best a tricky operation, it becomes harder when more than one network has to be fed, for one's lies have to be mutually consistent, and consistent with the information which the enemy will get from air photographs, intercepts, friendly diplomats and so on. Thus the most important work of wartime counter-intelligence is to be able to advise reliably on how the enemy can be persuaded to believe what you want him to believe, or not to notice or know that of which he should remain ignorant.

The biggest case of the latter kind was connected with PLUTO (Pipeline Under The Ocean). To save our overburdened shipping and tanker vehicles, the huge amounts of petrol needed by our armies would have to be pumped in a pipeline from Liverpool to a point on the Channel near Southampton. This would be reeled across to Normandy and extended in the track of the armies as opportunity offered.

The main invasion bases were actually Weymouth and Southampton, which was inconsistent with an attack on the Pas de Calais, about which the Germans were known – logically – to be sensitive. Our object was to keep them sensitive about the Pas de Calais, and the main bases were camouflaged and shipping concentrations were kept away from them. Once, however, the pipeline appeared on the air photographs, the position of its Channel outfall would give everything away. The problem was solved by digging. One ghastly day of pouring rain the whole Allied armies regardless of function was put to the puzzlement of digging trenches EVERYWHERE: fields, parks, hilltops, back gardens, farms. My platoon devastated the grounds of a school. We were not given the slightest idea why, and the affair remained the subject of debate and surmise for months – but the enemy air photographers, never spotted the track of the worm crawling slowly towards the south coast.

The advice, as I have said, concerns 'how', not 'what' lies should be told, for the fundamental lies have to be generated at a level of high policy by those who know what they want to conceal. Secret intelligence is not a dominant factor in policy making, in the sense that its practitioners make the decisions. They do not. They provide raw facts which help others to come to the right conclusions, and they can convey the polished lies upon which the enemy can base the wrong ones. Nor do secret intelligence services fight, or bring off weird coups, and contrive things which go bump in the night, because those who collect and transmit information wish, above all to avoid suspicion, which assassinations and sabotage necessarily attract. This sort of physical warfare was practised in various contexts, such as the rescue of prisoners, the instigation of strikes, the firing of ammunition dumps, but it was handled by separate specialist services which were usually warned off sensitive areas. Obviously the effects of the two sorts of activity sometimes coalesced, as when the Polish underground (easily the best in Europe) got its hands on a prototype V2 rocket somewhere on the Baltic and brought it to England.

Our advantage over the Germans was ideological. Nobody believed a word of what that gangster government said, especially as Goebbels was telling the Germans one thing while the diplomats were telling foreigners something else. Everybody hated them and told them as little as they could, whereas most of the population of Western Europe was rarin' to talk to us. Some of the information was of low quality; but the quantity was vast. When, later, we got over to Europe, it was worse still. Everybody had verbal diarrhoea. But it went further than this. Any dictatorial regime whether of the right or the left, Calvinist or papal, breeds preconceptions which make objectivity in the ruler difficult to attain; and since, in such a dispensation, the only way to get on in life is to please those in authority, informants, however well intentioned or loyal, can too easily pass on the kind of matter which the boss wants to hear. Indeed, the informant may be so imbued with the spirit of his ideology that he mentally censored it in ignorance that that is what he is doing. There have been many historical examples of this. The Papacy in the time of Elizabeth I, or the period of the Russo-Nazi alliance, when nothing would convince the Russians that Hitler was about to turn on them; Russian supply trains for the German war effort were still on their way when they were attacked. The Germans suffered from similar difficulties. People willing to collaborate sometimes had to suppress or slant reports to chime in with their masters' prejudices. It was technically possible to plant safe misinformation on the Germans if it struck the same chord. In comparison with us, therefore, they got less high level intelligence, and what there was, was less good. This was an important factor in the outcome of the war. They never, for example, had an inkling of the North African landings until the troops were actually wading up the beaches; and they believed till the last moment, that the Normandy invasion would indeed be launched against the Pas-de-Calais.

Chapter 24

BOMBING AND NORMANDY

Apart from the noises off, card-indexing German spies was a nine-to-five job but more entertaining. I also had as a secondary occupation, an Anglo-American working party at the Admiralty, in a compartment like a public lavatory without the thrones. The Germans were developing an organisation of naval spies, saboteurs and specialist contraptions similar to the Italian MAS 10 but more lavish. We, not the Navy, had stumbled on it, and as it was very land-based, the Navy had to ask the land-based services for information. I was the only junior army officer in the section with any knowledge of warships. This was a relic of a childhood interest. A great deal of *Jane's Fighting Ships* for 1932 and 1936 was, and some still is imprinted in my mind. I could name, recognise and describe almost every warship afloat except the smaller American ones with names like *Samuel B. Cronk*, even the Paraguayan river gunboat *Humayta*, or the fact that the Italian armoured cruiser *Francesco Ferruccio* was an unconverted sister-ship of the Argentine *Pueyredon*, the Japanese *Kasuga* and the brave Spanish *Cristobal Colon* sunk by the American fleet off Santiago de Cuba in 1898. This is me showing off; I am writing from memory.

This German enterprise was believed to be partly an intelligence and partly a fighting unit, which might endanger the cross-Channel invasion by discovering the concentration points and attacking the beachheads. In fact it was still very experimental and unsure of itself. It never had the dash and savoir-faire of the Italians, who sank two Austrian battleships in World War I and two British ones in Alexandria in World War II. Luckily the Germans were too arrogant to take their advice. A German military proverb said that the perfect life was to be in the German Army, with British food, French mobile brothels, the Russians as allies and the Italians as enemies.

London was still being raided at night. Everybody bored everybody else with their bomb story and I do not see why I should not bore you with mine. But first a baffling oddity. I woke up at about 4.00am. My head was on Fanny's chest, one ear pressed against it. Through her I heard the sounds of an underground station, the rumble of a train coming in, the peculiar sound of the pneumatic doors, the guard's warning shouts, another pneumatic rumble and then the train starting off and dying away into the distance. This was repeated several times, while simultaneously by the other ear I could hear the occasional quite other-sounding trams on the Embankment. I was not asleep or dreaming this: I was as wide-awake as I am now, and I was astounded and kept my ear in the same position for half an hour. Eventually I moved my head and broke the contact. It was at a time of night when the underground was not working. The only system which might have been was the Post Office Tube and though I have no idea where it ran, I sometimes wonder if I had tuned into it somehow. Fanny was fast asleep throughout.

Let me digress a while onto public transport. Apart from some of the South-suburban services, the railways were steam-powered, and therefore slow to accelerate and apt to be dirty. Some parts of London were served by double decker trams and lovely quiet – and fast – electric trolley buses, but the whole system was much more efficient and there was more of it. Trams and trolley buses ran all night, the Underground was closed only between 2.00am and 5.15am, and the railway net was so fine-meshed that there were few places, even hamlets, which you could not reach by rail plus a decent pair of shoes; mail never took more than 24 hours between *any* two points in the kingdom. In London, letters were sometimes delivered in four hours. These conditions were maintained against every sort of warlike interruption, and it was cheap. It cost in 1940 one twenty-seventh of the 1985 cost to send a letter.

In the early evening raids, Fanny and I used to distract ourselves by trying to do Lewis Carroll's logical conundrums; and at times we laid down mattresses on the hall floor and slept there, or occasionally in the basement, but gave that up because of the mice. Much of the basement was occupied, by a cheerful team of WRAF girls who managed a barrage balloon called Shirley Temple anchored to a circular brick stage in the middle of the Inner Temple garden. The girls were the toast of the neighbouring pubs. One night, when a bomb fell somewhere near, the whole of Paper Buildings – a very large brick, four-storey block – rolled, as one, a good six inches out of the vertical and back again like a ship. We were in bed and clung to each other for dear life, but nothing came unstuck. Then one night an oil bomb fell on the sixteenth Century Middle Temple Hall. There was a great sheet of roaring flame. I went out to see if I could help. It was a very noisy night with bombs, the London defences spangling the sky, the occasional intimidating rumble of a collapsing house, and showers of small metal particles from our own anti-aircraft shell bursts. There were, however, no fire services to be seen, but there appeared to be a great deal of activity in Fleet Street. When I got there, I found that the fire brigade had driven its huge vehicles nose to tail into the Serjeants' Inn cul-de-sac, instead of the Temple. I found a fireman and offered to show him how to bring his vehicle in. He was curt, not to say snooty. A little later, by the light of a burning building, I understood why. He was not in charge of 'a' vehicle. He was at least a Brigadier-General of Firemen and therefore slightly grander than God. Once they got in, they were a model of efficiency and sense, and had the Middle Temple fire out in half an hour.

One night I was duty officer at Ryder Street. A bomb fell on Sotheby's nearby. I heard it strike before it went off, and hurled myself to the floor. Then came the bang; the window, in one piece, frame and all, shot over my head and smashed itself on the wall opposite. There was a small moment of silence, and then everyone in the building, duty clerks, Victoria Jex-Blake the secretary and I began shouting: -

'Is anybody hurt?'

Nobody was. Everybody had done the same thing.

The street black-out was very complete. People hurt themselves, if there was a mist, by walking into lamp-posts, and once during a hissing downpour in Bond Street I nearly lost an eye in the pitch dark on the protruding spike of an invisible open umbrella. When the pubs all closed and the whores did a roaring trade in the Piccadilly area, it was quite usual to get into a taxi and find it already actively occupied. Petrol, of course, was rationed and this kept a Hansom cab in business from a rank in Leicester Square. I once came eyeball to eyeball with the horse.

The raids slowly tailed off as the RAF, with its radar, got mastery of the night sky over the South East, and the allied bombing began to reduce German industrial production. It was only when we reached Germany that we realised how appalling the suffering of its population must have been. Ours was no match for it, because we were better at making war than they were: for example they never conscripted their women.

The RAF did all the night bombing; the Americans, with their Flying Fortresses bombed by day. American troops swarmed everywhere and, though in general they behaved well, they were not particularly popular. They were large, rather slow men, who cluttered up the pavements, but the real cause of friction was that by our standards they were enormously overpaid. A private got about the same as an English major. The price of essentials was controlled, but it did raise the price of fun things, and it enabled them to drink the pubs dry and also to make away with other men's girls. There were fights especially as they were not used to English beer or the size of our pints, and American police patrols were busy and had to be efficient and tough. Their authorities were alive to the problems and maintained, after a while, a stern discipline which undoubtedly helped. All the same it was not an easy time. It was said that the Americans were 'overpaid, over-sexed and over here', yet many made lifelong friends or married into the States, and certainly at my sort of officer level there was the friendliest service co-operation. It was not a perfect situation, but I doubt if it could have been improved much.

As we moved through the winter into the spring of 1944 the excitement and tension grew. For reasons, some sound, some ignorantly based, some highly disreputable, the Russians had been stridently demanding premature western offensives almost since their alliance with Hitler broke down. Now everybody knew that the great western showdown was about to be launched and there was a now-or-never feeling. This thing simply had to succeed. I thought, and think, that the assault should have been made from the victorious Mediterranean, and that in insisting on a cross-Channel offensive, the Americans inflicted on the free world the greatest political blunder of modern times.

King George VI focused the national mood by a broadcast call to prayer when it set off. If ever a man struck the right note, it was the King, who, in spite, or perhaps because of his nervous infirmities – his rather thick stuttering speech – was much loved. Nobody doubted his sincerity or courage. He had fought at Jutland, the biggest sea battle of the age of steam. He had refused to quit London when the people were streaming into the countryside. The Boche had dive-bombed his home.

> 'The King is still in London, in London, in London;
> The King is still in London Town
> Though London Bridge is falling down...'

It was not only the general hopes of the free nations which went with that armada, but the fears of mothers for children, wives for husbands, boy-friends for girl-friends (women went too), the yearnings of refugee soldiers re-conquering their lost homes, and of course the gravity and ambition of those who planned it. In defeat all this would have been waste; in victory, a personal loss might be bearable. So when the time came to hazard everything the King spoke across the abyss. I doubt if the Almighty makes the sort of personal intervention which his message seems to imply,* yet I was profoundly moved, and not alone. People talked about it in undertones: flower girls, staff-officers, dustmen, doctors.

When the troops had established themselves far enough inland to make a beachhead, the full panoply of the nation's ingenuity staggered us. Petrol was coming in via PLUTO. There was the astounding MULBERRY floating harbour at Arromanches crowded with dozens of ships and landing craft, when I flew over it a few weeks later. There were the horrible Napalm bombs which suffocated, if they

---

* My daughter Katharine disagrees with this.

did not roast the Germans defending the concrete beach fortifications. There were bridge-laying tanks, and portable runways for airfields. An R.A.F survey had given us better maps of enemy territory than the enemy had. Every man's clothing was lethal to lice, and with a shuttle system of ambulance aircraft, a man knocked cold in the mud outside Caen might wake up among the gorgeous nurses of some hospital in Berkshire.

This meticulousness made us feel that everything would be alright; but meanwhile the Germans had a new trick which, fortunately, had been anticipated. We had known for a long time that something was in the wind, but were still rather startled by the details. There was, on the first night, the curious deep-throated grating roar, quite unlike the bombers. We were soon familiar with the sequence: the V.1 or flying bomb, if it had survived the south-eastern defences, came roaring peremptorily across the sky a few hundred feet above the roofs. Then came an abrupt cut-off and silence, followed ten or twenty seconds later by an explosion. Usually you only heard all this, and there was a strained feeling while everyone wondered where it would strike. Once Fanny and I saw it happen from outside a pub in the old Printing House Square.

These V1s, as she pointed out, may not have been a war winner in the quantities in which they were fired, but they caused much civilian hardship because they were sensitively triggered and exploded at roof level. They stripped tiles and smashed windows in a wide radius, and then, if it rained, houses quickly became uninhabitable before they could be repaired. On the other hand because they flew on predictable courses, the anti-aircraft batteries and barrage balloons of Kent, whither *Shirley Temple* was moved, accounted for 75% of them, and the RAF could find and shoot up their launching sites.

The V2 two-ton rockets however arrived vertically, invisibly and ahead of their own sound. They could not be intercepted and needed no special launching sites. A road or a hard tennis court would do. They arrived with such momentum that they often buried themselves deep before going off. They might demolish a house or two and damage might be locally serious, as when one of them broke gas and water mains in South London, but it was seldom widespread in the V1 sense.

The moment now came for me to set off for Europe. A plane-load of us took off from Northolt. It was a calm damp day of lowish cloud, and we circled several times over Arromanches where 25 ships were unloading peacefully as if the *Mulberry* had always been there. Then we landed on a portable airstrip near Caen. I had a serjeant, a driver, no vehicle but a very well turned out French serjeant-major (*adjudant*). I forget who else was in the aeroplane, but there was, unbelievably, nobody on the airfield. Here we were in the supply area behind an immense, if dispersing battle, and the airfield was empty. A figure now emerged from a shack half a mile away and walked towards us. It took him ten minutes to reach earshot: -

'Yer can't land 'ere: it's closed.'

We had an important colonel (Felix Cowgill, I think) who did not take kindly to this. The man, a serjeant in the RAF was told to find a telephone. He had one in his shack. The colonel returned in triumph. A lorry appeared and took us into the outskirts of Caen. Here my *adjudant* showed his metal. We marched into an undamaged house. He commandeered the lady of the house. He was a very handsome *adjudant*. And after they came downstairs, he commandeered her car. The war had thundered off northwards. We simply pointed our nose at Brussels and followed it. Somewhere in the middle of nowhere, the car gently petered to a halt in the dusk. There was a farm. I sent the *adjudant* to the farm, while the others manhandled the car up the drive. We were welcome, and there were beds for all.

It was a five strong peasant family from Grandpa to the son and his wife who were 40ish. There was also a *bonne* and her husband the ploughman. We gave them half a pound of tea, which they had not seen for years and some sugar, which they received with delight. When they proposed eggs for supper, it was our turn, for one had been lucky in England to get one a week. They put half a pound of butter into a vast frying pan and broke twelve eggs into it. They could not understand our pleasure: they were in fact rather apologetic. This, it seemed, arose from the dislocations of war. They had so many eggs, so much butter, oodles of milk, but bread had been short for a month.

Another day, we had stopped at an inn – the sort of place called an *estaminet* in the previous war. They blushingly said that there was only steak, and rows and rows of steaks appeared on a dish and nothing else. The battle lines had cut them off from the area to which they sold their meat, and from which they received their vegetables – so somewhere eastwards another *estaminet* was gleefully stuffing German officers with sprouts. In England the great shortages had been just of these luxurious things.

In the morning we got a friendly RAF vehicle to tow us to Valenciennes, where we cast off at a civilian garage. We explained. They asked if the car had been off the road for long. The *adjudant* said 'most of the war'. They disconnected the petrol system, blew high pressure air through it and said 'that's it'. It was a very common problem. We offered to pay. They said 'No; just make sure that the Boche doesn't come back'. So we drove gaily into Belgium.

The contrast between the *débrouillard* French and the happy Belgians was extraordinary. Precisely from the frontier the roads were lined with crowds, and the houses blazed with red, gold and black Belgian flags. The crowds were feasting their eyes, but knew, soberly, that if they got in the way it might hinder the victory. So, if there was a hold-up, a thousand grateful Belgian hands were ready to heave, pull or clear an obstacle, - and these were Walloons whom Englishmen find it hard to differentiate from Frenchmen.

The RAF's aerial pursuit had been devastating. About every hundred yards for miles there was a wrecked vehicle or a clutch of dead horses: all heaved off the road by enthusiasts, or the Royal Engineers' bulldozers. But beside it was the pipeline, which was already pumping as far as the frontier when I reached it, while gangs were already laying it to Brussels. And there we arrived towards midday.

There were still both euphoria and fires. The Bruxellois are not Walloons but something on their own, and they have, as have Belgians generally, a remarkable capacity for celebration. There are plenty of pictures of liberations: wind-screens covered with lipstick, boys and girls riding on tanks waving flags, and so on. The reality was much more fun. An elderly woman mounting the running board saying

'I *must* kiss an Englishman'.

A miscellaneous crowd dragged down a lorry-load of soldiers, hustled them into a café and gave them all flowers and Champagne. The bottles thrust through our windows cluttered those at the back to immobility. The whores declared a free night: so did the other women. The tower of the enormous *Palais de Justice* was on fire, and the surrounding open space was a mass of firemen's hoses and water. A British brigadier emerged, whereupon ten children joined hands and danced round and round him singing some Flemish nursery rhyme, all among the policemen and the puddles. Ah, Brussels!

I found my headquarters, lost my *adjudant*, obtained my regulation – G. Ten-ninety-eight* vehicle and was told to push on to Antwerp. So off we went, but now with a Belgian liaison officer. The Canadians ahead of us had taken the vital bridges at Duffel before the enemy could blow them, so we sailed cheerfully into the outskirts of Antwerp.

Something was wrong. Not a flag or a soul.

We drove a bit further. It dawned on us that Antwerp had not been taken. We had, admittedly, seen no Canadians, but had assumed in the fog of war, that they were already in the city. We hurriedly turned round and started back. After about two miles we met a surprised Canadian tank. The subaltern started talking into his intercom: then he said –

'Germans must be clearing out. We're all going up. You better get behind'.

So we ate our rations a couple of miles further back, expecting all hell to break out behind us. Absolutely nothing happened. After a while a high formation came along. Some of them said that the forward units were in the city. So back we went.

---

* G 1098 was the number of an army form which listed for each unit all the equipment reserved for active service. The 70th Buffs one had included two hundredweight of cheese. The phrase was commonly used of the equipment itself.

Transformation scene. The whole population was milling in the streets. People were singing, shaking out flags from balconies, weeping, climbing onto tanks, yelling, dancing. The confusion was an outburst of joy, the like of which I had never imagined and could not describe. Everyone ecstatic and especially because they had been rescued by the British. 'We knew you would come' they said over and over again, 'you always have'.

My Belgian emerged with a requisition for a luxurious billet in a flat owned by the elderly baroness Van der Gracht de Romerswael. She was a comfortable, energetic middle-aged widow of a shipping magnate. I dumped my traps and went out to enjoy the triumph. I had gone about ten yards when I was seized by a cheerfully tipsy group. We surged into a café. Everybody in it leapt into activity. There was so much Champagne that one could swim in it. It was deafening and kaleidoscopic. We talked, or rather bellowed at each other: these people were experiencing the first moment for years when they could talk without looking over their shoulders. The tables were pushed aside and we danced – with the barmaids, *la patronne*, people snatched in from the street, anybody. It was nearly dawn when I got back to my baroness.

But I was not allowed to settle; shortly after going to bed there was a rattle of machine guns and a small fusillade. I hurled myself into my equipment. La Baronne appeared, all of a twitter. I saw to my pistol and went out onto the balcony. There were a few armed soldiers going about warily: otherwise nothing. I went back to bed. In the morning there was firing in a small park nearby. It had been an amusing affair. The Germans had a fortified command post in the park and the Anglo-Canadians had come in so quickly because of the intact bridges at Duffel, that they had cut off the general and his staff in their bunker. The fusillade, in the presence of a huge audience crowding the windows and roof tops all around, was persuasive. They came out to roars of applause. It was the city's late commandant.

During the evening night parties and day work I had a grim duty. Breendonck was an old perimeter fort which the SS had used as an interrogation camp. A low concrete structure with a single approach across a wooden bridge, there were thought to have been SD men among its staff. The SS, quick in the uptake, got away. When I arrived, ambulances were collecting the poor surviving victims. The rest had been thrown into the moat.

The machinery of murder and cruelty is sordid and simple. Cells had been built of cheap naked brick on a concrete floor with internal windows covered with barbed wire. A kitchen table was used to strap a man down for interrogation; a single wooden joist across a corner to hang him. The place was at once horrible and dull.

Marie, mère des pauvres, aide nous.

I am glad to see that the place has been razed. I found these words scrawled in pencil on one of the bricks.

Chapter 25

BELGIAN POLITICS, GIRLS, BOMBS AND SPIES

I suppose that all suddenly liberated populations burst apart as the constriction of bondage disappears and the pent-up energies are released. In Belgium these were pretty varied. There were, of course, the traitor-baiters and hair shavers, and the frenetic demonstrators, and the business people who cut corners before civilised regulation could be re-imposed. Politics blossomed into about fifteen major and minor parties, each with its creeds, hatreds, intrigues and disruptive tendencies. Literary and artistic controversy, tinged with linguistic nationalism burst into flames. There were also those who took advantage of the unverifiable features of underground movements to give themselves credit for spurious achievements, or pretensions to rank. There were quite a number of unlisted colonels, and Richard Gatty, my boss, and I had to protect an Antwerp café *patronne* from the inebriated attentions of a very unemployed major-general.

For about eight months our work was now in Antwerp, and we lived there or in Duffel, with occasional sojourns in Brussels. We had two serjeants as confidential secretaries, and two drivers-cum-batmen one of whom, Seagrove but nicknamed Nobottle, was something of a character. He was young, immensely strong, and handsome. He always got whatever we needed, usually in return for services rendered to the locally most influential women; he was a marvellous driver and an immaculate mechanic. He was a Surrey butcher by trade, and I imagine that by now he is a millionaire.

I have already described the purpose of our work; our methods were three-sided. We listened to anybody who would talk to us about anything, and naturally everybody talked as if they had never talked before; we maintained a friendly relationship with the local forces of law and order, especially the *parquet* – of whom more hereafter, and we had the usual networks of informers and agents. Information got by one method could often be cross-checked through the others – not to mention the files in London, with which we communicated all the time by radio. In Ryder Street we had accumulated a little list of those whom the Germans would leave behind as agents. It emerged that these were mostly the heads of networks, and that we with our masters in Brussels were looking for far more people than we had originally thought. A few small fry were falling into our hands; mostly civilians arrested on irrelevant charges or denounced as collaborators by personal enemies, and then found to have skeletons in cupboards. Once or twice such people panicked and told all before we had any idea that there was anything to tell, and mostly they had little. Even the odd wireless operator was low grade. It meant, however, that one was constantly being called to police stations, prisons and internment camps to try and match people with what we already knew, and get lines on their contacts. The really striking thing about these captures was that it could have mattered very little if they had not been made. These 'agents' were untrained, unskilled and not very sensible. They could not have transmitted much information which the Germans could not have got from more reliable sources.

Business with the Belgian police was more interesting. The city of Antwerp had its own police and detective force, which branched out into the less conventional police work because of the port and the international diamond trade. Diamonds, whether industrial or ornamental, are heavily guarded, but once stolen they are easy to smuggle. The techniques of theft and transmission are much like those of secret intelligence and as the methods for combating them resemble counter-intelligence, the Antwerp police had a powerful detective department, with all the features of a secret agency.

There was, however, an important social factor. To Europeans the occupying Germans were the enemy. Since all is fair in love and war, a man felt morally justified in stealing from the Germans; he was helping the allied war effort, and the higher the value of the thefts the better, especially if they happened to be industrial essentials. A trading people like the Belgians, was always ready to earn a little something, and some were less scrupulous than others. A tremendous black market subsisted on evasions of the rationing system and stolen enemy property. The whole nation was in it, patriotically, up to the neck.

The consequences were serious. Moral values were blurred during the four year subjection, and besides, there were many whose livelihood had come to depend too much on this endless complex of illegal operations which wound, from the petty to the greater thieves, to gang organisers, bribed janitors and bent police, to receivers, to wholesale and retail businesses, and so to many of the most powerful and respected figures in the land. As soon as we arrived, these activities became not only illegal but immoral, but it was difficult for many and impossible for some to make the transition back to normality. By that time, too, the habits of years under an enemy had merged insensibly into a habitual amorality. When we arrested a prominent industrialist who had apparently consorted with the Enemy more than was thought decent, we found that since the liberation his flat had been used as a depot for the pornography trade. The speed with which that flat was emptied was truly remarkable. Much of the pornography, by the way, was beautiful. I wish I had collected some of it. It was in a different class altogether from the mass produced ephemerals of modern London or Amsterdam.

One reason why all this was not immediately obvious was the long honeymoon with the liberating armies. Belgian life and custom gave a kind of sacrosanctity to soldiers, and so decreed that you never, but never allowed a soldier (who was paid a pittance) to pay for himself in a pub. If the landlord was not looking, a bystander forked out as a matter of course. There were cafés which were still refusing to take payment from the thousands of British soldiers six months after we arrived. Another, important reason special to Antwerp, was that the port could not be reopened for some considerable time. The German plans envisaged a retreat behind the Dutch Rhine plus fortified zones designed to deny us the use of the abandoned ports. The seven mile Antwerp harbour complex had been set up so that all the quays and cranes could have been blown into the basins. In the greatest single achievement of any underground movement the control system was traced and the vital junction boxes found. At the last moment, when the Germans would have no time to remedy a fault, a brave and intelligent Belgian removed the junction boxes. The German demolitions officer pressed the button – and nothing happened.

Hence the Germans had to rely upon strategic measures. They held the mouth of the Scheldt at Breskens, Walcheren and South Beverland, and these had to be stormed. Breskens fell easily, but the islands needed a major operation in the course of which the enemy cut the dykes, let in the sea and turned the islands into atolls. Even then the port could not be used because, believe it or not, for two months or so a square mile of strategic suburb was held by the SS *Hitler Youth*[*] division. This force was isolated by forty miles and two large rivers from the enemy's main army. The Allies occupied the neighbouring streets and houses, blockaded them in their quarter and diverted traffic round it as if it were a burst main. The SS reserved their ammunition for the expected grand assault, and the Allies, having other things to do were content to wait while the SS consumed their rations.

Meanwhile apart from the traffic diversions, nobody really noticed the SS at all. There was the usual rush hour at 9.00am and 5.00pm. The restaurants and cafés functioned; the law courts were open; trains ran; trams clanged. There was trouble at the Flemish Theatre because the Germans had, admittedly without much success, encouraged a Flemish Nazi party and created political difficulties in the way of putting on a Flemish play. The French theatre, on the other hand, was busy. I saw Rostand's *l'Aiglon* there. One remarkable piece of British efficiency attracted

---

[*] This was its name, not its nature.

appreciation. Within three days, ENSA* was putting on non-stop performances of *Desert Victory* with Dutch subtitles. It was packed out all the time. I saw it myself.

I enjoyed Antwerp. Listening to people kept one permanently, if mostly agreeably, on duty. There were two avenues into local society. The higher, or at any rate richer society was only too keen to entertain you, either from patriotic friendliness or a desire to get a word in first. The lower was easily accessible in the cafés. The lawyers, bankers and industrialists who, with their wives and mistresses formed the upper level, were educated and intelligent folk, often tri-lingual (the third being English), with a wide conversational horizon and often much to conceal. It is hard to see how, the industrialists, in particular, could wholly avoid collaboration with the enemy. Apart from naked coercion by sequestration, arrest or worse, there was the genuine problem that refusal would put the work force out of work and later in the war, might cause wholesale deportations to the Greater Reich; but once the area was liberated, they could be represented at best as having backed the wrong horse, at worst as double dyed traitors – especially as many of them had made fortunes. Yet even such fortunes had their better side, for the more money there was for a Belgian the less there was for a German.

It was all very difficult; denunciations were common and often tainted with spite, jealousy or business competition. Fortunately we had taken a great mass of enemy police and intelligence records, from which we could often check these delations. We were soldiers not moralists, and the policy was to cause minimal disturbance, and, if possible, to leave such people alone – but, of course we could not speak for the Belgian authorities who might have sound legal reasons for prosecuting them. Our sole concern was to answer the question 'is the fellow a spy or not?' Mostly they had the best of all reasons for not being: the Germans were losing the war.

Our contacts with the Belgian authorities were not, even primarily confined to the Antwerp police. More important or wide-ranging offences were, as in France, handled by a national police with criminal investigation departments working in each province to the *Procureur du Roi*,** a court official responsible for launching proceedings. His office, consisting of police *commissaires* who assembled the material and advised him, was called the *parquet* and, again as in France, as soon as somebody was arrested for investigation, a magistrate, the *juge d'instruction* was appointed to hold the balance between the *parquet* and the prisoner. It was his function to prevent violence, and nothing said by the prisoner after arrest was admissible in evidence unless said in his presence. It could never have been easy for these magistrates to stay objective, considering that their lives were bound up over and over again with the same *commissaires*, but with a particular accused only once. After the Germans

---

* Entertainments National Service Association.
** King's Attorney.

everyone was tainted or thought to be tainted by contact with them: *commissaires*, *juges d'instruction*, accused, accusers – the lot. So suspected offences against the state had to be put in to the hands of rather cumbersome but undefiled courts martial consisting of officers and lawyers who had escaped to England. Either way the system would have worked badly. It was, in particular, far too slow.

Thousands, from unwashed managing directors to unwashed dustmen, wandered about in crowds in the unpaved areas of a huge nineteenth century fort, waiting for the preliminary investigations. Some months later, I returned and the numbers had not perceptibly diminished. The system, in truth, was designed for the more leisurely days of peace, not to cope with the torrent of accusation and back-biting bursting out after four years of bitterly hated occupation, and I have no doubt that there was too much wasteful and senseless injustice. An early amnesty would have worked wonders.

Antwerp life outside the higher and the old aristocratic society (distinguishable by double or multi-barrelled names – such as adorned my landlady) was snobbish in its outlook and matrimonial engagements, but remarkably free and easy in some other ways. Especially in the French Quarter there was a type of café waitress who was employed, if possible for her looks, but mainly for her conversational gifts. It was usual to order one's drink and when it was brought, to offer the waitress one; she would accept it, and sit to talk, but occasionally disappearing to serve someone else. She might introduce acquaintances to your table. If she was obviously in deep conversation, another girl or the *patronne* would serve and talk to the next batch. These girls were paid a pittance, but received a commission on all the drinks. Thus their living came from keeping you happy. Everybody went to these places which were numerous, and as the talk was usually of a high standard the girls were very well informed. If you wanted to know why the Flemish National Orchestra was refusing to play Grétry, or the size of mijnheer Van Donck's bank balance, you could get fairly reliable pointers in the course of a few beers, for though the girls were discreet – and anyway you respected their discretion if you were wise – somehow you were apt to find yourself being introduced to the person who might know the answer. It was, by the way, quite common for customers to bring their wives, girl-friends, or daughters.

Such a person was not necessarily a prostitute nor even a courtesan. She resembled, perhaps, the Japanese *geisha* or the Athenian *hetaira*. It would depend upon her temperament and the character of the establishment in which she worked, and whose character she very soon influenced. Some were faithful to husbands or steady boy-friends: at the other end of the scale, there were cafés which were properly equipped as brothels, with waitresses who were fully blown professionals, and most of them had a *back room* for a quick ride if you and the girl fancied it; or it might be something more elaborate, with broad sofas, and a bar. A friend of mine and Wanda his amusing wife, once began with dinner at their flat for ten: eight men, Wanda and the girl-friend of one of the men. They had taken a *back room*, to which we drove after dinner. This one had alcoves. There were a couple of waitresses when we arrived, and a benign *patronne* dispensing Champagne from the bar. The number of girls in the room slowly increased and the party became cheerful, not to say busy. To reduce inhibitions our host got Wanda and the other girls to take their pants off. This was still the age of the skirt. Couples would occasionally vanish upstairs for a while and come down looking preternaturally tidy; others made love in the alcoves. Eventually the whole lot, except the *patronne* who wanted to lock up, piled into cars and drove back to the flat where we drank, danced and fell in and out of bed till breakfast time.

The flavour of such parties is not capable of generalisation. Once, at a wittily ribald dinner, we became aware of a loudspeaker repeating back to us the last half-hour's conversation. Later a local accountant who liked middle-aged women, had a political tiff with one of them. She playfully slapped his face; he drunkenly slapped her a little harder; she retaliated with more steam; he really retaliated. She stopped the whole event with 'Eh –maintenant je ne noce pas'.*

Now this all sounds like a splendid and carefree life, and so up to a point it was. These people might or might not somehow convey indiscretions to an enemy and have to be put under restraint next day. Even when drunk we had to remember and make sense out of what we had heard. This became more complicated after the SS had surrendered (after a short sharp conflict) for then the port started to function, and the Allied supply centres moved north from Normandy. The port became a roaring emporium in which the losses from theft and corruption amounted to millions, though as a percentage of landings they cannot have been large. Our concern was not to prevent these thefts *per se* – that was someone else's job. We were worried about the possibility that the undiscovered enemy networks might finance themselves from the profits. Meanwhile the difficulty of coping with the black markets was now compounded. The patriotic theft which had yielded an incidental profit, now became a dishonest operation pure and simple, but the allied troops joined in zestfully. Purchases at officers' shops had to be limited, because you could get a good pair of shoes for £1 and sell it on the black market for £25. An entire American Transportation battalion was court-martialled for stealing eleven million cigarettes, and besides it was obvious that Belgian authorities were in it. The walled dockyards were patrolled and checked in-and outside by the city police, and still the goods poured onto the market.

---

* If it's going to be like that, I won't fuck.

Richard Gatty and I concluded that there was collusion between the Antwerp detectives and the racketeers. They had their agents there: they were producing precisely nothing. A high, if uncertain proportion of the 91 detectives must be involved; the *parquet* was, independently, worried from the criminal point of view. They broached the subject to us when our minds were already moving in that direction.

We had much theoretical information about German intelligence networks, but had caught few actual spies. A rich network is obviously safer and more dangerous than a poor one, and one way of finding our quarry was to follow the profits through their devious channels until we came up with the ultimate beneficiaries. If we had had the time we would have done this but in war, time is always short, and we knew that an allied offensive was being mounted and might be jeopardised by leaks. So we took a short cut. A Field Security man got the names and addresses of all 91. We arrested and interrogated them all. This decision was fraught with dangers, because their department was directly responsible to the *Bourgmestre* of Antwerp, a powerful politician who might make widespread trouble. One might have thought that the decision should have been taken at a higher level. We, two army captains, never hesitated. We were better informed about Flemish affairs than our masters in Brussels, and reference to them would bring possibly dangerous delay. So at three o'clock one fine and dark morning, the Field Security Police, organised by us, picked them all up. We felt like the Gestapo.

We recovered from these private houses and flats, half a kilo of industrial diamonds (these tend to look like shiny off-brown coal), 21,000,000 francs, a three-ton army lorry, six jeeps, unauthorised weapons such as pistols, tommy guns, many tons of rationed goods including food and medicines, blankets, shoes and underwear. The stuff poured in for days, yet it did not in a military sense render suspect all or even most of the 91. This suited us because we could hand over those involved to the *parquet* and represent the whole affair as a purely criminal operation. There were, of course, high level and press protests from the *Bourgmestre*, but these were easily smothered by the inventories of stolen goods.

Meanwhile the quick and careful interrogations on that cold morning yielded a good many disjointed but useful clues, including some new names and addresses. We left these alone for the time being, to see where they might lead.

At that time our requisitioned office was in the Lange Heerenthalsche Straat. In Antwerp there are long streets and short streets. We also had a nice flat in the Meir. We rented it deviously from a beautiful fishmonger with untraceable money. Oysters were like gold because transport to the Tholen oyster beds had broken down. The Antwerpers are partial to oysters. The oystermen were glad to sell them for a song to anyone who would fetch them for it was bad for the beds to get overcrowded. So once a week we fetched a fifteen hundredweight truck-load from Tholen, and let her have them minus what we wanted ourselves. I loathe oysters. She sold them at a vast profit, and as she had British officers in her flat she was safe from requisition. So for the cost of about four gallons of petrol a week, we had a large discreet fashionably placed and comfortable centre.

Once the Germans knew that Antwerp was being used as they feared, they diverted some of their V.1 and V.2 offensive from London to it. Relatively, Antwerp was more heavily bombarded than London, but there was a saving factor. The whole of the city was on the east bank of the Scheldt. There was not even a shack on the blasted heath called Hoofd van Vlanderen opposite the centre. The docks on the Scheldt were the German target. The V weapons were never very accurate, and an overshot of even 100 yards would fall harmlessly on the heath. Half of them exploded without damaging a hencoop.

All the same the other half added to our anxieties. If an explosion scattered our secret papers all over the city, there might be hell to pay. A V2 hit a cinema in the street next to the office and killed 400. A V.1 exploded in the glass canopy of the main railway station, and so on. Such incidents were grim – often horrible. I found parts of a woman's body on the balcony of my billet. On the other hand sometimes they were grotesque. Walking along the Meir, there was a loud bang in the market behind the houses opposite. I dived, as usual, for the open. As I lay flat in the roadway, a storm of vegetables and melons sailed over the houses and fell upon us in the Meir. An American colleague's ceiling fell on him in bed. He got a bit of sticking plaster from an American field dressing station; and received a few days later George Washington's Order of the Purple Heart for those wounded in battle.

Having to be on watch all the time is indubitably wearing, whatever the circumstances, but again I was lucky in two different ways. I had twice to escort valuable prisoners to England, which gave me unexpected blessed weekends with Fanny. My other solace was Josée.

She was a waitress in a Flemish café. She had been a prostitute, but preferred, with the greater freedom of café life to give up potential earnings so that she, rather than the madame might choose her clients. She had the ordinary Flemish peasant girl's face, but was dark in colouring, and she had the peasant's muscular figure, much as you see in Brueghel or Quintin Matsys. She appealed to me because she had, unlike everyone else, absolutely no interest in politics or public affairs, and again, unlike everyone else, she was invariably cheerful and affectionate without being pushing or possessive. The flying bombs did not worry her. She was perpetually yet somehow not obsessively happy in her work. Her service came perhaps with a carnation in a little pot. She could sit quite composed and listen to an old man in a cloth cap pouring out some tale. But the practice of sexual enjoyment was undoubtedly her great pleasure, and skill.

Though she was a Fleming working in a Flemish café, French was her usual language, even in the café. She was frank about herself. Yes: she preferred men, but girls could be fun too – and a foursome had some of the advantages of both. Was she in truth a lesbian? No: she fell flat for certain sorts of men, but had never felt even slightly involved with a woman. Generally, unless she was having an affair, she was most intensely aroused by the fourth man in an evening. Did that happen often? Formerly rare, depending on whom one got. Now it might happen more frequently, if a lot of one's friends came in together. One quiet evening she said 'do you mind waiting a bit longer? That man over there is supposed to have an enormous one, and I want to try it'. Another time she said 'come very early or late tomorrow. I've got a very rich friend, but he always goes home by ten'. I asked her if he was any good. She said 'only sometimes', and added that she was not going to borrow from me.

The relationship was undemonstrative. We never felt a longing for each other – that mental ache which I always feel for Fanny. I think that the need for a similar kind of stability in the dangerous and emotional atmosphere of that city was needed alike by the prostitutes and the intelligence men, and that it could be got only by sharing physical experience. Politicians, who are professional manipulators of emotions in a profession mostly concerned with emotions, need the same outlet, and are probably the better when they have it. Obviously it comes best by way of a happy marriage, but I find the prurient self-righteousness which deprived the public of John Profumo, the second Earl Jellicoe and Cecil Parkinson unlovely, inexpedient and silly. It is not as if these admirable public servants had done anything new. Most of our worst rulers – Charles I, James II, George III have been chaste. Our ablest – Henry VIII, Charles II, Lloyd George, have been libertines. There is a compensation factor at work which ought to be accorded a little more toleration in the media. The answer may be to reopen the Fleet Street brothel, which existed until some years ago near the *Daily Telegraph* building. I have naturally, wondered if others in my kind of position in Antwerp or Brussels did as I did. I simply do not know.

The aerial bombardment forced Richard Gatty and me to move to Duffel twenty minutes away. It made little difference to our habits or work. It was a macabre sojourn. Duffel had a large lunatic asylum run by nuns. Half of it became a military hospital, the loonies and their guardians being squashed into the other half. I was billeted with the chief psychiatrist. His wife used patients as cheap labour. In the early morning the door would open cautiously; then a cup of tea would appear; then a beaming vacant face.

We lived in a religious ambience. The nuns were cheerful bodies who wore enormous up-folded white flapping linen hats even when digging in the garden, as they mostly did all the time. There was a stream with a hump-backed bridge, over which they took their wheelbarrows, flap-flap-flap at a run. Also we messed in the front shop of a religious coffin maker, whose children were nuns, priests, a missionary and a whitefriar, with a daughter of twelve obviously being groomed for a like future. On Christmas Day we found her learning Latin grammar, which the curé intended to hear the next morning. We took her away to our Christmas dinner, stuffed her with plum pudding and sang carols. We also put on funny hats. I hope that we saved her for a fate worse than death. It was such a holy, joyless household.

The military hospital, on the other hand was festive. There had been few casualties at that stage, so that the nurses had nothing to do but wait. Consequently, if we were not in Antwerp or Brussels of an evening we were in the Loony Bin, and we naturally picked up the girls who interested us most. I acquired a sort of platonic daytime girl-friend called Fenella whom I used to take to the Brussels Théâtre de la Monnaie, the local Covent Garden, for concerts, and we used to read *L'Eventail* (The Fanlight), a literary paper published by the theatre itself.

One Sunday a naval officer attached to us had to go to the little Dutch area south of the Scheldt, which the Belgians sometimes call New Zeeland. We loaded ourselves and our sisters, into his vehicle and set off towards Hulst. This beautiful countryside is flat with wide horizons and endless green subdivided by long poplar avenues on the tops of dykes. Hulst looks like a lot more trees with a spire sticking out. Eventually we came to the estuary and laid out our picnic on a sloping dyke. It was a bright sparkling day, with little clouds making shadows which chased each other across the marshes. We sat on the grass and looked northwards, and began to notice that there was nothing between us and the Germans except these miles of empty flat-lands, flooded islands and great rivers. They were probably looking at us.

Then a long plume of smoke rose vertically to a great height from the distant shore, and began to topple towards the west. We realized helplessly that this was the take-off of a London-bound rocket which, in a few minutes might kill somebody we knew. Then another went up. The happy landscape suddenly became sinister, and it started to cloud over. We folded our blankets and left.

Another day began when our Belgian friends told us that the only beer worth drinking – if you did not like the *Gueuze* – was *Trappiste*. *Gueuze* is peculiar to

Belgium. It was a flat bitter sort of beer which came in wine bottles and was often laid down in cellars like claret. *Trappiste* is a conventional but strong malty continental brew which arrives in crown-topped bottles. As its name implies, it is brewed at a Trappist monastery.

We found the place, which looks exactly like a brewery complete with factory chimney, out in the country off the Louvain road. Trappists were under a vow of silence, and the emaciated Father who sold the stuff did not waste words. He was in a filthy temper. The convent had run out of cases, and we had to drive away with only half a dozen. A mile homewards, on the outskirts of a village, my serjeant spotted a rambling heap of empty Trappiste cases. We stacked the truck to the sky, and drove back. Our furious Father was just shutting up shop. I told him where the rest were. A thin smile parted those forbidding lips.

Now we had a run of luck. A vigorous man of about 38 walked in (he refused to be stopped by the serjeants) and came straight to Gatty. He identified himself as one of the names on our little list. It was a very familiar name. He then gave his cover-name. We knew this and he knew that we knew. Then, without much talk, he produced a typewritten list of about 70 names. We had already taken a few of those on it, and others were in our records: enough altogether for authenticity.

Over 50 names were new. Using every source we had, and the telephone directories, we had enough to pick most of them up. The problem was, what on Earth to do with him. He might be the centre of something infinitely dangerous, and, like a lizard, shaking off his tail. He might be a genuine convert or a traitor hoping for a deal. He might be purely mischievous. In this world of lies and sleight of hand, anything might happen. In the end we decided to leave him at large, go for the list, and then see what our captures could tell us.

We got the various authorities concerned to mount a great operation all over Flanders, and had them all under lock and key in 36 hours. It was a splendid haul. Some of them were bigger fish than he knew, and others led us to other big fish as well. By the time that the interrogators were through with them, it was clear that we had broken up the German undercover apparatus in Belgium. But still the puzzle remained. He ought not to have had that information; the Belgian, Dutch and French all denied employing him; he was not a member of any underground known to us. One theory was that he was a serious and identified criminal, perhaps a blackmailer or murderer, who was hoping for clemency when the police caught up with him. And anyhow, how did he know that we were the people whom he should approach? I think now, on very late reflection, that he may have been frightened by our operation against the Antwerp detectives, and had decided to make his peace; but he never said so. Indeed, to us he never disclosed his personal connections at all. In the end we gave it up. Others, however, did not, and while we turned our attention elsewhere, the Belgians arrested him. I do not remember why.

For, elsewhere there was a likelihood of political and possibly military sabotage. There was a strike in the docks. Militarily this was serious, but one thing was clear: it was not instigated by pro-German elements, because none existed. The alternatives were ordinary industrial unrest, or communists. It may, at this distance, look like a search for Reds under the bed, but the difficulties of objectivity were intense. The Grand Alliance contained everyone opposed to the enemy, for whatever reason. We had, however, already experienced Russian treachery: the alliance with Hitler in 1939, the massacre of the Poles in 1940. We had also endured the propagandist screams for a premature Second Front (as if there were not one already in the Mediterranean) at a time when a cross-Channel offensive was bound to fail, and we had heard the very similar radio demands for a Warsaw rising which the Russians never meant to support. At a more immediate level, we had encountered the ingratitude and unco-operative hypocrisy on the Murmansk convoys. It was logical to assume that, now that the Russians were moving forward against their *German* enemy, their intention was to ensure that their *allied* enemy was destroyed in the conflict. It is my belief that this analysis was correct in accordance with Marxist doctrine, and consistent with evidence of their actions.

There was, however, a good deal of other loose gunpowder lying around, on which Richard and I reported in great detail. The more politically disruptive Left fastened on the sacrosanctity of soldiers to launch an (eventually successful) attack on King Leopold III. He had, so the argument ran, by surrendering the army in 1940 implicitly undertaken to go into captivity with it and share its sufferings. Actually he had enjoyed the fleshpots of Laeken (the royal country palace) and taken to himself a disreputable concubine of doubtful lineage (this was an oblique reference to his Queen Astrid, a beautiful Swedish princess killed in a motor smash just before the war). He had even MARRIED her at a time when poor soldiers in prisoner-of-war camps had no one to marry. All this was grossly unfair. The King had certainly been open to criticism for his military conduct in 1940, but a king at liberty was obviously more useful to an oppressed nation than a king in captivity, and the lady, a Mademoiselle Baels, later ennobled as Princesse de Réthy, was the perfectly respectable daughter of the governor of West Flanders. She was, by all accounts, sensible, charming and nice, and the King's children were devoted to her. What made the mud stick, I believe, was a subconscious national desire for a scapegoat for 1940, but the agitation benefitted the far left.

The second problem arose out of the black market. Most people had profits from it. Some had fortunes in mattresses or under floorboards to avoid official and

German suspicion and taxation. This black currency formed much of the blood-circulation of the black economy, and it never went near a bank. It was a major agent of economic distortions and inflation. It also engendered hatreds, for these black market millionaires were conspicuous spenders enjoying a high life style. They could hardly do otherwise, for black money must, in practice, be spent. Nobody doubted that this particular cancer, unless operated, would wreck the economy and the social system, and if the crash came early, it might have serious repercussions on the war.

The Belgian government courageously tackled the problem by a sudden, well prepared ambuscade. A complete new currency was secretly printed in London. The banks were abruptly but briefly closed. The new notes were distributed to them in a matter of hours. Then the old currency was declared invalid but holders had 48 hours to exchange old for new at the re-opened banks. Panic! Vast queues, which those who had much to explain felt that they could not join. Thousands of millions of francs vanished in smoke in two nights. The grosser profiteers were tumbled: the currency unified. Inflation fell. Of course there were agonised shrieks from Ostend to Herbesthal but the good sense and justice of the raid were widely understood.

The third division in the land cut clean across the other two, and it was, if not wholly unknown to the British Foreign Office (as I have good reason to think) then ignored or certainly under-estimated. This was the linguistic, partly racial partly social problem, which was entangled with religion. Even in 1944 a majority – perhaps 55% – normally spoke Flemish, a dialect of Dutch. The reason why this was not appreciated by foreigners (who might have troubled to look at the bilingual street signs) was that all the Bruxellois and the upper layers of other big city society were bilingual and naturally spoke French, if not English, to strangers. Bilingualism, too, was a qualification for a government job. The best such jobs were in the capital just within 'Wallonia' if not of it, and the French speaking minority had long engrossed far more of them (perhaps 90%) than their numbers warranted.

The Germans had purposefully left a legacy of suspicion and disunion, but it is important not to overstate this. The nation was solidly against the enemy, and in any case a Roman Catholic society (of the four universities, two were professedly Roman Catholic) was profoundly opposed to the irreligious Nazism of the occupying power. This was more important in Flanders, for whereas the Walloons, like Frenchmen, take their religion sceptically, the Fleming is serious about his. Walloons were trying to tar Flemings with a racialist-Nazi brush because a few had joined a Nazi organisation. Flemings accused Walloons of insufficient patriotic and religious rigour, while enjoying all the best jobs. It is not hard to see that such controversies could be combustible.

On the other hand, like Willie in *Shoulder Arms*, we all, including the Belgians, had to pay attention to the war. Recrimination had to wait. Winston Churchill stated that the communists provoked the Antwerp dock strike. This was not based on the judgement of those of us at the docks. I thought that it was war weariness. The communists wanted to provoke it, but had no popular hold. I lived among these people and talked, drank, ate and slept with them for months.

One other incident related to this complex of issues, but raises a different point. I wrote a very detailed account of the Flemish political situation, mentioning all the real and spurious parties, and naming all the personalities. It was sent home via the usual channels. Exactly a year later I had to call on Jim Sillem, then in charge of the Belgian desk. He was in a rage, for it had arrived that very day. It would, he said, have saved him and others a great deal of trouble if only he had known about it. I originally thought that this was Foreign Office lethargy, but recent reflection puts it closer to Philby. One could not fail to know this nasty and intellectually arrogant man because he was constantly wandering about the Ryder Street building and speaking at meetings. The world knows that he had been the *Times* correspondent in the Spanish civil war, and not the least of his treacheries had been his biased reporting, not to say lies, about Guernica and the communist propaganda connected with it, and made respectable by the overshadowing wings of his newspaper, then an organ of high repute. This propaganda he and his sometimes unsuspecting colleagues poured all over us like a viscous political gravy, and bent the British away into still existing misconceptions of their interests. The captured German archives have revealed much surprise at the press reports of the bombing of Guernica, because its destruction would have been militarily pointless. Modern observation seems to show, in fact, that no aerial bombardment ever happened.

I never understood the media efforts to whitewash this murderous traitor of a Moscow resident major-general in the KGB, because he was so extraordinarily unpleasant. War shortages made for short tempers, and we were all used to them, but with him one had to tolerate the intolerable – unavoidably because in MI 6 he had reached high rank. I think that he was not exposed during the war because we all concentrated so much on the Germans that we had no time or energy left for the enemy behind us. Moreover Russian propaganda was so strong and deep that we could not or preferred not to believe that the Russians were our enemies. There was a suspension of common sense which, with my Oxford perceptions of Marxism, should not have happened. He may possibly have had a charm which he did not switch on in my presence. All the same, common sense – mine at least – reasserted itself when peace broke out and I went to Norway. Of this, more later.

We now became aware of the approach of a trained German sabotage unit. Counter-intelligence was our business, but, at anyrate for a while there was no local intelligence to counter. So we started looking round for idiots with bombs. There were hardly any. By that time the deplorable Arnhem attack had just happened and we were in control of an area of South Holland. It involved us with the Dutch *maréchaussée*,[*] and it led to a curious wild goose chase. I cannot remember the reason for it: only that the outcome was negative. I went to Nymegen by train, first to Rosendaal and then on the Dutch system. I kicked my heels in Nymegen for three days, most of which I spent reading a Dutch colonial encyclopaedia. Did you know that I knew Dutch? I didn't. There is, it seems, a Sumatran dignatory called the Soesoehoenan of Soerakarta who is the centre of the universe, and has to rest at intervals lest the spinning cosmos overheats. Later I read with sorrow that his historic and beautiful palace was accidentally burned down in 1985.

The train back, a row of box-cars (you know: Hommes 40, chevaux 8) was waiting when the daylight sky was illuminated by an enormous red flash far away to the North-West. Then we heard the rumble.

The line through Rosendaal had been destroyed and we would have to go round to Antwerp via Limburg. The engine, which had been extracted from a Dutch railway museum, was at the north end of the train, and there was no way of getting it round to the south end for the southward journey. So we went backwards.

My resourceful Nobottle had collected a tombstone from a wrecked cemetery. This he laid on the floor, built a fire and boiled water, while I sat with my legs dangling out of the windward door admiring the leisurely passing countryside. Soldiers climbed along the train with mess-tins, and we had a sort of ambulant tea party, with the smoke pouring out of the leeside door. Nice sunny day.

At Limburg the train backed happily towards another train moving towards us on the same line. My box-car as the leading vehicle was likely to take the impact. An enormous noise came from a group of angry Dutch railwaymen. I was wondering how to prevent the imminent, if slow-motion crash when a Royal Engineer serjeant appeared from a signal cabin and blew two whistle blasts which must have been heard in Stuttgart. Everything stopped. They got the engine to my end of the train. This was obviously an improvement, but as they could not turn it round, it had to rumble through the night, tender first covering us with steam and soot. Brueghel would have painted this monster, illuminating its own clouds from its red boiler fires and stopping for water every ten miles. The Flying Antwerper eventually made the journey in fifteen hours.

[*] Marshalsea? Their national police.

The explosion which we had descried, was the only important piece of German sabotage on that front or, I believe, anywhere. They had set charges in a shunting yard which happened to fill up with ammunition trains. Explosives, rolling stock, engines and permanent way went in one tremendous up-draught; the associated ground tremors wrecked the neighbouring villages. I do not think that this is what the Germans expected. They were probably hoping only to delay the use of the place by wrecking a train over the multiple points.

Chapter 26

INTRIGUES AND NORWAY

The Germans made their Ardennes offensive and then the western Allies invaded the Reich. Just before these events, I had a pair of visits to make. I record them for their careless allied euphoria.

It was thought that the sort of saboteurs who had blown up the shunting yard, might be filtering in across the Nomans-Mesopotamia between the two long mouths of the Rhine known locally as the Waal and the Lek; so I went up there to have a look, in a 100-mile per hour air-cooled Daimler-Benz, descriptively called The Elephant, which Nobottle had taken off a German admiral.

The mesopotamia was a flat agricultural plain with mostly straight roads. There is not much cover. I bowled along without a thought and ran slap through an enemy patrol which must, I suppose, have been resting in the roadside ditches. Anyway, it appeared from nowhere, quite suddenly. Nobottle simply put his foot down and I waved cheerily at them as we shot past. They waved back, and we vanished in the direction of enemy Holland at a rate of knots. Obviously we could not go back the same way; luckily another road converged upon ours as we neared one of the bridges, so we took the Elephant across the fields (four-wheel drive) to it.

The other visit was to Arnhem. The Germans held the ridge to the north of the river; the Canadians and others the flat lands to the south. Since the Germans had the view for miles, we had placed rows of smoke generators which were kept going all day. On this particular day, the wind was at right angles to the road, and driving across the smoke screens was like moving through a series of doors from one parallel sunlit corridor to another. They were sometimes as little as a hundred yards wide between their billowing grey walls.

After I had seen the Canadian Field Security, somebody suggested that I might go up to the front and have a look. A Canadian captain, the most solid lump of muscle you ever saw in your life, took me along in his jeep. We had food, and settled down in a nice dry ditch to eat it. The great river was 200 yards off; the Germans were above us just on the other side. They too were having lunch. Smoke rose from cooking fires. Soldiers pottered about. My companion suggested borrowing rifles and shooting them up. There was a section of, I think, Van dusens* along the fence. They lent us a pair of rifles. We made ourselves comfortable, I took a quick shot at a man with a bucket. The bucket spun out of his hand. All signs of movement vanished. There was a short moment and then uproar. About 200 assorted rifles, machine guns and mortars seemed to let fly. After a few minutes it all subsided and we crawled down the ditch and gave our rifles back. There was an officer there by then.

'Whatta hell you wan' to do that for? Somebody might've got hurt'.

Then the time came to leave our Antwerp and go forward with the army. We called in at the Brussels HQ where Richard Gatty was incensed to see a report to the War Office recounting in detail their brilliant clean-up of German agents in Belgium. Less than ten on their list had *not* been taken by us: but we did not even rate a mention. Richard, a born daddy figure of usually unshakeable amiability, blew his top. He wrote 'our business is to tell lies to the enemy'.

This was part of a complex of activities at Brussels and stretching back into Ryder Street which was giving us concern. As he and I were only intermittently in either place we did not get a continuous or comprehensive view, but we did see and hear enough for disquiet. I am writing this paragraph in 2001, and old men forget names and job descriptions. We were subordinate to the Brussels office, which itself was a sort of outstation of Ryder Street, but instead of the certainty of a military hierarchy with responsibility moving from rank to rank along a chain of command, the man in charge in Brussels (Robert Barclay) was not really in charge at all, but was overshadowed by powerful colleagues like Malcolm Muggeridge (who later made a TV killing and went all holy), Donald MacLachlan (later editor of the *Daily Telegraph*) with Kim Philby; these three had been recruited, like Sefton Delmer's *Soldatensender Calais*, from journalism to which they returned, but there were others whose image still appears on my mental screen, who were schoolmasters. MacLachlan had been both: he had taught me at Winchester.

None of these people had ever been trained in the rigours of military discipline or taught to concentrate for long on an enemy, and (as we now know) loyalty – in Philby's case not to his country – seemed at the time to be to themselves. When they did not bicker, they were more concerned with intrigues and negotiations about their personal standing as against people in equivalent positions in MI 5, SOE or elsewhere. Their energy, in short, was diverted from fighting the Germans to fighting their colleagues. One would, for example, have expected that a group of clever people who had access to the leaders (admittedly Francophone) of Belgian politics, industry and Society, would have acquired a real knowledge of Belgium. They did not. They did not heed the high grade material which Richard Gatty and

---

* Vingt-Deuxième = Royal Twenty-Second of Canada.

I supplied though, of course being a headquarters superior to us, they were very ready to intercept it and take the credit. It was fascinating to see some of the things which they did. For example I remember an agreement, rather like a treaty between Section V of MI 6, MI 5 and SOE. I forget the subject matter, but in the rest of the army, the arrangements which it set up would have been ordered by authority. Here I doubt if authority ever heard of it. I do not say that the treaty did any harm: only that those concerned had become a fifth wheel. Their job was concerned with Belgian conditions, of which they knew little. This, I suppose, may have been a factor in the diversion of my already mentioned report on Belgium. If anyone who mattered had seen it at the right time, they would have been found out.

My personal invasion of Germany got only as far as Cleves. The army had bulldozed a narrow track round the town. It was slow going, with transport and infantry filing gingerly along at a walking pace. The Germans had sown minefields all around, and an unfortunate man just behind me stepped incautiously and blew himself to pieces. It was only now that one began to understand the devastation of war. The British civilian public still thinks itself uniquely hurt and we hear of London's 90 day Blitz, the Baedeker raids, and the destruction at Coventry. Of course these were serious enough, but the truth is that the allies developed a destructive capacity whose effect, seen on the ground, dwarfed the German. It happens that we saw this for the first time at Cleves; the town fell upon its inhabitants in one apocalyptic holocaust, which blocked the valley with smoking cliffs of rubble.

In 1950 I went to Berlin to defend a prisoner before a court martial. The surrender was, after all, four years ago, but the city was in much the same state as the war had left it. In Berlin everything is excessive; the distances are too great, restaurants too luxurious, the night clubs too immoral. Minor side streets are often as wide as Knightsbridge. This separation of buildings would have been some protection against Luftwaffe bombing but the Anglo-Americans made a proper job of it. Imagine standing on the steps of St Paul's in London and having an unobstructed view as far as Earl's Court. Berlin was a rubble heap the size of Birmingham surrounded by a ring of crowded suburbs. The British sector proudly possessed half a hotel: the other half was a knitting tangle of wrecked reinforcement. There was only a rickety contractor's rubble railway along the Kurfürstendamm. Some enterprising souls had knocked together habitable boxes like open cubes, in the steel skeletons of wrecked department stores or set up tiny nightclubs or shops in them. In the outskirts, I found a modest four-bedroom house with 26 doorbells, some of which represented whole families.

It was now considered that with my background, I should be employed elsewhere. The German collapse was obviously imminent. There were large outliers of German power, which would have to be liquidated separately, especially the 300,000 strong Norway force. A counter-intelligence unit was being formed, and I was assigned to it. It is an oddity of my field experience that both my immediate superiors, Richard Gatty and Arthur Battagel, were of anglicised Italian extraction.*

The end of the war came with a confusing rush.

There was VE Day.** Fanny and I were at Chelmsford where the pubs stayed open and everybody danced in the streets. There were loudspeakers and a man playing the gramophone on the Town Hall porch till 'one o'clock, three o'clock, four o'clock or until you've all gone home'. It was a cheerful, happy and not disorderly affair.

Then I had to deliver three truck-loads of Norwegian officers to an airfield in Lincolnshire. We stopped the night in Huntingdon. The people at the large pub by the bridge understood the Norwegians' feelings and made them honorary residents. That, by contrast was a very drunken night indeed. They must have swallowed the town's beer ration for a week. It took some time to load them into the trucks next morning.

The Germans in Norway negotiated their surrender separately from Admiral Dönitz in the Reich. The terms were agreed at Edinburgh with Scottish Command, a body which had hitherto had so little to do that they issued a Command Order on Uniformity of Spelling. Our Norwegian unit was assembling up there and we took ourselves to the local variety show. I am bored with music hall and variety unless exceptionally indecent or exceptionally witty. I enjoyed the Concert Mayol in Paris until its lamented demise. As I have recorded in my 'Quacks and Quotes' the monosyllable is the polysyllabic periphrasis for pudendum which rhymes with punt (Regency slang). I once had a front row seat in the stalls. It was nearly under the stage and the chorus was naked. I never saw so many monosyllables in my life.

This affair, however, was banal, and I set off from Turnhouse next morning with relief. We did not know whether the surrender terms had been confirmed, so the Airborne Brigade destined for Stavanger was armed to the teeth: all except me. I did not have even a pistol. So we were glad to see Norwegian flags over the farms as we flew past Lista. The Germans at the airfield were peaceable. I thought it unwise to remain unarmed and took a rifle and ammunition off one of their sentries. Then I took a taxi to the town waterfront hotel. German officers were trotting down with their brief cases as we came up to a rapturous welcome, and

---

* Gatty: Gatti; Battagel: Botticelli.
** Victory in Europe.

a tremendous, and rather unfamiliar banquet. Enemy naval activity had deprived us of fish for years: Norwegians lived on little else. We were given five fish courses, which we washed down with Aquavit and beer, chaser fashion, and the whole performance took hours because of the speeches. But my principal memory was that dozens of school children wandered quietly among the tables, as if they had been sent to improve themselves unsupervised, by inspecting a liberation (*Liberatio anglicana postgermanica*) like an animal in a zoo. Swarms of them in a good tempered gaze, getting in the way of the waitresses.

By bedtime EVERY sign of German occupation had been scoured away. I had a lovely balcony overlooking the quay, where, however, German sentries were still on guard. There was a bit of trigger happy Bren gunfire in the night, but nothing worth bothering about. In the morning the Germans woke us by changing the guard ceremonially with fife and drum. We watched this entertainment from our balconies, pyjamaed, three mornings running. Then a furious English general appeared and stopped our floor-show *in medias res*. Something to do with making the Germans realise that they had been defeated.

I have mentioned Churchill's views on Prussia. Other aspects of the same issue were the related concepts of unconditional surrender and the strangulation at birth of any myth, such as bedevilled the 'twenties, of unreal defeat. The Reich government was dissolved, the country occupied, the administrative geography rewritten, some war criminals hunted down. I suppose that stopping a small display by a subaltern's guard on a distant Norwegian quayside fitted in with this, but it seemed a silly way to go on. What we needed was to harness the will of the many decent Germans to the work of cleansing their Augean stable; indiscriminate public insults like this were counter-productive, and created an early scepticism of the justice in whose name we had fought the war. There was, of course, no reason to spare the feelings of real Nazis. I nailed one of their flags down on the threshold of my office so that they had to walk on it, and we began a systematic search for suspects. If we had at the outset exhibited Justinian's constant and perpetual desire to render to each his due, and therefore sought earnestly to separate sheep from goats, that search would have ended sooner and we might have anticipated scandals such as the Eichmann affair and the institution of so-called Holocaust studies at universities to support the policies of the Israeli foreign office. 'Vengeance is mine saith the Lord.'

Meanwhile we had to get the military used to the idea that there were now no Germans to fight. In our case there was no German command to which an intelligence service could report. Securing their records, breaking up their organisation, exposing their agents had become mere police work in which we should not be involved. We should give our records, suitably expurgated, to the Field Security and the Norwegians and leave it to them. It was really a sort of archeology.

There was an admirable interrogation centre near Oslo, which was run by Major Barnett. I mention it mainly because he interrogated (I did not know) and released my cousin Wulf-Werner von Blumenthal who was a full colonel at the time. The centre turned out reports on all sorts of German specialist units. It took great trouble and it was all interesting reading, but it seemed to have escaped the notice of the responsible staffs that these units had all been dissolved, disarmed and their members repatriated as civilians.

Our true function was to concentrate on existing intelligence organisations still likely to have a purpose, and I found myself arguing this against odds at a headquarters conference in Oslo about three weeks after the surrender. I was in Oslo because I had not been given a wireless or cypher link with the rest of the organisation. I had to make up a cypher of my own, whose key I had then to convey to Oslo by train. In theory comfortable, the train was so crowded that I was unable to leave my seat for 23 hours. Hence I am the only person I know who has read the whole of *Gone with the Wind* in a single session.

Two organisations were suitable for our attentions. One was the relatively friendly Swedish one: the other the undoubtedly hostile Russian. That the Russians had been infiltrating ours for years is now, since Burgess, Maclean and Philby, a matter of public knowledge, but we had already experienced other Russian efforts. They had subverted a Canadian officer who was to be posted to our unit, but he was unmasked before he arrived and there had been two brazen incidents. The Russian liaison officer at 21st Army Group suddenly asked to visit our Brussels HQ, and one day a Russian mission had appeared at our London HQ on the pretext that they were hoping to take a lease of the building and wanted to inspect it.

The Swedes, by contrast, had played the role of international double dealer. This was not entirely their fault. A government's duty to its own people comes first and it conceived it to be its duty to keep out of the war at all costs. The Baltic had become a German lake. The German invasion of Norway was aimed mainly at the Swedish copper and iron deposits at Kiruna, which could only be exported across Norway, and Sweden herself had been surrounded by German armies and naval minefields. Her economy was now perforce harnessed to that of Germany, and they let the enemy use the railway from Malmö, opposite Copenhagen, to Oslo for military purposes. So much for neutrality. Many Swedes favoured this pro-Germanism, and this explains the railway concession. The much worse situated and weaker Swiss never made any such concession.

Nevertheless any Swede could see that if the Germans won, Sweden would be swallowed next, but yet that collaboration might have dangerous consequences if things turned out otherwise. Hence much secret and semi-secret wartime correspondence with the British. There was the romantic trade in ball bearings, which we badly needed. Fast aircraft flew across enemy territory to Swedish airfields, loaded up and disappeared before German agents could signal them for interception; our agents would head these gentry off with false information or other gentle or less gentle methods. Stripped down disarmed MTBs wearing the red duster would make whirlwind runs from Immingham across the minefields to Kattegat ports. No ship or plane was ever lost. Obviously this would have been impossible without Swedish help, particularly from their counter-intelligence which was highly developed and had even cracked the ENIGMA cypher on its own. They naturally had dealings with the Abwehr and perhaps with the SD. After the surrender, they were happy to tell us a good deal about both. Then Russia replaced Germany as their most dangerous neighbour. The Russians had extorted a base at Hangö, ten minutes flying time from Stockholm; this base had been since released, but across Finland, Russian air bases were not much further from the mines at Kiruna.

The first sign that the Swedes were continuing to take a professional interest in us was a simple ruse. They let all British troops travel through Sweden on production of a pass stamped with the official unit stamp. Copenhagen being a favourite leave resort, they might have built up the British order of battle very soon through their stamp collection. I rather enjoyed myself forging the stamps.

The truth was that the policy problem was political, and the decisions on the redirection of our efforts had to be made at a political level. I do not know what decisions were made or when, for my position was lowly and we were all looking to demobilisation, but meanwhile one got on with a decreasingly worthwhile job. It involved working and living with the Norwegians, who were at once both friendly and impatient.

We were there because they could not handle the 300,000 armed Germans. Norway is huge. If you swivel it on Oslo, so that the North Cape is at the south, it falls somewhere between Rome and Naples. It was very disjointed. Apart from the many islands, many mainland areas were too, because of the mountains, approachable only by sea. The sea-water-filled fjords had sides so steep that there was little room for habitation. The climate is not benign. The sparse rural population lived isolatedly, farming in the short summer and otherwise fishing. There was a steady drift up-country to the few towns or to merchant shipping. The people were inward looking and were concerned more with their cabbage patch than with the wide world. When for example, they drank, they deliberately drank to excess, as if to shut out the landscape.

This was noticeable, too, in the towns. Their history had isolated them. For centuries ruled from Copenhagen, and from 1815 to 1907 under the Swedish crown, their difficulty was to create a national image or culture, with only one composer, one sculptor, one play, one small university. I gather that other practitioners, especially composers, have now emerged, but meanwhile they created artificial controversies of a peculiarly provincial kind. For example, Norwegian and Danish are slightly different versions of the same language. They set about increasing the points of difference. They invented an official language for official documents (*Landsmål*), which nobody speaks. Its virtue was that it was not Danish. They had had no fewer than four spelling reforms of the usual language (*Rigsmål*), which confused the educational scene, but differentiated the language increasingly from Danish. Such a people would naturally have little time for foreigners. One got used to being asked when one was going to leave. The trouble was that until most of the Germans had been safely disarmed and shipped home, we simply could not go.

Apart from the shortage of shipping caused by the continuing Japanese war, numbers of Germans in Norway had, even from a Nazi point of view, no business to be there. Many were wanted men, evacuated from Russia, Poland, even Czechoslovakia and Hungary. It was sensible to put them all through a filter at the Norwegian ports before they got lost. Moreover much of the central Gestapo records had found their way to Oslo, and these were too valuable to ignore.

We all had surprises. We picked up, for example, the deputy commandant of Auschwitz, a little runt of a man called Fritsch, whom we naturally put into the custody of a Jewish guard – with strict instructions not to damage him, of course. I found among the Budapest records an order to arrest my old Oxford friend Edmund (Ödön) de Unger, on the ground that he might be a Jew. I said a prayer. Two years later, I met him in Chancery Lane.

I also had an interesting week with a high ex-official in the German administration of Occupied Russia. He came forward as a volunteer. The likelihood of a former official of a destroyed offshoot of a dismantled state being able to make much trouble was obviously remote. His name was von der O or Ow. A group photograph which I saw 50 years later suggested that my father and a relative of his were Rhodes scholars together in 1908.

In his view Hitler lost the Russian war for political rather than military reasons. Herr von der O was a Russian-speaking Balt, Rosenberg, his minister having been brought up in Russia. He came in behind the German invasion as a civilian administrator, and discovered to his surprise that the rural population was not at all hostile: rather the reverse. The reason was the long and ruthless oppression arising from industrialisation and the forcible creation of the hated state and collective farms. In some parts the Germans were even greeted as liberators. Bearing in mind the recent murderous campaign against the *kulaks* (Stalin said that it was worse than the civil war), there was nothing inherently unlikely in this. As more and more Russian territory was conquered, this aspect of Russian life raised issues of increasing urgency, and there was a policy dispute between Rosenberg's Ministry and the industrialists and war technicians led by Funk and Speer.

Rosenberg advised Hitler that the goodwill of the rural population in the western areas, especially of White Russia, the Ukraine and Great Russia would be secured by breaking up the great farms and returning the land to private ownership. This would create an enormously powerful interest which, if not exactly pro-German, was certainly anti-communist enough to stick to the German side in the war. The policy would in the long run raise agricultural production and so provide the cheap food which, in exchange for the industrial products of the Reich, would confirm the prosperity of the New Order. He thought that these people were waiting for a signal and that a quick land reform was a war winning policy, for it would spread disaffection eastwards far beyond the front line into the Red Army itself.

The technocrats thought otherwise. They believed in absolute priority for the ability to train vast armies and to equip them to unassailable standards. They did not believe that their enemies could ever be reconciled in large numbers: they had therefore to be destroyed. Such overwhelming violence needed a superabundant industrial production. But – and here was the snag – the western Allied industrial potential would, perhaps soon, outrun that of the Reich. Everything in the immediate or short run had to be concentrated on the great effort: the war had to be won now or lost forever. A land reform would create immense distractions and absorb time and talent.

Worse still, it would in the vital short run disrupt agricultural production by destroying the existing management units. It would be better to draw to the Reich the surplus production which had hitherto fed Russian industry, and if this created Russian urban unemployment, the starving hands could then more easily be deported westwards as slave labour.

The champions of this argument had the powerful support of Hermann Goering, whose *Luftwaffe*, suffering serious attrition, needed speedy material reinforcement. Rosenberg, on the other hand, never had a strong influence with Hitler. He was too intellectual, and too specialised in something – Russia – which the others knew nothing about. His Russian mother probably told against him. He lost.

The result was a catastrophe. The Russian farm workers, finding that the same hateful system was being continued by their new masters, preferred to operate it at least for their own kith. The very loss of production expected from land reform now took place through lack of it. Norms were never fulfilled. Machinery unaccountably broke down. Guerilla, hitherto ineffectual, acquired some indigenous support. The endless overstretched communications were constantly interrupted, and forces which might have been fighting the Red Army had to be wasted on police work; especially, the Russians to the east now had no motive for mutinying against their tyrants. As the Stalin regime rectified its military mistakes, the Wehrmacht found itself isolated in a huge sometimes hostile country where there should have been co-operation. It was not big enough to do the job without help. If on the other hand, help of the kind proposed by Rosenberg had been forthcoming, the Russian empire would have collapsed, the eastern armies would have been free to fight the Anglo-Americans to a standstill and to a compromise peace.

I suspected wishful thinking. He was talking, as he thought, as a gentleman to an English gentleman, but the interest of all this lay rather in the picture of rural Russia. Was it real? Was the regime really as detested as he said? As we advanced across Europe, we had swept up many derelict Russians: labour conscripts, industrial slaves and soldiers of a uniformed force on the German side. We even had three Russians, known as Omsk, Tomsk and Minsk, as batmen in our Brussels HQ. Many of these were true volunteers. They showed signs of relief at falling into western hands, and evinced no desire at all to return to Mother Russia. I remember Minsk's consternation on seeing a Russian officer. It is idle to call these people traitors. They had an enormous grievance, and they crossed to the other side to seek redress. Their oppressors never had any scruples about subversion or treachery. 'Workers of the world unite'. Well, why not?

Murderous savages, like their imitator Hitler, though they were, the Russian government were not fools. They regarded the large Russian and especially Ukrainian diaspora as a danger presumably because they knew too much, and knew how a similar diaspora had overthrown the Czars. It must have been big enough to be worth fearing, for they tricked, bullied or cajoled the western Allies in to rounding up and sending their own best friends to death. In 1984 it emerged that we had shamefully sent captured Chetniks to an identical death at the hands of Tito's partisans. Harold Macmillan, then Cabinet representative was involved. In a record breaking libel action against Count Tolstoy and another, my old friend

Toby Low, who had been the local Brigadier, General Staff, now Lord Aldington proved that he was not. Meanwhile another punitive operation was in progress behind the shield of the Red Army, and in due course Solzhenytsin's labour camps were filled. The only explanation, I think, is simply wickedness: these miserable people like Hitler's Jews, had to be exterminated.

All the above was written long before the overthrow of the Russian Communist Party and government in 1989. This epoch making event, I think, corroborates it.

The sorting out of Germans meanwhile had to be done with Norwegian good will which we had on our initial arrivals to an embarrassing degree. You have to go by boat from Stavanger to Haugesund across the island studded Boknfjord and then up Karmsund between the mainland and the large island of Karmöy. At Koparvik, the chief village of Karmöy there were speeches on the quay and then we went to the mayor's house for drinks. We were received by his daughter, who was dark, enormous in height and muscle – a giantess of a girl. She wore a blue lace dress – with absolutely nothing on underneath.

Thence we reached flag-bedecked Haugesund. More quayside speeches. At the hotel the mayor announced that when the Germans landed, he had buried a case of Scotch and sworn to dig it up again only when the British came. He had now dug it up. Cheers. We were to drink it ALL. Cheers. Here IT IS. Frantic cheers. And twelve bottles were duly placed on the bar. This charming gesture perceptibly dulled the evening; the company had been lacing itself with Aquavit and beer ever since they saw us leave Koparvik, and I could see people being pushed or carried home. I was assured that if I ate enough *Lutfisk* all would be well, so I started on this strange delicacy which is grey, jellyish and made of cod which has been buried for several months.

Prandial speech-making was a great Scandinavian habit. At the end of dinner the man on the hostess's right got up and made a speech. The host replied and then anyone might join in. They mostly did. Fanny and I experienced this in Finland, at Saarijärvi. We were five at table and it was *breakfast*, but, presumably under Swedish influence, they all spoke – and of course I replied.

At Haugesund that evening snores finally ended the proceedings.

My life at this time was punctuated by a running fusillade of complaints from my mother. They came about twice a week, and sometimes I answered as best I could. Sometimes, on the other hand, I had a nice letter from Pater who, it seemed was ill. These I answered with pleasure and such comfort as I could manage in the face of his reticence and my mother's silence about his condition. Then I had a long cruel accusing letter from her and at last I replied as she deserved. I got, in answer, a letter from Pater. He said that she had come in to see him in such a state of distress that he had forced her to show him my letter. I can picture the scene. And then he upbraided me with ingratitude. As he obviously had no idea what had been going on, I replied at length describing it, but I never sent the letter.

Chapter 27

SWEDEN

I went home several times from Norway. One return flight on a Lancaster bomber frightened the pants off me. The navigator, all among his sparkling electrical equipment, said that he did not know for certain where we were. I knew that several aircraft had crashed on Norwegian mountains, and he explained that some of these had magnetic deposits which blinded navigational instruments. He seemed uncertain how to read a map; I suppose the high speeds made attempts at map-reading a waste of effort. At that moment I recognised Lista beneath us. He thanked me! The aircraft began to climb.

I was now permanently in Oslo. Not a distinguished town, it has one of the most beautiful situations in the world, on a series of hills looking south on the outer rim of the great arc of the Oslofjord with its woods sloping down into the tranquil water. Here it is about five miles wide. In the summer all is green. in the autumn the occasional birch tree turns scarlet like a flame amid the black pines.

I happened to be there on the 17th May. This was the first national festival since the liberation. There is a park-like street from the astoundingly ugly dirty-brick parliament house, down to the funny little palace at the bottom. It is called Carl Johan, the regnal name of Bernadotte, who as king of Sweden did much to encourage the Norwegians. King Haakon VII was on his balcony while an enormous intermittent procession, which included just about everyone marched gaily at him down Carl Johan. Each batch would stop below the balcony and yell, waving hats, flags, or malacca canes with little red bows attached. These seemed to be an academic symbol. He would wave, or salute and speak to them. In a country preoccupied with its private linguistic arguments, the joke was that the King spoke only Danish….. but then he was the exception to every rule. They would not have worried if he had addressed them in Choctaw.

I had to go to Copenhagen that autumn. An American colleague and I drove through Sweden. Having been at peace all these years, it flowed with milk and honey. The food in the Oslo officers' messes had been the sort of careless rubbish which the army had been trying to abolish. Suddenly, at a minor hotel at Halmstad, a small coastal town (frequented by our ball-bearing MTBs) we were faced with a Scandinavian meal. They expected us to eat a *Smorgasbrod*.* 28 dishes by twos and threes passed across the table. We were famished. Eventually we came to a halt, puffing and slightly drunk. Then they said: -

'And now, what would you like to *eat* ?'

We felt that as victorious soldiers we simply had to show them. They suggested ptarmigan. Ptarmigan it was: a dish big enough for six cooked in cream to be washed down with lots of claret. Lots of Swedes drank with us. A drunk officer insisted on exchanging one of his pips for one of mine. They called for English songs and half the bar bellowed *John Brown's Body*.

I remember the beauty of Copenhagen on that occasion, but my visit was short and wholly businesslike. We then copied all other allied visitors and loaded up with the locally plentiful butter, eggs and cheese to share with our Oslo friends. But the impression of Sweden and Copenhagen remained strongly in my mind, and I determined to go there again.

The seasons move rapidly in northern climes. The Shetlands, Oslo and Stockholm are on roughly the same latitude as St Petersburg. The summer days are long: there is still a glimmer of daylight at the midsummer midnight when the Norwegians hold a great fire festival. Arthur Battagel and I were bidden to a family party at a forest house whose land fell down to the water's edge. A huge bonfire roared on a raft floating in a small pond among the pines. As far as the eye could see through the trees there were other fires in the woods and floating on the fjord while people talked and danced, or went down to and bathed naked in the still water. This ancient and beautiful custom must have come from pagan times when, perhaps it reeked of old gods and sacrifices. Now it had become a calm affair in which people spoke quietly of their condition and their hopes. I had a platonic but agreeable friendship with a girl who was a potter. She had supported life under the occupation by making useful things for friends and neighbours, for if in those hard days, you broke a saucer, you could not otherwise replace it.

But from midsummer onwards the days were progressively and noticeably shorter. The sun's rays reached me ten minutes later every morning. By Christmas it was dark by half-past three and not fully light until half past ten in the morning. It was also bitterly cold. We had all done most of the work for which we had come.

Before we had to go we had to cope with the problem of Our Dog. This astonishing animal, taken from the SS, was enormous, standing thigh high. He resembled a sheepdog with a glossy black back, and a white front changing to brown along the belly. He spoke English, German and Norwegian but preferred

---

* It comes as a surprise that this word means 'bread and butter'.

English. He was a very strong character. If you wanted to get rid of somebody in, say, the outer office, you simply said 'George, show the gentleman out' and he would go out quite silently and look..... and the man would invariably leave. He knew everyone he had ever met and he also knew if they had business at the office. He disliked Germans but would be polite to one if the need were explained to him. Naturally we all respected him. He could probably have run that office himself.

A Swede used to visit us from a Swedish township somewhere near Halden. He and Our Dog would sometimes talk in the outer office; perhaps he was teaching him Swedish. We and Our Dog knew that he could not go to England, and the Swedish quarantine was extremely severe, but the Swede said that he would like to have him regardless. So we explained this to Our Dog and a few days before embarkation we took him to the frontier. The Swede would be waiting on the road about half a mile on the other side. We got out of the car and told Our Dog about it, and that he should give the customs posts (which we pointed out) a wide berth. We said good-bye. He made a long circuit and disappeared over the frontier. That evening we had a telephone call, thanking us for our handsome present.

Our Oslo offices had had a joint quarter-masters' store for the SD and the Gestapo. The stores naturally included several gross of portraits of Adolf Hitler: G 1098 no doubt. In our off moments we used to play ducks-and-drakes with these on the ice: plink-a-plink-a-plink, plink. *Crash*. The Norwegians helped. There was also a telephone tapping installation the size of a tennis court with a very splendid series of recording consols. We took a sledgehammer to all this but the Norwegians were less enthusiastic. Indeed their police were rather upset. Arthur Battagel assured them that their concern was a matter of great public interest. We heard no more.

And so at last we left. I have been lucky in my North Sea crossings. Our troopship was (for the second time) the *Stella Polaris*, an old pleasure cruise ship much favoured by rich tourists before the war. This time my baggage included 26 strong-boxes each sealed like a diplomatic bag, and I also had a corporal and a serjeant. I had my boxes put in the ship's strongroom and after that we caroused our way – against all regulations, for troopships were dry.

Some of us got very sentimental about Belgium and sang the *Brabançonne*, a very long and loud song, at about 3.30am against protests from half the ship. We said, loudly, that they could sleep all day if they wanted, and continued the concert (embellished with knives on mess tins and boots on the deck) with the immortal words: -

'Tum-ti tum, Rum-ti-tum ti-tum ti-tum, tum
Rum-ti tum tum, ti-tum ti-tum ti-tum...'

and so on for six more irregular lines to the triumphant *ralentando*: -

'Ti TUM tum tum ti Rum Tum
Ti rum tum Rum-ti-tum ti tum tum ti tum'.

I think of the Atlantic as a raging monster decorated with wrecked Tobermory galleons and huge combers at Cape Wrath (suitable name). In fact I have seen, with Pater or otherwise the Minch with its islands and the Scottish mainland all cheerful in the sparkling sunlight. One could stand on the deck and dream. Eventually, with the weather getting increasingly hazy, we turned into the Clyde. There was a smelly peasoup fog, and the tugs had to grope us up the canal-like river in the murk to a quayside.

Absolutely no arrangement had been made to receive the 600 troops. We had all forgotten that sensible armies did not arrive at Scottish ports on New Year's Day. The authorities had simply not bothered. No shops or canteens were open, nor anything else. Our infantry colonel was furious from head to foot. No RTO was available at Glasgow station. There appeared to be nobody above an orderly serjeant at the local military headquarters. While the colonel stormed over the telephone at increasingly senior HQs all over southern Scotland, I went down to the station to find out if there were any scheduled (civilian) trains.

It turned out that there was one in the mid-afternoon.

'Alright', he said, 'we'll take the whole damn' train.... railway passes or not'.

So we piled all the troops into it, and off we went. There was nothing to eat or drink, but we were on our way. The railway people were sympathetic and raised no questions. We made the few civilian travellers welcome.

I had telephoned for a Ryder Street truck to meet us at St Pancras. At about seven in the morning we reached the Temple and staggered upstairs with the 26 strong-boxes to our flat. Fanny gave us breakfast and then we held a great unpacking. 26 strong-boxes hold a lot of bottles, even when padded out with secret documents, and even after the serjeant and the corporal had taken their share, there was enough to keep us in high spirits for many months.

This serjeant, Geoffrey Brazier, became a personal friend. He was linguistically gifted, speaking Norwegian perfectly. He had a passion for skiing and mountaineering, also great skill of hand and eye. He was an artist as a serjeant, and in the days of really obstructive exchange control, he could go to Norway with no money at all and keep himself there on extended holidays by painting and selling pictures as he went. I have two of them. Later he decided to become a cabinet maker, and made an enjoyable living in Bristol, where he married a musician, making beautiful and elaborate things out of every known wood.

After delivering 24 empty strong boxes and two of secret files to Ryder Street, I came home to Fanny. The conversation naturally veered round to family affairs, and I told her about the harassing letters from my mother. She asked me if I had had anything from Pater and I began to say something when she stopped me. He had died of cancer in the London Hospital just before I left Norway, and my mother had put an announcement in the newspapers. Later when I saw her, she asked why I had not come to the funeral. I am afraid that I told her that I was obviously not wanted. Much later, she handed me a note of her purported last conversation with him. He was supposed to have said that I had put myself outside the family. I doubt it. It was not his style. But I am still unsure whether I was right to refrain from sending him that letter. Had I had the faintest idea that he was dying, I would certainly not have sent it.

Demobilisation was in full swing. Everyone in uniform was looking to their future, and in MI 6 there was much jockeying for jobs in the diplomatic or consular services, which were at that time separate. I was sounded out for the Vice-consulate at Narvik, but having seen how British missions were tied to London by their radio links, it did not seem to be a very responsible way of life. I decided to read for the Bar, as I had intended all those years ago.

I had to wait six months for my demobilisation because of the principle of 'first in, first out'. The dissolving War Office was sending officers back to their regiments. I saluted my Regimental Adjutant at Canterbury. He looked me up and down and said: -

'Your battle dress is far too large'.

Indeed it was, for I had become as thin as a rake. I had contracted that variety of tuberculosis which, as it turned out was curable in 1945 with milk and eggs, like my father in 1917.

I continued to live at home but visited Ryder Street monthly to empty my in-basket into my -out. In the intervals, with Fanny's aid and a set of Question and Answer Books, I taught myself Law. I had to go to lectures at the Inns of Court Law School to qualify for a grant from the Ministry of Education. Enough signatures in a book qualified you: a signature missing did the opposite. It treated Henry Brandon (who became a Law Lord) in exactly the same fashion. In his case they even had the impertinence to say that they did not support potential failure. Our lectures, though delivered by lawyers of distinction were of startlingly low quality. I expected barristers to speak and to speak clearly. What we mostly got was confused exposition sometimes audible through confused or weak diction. The Greeks believed in rhetoric: it was obvious that these people had never heard of it; and I have noticed that this defect is spreading everywhere in the intellectual world – a defect not improved, by the microphone. To explain something to an audience, the thing must be analysed and the analysis communicated. Modern lecturers too seldom do either.

Fanny worked as hard as I did. The first dividend was that I got a First in Roman Law. This may have been due in part to the material sinking at St Tropez into my subconscious and then popping up again. In 1960 (I think) the Bar Council (or someone) deleted Roman Law from the syllabus. This reform was not a good thing. The derivation of Roman order from principles is a desirable antidote for the 'sometimes barbarous casuistry of the Common lawyers', and anyway it has now put English lawyers at a disadvantage in the Roman based systems of Europe.

Demobilisation found me with a new suit provided by the government, a minor Norwegian decoration (which came by post), a £400 gratuity and another £400 saved from my pay.* We decided on a second honeymoon in the fleshpots of Sweden.

British wartime food administration had been brilliantly managed by Lord Woolton. It encouraged economy by, for example teaching army cooks to cook enterprisingly, and by circularising recipes which most people might otherwise have missed; and rationing was gently applied so that each separate increase of pressure was, if not barely perceptible, at least acceptable. The cumulative effect was however very great. At one period the week's civilian ration of butter sank to 1 oz, of bacon 2 oz, of sugar 4 oz. One Christmas the cheer amounted to only a few ounces of pork. Cheesemaking except Cheddar was suppressed, and vegetables were of the dullest kind. Most Trafalgar Square pigeons disappeared into the Soho casseroles.

In truth the victorious nation was quietly starving. I was not the only thin man. Food and cookery were major subjects of conversation, publishing, day-dreaming, anything. I learned to cook partly at an officers' cookery course at Maidstone designed to demonstrate the uses of unexpired rations – army jargon for leftovers – but mostly from a Chinese cookery book which, in an era when meat was a trace element, represented the ideal system.

So we took the Swedish boat from Harwich to Gothenburg.

The trip was a sudden and very complete release from war. We went to eat but thought that we might visit historic places. We found a hotel, and went to the railway station to look at timetables. There was a train to Trollhattan, and of course we went. You cannot miss a place called Trollhattan. It had lock-staircases down

---

* Worth about £24,000 in 2003.

SWEDEN

from Lake Vänern to the Gota River, and we sat on a cafe terrace looking over the plain and thought how sensible we were to be at Trollhattan. Somewhere in Scandinavia there is an island called Torghattan. The giant Torg had an argument with the god Frey. Frey threw his spear at Torg. It went through his hat and knocked it off. Naturally spear and hat were both turned to stone, and there they are to this day: the island hat with large hole, the great bolt-shaped stone lying beyond. At Trollhattan we observed nothing like it. We must have looked the wrong way. Do not trolls (according to Tolkien) turn to stone in the sun?

Then we took the train to Calmar (of the Scandinavian Union) in order to catch the twice-weekly boat to Visby on the Baltic island of Gotland. We boarded it late just as two elderly men rushed up the gangway. They were the tall long-limbed sort who play the heroic sheriff in Westerns – complete with hat.* The difference was that they were rather drunk as the floodlit Calmar castle disappeared over our wake. They settled down on deck chairs, each with a double dozen of beer beside him. At 7.00am next morning at Visby the 48 bottles were empty and they more or less fell down the gangway and staggered away. Drunkenness evidently was a major problem, which had led to an ineffectual form of prohibition. We saw more really drunk drunks in Sweden than anywhere else in our lives. The causes must have lain deep in the roots of Swedish life. Meanwhile the law-abiding had to endure a silly regime under which, for example, a woman could be allowed only half as much Aquavit in a restaurant as a man. Naturally one pooled.

We had other impressions of Swedish *malaise*. The film industry seemed mostly sick or grotesque: a Parisian audience got indignantly bored with *The Silence*. There was a hollow materialism with, I suspect, guilt for the country's recent behaviour. Sweden's past has been nobler than its present, and governments have been doing their best to make the nation forget it... In 1977, according to the Swedish embassy, no history earlier than the French Revolution was being taught in schools. Later Fanny and I saw *Un Ballo in Masquera* at the Royal court theatre in Drottningholm. It is based (roughly) upon the spectacular assassination of King Gustavus III at his own court masque in 1792 – just within the period.

But we did contemplate the evidences of the great past. Many-towered Visby is a ghost city of traceable streets and ruinous houses. Two churches are standing: twelve are roofless. Grass silences the footsteps. Yet this Hanseatic island city had been, till Waldemar Atterdag's Danes attacked it, the greatest emporium of the north and the focus of a world trade. Its vast treasure troves have so far included coins from everywhere between Berwick and Baghdad. The commercial web concentrated upon the warehouses of Novgorod Street, while the peasants of Roma

---

* There seem to be a lot of hats in this passage. I cannot take them seriously, singly or in combinations such as Hatushash, the capital of the Hittites at Boghaz Keui. Only the quiet Hattifatteners of Tove Jansson's charming Moomin books can be taken without salt – but they, of course worshipped a barometer.

fed the citizens. Then the whole fragile centuries' old complex fell to pieces in twenty years. The business men offered Waldemar money: the peasants stood up and were massacred. Then pestilence decimated the businessmen, and anyway the Danes meant to take Visby's prosperity for themselves. The international traders, unable any more to rely upon the City's facilities, went elsewhere. New commercial routes passed Gotland by, leaving a magnificently fortified ruin.

Stockholm, the real rival, is a few hours away in a channel between the Baltic and the sprawling island-bedecked Lake Mälar. This formed the arterial system of old Sweden, and being ringed with woods, had endless supplies of ship timber. Most of Sweden's historic places are on its shores. We promptly set off for ancient and much dreaded Uppsala where the pagan Swedes met to perform the rituals needed to ensure good harvests and calm seas. The monarchy probably started from a sacrificial religious confederacy (as *Heimskringla* seems confusedly to relate) involving the Kings. Three great howes cover the earliest of them; for divination, men were thrown alive into a well; if they did not come up again the omen was good. King Aun sacrificed all his sons. Other victims were hung up in a wood.

St Henry, that redoubtable missionary Englishman laid the cold spirit of this place. He founded the cathedral, still the see of the world's only Lutheran archbishopric. There is no building stone, so they used brick. It was conceived at a high design point of gothic, which is an engineering system for stone. The climate is clean: the building well maintained. To the untutored English eye it looks as if it had been put up in the 1880s by Gilbert Scott. It is five centuries older, and it disappoints because, like the Victorians, its French architects copied their original without regard for the materials.

Strängnaes has another, less ambitious and more successful brick cathedral built partly on arches projecting from a hillside. It forced on us another aspect of Baltic civilisation. It has a carved wooden altar-piece of blazing splendour, such as makes one vigilant for other such creations. Of course, we knew of this art, whose famous exponent was Tilman Riemenschneider; but it was simply that this beacon, high in the sunlight, threw so strong a light that one had to follow it.

Vesterås, the Swedish Runnymede, was as interesting as Egham, but the seventeeth century interior of the island castle of Grypsholm in its leafy creek holds a portrait gallery with pictures of the strange Eric XIV and his charming mistress Carin Mandsdotter, and also a modish version of Elizabeth I. Diplomacy sent portraits of great ladies long distances; of, for example the splendid Gonzaga Duchess of Mantua who spiritedly refused Henry VIII on the ground that she did not have two heads. The diplomats obviously reckoned with Carin, and had Elizabeth painted to suit the King's fancy as a withdrawn young woman of high society. It is immaterial that the great Queen never meant to marry Eric XIV. The possibility only had to be plausible. He, therefore, had to be at least attracted.

Then we crossed Sweden via the Gota Canal. This little steamer was full of solid middle-aged Swedes. We had a tiny cabin, and shared meals with them. We had noticed a Swedish tendency to bump into things. We put it to the test. There was a small square empty deck outside the dining room. We put a single chair bang in the middle. There was plenty of room all round. They all came through that door and fell over it.

We set off from Stockholm in the morning and turned south through the coastal skerries. A pilot took the wheel himself and his abrupt turns noticeably heeled the ship. The sea was flat calm but everywhere there were rocks, reefs and broken water like a watery desert at the end of the world. The only life was the occasional seabird and, in the middle of nowhere in particular, the old cruiser *Fylgia* (my old hobby raises its ugly head) at anchor gently perspiring.

At teatime we reached the sea-lock at Södertälje. The pilot shut his book with a snap and jumped onto the quay, and we started along the canal. The rural scene sauntered gently past our grandstand. At night we made fast.

At the morning rumblings, Fanny got up and, looking just like a dormouse, peered through the scuttle. The ship was entering a staircase of locks. It would take time, and it was suggested that passengers might like to go for a walk. This brought out a striking facet of Swedishness. They felt *obliged* to go, and in one grand collective. Fanny and I dislike gaggles, and we wandered off ahead. Protests. We took no notice. An irritable crowd poured past us. We slowed down to be alone behind. They started looking round, beckoning, waiting for us, and eventually coming back to hasten us on. There was no possibility on that towpath of anybody getting lost or delaying the boat. We remembered Jim Sillem telling us that if you were strap-hanging in a Stockholm tram alone, the first Swede would hang onto the strap next to yours. Swedes too were very keen on minding each others' business. Their Inland Revenue published everybody's assessed income annually and sold it on the bookstalls. If someone thought that someone else's child was misbehaving, they complained to the courts, and the child might be taken away and fostered at some place kept secret from the parents.

25% of children were said to be victims of this official child-stealing. This iniquity had provoked a few protests and someone was trying (with difficulty) to form a League of Deprived Parents. A milder version of this has spread to Britain where 'welfare' authorities may inquire into the condition of children, but may not disclose who their informants are. Katharine, a mother of two, was thus harassed. Perhaps they suffered from an unendurable loneliness, provoked by the country's size, emptiness and division by woods, bogs and lakes.

There was also a fibre-sapping dependence upon the state. At an international seminar on the techniques of democracy, a Swede read a paper about a local television station at the rich mining town of Kiruna which he directed. It was well developed, with plenty of professional and amateur talent, but after some years it collapsed. We asked, why?

'Because the government wouldn't give us any more money'.

This whine provoked polyglot indignation. Were there not other sources of income? Could the municipality have helped? What were the alternatives? Had he campaigned for funds? How much notice had he had? He seemed stupefied. It had not entered his head that we would question the outcome. Whatever the reasons Swedish social democracy seemed pretty unattractive. When the politician Mr Erlander, its architect, died, his English obituaries lamented him with an undiscriminating fervour which seemed to me embarrassing and wrong. Destroying a nation's courage is not an achievement. Drunkenness, drugs, promiscuity and suicides were the natural results – and this was not the swinging sixties, but 1946, nor was it the Erlander type socialism of Blair's Britain with its parallel features.

Svealand, the Swedish country, is centred on Lake Mälar. The Goths lived further south where the many lakes tended to divide rather than unite. Our steamer passed through two of the largest: Lakes Vänern and Vättern. Vänern is about the size of Devonshire. We were out of sight of land for half a day between Kristinehamn and Trollhattan. The Goths can have had no cohesion. This must be why the Swedes gave their name to the whole country.

The Goths were civilised from the Swedish inspired convent at Vadstena by St Bridget. This strong-minded lady helped to move the Papacy back from Avignon to Rome. Vadstena occupies the position in Swedish (or Gothic) history which St Hilda's convent at Whitby has in English (or Northumbrian), but it all happened seven centuries later. The convent became rich, and still stands huge and alone with its tubular copper spires surmounting the sloping roofs of its bastions.

So, naturally, we returned to Trollhattan, and the steamer vanished down the deep three-lock staircase. The end of all good things was in sight. We took the coastal train to Lund, which has a French Romanesque cathedral, and then from nearby Malmö, we boarded the ferry to Copenhagen, a morning's run away.

It now becomes important to understand that though Copenhagen is at an international cross-roads, until the Swedes seized the three provinces of Blekinge, Halland and Scandia (after which Scandinavia is called), it was at the centre not the edge of the Danish world, and much Danish is still found in the speech of the three provinces.

The city is a true-spirited cosmopolis. Supported on a rich hinterland, it received the traffic of all the Baltic with its connections into Russia, Poland and Germany, and of all the North Sea with its extensions to England, America and the East. Its splendour commemorates its renaissance power and the far-ranging tastes of its great men. The spire of the palace of Christiansborg is a tapering pile of crowns; that of the Exchange, the intertwined tails of crocodiles. One church, with a green and gold Tower of Babel, supports its transept vaulting on the backs of elephants. The Copenhagen porcelain factory turns out a standard ware known, after an Indian colony, as Tranquebar, and the Danes make a delicious mild curry all their own.

The older town was pretty uniformly built up with five and six-storey houses for the merchant families with their roots in local trade and their branches all over the world. This has influenced life ever since. The ubiquitous half-basements are occupied by shops, now seldom in the management of the household, but originally part of Copenhagen family life. This rich frame no longer encloses a society for which it was designed. Denmark had ceased to be a great power by 1700, and its merchant nobles saw worse days, but the population expanded and, as everywhere in post-Bonaparte Europe, migrated towards the towns. The great could no longer afford the whole of their houses, and without accumulated industrial capital, no one could afford to build slums. So the big houses were subdivided. We had missed the weekly boat home from Esbjerg and were by now very broke, so it was in one of these houses that we found a room at 10s* a day. The Musicians' union was above; a metal turner along the passage; a convenient grocer immediately underneath, and our room had 23 wall clocks – none of which, thank God, worked. We bought a penknife and lived by buying pic-nic food downstairs and eating it in the gardens of Christiansborg. We mostly walked.

Sometimes we went to the Tivoli, an enclosed park with splendid lawns and trees. You have to pay a small amount varying with the day of the week to get in. It contains every civilised amusement: a classical concert hall; an open air theatre; original Italian pantomimes; you can climb a high pagoda, drink coffee among ornamental ponds or get yourself a gorgeous or a merely necessary meal. If you want to dance or listen to pop or just moon about, you can do it, and people of differing inclinations will not interfere with each other.

After Copenhagen and Frederickborg (a sort of renaissance Windsor) there was naturally Elsinore, an eighteenth century fortress erected to control the narrows of the Sound, with, inside, the remains of a Baroque palace used as a barracks. We

---

* 50p.

were shown round with a party by a woman who spoke only Danish. Danish has more glottal stops than any other known form of utterance. The locals care nothing for Hamlet: Elsinore is the home of Holger Danske (Ogier the Dane) who sleeps under the foundations ready to arise at the call of disaster to the Danish race. So we wandered about in the cellars in the wake of this hoarse woman and her glottal stops. I dislike dungeons; having seen the *piombi*, Chillon, Windsor and Breendonck; enough is enough.

Holger Danske not having risen, there was, plainly nothing rotten in the state, and the view from the ramparts explains a few things. The narrow sound was impassable against the will of the fortress commander long after the opposite shore became Swedish. Hence the Danes could substitute for piracy a toll against foreign shipping from the middle ages to 1857. It was based on the outside measurements of ships, and this engendered the 'pink', for five centuries a standard trading vessel north of Biscay which held its ground simply to reduce Sound tolls right into the age of steam. The Bakers owned a beautiful eighteenth century painting of their ancestral Smart Millwall slipway, with a pink in full sail under the Danish flag.

Next comes Aarhus in Jutland. This place and Stockholm have living open air museums composed of old houses picked up from their original sites and rebuilt bodily as a village. In these were assembled the furniture, pottery, utensils, which pertained to ordinary life as lived in them; and people dressed in the right garments carried on the right crafts: cloth from a Sleswig loom; a coppersmith making a kettle, or vegetable dyes being distilled. The people worked for profit and therefore seriously and only incidentally for show. The old crafts thus continued to live, and the exhibits – the houses and their contents – were managed and unobtrusively policed. This idea is spreading too slowly. In 1971 I saw such a village only in Canada, but surely there must be some more by now?

In 1961, however, I stumbled upon an open air sculpture museum outside Antwerp. It was a revelation. The pieces, some copies, many originals, were arranged in historical order and widely separated among trees and lawns. You can go as you please, or follow a route discretely suggested, or you can hire a guide. I did the last and spent a very agreeable afternoon in the sun discussing Maillol, Thorwaldsen and Barbara Hepworth (whom I do not like), for it was a very complete collection to which they were regularly adding. They had indeed just installed a large, brazen twisted thing called KRONKEL.*

---

* I believe, without much evidence, that this Flemish word simply means 'ring'. I hope not. Such a word should stand on its own like a sculpture or a brillig afternoon.

Chapter 28

THE BAR

I had decided to go for the examinations in the Autumn of 1948. In the spring I thought that with Fanny's help I knew enough to give it a trial. In those sensible days one could fail as often as one liked, but a pass would put me ahead of some of the competition. I passed by mistake.

Meanwhile more important things had been happening. We had decided to have a child as soon as the war was over, but poor Fanny had a very late miscarriage. This is a misfortune which no man can fully comprehend. The shock of disappointment and frustrated love is terrible, and there was nothing but to set about making another. This time we were very happy. Katharine was born just after the results of my bar finals.

In the Inner Temple, Call Night was a muted ceremony. The Great Hall had been burnt out during the war and they used the rather depressed Niblett Hall, now demolished. You dined there, having been already called in your absence at a previous meeting of the Bench. At the end of dinner you were given a glass of port and lined up in front of the high table, and the Treasurer made a speech and drank your collective health. The Treasurer of the year was Lord Simon (John not Jack) and his speech was ill-prepared and perfunctory. There were 61 of us and it was rather a scrum. Then the senior man called, made a reply and we drank a health in return – and that was it. I returned slightly drunk (on other beverages) and Huss, our midwife suggested Champagne. So I went into the rain to buy a bottle. I recognised a back in front of me in the 'bus queue: it was Roland Adams, whom I had known in MI 6.

'I've jusht been called to the bar' I said.

'Looking for chambers?'

'Yesh'. Chambers were nearly impossible to get.

'I think I can find you a seat in mine'.

So next morning I had a seat as a pupil. I paid him the usual 100 guineas and five to 'John' (Basil Beman) his clerk. I just had time to see that Henry Brandon was my room mate when Roland said:

'Put on your hat. We're going to Church House'.

It was, he said, a wreck inquiry. Roland, it seemed, was an Admiralty practitioner. The bar curriculum made no provision for Admiralty practice.

We settled down at tables, the Commissioner facing us; people bustled about with papers and exhibits. Sudden silence. A little man got up and said that he wanted legal aid. Someone tapped me on the shoulder. It was a large, cheerfully serious man sitting just behind me. He said:

'You haven't got anything to do. Why don't you take him on?'

I didn't see how I could very well refuse. So he made out a backsheet for me and said:

'Better ask for an adjournment'. I did.

'How long do you want?', said the Commissioner.

'Three days', I said disbelieving the sound of my own voice.

'You can have twenty minutes'.

So I hustled my client downstairs into the café, ordered coffee and a bun, and asked him what he had to do with it.

'Oh', he said, 'I wrecked the ship'.

One dark and stormy winter's night off Belleisle, the good ship *Something or Other* had run full tilt onto some rocks. My client, the ship's first officer, had been on watch. The issue at the inquiry was whether he should lose his master's ticket. This made him the star of the proceedings: and the wretched man was being represented by a barrister of sixteen hours standing, who had never heard of the court which was to decide his professional future. He could give me no proper instructions for he did not understand the situation. Fortunately he had a marked chart.

The only thing was to brazen it out. In those wild areas there are two lighthouses, and he had navigated in the belief that he was taking bearings on the one when it might easily have been the other. His case (my case) was that on the course proved to the inquiry, he should not have hit anything, no matter which lighthouse it was. At this point they asked him how he had laid off his course. A four-point fix, he had replied. The whole inquiry now revolved round this four-point fix, but I had not the faintest idea what it was. I could not get him to tell me, because he was out there in the witness box. I could not ask Roland, who was on the other side. I knew no one else in the hall, not even my own solicitor. By the evening adjournment I had been on my feet quite a lot; I had nailed my colours to the mast, and evolved a theory of my own.

The inquiry lasted three and a half days, and I ended with a rousing speech. People came and congratulated me. More to the point, though I did not get my client exonerated, I did get him off all effective penalties. He was grateful and surprised. So was I. I would have been even more surprised if I had known that my contentions were based on a total misunderstanding. It was four years later that I found out what a four-point fix was. Also, of the two Belleisles, I had had the wrong one in mind throughout. Luckily I had said nothing to give the show away.

Let me return to Henry Brandon. We had, as I mentioned long ago, been to rival prep schools, and had met and remembered each other on the hockey field. He was a fast and efficient forward: I was a large and rumbustuous back. My method was to hit the ball wherever it happened to be. In these Allen House – Ripley Court matches the ball was usually with Henry somewhere near my goal. So I bashed away until, sometimes, his grip loosened.

Then I went to Winchester, and after two removes I met him again in a classical div: under The Jacker. Henry was now a scholar and already showing, that strong intellect and learned determination which informed his career. We parted academic company very soon and then we parted further still, he to Cambridge, I to Oxford, and yet still further when he as a gunner took part in the seizure of Madagascar. This set the scene for the first meeting of two legal luminaries, for Major Jack Simon commanded the tanks supported by Major Brandon's 25-pounders. In the fog of war surrounding Diego Suarez, Major Brandon bombarded Major Simon who was well ahead of his expected position. With his armour, he, as usual, good-naturedly shrugged it off.

Then Henry got himself a distinguished law degree, and somehow he and Roland met. Roland instantly recognised his quality, and he was already in chambers when I took my seat. I shared a room and gained from his abilities for four years. Learned without arrogance and helpful without overthrust, he could not have been a better or more interesting chambers companion. Save that I listened to his accounts of his affairs of the heart – for he had a passionate nature – I doubt if I did him much good in return. He took silk when unusually young and became, if not the youngest High Court judge in history, the youngest in the century. On the very day when he took his seat on the Bench, he electrified the Bar. A barrister before him had not looked up his cases properly. Henry adjourned until he had. As a Lord Justice he observed characteristically that the work was 'as hard as the front row of the chorus at the Windmill'.

Not surprisingly he reached the House of Lords before most judges do. Three other features of this distinguished Wykehamist deserve a mention. Since his middle 50s he had never been without pain, being forced to sit in court in one of those surgical collars. The second was endearing. He carried a nail file, not to file his nails but to do useful electrical jobs like mending a radio, in which he was highly skilled. The third, also in character, was that he married the strikingly beautiful Jeanette Janvrin.

I was among the last generation of barristers who practised under the ancient dispensation before legal aid and Lords Beeching and Gardiner pulled the system apart. Its era began in the thirteenth century and still carried on, diluted with practical modernity, since the Judicature reforms of 1873.

To begin with, there were the physical conditions. The old Common Law courts had sat in Westminster Hall, the Chancery mostly in Lincoln's Inn. One normally went to Westminster by boat from Temple Stairs to avoid the robbers, conmen, doxies and mud infesting the Strand. Hence Common Law barristers had their chambers in the Temple, Chancery lawyers in Lincoln's Inn, each accessible to the Thames at Temple stairs by way of Middle Temple Lane. No barrister ever had chambers in Gray's Inn – too dangerous and inconvenient. The effect was still visible. The courts had been in the Strand since the '80s, but nobody ever practised in Gray's: indeed the head of my chambers in the Inner Temple, Noel Middleton, was a bencher of Gray's Inn.

As the number of courts had greatly increased, so had the number of barristers and there was congestion in the Temple. Of the impressive list of names on a door, those at the top were probably judges and never came near: those near the bottom had probably just come or just gone. In the middle were the well established, who made do with two or three rooms between seven or eight of them. The clerk, of whom more, shared a cubby hole with the accounts clerk and a couple of boys. We had no typewriter but wrote our opinions in long hand, often on the backs of the instructions, and if they were needed again, the solicitor sent them back at the next stage. It was for him to keep the files.

The second peculiarity was the method of remuneration. The media always distort a barrister's life. A good one avoided criminal work because criminals, almost by definition do not pay. In civil practice, however, there is a series of paper stages before a hearing, which take up most of a barrister's time. Each might, in fact take days for which the fee would be only two guineas. When the great day comes the brief may be delivered marked 50 guineas for the first day plus two (for a conference)[*] and there would be daily refreshers at two-thirds of the brief fee. One could do nicely in a five day case. But supposing that great issues were involved, then one's solicitor might brief a QC to lead you. This was splendid, for he had to be paid at least 100 guineas for the first day, and your fee had to be two-thirds of whatever he got, including the refreshers. As he did most of the talking, you were paid much more for doing less. It is quite easy to justify this pattern, but it could result in long periods of indigence for a newcomer. Court appearance was

---

[*] £52.50 – at 2003 rates about £1,200.

his only public relations forum. If all cases matured into hearings late, he might drudge and pinch for months with nothing to show for it; for solicitors, though supposed to pay at delivery of instructions, actually paid only when a case was over. Indeed some, even reputable solicitors, calmly banked the fees, took the interest and kept you waiting. A small fee of mine turned up eight years after I had left the bar. A friend lately had £80,000 outstanding. This state of affairs arises because a barrister has, in law, no contract with a solicitor, and so cannot sue him. His only resort is to report a defaulter to the Law Society – and lose the client. Hence you report only the solicitors whom you want to lose. This analysis was correct in the 1940s. I gather that in a different way, it is much worse now.

To get experience and an occasional audience, most newly called barristers had to take on, however unwillingly, some criminal practice. The paper was negligible: the brief fees, on the other hand were low and late, but at least one was in the open but one had to be very good at it to get a reputation, and it took one away from the Strand, where one hoped to make good, and hid one among the wrong sort of professional audience at Assizes or Quarter Sessions in Brixton, Dorchester, or Bodmin.

The judges held an assize for each county three times a year. Some cities were counties in their own right as well as county towns. At Exeter this had comic effects. The City Corporation sent their state carriages and trumpeters to bring the judge to the City Assize at the Guildhall, where the eight City Macemen surrounded the court. You could hear his triumphal approach. The great man was scarlet robed with peruque on his head, tricorne in his hand, and a huge bouquet to keep the gaol fever away. The stately words of the Commission of Oyer and Terminer, Assize and General Gaol Delivery were read and concluded with the words 'God save the King and my Lords the King's Justices of Assize'. Everybody bowed. My Lords, one of whom was the mayor, retired. As soon as they were out of sight, one rushed madly for the door, taking off and rolling one's gown as one went and bolted up Rougemont Gardens to County Hall, because the county Daimlers could take the judge to the County Assize more quickly and quietly than the City coaches. One hurled on one's gown, adjusted one's wig and sat down in court just in time to get up again to bow to my Lords – one of whom was now the Lord Lieutenant. The stately words, with minor alterations, were read. 'God Save the King and my Lords the Kings Justices of Assize'. Everybody bowed again. Business could now start.

Barristers were not allowed to go into partnership, though they commonly shared the upkeep of a set of chambers; nor could they have direct financial dealings with clients: they had to arrange these through their clerk. The congestion resulted in an average of six barristers to one clerk. By 2001 the proportion had risen to one to sixteen. A clerk was paid a scale-based commission on his barrister's fees by the solicitors. Thus he had a personal interest to press his most successful and therefore most expensive barrister, to the disadvantage of the others, and as the latter were not allowed to practice without him, he could demand, ahead of his fees a small non-returnable salary, which relieved him of the need to do anything much for the newly called. Thus the successful were chronically overworked, which under graduated taxation was decreasingly rewarded, while newcomers were underworked and sometimes starved. Most clerks became much richer than most barristers. One came to the Temple daily in a chauffeured Daimler. This imbalance still exists. In truth a clerk employed his barrister not the other way round.

The clerks represented the soft underbelly of the system; there were no professional qualifications for them. They started as messenger boys and worked up from chambers to chambers. A clerk sold his blokes in the Fleet Street pubs to solicitors' litigation clerks and arranged cases so that none of them had to be in more than two places at once. Two? Yes! Some devil (another junior in his chambers) might be got in to cover the greater man while he was elsewhere. With luck he might be back to prevent a forensic disaster. Sometimes the devil was paid: mostly he had to make do with the hope that somebody might notice him and send him work in his own right. What is surprising, is that the layman who paid for all this, suffered so little, but there were of course unfortunate accidents (the comic film *Brothers in Law* exaggerates only marginally), but on the whole this apparently outrageous system was saved by the rocklike intellectual application of the average barrister. For once things get going, a barrister's life is very demanding.

Most of the work is paperwork, but by definition you cannot do paperwork in court; hence, if you are in court on a Monday, you cannot start Monday's paperwork till the court rises at 4.30pm; if the case is to continue next day you are preparing for that day, and so Monday's paper has to wait till 4.30pm on Tuesday, when Tuesday's paper will have joined the queue. After a long, difficult case, you may be faced with a fortnight's or three weeks paper all at once. A very long case makes your clients restive. The only thing to do is to work far into the night. Lord Goddard worked a whole night through per week.

During my 60-odd years living in the Temple, I have hardly ever seen all the windows in darkness, no matter at what hour. To be a success at the bar, according to Richard Gatty, you must be either all bull-muscle or made of whip cord and able to live on your nerves. But for all its vices, the system encouraged critical discussion, to which everyone contributed ideas or experience. This was the real training ground. You got your law through the pores. If there was arrogance, there was also intellect and courage. It was this which served the interest of the client.

The media have made most people familiar with ordinary law courts, or with the American gavel-banging kind. I mostly experienced the less usual ones. They were distinguished by a special attitude either to facts or to law. Of the former class, the courts concerned with sailors were characterised by a disposition to disbelieve witnesses. There is still a piratical streak in seamen, and centuries of experience has bred an official cynicism. I remember the difficulty I had in getting a hearing before a bored group of Brethren of Trinity House, when defending a Thames pilot. The pilots were paid on a tonnage basis, but were naturally required to take their turn. My old villain had jumped the queue. He said that it was a mistake. The Brethren assumed that this was hardly possible. They were no doubt right, but I had to argue with them. They were sitting on one side of a table: I was standing on the other. The chairman ostentatiously looked at his watch. I can read upside down. It had stopped. I told him that lunch was sooner than he thought. Then they listened.

The Admiralty courts institutionalised this assumption that all men are liars. In a collision action each side had within one week to lodge with the court a sealed so-called *preliminary act*, containing the answers to fourteen standard questions ('What was the bearing of the other ship when first seen?'). The judge opened the rival acts at the beginning of the hearing, and neither party was allowed to adduce evidence inconsistent with his own Act. This was very necessary: the sums involved were usually well worth a little perjury or subornation. Forgeries, especially of logs, were not infrequent, and witnesses might be pressurised by their owners. The English Admiralty Court had a world reputation, and as the sea is common to all, shipowners had their cases tried there rather than at home. It was, to a remarkable extent, an international court.

I was brought up to regard sea captains as alarmingly adequate men who defied wild situations with calm calculations based on spherical trigonometry, tide tables, hydrography and other mysteries, while passengers bit their nails. They probably are, and doubtless only the bad ones end up in the Admiralty actions. All the same...

The first officer of a ship going up-Channel saw the blip of an approaching ship on his radar screen about ten miles off. Such screens were known to be ineffectual at short range because of ground echoes. It was a dark foggy night, so he put his feet up in the blind comfort of the charthouse and watched his screen. He sensed danger only when the bows of the other ship came in through the charthouse window.

Another ship was bowling along the North African coast on a clear day. Her new fourth officer on watch re-plotted his course by the landmarks, and concluded that the ship would run ashore on some islands 60 miles ahead. He telephoned the First Officer and then the Captain. Both told him to fuck off. After 60 miles, the high cliffs of the islands rose, as predicted, above the horizon straight ahead. More telephone calls. Permission to alter course refused. When the islands were two miles off he could stand it no longer, and rang the engines for slow. A blasphemous Captain came staggering up in his shirt. At that moment the ship hit a sunken outcrop and had to be abandoned with £750,000 worth of oil rigs.* A third ship left New York for Genoa so ill found that bits kept fall off in storms, and she ended up adrift somewhere near the Azores without a propeller. Radar has not helped much. Ships with radar do not pass in the night. Perhaps out of loneliness they seek each other out in the ocean wastes and ram each other.** My brother-in-law, Ernest Sandon, a merchant Captain who held the very rare rank of Captain RNR, believed that collisions were caused simply by ships getting too close to each. Even the fastest ships move slowly by land or air standards, and at intervals of half a mile or so, yet traffic regulation rules have been imposed between Brittany and Hamburg since the advent of Radio Directional Navigation.

Another agreeable source of income was salvage. You can expect payment for salving a ship, cargo, or lives at sea, but not for saving someone's Leonardo or wife on land. There are solid reasons for this, but historically it is the consequence of the different sources of our law. On land you would have to found a claim on a contract (which had, of course, not been made) or on an injury (which you had not suffered) and you would fail. But below the bridges where the great ships go, you could found your claim in the Law of Admiralty derived from international practices codified at the tenth century republic of Amalfi, a picturesque little place in a coastal cleft near Naples. Before 1875, you would have sued in a different court.

The international maritime community thought it against the public interest that ships should be lost, and insurers preferred to pay the partial expenses and reward for salvage than for total loss. Thus salvage has for a thousand years been part of maritime law. In practice it arises in circumstances of danger and confusion, so Lloyds of London, as the world's greatest insurance institution, established an arbitration system called 'No Cure, No pay' whereby salvors and those whom they rescued, fought off disaster, leaving the reward to be settled cosily by an Admiralty barrister-arbitrator in London. Other barristers appeared for the parties. The evidence was all written and circulated in advance. We all sat comfortably round the arbitrator's table smoking and drinking tea, with our solicitors sitting with us. It was far cheaper than court proceedings, because of simplicity and speed, yet it was good for the bar because of the number of counsel who might be involved. An important arbitration might involve all the

---

* 1980 values. About £11,000,000 in 2003.
** In September 1986 two Russian ships did this in the Black Sea.

Admiralty practitioners. The system worked so well that salvage actions in court had virtually disappeared.

Admiralty actions are in fact, if not mostly in name, contests between rival insurers, and large sums were commonly at stake. Hence appeals were worth the candle, and Admiralty chambers often appeared in the highest courts. Under our system, the higher you go, the less formality you encounter. The assize judges went with scarlet and trumpets; the Court of Appeal is stately in black; but the Lords and the Privy Council were, to say the least, casual.

The Commons, bombed out during the war, were still using the Lords' chamber, and the Lords sat in the King's Robing room. Lawyers, leaders in court dress and full-bottomed wigs, were crowded into some dark pews under a temporary gallery. The Lord Chancellor presided in robes on the woolsack. Somewhere there was usually an uncomfortable looking bishop. Their Lordships, four or five of them, in ordinary suits, lounged on the benches or put their feet up on the table, and, of course, being a House of a legislature they delivered their judgments as speeches and made their decision by vote.

The Privy Council sat in Downing Street. You arrived at 10.00am and a waitress took your lunch order while you gossiped in the anteroom. Counsel were fully robed as in the Lords. Then you were summoned before the Board in a high big-windowed room going through two storeys. You entered a pen with benches backing onto the sides; the front was bounded by the straight side of a large semi-circular table, and in the middle was a lectern. My Lords of the Council sat on the other side round the curve of the half-circle; and who do you think they were? The same people whom, as peers, one had seen in the House of Lords last week. There would be one exception: the Chief Justice of the country being appealed from would be there, not by virtue of his office but as a privy councillor summoned for the occasion to advise the Sovereign (or the Malaysian Yang di Pertuan Agong), and as it was a council its members did not deliver individual speeches, but offered a single written advice. This has since been altered to approximate to the practice of other courts. I cannot see why, and I am not sure of its constitutional propriety. Barrister after barrister would take turns at the lectern; the Privy Councillors drank tea from little pots brought to them by aged waiters, and juniors on our side of the table found references and handed up precedents. On a summer's day the sun pouring through the windows made the room uncomfortably hot.

For over two centuries this had been the only truly international court in the world. I forget the number of legal systems in its remit, but they included: for example for the Channel Islands, the Coutumier of Rouen of 1207; for Quebec the Paris coutumier of 1763; for Mauritius the Code 'Napoleon'.[*] Roman-Dutch law

---

[*] My inverted commas arise because Bonaparte appropriated the credit for a draft which was made by Cambacérès before the Revolution.

obtained in South Africa; several varieties of Hindu and Moslem law in India. It could, in its dry way be quite exciting.

And finally, there was parliamentary practice. The Houses dealt with much legislation which is private or local in its effects – as much as 400 pages of it each year. Bills and orders of this sort were introduced not by members but by outside petitioners who had to prove that the general law should be altered in their particular interest. They are mostly public authorities, and their bills, after Second Reading, were referred to a committee of four MPs or, as the case might be, five peers. The proceedings were just like trials in court, with robed counsel calling witnesses, and where the issues were important or technical, the proceedings could be prolonged. I once appeared behind Roland Adams on behalf of Oxford University against an order which, if passed, would have allowed a Gas Board to erect an enormous gasometer among the dreaming spires. We, it turned out, did not have much to do. The five noble Lords, all peers by inheritance, knew more about gas than the Gas Board's experts, and made mincemeat of them. All we had to do was to draw attention to obscure topics and take our fees.

Chapter 29

PARISHES

In the summer of 1951 I had cerebro-spinal meningitis. I will describe the symptoms of this fell disease in the hope that I may save some distant reader's life. It starts with a headache and pronounced rises and falls of temperature, which are cyclic over a period of about an hour and a half. The headache gradually takes possession and creates a sensitivity to light so acute that I could not stand a shaded lamp even with my eyes shut. The ache spreads down the spine and it became impossible to lie long in any one position. Time is of the essence: if it is not caught in a matter of hours, you die.

My doctor, Patrick Mitchell-Watt diagnosed it over the telephone and came straight round with the serum. I was out of bed in ten days but was warned not on any account to work, for though one does not feel it, it induces weaknesses in the brain system which is easily and fatally damaged. I did nothing for six months. I recovered well, but ten years later I again had meningitis but of a different type. I got apparently well, I took only six weeks instead of six months off. Of my many mistakes, this was (so far) the worst. I never recovered my sharpness of mind; it seriously interfered with my sex life and it had repercussions in my marriage. Some twelve years later still, my friend Charles Pollitt had it. I wrote and having related my two experiences, urged him to take at least six months holiday. He could easily have afforded it. He was a restlessly active man and did not feel that he needed it. One never does. Two years later still, one wet Sunday, he hanged himself in the garage.

My bar practice could not stand a six month break. I looked half-heartedly for a job, but accident intervened. The telephone asked if I wanted a job. I had not made my intentions public so as not to destroy the practice, so I said 'not particularly', and then, out of curiosity, 'what sort of job?' 'Local government', she said, 'parish councils, actually'. I tried to sound well informed about parish councils. She asked to come up and see me. I was puzzled; and as I had never heard of parish councils I did not see how they could have heard of me. Betty Searle turned out to be a talented lamp-post of a lady barrister, and she had got my name from the Bar

Council's job register, where I had forgotten that it was. The job, the Secretaryship of the National Association of Parish Councils, looked possibly exciting, with scope for development. The pay, at £750 a year,* was unimpressive, but there might be possibilities. A safe income was becoming necessary because Katharine would soon be going to school.

I was interviewed at 26 Bedford Square during the lunchtime adjournment of an aircraft inquiry. The twelve interviewers seemed a rum lot. An Admiral was in the chair; there was a weather-beaten lady and a fiercely bearded egg-head. It took a long time and the Admiral startled me by asking what games I played. Years later when I knew him well, I asked him why he had asked that particular question. 'Oh', he said cheerfully, 'you have to ask people questions, but it doesn't much matter what'.

I managed to make them laugh, and said to Fanny, that the job was in the bag. As usual I was wrong. Someone else had refused it, so they had to make do with me. Some twenty years later, Brian Keith-Lucas (who was not there) told an audience that it was a decisive moment in the modern history of local government. I think that he must have said it, because five years later still when I resigned, he wrote that I 'had changed the course of history', whatever that means. But supposing that it was so important, it happened because a stranger had changed his mind.

This was mid-November, and I was due to start on 1st January 1953. My predecessor regaled me with horror stories about the burden of work, the shortage of money and the Association's murky past. The worse she made it appear, the more I liked it. I was casting caution to the winds for something in which I could believe.

All the same it was alarming. The organisation originated in a NCSS (National Council of Social Service) committee for servicing (mostly with legal advice) the parish councils (which have nothing to do with the church). The NCSS was a love-thy-neighbour body which tended to put more into its causes than the beneficiaries ever paid back. Legal advice, often of great complexity and unlimited quantity, was being dispensed for an annual subscription. Paid by local authorities with power to levy a local tax, it varied between £3 and 10s a year.** The Association was a federal body of county associations which kept two thirds of this magnificent sum themselves, so the national office was getting between £1.3s.4d and 3s.4d a year. Publications were all losing money. There had lately been expensive but useless conferences and threatened writs. At the start of Betty Searle's seven months, her tiny office had been stacked six inches deep with unanswered letters. There had been choruses of complaints. Of the 7,000 parish councils only about 3,200 had ever belonged, and there was a steady dribble of desertions. When I first sat down

---

* At 2003 rates £16,000.
** The equivalent in decimals of £1.17p, to 17p. In 2003 these amounts would have been negligible.

at my desk in the attic of 26 Bedford Square, I used to receive two or three abusive letters a week. Since 1947 the association had been formally independent of the NCSS and could expect no money from it. I was not much helped, either, by the Treasurer, a Mr Veit. He was not only difficult and ill-mannered – so that in the end I refused to see him without a witness – but he obstructed the raising of funds, even to the point of stopping the passage of a subscription scale which it was his business, as Treasurer, to defend. Death, however, supervened. Perhaps illness explained his behaviour.

Also, the Association had quarrelled with its natural allies. I met hostility even in the NCSS. I had infuriating and disheartening discussions with bodies like the Women's Institutes and the Preservers of Rural England. One of them told me that we were over ambitious and demanding. The organisation of local government was under discussion, and one major issue was whether parish councils should, as in Scotland, be abolished, yet at that moment their case was being advocated by a minority body, divided against itself, friendless and all but bankrupt.

On my very first day I went to my first experience of local government negotiation. It was in a room at the (since demolished) offices of the (now defunct) County Councils' Association (CCA) in Eccleston Square. There were four of us: Admiral Oldham, two others and myself. The CCA were led by Sir George Mowbray. The Urban and Rural District Councils had half a dozen each. We had just published a policy document which set out our objectives. An innocuous little thing (mostly about public benches, footpaths and waste-paper baskets) it was, but you should have heard the uproar. Everybody bellowed at us. We might have tabled the Surrealist and Communist Manifestoes rolled into a UDI. These people hated our guts, but were wondering whether to get us in as allies against the Association of Municipal Corporations (AMC). And thereby hangs a tale.

When the Battle of Alamein made us think that we had a future, the mandarins began discussing reform. By 1950 the four other English Associations had reached an impasse. The counties and the two sorts of districts were satisfied with the existing system, but wanted to tidy it up. It was based on specialisation rather than hierarchy, that is to say that the difference between county, district and parish authorities was comparable with the difference between, say, infantry, artillery and engineers, not between officers with a widening power of command; but history had confused the system. Counties like Rutland were smaller than districts like Hornchurch. The most populous parishes with 30,000 people had many more people than small boroughs and urban districts like Bishop's Castle (1,200) or Llanwyrted Wells (700). Hence many authorities were suitable for the functions of councils in a category not their own.

Had this been the whole picture some boundary changes and transfers between categories would have settled, if with heart-burning, most of the problems, but it was not. The urban districts and the boroughs combined in themselves the powers of parishes and rural districts, in the middle of which they existed as islands of independent power. The county boroughs had the functions of counties as well as districts and parishes, and formed power islands in their surrounding counties. To transfer a council from a more to a less powerful category was to wound susceptibilities and pockets; to alter boundaries so as to enlarge an urban authority meant extinguishing locally cherished institutions in the transferred areas. Either process incurred hostility and protest.

The financial system also created trouble. The big cities had the most to do and therefore to spend. All local authorities got money from the 'rate', a tax which they levied on the annual value of occupied property within their boundaries. A boundary change therefore altered the amount of property which an authority could tax. But national and international politics had bedevilled the situation. Rural authorities could not touch their main resource, agricultural land. Industry was derated by 75%, so urban authorities could not touch most of theirs. The war had destroyed much rateable property, mainly in the big cities, which were therefore ambitious to extend their boundaries; and besides, there had been no systematic valuation for rating since 1939. Old property was now undervalued and new, the product of enterprise, was overtaxed.

Overshadowing all these technical factors was the encroaching power of the central government. This took two forms. There was a tendency to take over existing services such as roads, hospitals and gas, and also, on the excuse that local services should be improved and equalised, to pay Exchequer grants to them for these purposes. The grants grew to enormous dimensions, and were welcomed by councillors who thus avoided the local odium of raising the rates. Local councils became decreasingly independent in fact and mind, and intrigued for central money. Hence, they acquired a material motive for getting into national party politics. The parties loved it. They wanted to keep their constituency organisations in trim between the irregularly spaced general elections. How better than to involve them in the more regular local ones? Thus national parties barged into local affairs, where their policies were seldom relevant. Is there a political doctrine on lamp-posts or playing fields? The reform of local government, originally a series of technical issues, became artificially political, especially in the areas of large population. In 2006 enormous centrally sponsored publicity was urging everyone to vote in local elections. The loyalties of the urban authorities were divided. The boroughs had ancient charters of incorporation and often, as in the Cities of London and York, dignity and repute. The urban districts, created in 1894 as well as rural districts and parishes, had virtually the same functions but had succeeded sanitary authorities which laid drains. Both sorts of boroughs had long had, in the AMC, an organisation of their own. This included huge cities like Birmingham and villages like Montgomery, which shared the same chartered status. Not surprisingly, the big county boroughs dominated the Association's affairs. They provided most of the money and talent.

Now the AMC was, on the whole Labour dominated, the CCA and its allies on the whole Tory. The AMC favoured the idea of the multipowered authority like its dominant membership. The other three supported the older concept. The AMC wanted to redesign the system in its own image, and tear up the ancient maps. What, I asked, was to happen to county cricket?

The CCA were now seeking allies because the AMC's membership seemed to represent most of the voting public. They did not know how weak my association was, and I did not regard it as my duty to tell them. If we were ready to support them, they would have another name to conjure with. We, on the other hand, were friendless, for the AMC's unitary proposals seemed to hold out no future for us. As the only point on which the warring factions might agree was that the parishes should be abolished, it was common sense to get into cahoots with one of them.

So there we were in a shouting match at Eccleston Square.

Actually the situation was not quite as those concerned thought. The leaders of the other associations underestimated the apathy or hatred of the public. It was not true that because the municipal corporations contained most of the voters, their position was dangerously strong. The voters knew nothing of the issues and cared less and had never heard of the AMC. Similarly, the other associations thought that they had us at their mercy while being able to use our name. We had no parliamentary influence, and once we were in the fold, they took a high tone with us.

I set out to change all this. Having worked at the parliamentary bar helped. I thought that we needed a coherent doctrine founded upon a principle distinguishable from that which justified other types of authority, namely the idea of the human or personal community: the body of neighbours who might know each other, at least by sight. The obvious case was the nucleated village with its cross-roads, green, church, pub, post office and village shop; but of course there were villages of many other types: the specialised ones centred on an engrossing activity like a coalmine, or dominated by a physical feature like the 700 seaside parishes. The variety is remarkable: parishes ran from a few acres to 100 square miles. Agriculture, animal husbandry, gardens, fruit growing matched the tourism of the Cotswolds, the harbours of the Humber and the Isle of Wight, the oil refineries of Southampton Water and the Thames. Their shared characteristic was the personal contact and knowledge of their people. Public effort could be based less upon administration defrayed from taxes, more upon neighbourliness and humanity – the willingness to spare a little time for others. The differences between parishes and larger authorities were those between personality and anonymity, between natural growth and functional convenience.

Once this idea and its ramifications could be established, the controversies between the other bodies could be seen for what they were: struggles between rival groups of technicians in which we hardly needed to join, for our case did not depend on the state of technology. We could in good faith choose those parts of the opposed cases which suited us because our basic assumptions were different. We were no threat to the others because we had no ambitions in their territory. Smallness was the essence of our existence and we wanted to do things suitable to our size.

Our moral detachment, too, was attractive to a good many. Politicians were not esteemed. Many distinguished people avoided politics and pursued their public ambitions in other fields such as law, education or philanthropy. We had, in fact, already attracted one or two. Our first President had been Lord Justice Scott. I doubt if the Association could have got off the ground without him. He had recruited William, 3rd Lord Merthyr as a vice-president. Scott had also managed to interest the well known Lord Justice Denning, and it was on Merthyr's recommendation that he succeeded Scott. I shall be saying more of Merthyr, but it is proper to acknowledge his objectivity. Denning's was a name to conjure with: Merthyr's was not. Therefore it was evident to Merthyr that Denning ought to come in over Merthyr's head.

Our third pillar was A.R. Watson, the secretary of the Lancashire Community Council and Parish Councils Association. In the rather smug world of social service, Watson was suspect. He was an influential Labour Alderman and an excellent speaker, and a good and sophisticated adviser. Many hard things were said of Watson, but the proof that he was not wholly self-regarding comes from his behaviour at this time. Once convinced of the need for a parliamentary lobby, he cast about for suitable personalities and came up with – a Tory MP, Richard Fort of Clitheroe, and with him we began to build up a small but useful parliamentary interest. Richard was as objective as the others. Most of his friends were, naturally, Tories, but others respected him and he saw, without argument, that a non-political lobby must find support on both sides. So he found supporters among his opponents. This was difficult because Labour MPs mostly represented urban areas.

In the end he and Watson both died suddenly: Watson in the middle of a speech, Fort while driving his car.

Meanwhile I had got to know Merthyr. Betty Searle had told me that he spent his life in unremitting public service and that he was the best chairman in the world. Nine months after I came in, the parish councils' national conference was looming uncomfortably, so I made a point of booking him for the Two Great Days, and naturally we met. If ever a camel could go through the eye of a needle, that camel was Merthyr. Born to title and riches, his health had been shattered in a Japanese prison camp where he became a shoemaker. He was only about fourteen years older than I, but he looked as if he might have been my father. Nothing was too much trouble for him. Like all busy people, he always had time for more. He would concentrate on anything, however important or trivial, which you put before him. Though not without humour or passion, his cold logic was an undisguised blessing. He saved us from countless snares by his ability to look at a thing and see what it was. He was a good man. His wife said that if he found a speed limit sign on the moon, he would obey it.

Chapter 30

UNDERNEATH PARLIAMENT

Even when we were trying to get the Association onto an even keel, we had to make an impact on the powerful. We were unlikely ever to make national headlines or occupy much time on the air. We could however, court the specialist and local press. Fanny wrote a witty and valuable piece of tactical advice on this from a time sample. Maureen Fitzgerald, the talented editor of the *Local Government Chronicle* was a sympathetic and wise friend. Introduced by her, I wrote much for the local government press: I had something which had so far had been left unsaid, and besides, I needed the money. It led me into some curious, occasionally hilarious situations, as when I was once commissioned by two deadly rivals to report a ten-day conference in Brussels. Each journal congratulated itself and me on how much better its own Man In Brussels had been than the others...... And then Jeremiah Snodgrass, who still lives (unlike Bunbury) once waged an acrimonious correspondence with me about cemeteries.

If we made our impacts, the Association would, I thought, grow of its own because people would see that it was not just another mutual admiration society. The soft point of entry was the anomalous, often daft condition of parish law. The Ministry of Housing and Local Government had been asked to negotiate on the future of the system, and all the associations had put in memoranda. In ours I included a proposal that the law should be rationalised. The parish laws had been made at irregular intervals since 1812. The concerns of these small bodies, which the laws were supposed to regulate were well below the horizon of the Great, the Good and the Very Bad. The results had sometimes been laughably maddening. The law on their churchyards and burial grounds was scattered through 83 statutes, half a dozen statutory instruments and some thousands of local acts and orders. To provide a public shelter, a parish council had to be given the power by an electors meeting on a simple majority which might entail a poll, but it had to raise half the money by public subscription. A two-thirds majority, but no subscription, was needed for a lamp-post in a street, but for one in an open space it had only to seek the power from the county council.

It happened that another nonsense was entangled with a grievance and a quarrel. Parish councils, like other councils, paid for their own elections, but the clerk of the Rural District Council (RDC) conducted them, for a fee. There were complaints that they cost too much (a reflection on his competence) and that the fee was too high (a threat to his pocket). RDC clerks should have been our friends, but nothing upsets friendship sooner than a threat to the pocket. We badly needed friends. The legislation had created a Mad Hatter's tea-party procedure. The clerk of the RDC ran the election, and sent the bill to the parish council. The latter issued a precept for the money to the RDC, as rating authority. It paid the parish council. The parish council then paid the clerk of the RDC.

I made a private deal with John Macintyre, the secretary of the RDC's Association. Let the RDCs pay the expenses direct to the clerk, but charge the parish ratepayers. This would make no difference to the latter who would have to pay anyway. The 'Tea Party' would go, the item would cease to appear in the parish accounts, so that the parish councils would stop complaining, and the RDC and Parish elections would be held together, with a real reduction in cost.

We went to the government and I persuaded ministers to get it announced in the Queen's Speech. No government which meant to abolish parish councils would take up valuable parliamentary time on such a point, so this piece of diplomacy assured us that we were safe. The resulting overdrafted and trivial Local Government (Elections) Act 1956 represented the little remarked turning point in our fortunes.

J.D. Jones (later Sir James) was Deputy Secretary at the Ministry, and responsible under Dame Evelyn Sharpe for the reforms. My request for rationalisation had caught his eye. He doubted if all that small detail could be squeezed into the more general reform bill. I said that if I could get a private member to introduce a bill to do it instead, would the ministry perhaps offer time? He could make no promise, and anyway it would depend on the bill. I said that I would be happy to agree its terms with the ministry. He laughed and said that I would probably have to lobby a lot of others as well. I thought so, too, but it was worth a try.

I had to rush round. I made the draft, showed it to everyone who might be worried, amended it to suit them, put in things to please others, explained to maddened committeemen why their pet idea had to be left out, argued with government departments, got them to help me with redrafting, made speeches about it, saw MPs and peers, and generally enjoyed myself. The problem, as always with legislation, was the time factor, made more pressing by the increasing demands for advice from councils. I had no other lawyer to whom I could turn. I had to do everything myself.

A bill had to jump all its fourteen or sixteen procedural hurdles in a single session – about a year – and if it failed at any one of them it is a nullity, and you had to do it all over again.* This excellent rule forced everyone to have it complete, ready and lobbied before the session, and it forced governments to think out their priorities. A Session began in November, but parliamentary holidays cut the working year down to about seven and a half months. The government pre-empted all sitting days except the Friday half day, and half of the Fridays were kept for motions. This left about sixteen periods of two hours in a session for private members' second readings. The whips usually shanghai the 500 members into bidding for this time, and they ballot for it. The first sixteen in the ballot have a prospect, but bearing in mind the fourteen or sixteen stages, it is only the first six or so introduced before the end of January which had much chance. Moreover on the day of Second Reading the House does not have to throw a bill out to kill it. A member can kill it by talking the two hours out, and if it is the second or third on the day's list, he can kill it by filibustering the bill before.

We were nearly wrecked. Our MP Vice-Presidents, unlucky in the ballot, had persuaded Wing-Commander Bullus, MP for Hammersmith (a place sadly deficient in parish councils) who had a good place, to take up our bill. He was interested in another one (to abolish borough polls) which was hotly opposed in committee. We squared everyone for our second reading and had a nice polite two hours. The government moved a financial resolution in support (stage three). Then, at stage four (committee) we were stuck behind Bullus' previous bill. Time trickled away, while MPs talked interminably about the constitutional rights of borough electors, and even about the effects of the precedent on the colonies and dominions.

I told Bullus that if things went on like this, he would lose both his bills. MPs like to have an Act to their credit; he waited another week and then dropped the earlier bill. The committee atmosphere changed at once. It passed our fifteen clauses and two schedules in a morning and without amendment. So, back to the full House where, a fortnight later, the report, third reading and pass were taken on the same day (Stages five to seven). Now for the Lords.

Lords' procedure was similar in theory (though they did not deal with money) but very different in practice. There are less politics and they will not block Commons' bills save on an issue of overwhelming national importance. Collectively, however, they knew more than the Commons. The membership was bigger but peers mostly attended only when they had something to say. The result was a smaller alert assembly, which scrutinised wording and detail with valuable effects. They had few rules, and though the Lord Chancellor presided, the peers managed their business themselves. In the Commons, if you want to speak, you catch the

---

* I gather that the Blair parliament has, wrong headedly, altered this.

Speaker's eye; in the Lords you put your name down on a list with a rough estimate of length, and nothing can stop you save a rare motion that you be not heard. Mutual forbearance replaces procedure. It does noisy promoted politicians a power of good.

Lord Merthyr, of course, took the bill and got it through with so little fuss, that I remember little about this occasion. He got me a seat at the bar, and I have an idea that the Second Reading (nine) took only about an hour and that the committee, report, Third Reading and Pass (10-13) all happened about a fortnight later. I had to lobby rather hard to prevent a committee amendment because an amendment in one House must be agreed (14) by the other, which might mean a fatal delay.

And so we came to the great moment (15) when the bill, by receiving the Royal Assent, was to become an Act. Nowadays this is mostly given in private and announced to the Houses by the Speaker and the Lord Chancellor. The Sovereign could come down to parliament and give it herself in state from the throne, though this has not happened in England for centuries. The ceremonial way of doing it – in 1957 still the only way – was by commission, which happens only at the end of a session. The Sovereign issues a royal Commission under the Great Seal appointing all sorts of grandees – a royal uncle, an archbishop and a row of other peers – 'or any three of you' to signify her assent in the Lords. This arduous task is left to the three at the end of the list. They appear robed in scarlet and take their seats on a bench in front of the Throne wearing three cornered hats. Black Rod is sent to summon the Commons. The doors are left open. There is a pause. Those in the know, cock an ear. Then, considering how far away it is, there is a remarkably loud crash. The officials of the House of Commons have slammed the door in his face. After this ceremonial insult, he knocks on the closed door, they open, he delivers his message and they all follow him to the bar of the Lords, where they stand in a sort of gloomy gaggle.

The Clerk of the Parliaments now reads the Commission. Every time he mentions one of the Lords Commissioners, he bows to him, and the commissioner raises his hat. This is the purpose, I suppose of wearing it. It takes some time to read the commission. The commissioners then signify that the Queen's Assent may be given in the manner accustomed. In fact they *do* no more. There is a sort of litany between the Reading Clerk on one side of the Table, and the Clerk of the Parliaments on the other. The Reading Clerk intones the title of a bill, and the Clerk of the Parliaments replies on behalf of the Commissioners – in Norman French. When they have got through their list, everybody bows three times and silently walks out.

I have devoted space to this bill to illustrate how parliamentary work occupied much of my time between 1955 and 1974. I have never been a member of parliament, but I am one of the few outsiders who has got public legislation through that body;* none of it was, exactly, spectacular and most of it has been regurgitated in later statutes; yet it represents some sort of claim to have done something useful.

Promoting one's own bills was one thing. Battling with other people's was quite another. Between and above these two extremes was the advancement of legislative changes of principle likely to invade the assumed interests of other bodies. Until 1974 I was uninterruptedly memorialising departments, seeing civil servants and ministers and tramping corridors.

The Association was still rickety. It was not only the over-small, if growing membership, or the insecure finances. There was an amateurishness among clerks and councillors which made it hard to make claims on their behalf. Requests for advice, for example, could only seldom be answered instantly because councils failed to explain what they wanted or give the essential facts. I treasure (if that is the right word) a letter from Anglesey:

> 'Dear Sir,
> the parish council is very worried about the water rate.
> Yours faithfully
> A. Squiggle'

We had to try and educate our people, but where to begin? I once, myself, ran a joint session for parish councillors and secondary school children at Brockenhurst, and during my first year I was away for 40 weekends helping county associations to teach. There was, however, an obvious and relevant centralised piece of work which I could do. I condensed the eleven handbooks into two. When we published they began to sell in thousands.

I now ran into Tony Forster. He, the poet Frank Thompson and I had been close friends at Winchester, but the tides of war had carried us apart, and it was from Tony that I heard of Frank's terrible and heroic fate. Parachuted into Bulgaria, he had organised a communist resistance to the Germans. He had been caught, tried, and shot while trying to escape. He became, for a while, a Bulgarian national hero.

I had known him well, and stayed with him and his parents at their home on Boar's Hill by Oxford. His well known father, Edward Thompson, had spent much time in India. The house was full of books in Sanskrit and Hindi. Edward was a friend of Jawaharlal Nehru, who occasionally stayed at Boars' Hill. Jawaharlal was,

---

* Five Acts actually: the Local Government (Elections) Act 1956, The Parish Councils At 1957, The Physical Training and Recreation Act, the Parish Councils and Burial Authorities Act 1970, The Dangerous Litter Act 1971.

of course, an extreme socialist. Edward imbibed his political views and passed them on to Frank who was not a politician but a starry-eyed (and good) poet. I put the blame for his death on his father for his influence on Frank. His mother too may have had a hand in it, for in about 1946 she invited me to a celebration for Frank. The language of the invitation was so obviously communist that I declined to attend. To claim a personal friendship as support for an opinion is fraudulent.

Tony was now a director of Methuen's. He invited me to write a book on parish law, for the books on the subject were bad or out of date. This seemed a splendid way of getting my ideas straight and – most important – of making some money; for I was still badly paid and Katharine was going to school.

> 'I'm tired of life and still more tired of rhyme,
> But money gives me pleasure all the time'.

So I wrote *Parish Administration*, and Methuen's published it. It went well, though, as I shall relate, not as well as it might have done. But it added to my hard pressed income.

I do not regard money with much respect, and I do not judge a man by his bank balance. I find possessions an incumbrance. Obviously one must have a living to support one's family, and it is nice to enjoy decent food, wine, beautiful glass and silver, or have a nice picture on the wall. One should not despise these things. Therefore I take on work in order to be paid for it, but I prefer responsible to irresponsible work, and the latter means thinking of other people, yet I am a bad volunteer. If I accept a place on somebody's Committee for Improving the Universe, I am at best a spasmodic attender. I do not do a job well unless I am paid for it. This is not deliberate. It is simply a fact which I have observed about myself. On the other hand I have quite often done jobs for nominal payments. Even the acceptance of underpayments has, for someone with dependents, its moral drawbacks.

In 1955 I was asked to serve on the proposed Royal Commission on Common Lands under the famous Sir Ivor Jennings.

Despite the pile of work which I have described, I accepted. It might be hard and, save for expenses, unpaid, but parish councils were involved with hundreds of commons and owned thousands of village greens, and it might take me (free) out into the country a bit more.

The Commission met for the first time on 7th December 1955 in one of the beautiful Regent's Park Terrace houses. Jennings was fresh from drafting the Malaysian constitution, and was Master of Trinity Hall. A very nice, unassuming man, you never suspected the immense learning or strong intellect which lay underneath, nor did he ever ambuscade lesser mortals like me. His strength lay in his ability to produce the acceptable acceptably. In the commission's three year labours, its members had arguments but never quarrels.

The only person whom I knew already was the geographer Dr Dudley Stamp, who like myself was on the national committee of the Council for the Preservation (now Protection) of Rural England. I eventually served on this body for seventeen years and probably went to nine out of eleven meetings a year. It was large, full of people with local knowledge and interests, and it met at the National Trust offices in Queen Anne's Gate, a building distinguished for the spectacular beauty of its Dutch tiled 'loo. Sir Herbert Griffin had long managed it, with Mervyn Osmond as his deputy. Osmond suffered the misfortunes of a crown prince, for Griffin, who had brought the Council up from very little, had stayed too long.

It was addicted to case work – an approach to rural amenity not to be despised: particular eyesores and attempts at economic or bureaucratic vandalism should be resisted; but the Council had got into the habit, which suited Griffin's temperament, of doing nothing else. It behaved like a firm of solicitors, for ever preparing briefs and engaging advocates at public inquiries, and generally shying away from issues of principle. I raised several such issues myself – for example, whether the Council should favour high density urban development to discourage suburban sprawl, or have a policy on electrically powered rural industries. All to no avail. Sir George Abercrombie, the chairman, and the very able (but mostly rather old) public persons who composed it, understood the problems as individuals, but seemed unable to change as a group. Even after Sir Herbert retired, the Council was carried on by the momentum of its past, and so deprived itself of decisive influence by its approach and methods, just when the country was changing from individual rights rooted in law, to mass demands supported by political power.

One of these mass demands, canvassed by the Labour Party, was the use of the countryside for recreation. The (erroneous) belief that commons were common to all was one factor which caused the creation of the Commission. It had, of course, its statutory woman, a forgotten Labour MP called Florence Paton who urged upon us the good old labour doctrines. All the same we had to take these demands seriously for technical reasons. Most commons were abandoned lands, neglected and often useless or degraded, because everybody had forgotten who had what rights and duties over them. It seemed dog-in-the-mangerish to keep strangers out when no one else apparently bothered with them; and besides, there was the huge miserable urban proletariat with nowhere to go.

This picture was out of date. The amenity lobby contended that if you let loose hoards of trippers upon these scattered lands, they would self defeatingly erode and destroy them. Actually, the urban proles were car-born or on the Costa Brava. The ecologists said that they contained rare plants and fauna, some close to extinction. Professor Alun Roberts was a rural scientist: Colonel Floyd a leading arboriculturalist, and Sir Alan Lubbock, a friend of the Sitwells, saw the world from a literary and aesthetic point of view. None of these accepted at their face value the extremist arguments, especially when backed by Trevor Evans, the Duke of Norfolk's agent and Sir Donald Scott, a Land Commissioner, level-headed men with a lifetime of land management behind them. Nor, in the membership was history forgotten. Commons are mostly the residue of an Anglo-Saxon manorial system, and so we had Dr William Hoskins, a well known, especially local historian.

In this talented group I, obviously, was the odd man out. I was less endowed, and less experienced. They were mostly in their 50s and 60s, I was 37. My only contemporary was George Wilde, the Commission's energetic and articulate secretary. He was a recent and, I fear, almost the last example of the long line of literate civil servants. He had a golden English style, and the Commission's report, when it emerged in 1958, was besides a forceful statement of proposals, a work of art which anyone can read for pleasure. The witnesses provided the raw material and the Commissioners the means of digestion. George Wilde converted it all into true prose. Hence it had an impact denied to other and weightier reports. That the impact was not exactly as he, and we hoped, was the fault of timid or slothful politicians, and less intelligent civil servants.

The Commission advertised itself and met for two days a fortnight. Organisations, pressure groups, idealists, lords of manors, commoners, cranks, ministries and nationalised industries sent us memoranda between weighty documents with many appendices and a few sentences scribbled on cheap notepaper. Converted into double-sided foolscap* we eventually read a stack a foot and a half deep. Despite the repetitions – for everyone thought that what they said had never been said before – I am certain that we read it all, for we debated these documents at our fortnightly meetings.

Our proceedings fell into four overlapping stages: written evidence, oral evidence, visits and conclusions. Our first batch of human witnesses consisted of civil servants. Later on we had the main interested organisations such as the Commons Society, the National Farmers Union and the local authority associations. These last were of special interest to me for obvious and less obvious reasons. As secretary of the NAPC I had drafted its evidence, which I would then have to consider as a commissioner. Of course everybody knew this; and the oral hearing of the Association's witnesses was bound to be something of a charade. I was not sure how many of them understood the evidence for much of it was unavoidably

---

*A forgotten standard paper size now superseded by A4.

technical. I held little seminars for them and wrote it out privately for them in non-technical terms. When the day came I had intervened very little, and they had had plain-sailing. They even managed to interest the Commissioners by avoiding the standard clichés.

In every public proceeding there is a silly fool. Alderman H, the Association's Vice-chairman was a very nice, kind, rather deaf man with his heart in the right place and his feet in his mouth. I remembered with apprehension when he deputised catastrophically for the chairman at one of the Association's meetings. I had to save his bacon by saying what I hoped he would have said, had he known what he was doing. On this day at the Commission the witnesses had finished and were about to withdraw when up spoke the Alderman. There was just something which he wanted to add. The Commission waited politely. He then launched into a statement which contradicted everything which his colleagues had just said: - and he had no idea at all that he was doing it. One could only let him meander on. Luckily the Commission detected the springs of this private frolic. It was no good upbraiding him (though some tried) afterwards. Nothing penetrated that armoured skull.

We travelled too, all over the country. It is largely a result of social geography that most of the commons were at the periphery. In some areas, our reception was not elaborate. Arthur Blenkinsop, the articulate and civilised Labour MP for Newcastle, helped us a great deal especially in the north where he was widely respected. With him we arrived in a rather battered hired bus at a village pub in Westmorland. The commoners, a rascally looking lot, were standing about in their overcoats. They wanted us to let them do something which, in effect, would have made them the private owners of the large nearby common. We explained, as we had already said in writing, that we could only investigate and recommend, that we had no power to change the law one way or another. This seemed to annoy them. We had, they hinted, wasted their time. We asked them whether they could produce the documents mentioned in their memorandum (Inclosure Awards or Parochial Agreements, I think). Documents? What documents? What they wanted us to do was...

By the way, I last met Arthur, charming and modest as ever, getting off a *Vaporetto* at the Molo by St Marks.

Epping Forest, owned by the Corporation of London, is the most notable common near London. The visit to it was notable indeed. They fetched us in a convoy of splendid cars, and after showing us round this interesting territory, with its deer, its cattle customs and its woods, they took us to a hunting lodge – one of several. It consisted of a single square room rising through two storeys, with a single entrance and three huge fire places ablaze with vast log fires, for it was a cold winter's day. Here they spread a large and delicious meal with oodles of drink served by their foresters in heather-brown liveries – and heather-brown bowler hats. That is the way to treat a Royal Commission!

Chapter 31

LOCAL GOVERNMENT REORGANISATION

Henry went to Westminster under Dr John Rae in 1974. He won no school honours, being something of an original but he was respected. This came out forcibly when a boy in another house was in trouble for drugs. The Headmaster asked if there was anybody whom he might wish to consult. The boy asked for Henry, who powerfully defended him.

Some years before, we had bought a small house at Hampton Court. Long before when Katharine was at Margery de Brissac's school near Sloane Square, we had lived on a boat for a long lovely summer, just above Hampton Court weir. This was connected with Fanny's health, and we often slept under the stars. Katharine and I commuted across the walk-way over the thundering weir, while Fanny minded the boat and did the shopping.

When term ended, we went up-river. This was a halcyon time in both senses. We watched kingfishers at a small ayot near Maidenhead (the River was already busy but not yet a floating scrum) and pressed on to Oxford where I daily visited the Codringtom library and wrote *Parish Administration*. Financed by the grandfather of Nelson's colleague at Trafalgar this library is one of the lesser wonders of the world. It is said to be the biggest of all European rooms with an unsupported ceiling. I showed it to my cousin Marion, who, though well informed, had never heard of it.

So now we returned to Hampton Court. The house had been part of a bigger house which Charles II built for one of his physicians. There was a tiny garden in front: then a road, and then the Palace and Mary II's gardens. The excellent view across them from the bathroom was a strong motive for having a bath. Early one morning in 1986 Fanny looked out of the bedroom and said 'the Palace is on fire!' Henry and I leapt out of bed. There was a high column of smoke in the still sky, and huge flames rose at least as high again as the height of the roof. He and I rushed down there while Fanny interviewed press people. We found an incredibly efficient fire brigade operation in full swing, even though the nearest hydrant was over a quarter of a mile across a traffic roundabout.

Then Fanny sent herself on a training course and got a job as an English teacher in a large comprehensive near the White City. More money and new insights. Of 1,500 boys 65% were black or brown with Yugoslavs, Cypriots, Chileans and other members of our cosmopolitan society. They all worked together without noticing the differences which the press loves to emphasise, and the school, in common with others under ILEA, did and taught all the things about whose absence politicians have so unscrupulously complained since Mr Callaghan suddenly decided that there was a Great Debate.

Fanny taught at the Christopher Wren School for ten years, and her, by no means unique, experience argues for more independence in the schools, not less. It would reduce political interference and the parasitic educational bureaucracies. In 1985, the office costs alone in the Department of Education were running at £50,000,000[*] and Local Education Authorities, were, in total, running much larger bureaucracies. These computer pushers do not run a single school or teach a single child. Yet, when money is short, they complain about standards and cut school staffs rather than their own, because it is they who allocate the funds. It is a scandal in the Teaching profession that you can do better by not teaching than by doing that which attracted you into the profession in the first place.

Teaching is not alone in acquiring too many ancillaries at the expense of the cutting edge. Churchill inveighed in my presence against vast military back-up organisations supporting only a few men who actually fought the enemy.

Now there is a rule of thumb for appraising the proper size of a bureaucracy. The purpose of administration is to increase the value of the labour of the rest. It is necessarily too large if it costs as much or more than the annual growth rate of the Gross National Product. 'Bureaucracy', of course includes not only state bureaucracies but the mass of non-industrial office workers in the private sector, without whom the economy might grind to a start.

There were other activities at Hampton Court. Once Fanny looked out of our Temple flat and noticed some officials evicting some nice neighbours. They were carrying their things to their car. She caught up with them. They had nowhere to go, so she guided them to our Hampton Court house where we put them up for a fortnight, while they fixed things up. There are real advantages in a second home.

Here comes a blomp. I do not know all the places where my mother had made a home during her long life, but I have identified 22 in England, Germany and Switzerland. She was energetic long after most people are content with a rocking chair. Increasingly deaf, she attributed deafness to others and talked at the top of her voice. Once, at 76, she complained that she was not very well, but that was

---

[*] Perhaps £100,000,000 now.

because she had been redecorating a ceiling and had fallen off the ladder. She was 89 when she bought a flat at Hampton Court. I persuaded her not to go elsewhere because it might be better than ending prematurely in a sunset home. Age had slightly smoothed the rougher edges of her abrasive temperament and reduced her ability, if not her inclination to make trouble, but her demanding nature was now reinforced by the necessities of her condition. She had to be visited daily if only to compose some unnecessary quarrel with a neighbour. It was difficult to recognise advancing senility but her later years constituted an emotional and physical drain (for I was still perversely ready to be fond of her) which I hope not to inflict on my successors. In 1978 she died in her 96th year.

Words have to be written consecutively, but the events which they describe often happen simultaneously, so that the reality is distorted by the very nature of narrative. This is the disadvantage and temptation of specialist history. It makes a lovely story, but is untrue to life. Poets can appeal to more than one level of understanding. If only we could return to a more poetic prose such as that of Kipling, who could convey atmosphere as well as description and action, and strike chords simultaneously in different faculties. Nowadays the language is degraded by semi-literate sensationalism, or propagandist manoeuvres or fragmented by the dense private codes of scientific dons or by hasty and inelegant efforts at precision. There have always had to be technical terms, used as a kind of short-hand between specialists, but in modern English, jargon is encroaching upon communication. It is no coincidence that there is a growing passion for minority languages, sometimes evidenced by bombs. If sociology students and motor mechanics can have their private language, why not Basques* or the Welsh?

We were beginning to feel the early stirrings of Welsh nationalism in the Association. In the 1950s about a third of the Welsh spoke Welsh at home or in the shops, but monoglot Welsh speakers were already rare. Our thirteen local county associations could find only 80 potential customers for a proposed Welsh translation of one of our handbooks, whose English version had been selling in tens of thousands. I shelved the project, with regret. We had, all the same, our finger more sensitively on the pulse than most. I once discussed Welsh nationalism with William Dacey, the secretary of the CCA himself not only a Welshman but a Methodist lay preacher. He scouted the whole idea as a literary fashion of no consequence. There is now a Welsh assembly.

We were in fact discussing the proposals which took shape in the Local Government Act 1958. In the controversy which I have already partly recounted, the CCA and its allies (including ourselves), and the AMC had published rival manifestoes. The government was Tory, and the CCA was anxious, since reform

---

* Written four years before my son married a Basque.

legislation seemed inevitable, to have it passed before the electoral pendulum brought in their more radical rivals. The details were astonishingly trivial, and were trivially presented by the envoys of our Four Associations to Duncan Sandys, then the responsible minister. Sir George Mowbray and Dacey did all the talking. Sandys was prepared for a wide sweep. They could not get away from details. As we left the presence, he buried his face in his hands and muttered:

'My God, I offered them the earth, and all they could talk about was weights and measures'.

This was not the only misjudgement. Their assumption that the Labour Party would hotly support the AMC was quite wrong. We in the parishes had the best of reasons for knowing this, for we had invited Clement Attlee, the respected leader of the Labour Party, to speak to our national conference at Central Hall opposite Westminster Abbey. He returned from China only the night before, but that made no difference. Fanny met him at St Pancras. He said to those thousands of councillors that he was a two-tier man, that is, that he was against the simplicities of the AMC. This raised our stock with our allies, who, however, drew no working conclusion.

The outcome was that the Act of 1958 did not reform the system, but set up commissions for tinkering with it, by an elaborate procedure which was so slow that too little was done. I am sure that in spite of this, the objectives of our Four Associations were right. Most defects could have been cured by intelligent legal and financial reform and boundary adjustments. It was the CCA's determination to reduce and delay change which brought the scheme to nought, for in the end people began to wonder if any improvement was intended. I urged the English Commission to begin with some large easy areas such as the West Country, so that they could be settled and obvious, but it preferred (for good reasons) to tackle the confused and time-consuming urban agglomerations. This was a political mistake, for it *seemed* to get little done, and the system did not acquire the prestige of a modern reform or withstand the doctrinaire assault which was made upon it.

Personally, these were busy years; I was increasingly involved in the international business of local government, which took me to meetings in unexpected places like Stockholm, Toronto and Dubrovnik. I also had a Gwillym Gibbon award at Nuffield College in 1959-60, with rooms in College and free travel to Europe. I spent some time reading the accounts of the Principality of Liechtenstein and pursuing Austrian cadastral surveys. These studies were not remote from English village administration. I learned that continental local government managed very well without being, like ours, hog-tied by legalism and accountancy. By this mass of examples I persuaded the government, for the first time to legislate so that councils might use their own judgment in spending a limited annual sum.

Wilson's Labour Party was quite unlike Attlee's, and the Wilson government's attack on local government was political. Labours' voting strength was in the great cities, which were isolated from the surrounding countryside by their own semi-independence. If town and country were thrown together, the Labour swarms would capture wide areas hitherto dominated by older interests. So, Richard Crossman, the reigning Minister set up the Redcliffe-Maude Commission, with fanfares, to propose reform. Many observed that finance was excluded from its remit: far fewer, that it was required to assume that the amalgamation of urban and rural areas was desirable. This vast premise stopped the Commission from conducting the wide-ranging inquiry which onlookers were led to expect. All the same, its labours attracted much interest; and could make or break parish councils, because on them the Commission was free to say what it pleased.

It was about now that I did something which looked as if it might be interesting. I decided to supplement our income with additional work. I had written *Parish Administration*, and there had been an edition of *Everyman's Dictionary of Dates*. The Clarendon Press now asked me to write the *Oxford Companion to British History*. Also I have always had an urge to write, beginning, I suppose in Norway with a satirical fairy story called *Arson and Old Hake*. Somewhere in the 1950s I drafted a novel about the Biblical Jezebel and after her, I got interested in another alarming lady, Justinian's Empress Theodora. Publishers please note.

I accepted. Its compilation formed the ground bass beneath all my activities till 1985. I had plenty of energy and could sustain the work burden. Had I realised the nature of the shoals, I would have thought more than twice about it.

When the Redcliffe-Maude Commission met, most of its members variously regarded parish councils as helpless, unnecessary, obsolete or absurd. My chairman, Brian Keith-Lucas, and I did not know this, but were instinctively clear that we would have to organise a great effort to survive. In the rhinocerous battle where small people were liable to be trampled underfoot, the Commission was going initially to be interested in the technical controversies. We were not concerned in these.

Our problem was Irishly to compel the Commission to listen willingly to something else. The willingness was to be induced by the style: the compulsion applied by a demonstration of popular interest. We sounded alarm bells, called for suggestions, and investigated the parish councils' activities statistically. In about a year we were able to see what they were like, what they did and what they might wish to do.

Next, we drafted a trial document. Brian and I had both been members of a royal commission and were aware of the importance of not boring the commissioners. Most people who come to urge a case before such a body, do it without charm or style, and anyway style is conspicuously lacking in a committee ridden local government system. A camel is a horse designed by a committee. The only successful work written by a committee is the Authorised Version of the Bible.

So we adopted a principle of lay-out and a method. For lay-out we followed the Churchillian precept of keeping our argument brief and pithy, while relegating detail and statistics to appendices. We even printed the latter on green paper so that busy men might know which bit to avoid. As for the method, the whole document was to be written by a single hand and no textual amendments were to be allowed. Instead, changes were to be proposed and explained to the draftsman (me) who incorporated them so as to preserve a stylistic unity. When complete, the draft was circulated to every parish and to every county committeeman, for comments.

We refused to be monolithic. We could represent a consensus, but we stressed the variety of outlooks, circumstances and resources behind it and encouraged councils with their own point of view to express it not only to us but to the Commission. We thought that this would itself be practical evidence of vitality. It was indeed. Some six hundred wrote to the Commission. Their views made up a fat volume of its report. The Commissioners sat up.

Meanwhile the comments on our draft were coming in. We analysed them and in the light of what they said, it was rewritten. The Association's Council made the choices between incompatibles but the changes were, again, incorporated by rewriting. The resulting representation to the Commission stood out as the only one that was not leaden-footed, portentous or prolix. It was certain to make an impact, if only as a welcome relief. Moreover, it had the authority of the whole movement, and was not merely a puff from a caucus.

We were, too, luckier than we had any right to expect. There is an enormous advantage in debate if your preceding speaker is a bore. I had this happy experience once at Strasbourg. I was waiting to speak at a European assembly. The Italian cabinet minister ahead of me arrived with 21 pages of closely typed foolscap, and in two paragraphs emptied the chamber – all except the President, who was trapped, and I who was batting next. He thundered through his dramatic monologue line by line like Mussolini from the balcony of the Palazzo Venezia. Of course, the man was speaking to the Italian press; assembly delegates had every justification for not bothering, but curiously enough, the Rt Honble Signore did not seem to notice that there was nobody there.

After about twenty minutes, I gave up trying to understand him and switched to the simultaneous translation. Here I must turn aside into the field of interpretership. Even in 1980 really good interpretation could be reliably found only between English, French and German. The Council of Europe naturally attracted the best, but first class practitioners are rare and mostly pro-tem freelances in short supply amid the many-sidedness and rising technicality of international business. This was illustrated as by a flash that day. The English version was unintelligible, and I had to switch over to the German.

By now the Italian in the hemicycle has reached page fifteen. All the other delegates are, of course, in the café. Occasionally someone peeps in to see how much remains unread. You can drink quite a lot of coffee in fifteen pages. At page nineteen delegates begin to drift back. Here comes the peroration!... And then everyone cheers and claps from sheer relief while the speaker bows in all directions. It will be good for at least two columns in the *Corriere della Sera*. The longer and louder the applause the better for me, for the noise attracts people back and its duration has given time for them to sit down. The Italian journalists with their flashbulbs are a help.

Then calm is restored and I can begin before a full house ready to listen to almost ANYONE else.

I make only one – and that a new – point, with its exposition. I simply scrap my speech if someone gets in first; and I try to keep it light. A joke is difficult at an international gathering: the translations dawn on delegates at different speeds, so that they laugh at different times, but it is worth the making because these assemblies are so appallingly solemn. I am not exactly the world's most amusing speaker but I have addressed many international audiences and I have been the only one who has ever dared to make a joke. This time I spoke for seven minutes. I made everybody laugh and was much congratulated. My success was due, almost entirely, to the oratorical qualities of my predecessor.

Now, our document had already caught the Redcliffe-Maude Commission's eye, but when it came to personal appearance we were luckier still. We came immediately after the ministries, who had been long-winded and evasive. The Commission was ready to listen to almost anyone else, if only for light relief.

Sir John Maude, later Lord Redcliffe Maude (he was a Bristolian), had been the civil service head of the Ministry of Education – I once teased him about being the ghost of Sir Robert Morant – and an ambassador. Now he was the only man who ever interested the public in local government. Modest, charming and infinitely courteous, he greeted us in the anteroom and ushered us into the presence himself. Brian, who knew him well, said that this was his technique. Good manners may or may not be a technique, but good manners are good manners. The natives seemed friendly.

Brian, leading us, was an excellent and amusing witness. In reply to a question, he cheerfully said that a parish council's most important function was to 'raise Hell', and hit the headlines. Would we be content with a purely protest function? No, because all protesters, to be useful, must have some responsibility. Were we big enough to exercise responsibility effectively? It was too generalised a question: many were, some were not. Would we like substantial enlargement of our administrative functions? Not if it meant the wholesale enlargement and amalgamation of parishes. Even with government grants? Get thee behind me Satan. Our strength lay in the familiarity of neighbours: if we became second class rural districts we would lose that asset and gain only ineffectual powers. Did we then wish to stay as we were? Obviously not. We wanted freedom from legal constraints so that we could do whatever we wanted within our limited resources. Surely we did not want legally unlimited powers? Why not? The relative poverty inseparable from our community of neighbours concept, would prevent abuse. Our main principle involved us in no conflict of ambition or professional interest with other types of authority. Variety was the very stuff of our existence.

When we left, we felt intuitively that so far, all was well, and that this distinguished body would include at least a favourable reference to us in its report. This was as much as we hoped, but it turned out, that we would do better.

The Society of Authors occasionally criticises the business methods of publishers, most of whom seem to think that a book will sell itself. In the case of *Parish Administration*, I was entitled to complain. I had written it for a particular market about which, as it happened I knew more than the publishers. This, indeed, was why they had commissioned the book; but they took no notice of my advice. They under-printed, under-publicised and, as usual relied on critics who did not in this field exist. Hence, less than a quarter of the parish councils bought the book. This affected both my pocket and my work.

So when the edition ran out (many copies were apparently lost in a fire) I wondered what on earth to do. I was bound to Methuen's by my contract, and they, having had no great success, might be unwilling to finance a new edition. I then had a stroke of luck. A company unknown to me called, I think, Associated Book Publishers, informed me that my contract had been 'transferred' from Methuen to some other company. I naturally accepted this as a termination of my contract with Methuen. I withdrew the book. They wrote me a surprised letter. I was summoned by an important person. He kept me waiting in his anteroom for a quarter of an hour, and then when I was admitted to the presence, he motioned me to a chair and dictated to a secretary. After ten more minutes I suggested that I might go away and come back when he was less busy. 'No', he said, 'you're no trouble to me'. After a while he turned blandly in his swivel chair and said:

'And now, what can I do for you?'

I said patiently that it was he who had sought the interview. Three minutes later, I left. Long afterwards somebody told me that his behaviour represented tactics taught at business schools.

I decided to publish the next edition myself. There is trade propaganda against this, and an author pure and simple might get into difficulties. I was not an author pure and simple. I managed the organisation which could sell the book. I rewrote it, rechristened myself 'Longcross Press', saw my bank manager, who was enthusiastic and got the Association's admirable Kendal printer, Titus Wilson & Son to set it up. It went like a bomb.

I have already depressingly mentioned the remarkable Charles Pollitt, of Titus Wilson. He and a partner called Wilson (no relation) had bought this firm cheap. One of its assets was the *Westmorland Gazette*, and the fall of the *Gazette* would drag down Titus, so Charles decided to go into the newspaper business. Its reporter, Charles Pollitt, attended all the events. The editor, Charles Pollitt got all the right copy to the presses on time. Its printer, Charles Pollitt got the papers steaming off the rollers and there, rushing down the Highgate at Kendal was Charles Pollitt, newsboy, shouting 'read all abaht it'.

Like many fun persons, he had hardship in his background. One-eyed from a school pen-nib arrow, he lost half a leg as Colonel of a commando. He was, I suspect, never without pain, but you would never have known it, and I do not believe that it was a factor in his tragic death. He was the most practical, delightful, and well liked of associates. Kendal has a huge, five aisled parish church. His funeral packed it.

When the disaster happened, Charles had already sold his interest to Oliver Turnbull, who became as close an associate as he. The firm has figured prominently in my life. The contact originated with the *Parish Councils Review*. When I joined the Association, this shilling magazine was losing money. The editor was on the verge of retirement and in 1956 we advertised for a part-timer at £100 a quarter. We interviewed eleven, and took Campbell Nairne, the deputy editor of the *Radio Times*.

If you go back only about seventeen generations, you come up against the Black Death, many of whose few survivors were probably related anyway. Pater's mother was Helen Catherine Nairne, and Campbell's family's women were mostly called

Helen or Catherine. Meanwhile Pater's sister Catherine had married a Turnbull. Nairnes and Turnbulls are lowland Scottish clans. To put a sort of lid on it, in 1986 my nephew James Arnold-Baker became, in effect, the publisher of the *Radio Times*.

Nairne soon transformed this dying magazine. Then Courtney Marshall confidently suggested that we might write to every parish council about it. He was a shrewd, wiry old man, Clerk of a council near Tattershall in Lincolnshire, and one of those sterling characters who was in everything in his countryside. So I wrote a careful and rather modest letter pointing out that the 63,000 parish councillors needed to exchange opinions and information, and that the councils could buy them. I had 9,000 copies run off, and decided to sign them ALL myself. Have you ever tried to sign 9,000 letters? Ann Rowen, my admirable secretary (later MBE) used to put 300 or 400 under my nose every day. I got sick of my signature, and writer's cramp, but eventually all the letters were despatched. I went home on the 'bus and day-dreamed that it would be lovely to get the circulation up to 13,000. I forget why 13,000 but that was the day-dream.

Then the orders staggered us. We were well over 13,000 in a twelvemonth, and when I left in 1978 we were knocking 30,000. It had, undoubtedly, a powerful stiffening effect. Apart from the merits of the journal itself, one reason for this success was that because of my speech making many of the potential readership knew me by sight. A personally signed letter was thus a personal approach; a facsimile signature, no matter how good, is not the same. I have gritted my teeth and done it again and it always worked. There is a moral somewhere in this. In the vast operations of the publicity industry, a 5% response is considered good and 10% as bloody marvellous. We never fell below 30% – and incidentally recruited new membership as a bonus.

We were, of course, using our advocacy of the village council idea with the Redcliffe-Maude Commission to boost our membership. The Commission's findings and recommendations proclaimed our success. They wanted to abolish the counties and have uniform districts, within which parish councils were to have virtually untrammelled opportunities and widely drawn powers. It was almost too good to be true. The Wilson government loudly accepted the report. Unfortunately it was tottering to its fall. The Tory opposition agreed, during a perfunctory debate, that local government needed reforming, but, being in opposition, they did not accept the recommendations. It was the abolition of the counties which at that time stuck in their gullet, as, indeed it did in mine. We were not out of the wood after all. We thought that the Tories would win the general election, and set about courting them. We had a friendly meeting with Peter Walker, the likely responsible minister.

When his party had won he got the job under the title of Secretary of State for the Environment. The new nomenclature was related to the effects of the machinery upon society and its surroundings. Such statesmanship was timely, but precluded a detailed interest in the machinery itself. This was left to underlings while he busied himself in the Cabinet.

Graham Page and the civil servants framed the Local Government Bill. Graham Page was a practically minded solicitor whose private member's Cheques Act, simplified banking, saved millions of man-hours and eventually ended that old nuisance, the 2d receipt. He presented a front of agreeable reasonableness to MPs on both sides. The bill was long and complicated; I see from my preface to Butterworth's edition of the Act that it 'took nearly a year to pass, during which some 4,000 amendments were considered and many hundreds made. The Lords referred 630 new ones to the Commons in the last week.'

In negotiations with the departments on the draft before introduction, I had already managed to carry some important points, but I found that of the 4,000 proposed amendments at the committee stage, some 300 had to be mine. Our good parliamentary connection came in handily. One of our vice-presidents, James Ramsden, a modest and generous-minded public servant who had been in the Cabinet as Secretary of State for War, conscripted Charles (now Sir Charles) Morrison, a well-liked Wiltshire MP to take on the protection of our interests.

We had not only to push our own ideas, but sometimes to resist the ambitions of others. This meant keeping track of events in the office. The layman has no idea what this is like. We had to paste the bill clause by clause into the middles of 300 3ft x 3ft sheets of paper, and then, as proposed amendments came in, we pasted them with arrows, by the affected part. Sometimes there were amendments to amendments and alternative amendments. Sometimes accepted amendments would alter the context of one of ours waiting in the queue, and force us to rewrite it. Between twenty and 200 drafts came in every day for four months. It kept Paul Clayden, my assistant secretary occupied. Unsurprisingly, in due course, he rose to occupy my job.

Once one had understood a proposed amendment, one had to decide whether to support, be neutral or resist, and if not neutral, write a short brief for one's interested members. One had also to draft one's own amendments each with a brief, and separately without a brief for handing in at the Table under the signature of an MP. This all had to be done at speed. A hostile proposal might appear on the sheet on a Tuesday for debate on Thursday. One's opinion had to be drafted, typed, converted into sixteen copies and delivered into the right hands before the committee met at 10.30am on the Thursday morning.

The 'right hands' was itself a problem. As you watch you see that certain members have ideas or interests which you may need to meet or placate. Your own pet MPs have other problems besides yours. You must not outstay their goodwill: you therefore have to take some of their behind-the-scenes work off their shoulders. I met and had, often animated, discussions with nearly every member of the 40-strong committee during those months. It is almost impossible to persuade an MP that he is wrong, therefore you have to get in before he has thought about it, or else do some horse trading. Alternatively, you try to get the Minister interested (if the issue is political), or the civil servants (if technical), for the minister's 'advice' to a committee is worth more than any argument.

And what is such a committee like?

Off the wide high committee corridor the rooms are ranged along one side with windows overlooking the Thames. The stairs come up in the middle, and you turned right for the Lords and left for the Commons. The Grand Committee Room, where I once organised a meeting about canals, will at a pinch hold 200, but the others hold about 40, which is the average size of a Commons' Select Committee. This bill was before such a committee.

There is a row of desks on a low dais at one end. The Chairman takes the middle one, House officials sit to his left, civil servants and legal advisers to his right. The length of the room is occupied by two double rows of desks facing each other, for supporters (to the right of the chair) and opposition (on the left). The sponsor of the bill, in this case Graham Page, sits at one of those nearest the Chairman. Other members take, subject to their political allegiance, what desks they please. At the foot of the room, facing the chair, are uncomfortable benches for the small public. The shorthand writers work at tables in the middle. The large windows can make these rooms hot in summer, when the light on the opposition's faces must be trying. Perhaps that is why summer opposition can be pretty testy. Though the room is quite high, the general feeling is crowded and a little stuffy.

The first business is a government motion to settle the order in which a bill is to be considered. Debate on this can be animated because, if something important is postponed and the committee's proceedings protracted, the government may wish to set a timetable (or guillotine), and important matters may end up by not being discussed at all. In 1984 a committee threw out such a motion and disorganised the government's timetable. The bill is then considered section by section and schedule by schedule, the Minister explaining the meaning and purpose of each, and amendments being moved, discussed and if necessary voted in succession. Sometimes a provision is simply accepted. At other times everybody has a great deal to say, and members become quite heated.

There is constant movement. MPs and officials wander in and out. Lobbyists like me pass messages, or MPs come down to whisper to them or to take them out to talk in the seat-lined corridor. Knots of people gather at the doors. Votes are taken, firstly by voice and then, if a division is demanded, the public is pushed out into the corridor and the members troop through separate *Aye* and *No* doors. In the afternoon, division bells for the full House may ring: a House servant opens the door, bellows 'Division', and everyone gets up and rushes out. You can hear them saying 'what are we voting about, now?' as they hurry down the stairs. And then after about ten minutes they all come cheerfully back chattering.

Most Honourable Members come in with sheaves of papers, and writing cases, and write their letters. They cannot do this in the chamber because there are no desks. You might think that they were paying no attention, but they develop an ear, and when something vital is coming forward, their papers are ignored and they are all attention.

I was the only lobbyist present throughout the entire proceedings in both Houses on this bill. Having nearly 300 amendments at the Commons' Committee stage alone, I could do nothing else. A private member's amendment is usually treated in one of three ways. If the government resists it, somebody may insist on a vote, which will usually fail. If the government accepts it, it may, if plain or unimportant, be added to the bill then and there, but more often the mover will be asked to withdraw in return for a government undertaking to reintroduce something like it later on. This gives the back-room boys a chance to ensure that the wording is proper and will not create difficulties elsewhere. Such undertakings are invariably honoured, but they lead to further discussions behind the scenes. I was involved perhaps twice a week in such office confabulations with ministers or civil servants.

At the end of the four month committee stage, I had secured about 130 of my amendments, and the question was whether to try for the other 170 at the Report Stage, when the bill, as amended in committee, is considered by the full House. It is a ticklish problem for a lobbyist with a weak hand, for if you are urging a series of small cases, none of which, in the grand perspective of national or international affairs are very important, you risk boring or worse still irritating the whole House of Commons. Parliament was much concerned at this time with Ireland and the Common Market. On the other hand I had built up a fund of good will among ministers and their civil servants. *They* knew what was important to me and still missing.

Actually I had to make the decision in ten seconds flat. It happened like this. There was an official party on the evening when the committee ended. I found myself next to Clifford Pearce, the amusing and elegantly minded civil servant in charge of the bill. He faced me directly and said:

'Is your Association going to press its amendments on Report?'

I simply said:

'No. I think Hon. Members might not like it'.

He said:

'That's very statesmanlike of you'. And we spoke of other things over the gin. We both, of course, knew what was in each other's mind. If I tried to press, much House time might be wasted and other bills jeopardised, or we might make ourselves ridiculous. But if the government gave suitable advice to the House, we would probably get what we needed without much fuss. And so it turned out. Graham Page prompted by Clifford Pearce moved nearly everything we wanted.

In this kind of bill, the important stage is the Commons' committee upstairs but Lord's procedure, though theoretically the same, is actually quite different, both as to procedure and atmosphere. It is very rare for a bill to be sent upstairs. The committee stage was taken on the floor of the Whole House, with the Lord Chancellor absent and the Lord Chairman of Committees seated at the table in the Lords' Chamber. The numbers present from day to day may vary from three[*] to several hundred. The discussion on a bill would mostly be confined to technical, drafting and minor matters, because the Lords did not, generally, provoke clashes with the elected House on matters of political principle, unless the issue was of outstanding constitutional importance, such as the deplorable abolition of the rights of hereditary peers in 1999. In the case of that bill (and it illustrates another facet of parliamentary life) opponents got it amended by throwing out the European Elections Bill so often that the government was forced to bargain.

The final Act of 1972 had 274 sections and 30 schedules. In my annotated edition it took up 493 pages.

---

[*] Lord Methyr explained that the Lords' quorum of three was very convenient. With the Lord Chancellor on the Woolsack and one Lord addressing him, if another Lord came in to object to the quorum he himself made up the number.

Chapter 32

DISILLUSION AND CBH

The eighteen months between the passage of the Local Government Act 1972 and its coming into force in April 1974, were a watershed in our social development. We now saw, for the old organic structures, a new system which, being devised by technicians, was nakedly technical. They had a long opportunity to pre-empt the best places, while the public, kept in ignorance by the obscurity of the texts, continued to be represented through the dying institutions of the past.

It is a misfortune of some magnitude that the British public was so uninterested, for what now began, the exact opposite of what was intended, was simply not news. It was assumed that the new greater facilities for co-ordination, economies of scale and the elimination of outmoded practices, would provide economically more viable services. On the contrary, during the transition, the staff quite legally feathered their nests. In the following example I have changed nothing but the names.

The pay of higher officials had long been regulated by scales based upon population. A chief officer or his deputy working for 120,000 people would, very reasonably, get quite a lot more than one working for 40,000. Very well! Tom, Dick and Harry are respectively clerks of Eggville, Chickton and Cockerby, each with 40,000. They are to be amalgamated into the new 120,000-er borough of Battery. Tom is due to retire in three years' time; the others are younger. They easily (in the general chuminess) persuade the dying joint committee of the outgoing councils that the work in Battery would justify two deputies. Tom gets the new polysyllabically rechristened Chief Executive's job at £120,000-er salary; Dick and Harry get deputyships paid, under the pay scales, rather more than their previous top jobs. They then divide the work on the basis of the old component areas, but actually have less to do because the reforms transferred some of the old functions to other authorities. The trade unions prevented other dismissals, so Battery ended up with much the same combined staff as before, and the new transferee bodies like the Cluckshire County Council and the Hen Valley Water Authority, zestfully recruited new people and started building themselves new offices. So, more people at higher pay in more offices ended up doing the same work.

This was not all. The cost of some hundreds of mere changeovers amounted (according to Lancashire County Council) to something over £600,000,000 at 1975 values.* This was not news either. In truth there was no real control. The departments simply told the outgoing joint committees that it was unavoidable and most of them could not have cared less. This had a powerful secondary effect. The authorities, searching for ever more cash to pour down the drain, feared to raise the rates (which would have converted the whole nonsense into news overnight) and bullied the government into finding the money through the grants system. This represented an old trend now exaggerated by another factor, namely rising interest rates and the vast increase in local government indebtedness. Between 1914 and 1980 the debt had risen a thousand-fold and the rate of interest five-fold. In 1974 I asked whether we had all gone mad.

Thus ambitious Westminster centralisers found willing allies in local officials, whose fleshpots would be threatened if their employing councils became, by rejecting government grants, genuinely responsible. The other Associations were dominated by officials and looked increasingly like trade unions. The really important local government politics became the national politics of trade unionism, of pay scales and pension rights, in which the elected local representatives of the people had been elbowed out. 30 years of subsidies had sapped their morale, and the national political parties now intervened in earnest.

It is important not to over-simplify this. The degree of involvement varied with places, times and parties – especially left wing parties, but it was not always the party organisations which were responsible. All the parties, even the communists came to a Home Office conference on electoral practices. It considered whether political affiliation should be stated on ballot papers. *None* of the politicians favoured this. Nor did I. There was something comic about party-lines on lamp-posts and sewers. The Home Office officials said, and I believe them, that the demand had come wholly from 'the public' – which probably meant a few journalists, but, as all the world knows, the decision to do it was taken. The encroachment of national upon local politics was a combination of short-sightedness, accidental infiltration and erosion rather than calculated assault, but by 1970 it had gone far. During the Suez crisis Surrey County Council by-election posters spoke entirely about the Suez Canal, no part of which, I believe, passes through Surrey.

This represents a malign irrelevance. Social policy, foreign and military relations, taxation, justice and so on, which interest parliamentary parties, do not remotely resemble the local councils' issues such as planning control or

---

* About 8 billion now.

amalgamating schools. A parliament can decide whether grand – say educational – policies shall be adopted. A local council can say where its schools shall be: it cannot refuse to have schools. It is not a sovereign body writ small.

National parties now pushed in on a large scale. Parliamentary general elections happen about once in four years. It is hard to keep up enthusiasm in a constituency party if nothing happens in between, therefore idle hands must be kept at work locally. The framers of the 1972 Act let the cat out of the bag: they geared the electoral cycles to ensure that party activists would always have something to do.

Candidates now stand for local office because they support particular attitudes to non-local issues, and as the reformed authorities have large areas but few members, it is difficult and uninviting for councillors to know much in detail about their wards or districts. If, in law, the councillors make the decisions, in fact others or predetermined factors make them. Local government is run by paid unionised professionals variously influenced by committees of elected critics, in whom the electorates take too little informed interest.

We had got the local* councils through their greatest crisis, and we had now to nurse them through a geographical reappraisal undertaken by new urbanised district councils, with little understanding of the subject. I was enured to hostility, but the enemy were a different, less attractive breed, with new ambitions and power-bases. The time of reaction after crisis was thus, for me, a time of decreasing enchantment. I began to tell people that I had been there long enough. 21 years is a long time.

I had other, personal, reasons.

The work on the *Companion* was fascinating and took up much time. I suppose that a remote and ineffectual don might regard it as a full time occupation for seven or eight years. I did it while carrying on the multifarious business of my employers. It was a blessing to return from an argument at the Ministry of Malfunctions to the life of the Venomous Bede, but it kept me at work at times which others enjoyed with family and friends. Moreover, after a while it became unexpectedly controversial because of the way in which the Clarendon Press conducted the business. As the thousands of entries were sent to them, they referred them to advisers. Though my identity seemed to be known to them, the Press, of set policy, refused to disclose their identity to me. And this seems as good a moment as any for a blomp about this book.

I met him in, I think, Old Compton Street. He had been at Winchester with me but we knew each other only by sight. That was ten-minutes' worth on the kerb. He was working for the OUP. About four years later I had a letter. He said that he had found my name in a box and would I be interested in editing or writing

---

* i.e. English parish and (new) Welsh community.

The Oxford Companion to English History. We all, of course, knew of the brilliant *The Oxford Companion to English Literature* and it was said that a History one was badly needed. I had a funny feeling that my name had escaped him at the kerbside just as his escapes me now. I replied civilly and examined the Eng: Lit *Companion*. It seemed a vague sort of assignment partly shrouded in mist.

The mist continued to shroud.

Eventually the Secretary to the Delegates of the Press (alias managing director), a distinguished New Zealand poet called Dan Davin, got me to make a written proposal. So I went away and wrote it. It had to be pretty vague because the content and so the size was unpredictable, and therefore there was no knowing how long it would take or what or how I should be paid for it. But I was interested because history interests me, and I was interested in pioneering an uncertainty. 'When in doubt, eat it' is my motto. I signed up for £7,000 payable as and when I asked. £7,000 then was worth about £140,000 now. But what exactly had to be done was nowhere specified, save that I had to produce a manuscript to the satisfaction of the Delegates.

I started by trying to list all the things which might become headings in the book. Decisions to keep or bin and if keep, what to write would come later. I searched encyclopedias, gazetteers, atlases, historical indexes, biographical encyclopedias, telephone directories, even timetables, for headings to which a compiler might draw a reader's attention. This work could not be done in alphabetical order, because sense, which does not respect alphabets, kept intruding. It had to be done by subjects which scattered their blessings unevenly across the spectrum. This was all very well but these had, themselves, to be chosen. After much intellectual manoeuvring I realised that I was not getting on with the job. If you insist on perfection, nothing happens. If you adopt a major philosophy you eliminate much which people might like to find. Eventually I decided to go bull headed at it and see what happened. Even that rather Philistine principle was hard to follow. It involved a vast amount of miscellaneous reading because in history the only really bull headed man is a polymath.

At this point the OU Press helpfully appointed a minder, and sent me a set of the *Oxford English History*. This is not a compilation like the *Cambridge Modern History*, initially planned and informed by the learned Germanic giganticism of Lord Acton, but a collection of books on successive periods each by a different hand. The lack of apparent direction in this arrangement was matched by variations in quality, but it was balanced by the differing attitudes of the writers. There was no domineering line of thought as from a Marx or a Toynbee, and this was fortunate and interesting. But especially it showed me, as nothing else might, the crying need to read around every subject, and since this was not always possible in English I resorted to French and German (the other members of the interpreters' Holy Trinity), and later, with hiccoughs, to Dutch, Italian, Spanish and Latin.

> 'Ich sagt es auf Jiddisch, auf Englisch und doch
> Auf Paschtu, Walesisch und Ghizz;
> Ich vergass überhaupt, und es ärgert mich noch
> Dass Deutsch sei die Sprache Ihr spricht'
> Die Scharckjagd* IV v 5.

I am, as I have said, not a good linguist but I had access to linguistic talent. Henry speaks Russian well and Spanish fluently, my daughter Katharine is fluent in the Holy Trinity and even more fluent in Italian.

I also found that I could not safely confine myself to historical works. I had to widen the net into, firstly, literary material likely to convince its contemporaries by verisimilitude; then into solid objects like buildings or geography; then into specialisms such as law, diseases, theology and, God Help Us, statistics and criticism of them, and not omitting quirks and oddities. The Anglo-American Pig War of 1859 began with the shooting of an American pig on Vancouver island. I thought that atmosphere was important and best conveyed by anecdote. Did Elinor Glyn sin on Milner's or Curzon's tiger skin? The great tenth century bishop, St Wulfstan of Worcester commanded armies, looked after hundreds of orphans, and walked his diocese. The Albigensians, whose overthrow outflanked the English dominion in southern France, held a form of dualism which elevated buggery to a higher moral level than fucking. And Winston Churchill's only novel *Savrola* written in 1900, predicted a war in which a great personality saved this country from conquest.

This listing phase took nearly two years and I now had to write about the listed headings. Many had been overtaken or needed reorganisation, and also the difficult related issues of cross-referencing and caution had to be settled early.

Caution is a besetting problem. Do you assert something and accept the likelihood of attack or do you hedge in the hope of remaining unscathed? The latter seems justifiable on grounds of potential accuracy. The former is crisper, more interesting and not necessarily inaccurate. I prefer the gamble – *When in doubt eat it* – and there is a larger issue: a book like this must be compacted within a single volume yet contain a vast factual array. Much must be sacrificed to this: historiographical discussions for example must be curtailed because they concern historians not history. This space consideration also affects cross referencing, which

---

* My German version of *The Hunting of the Snark*.

takes up space, or disturbs the grammar by weird typography or the mind by the hallucinatory effects of asterisks, double-daggers and footnotes, but, on the other hand one can avoid repetition by including particular cases under generalised headings, and turgidity by calling in aid the poets, with their knack of saying several things at once. I decided to avoid the typographical methods: to call everything where possible by its popular name (I prefer CANUTE to Knut) and to make cross-references only inwards to major entries or outwards where the subject was not raised verbally, or was unexpected.

The contract was made in 1960. The next twenty years is history. I had got on well with my successive minders. The last of these was the late Peter Sutcliffe, who wrote a witty informal history of the OUP. By now the *Companion* consisted of a growing flimsy half-foolscap card index which made a double row in each of eight steel deed-boxes. I had been sending bits of it to my minders for some years for comment or consultation. A team of supervisory experts had been recruited. This sounded admirable. My texts would be checked and would become watertight. Nothing could be better. One makes mistakes and, in a reference work of this potential repute, a longstop is obviously sensible. This was not, however, what happened. The commentators never tried to correct mistakes or rectify errors. They simply scribbled negative comments or crossed things out or raised editorial points such as whether there should be an entry on a particular subject at all, which was my business not theirs. Worse still, they lost cards. After a year or so I demanded the names of these people so that I could speak to them. The reply was that it was the policy of the Press never to disclose the identity of its advisers. My minders were cut-outs in the standard MI 6 style. I later learned from a literary agent that this was a common practice among academic publishers. In that case, I said, it was my policy never to accept anonymous comment unless the reasons and authority for the comment were given. No decent man can be expected to change his mind at the behest of someone unknown who will not say why. It produced no effect whatever. They continued to behave as before. I twice put my case into writing. The Secretary to the Delegates was no longer Dan Davin but a Pharoah who knew not Joseph. I asked to see him. The discussion was amicable in tone and manners, and the Pharoah went so far as to tell my minder that only positive criticism should be made.

This instruction, if such it was, would obviously be a dead letter. My minder, without active support, would not influence the advisers. And so it fell out.

Things got worse. Comments of under-graduate standard began to be pencilled on the cards. I rubbed them out and returned the cards. At the same time I took a sample inventory (of the letters B and C) by checking the main cards against my duplicates. If grossed up to the whole alphabet, this showed that 3,000 entries out of a projected 14,000 would be missing. When I wrote this to Peter Sutcliffe, he said that this was inconceivable. I hoped so. They also managed to miss a year long opportunity to take some photographs which could not wait.

It now seemed that notwithstanding anything I did, this Companion could not emerge from the OUP as the work which I had written. I indicated that it could not, unless I had proper editorial as well as author's control, be published under my name. They suggested giving me a collaborator and in due course found one for the more modern years, because, they tactfully indicated, time was getting short. They seemed to have forgotten the size of the task or who created the delays.

The alphabetical arrangement of any such book, arises out of the irrational western reliance upon a third century Roman list of alphabetical symbols, corresponding inexactly with a different Greek symbol-list many centuries older. This cannot, obviously be used as a very convenient way of classifying modern English information, but it is so deeply and universally engrained in popular habits, that no other arrangement is possible. To alleviate its inconveniences, I built the whole book round a spinal narrative starting at BC55 and finishing now, but chopped the narrative up into component alphabetical parts named, as convenient, after reigns, or eras or administrations. Hence the parts, for example, named after Edward VI, Mary I and Elizabeth I are continuous with each other, but the alphabetical imperative places Edward VI and Elizabeth I before Mary I.

Having composed the spinal narrative for an era I then tried to envisage what outlying matters in such era deserved separate notice. Under Elizabeth I, the Armada is plainly important to the reign, but the actual details of its defeat are gathered together in an entry on Armadas – of which there were, in fact, five. The underlying coherence is there, if obscured. At the launch of the first edition of *The Companion to British History*, as it eventually emerged, at the City University, a beautiful Dane asked me why it was alphabetically arranged. I replied that I was not clever enough to think of anything else.

At the time when these disputes arose, the spinal narrative had reached about 1904 and my proposed collaborator (whose name I forget) was therefore to be a specialist in twentieth century history. The proposal confirmed my suspicions. Even if my name alone appeared on the title page the book would be only partly my book. 'Struck' as they used to say in parliamentary practice 'with Hybridity'. He and I talked amiably enough together and then he went off to do his stuff. He did not last long. The advisers continued to behave as before; I continued to fight them and eventually it was agreed to end the relationship: I was paid the balance of my now much depreciated £7,000, and my deed boxes were returned to me at the

Temple. The divorce was without rancour. My nephew, James Arnold-Baker, who later became Secretary to the Delegates, remarked that the history faculty were a quarrelsome lot, and when I told my printer friend Oliver Turnbull about the divorce, he said that being published by the OUP was like going to bed with a Duchess: the honour was great but the performance disappointing.

The deed boxes glowered for some years in my little room. I had had, as you will already know, much else to do and had become a visiting professor at the City University where I taught Law and Architecture. Not doing anything about the boxes was, for a space, a blessed relief: more time, no haystack. The space lasted till 1993.

At this point Henry said unanswerably 'it's a pity to let twenty years' work run into the sand with only 5% more to do'. So back I went to the grindstone, not very reluctantly. Having forgotten what was in the deed boxes, I started at A, and worked methodically through to Z. Things were worse than I had feared. Of the 13,000 existing entries not 3,000 but 4,000 were missing. Some 3,000 more were made unusable by scribbling. Fortunately I could make quick improved reconstructions from my duplicates so that only 700 remained to be written from scratch. The whole process took eighteen months while, simultaneously, we all looked for a publisher. We examined year books, and trade catalogues and inquired at bookshops, for Fanny had worked in old Simmons's well known bookshop in Fleet Street and had contacts. We 'phoned and wrote letters endlessly. The answers mostly threw up clouds of dust. The book was too big: too learned: over the heads of the average readership: as it was novel, the readership was unascertainable. It would be too expensive. We sought introductions through friends. We showed the manuscript in its boxes to a publisher from New Zealand. We took boxes out to Cambridge and Oxford. I got indigestion from business lunches.

The atmosphere of this time may be encapsulated, if with sinister overtones, by the incident of The Lady from a Publishing House of Note. The LPHN had given me lunch (much *Kleftiko* and *Retsina*). It seemed that she was bettering herself by moving to another Publishing House. She was interested in the *Companion* and would like to show it to her new employers. I had misgivings because I was dealing, I thought, with her present House not another. She assured me that both houses would consider the proposition. She moved house. I heard nothing from her original house and when Henry saw her to continue the discussion about methods of payment, she showed him the door and wrote me an irrelevant and abusive letter. I understand that the LPHN is not now employed by the second house.

By the time that this had blown over and the 1,800,000-word manuscript was as complete as I could manage, we had all, in conclave, decided not to put our trust in princes. We had an instrument of sorts ready to hand. Fanny and I had been united in the bands of Holy Matrimony in 1943. In 1953 we had reinforced the bonds under the provisions of the Companies Acts. We were, in fact, a £502 publishing Company called Longcross Press. It was named after that Surrey hamlet where Flutters Hill was. It mostly published works by me to captive audiences. Its main importance was that we had long been familiar with the techniques of publishing. The trouble was that it had little money and no independent organisation.

So now we had a sort of publisher, no money but a song in our hearts. We decided anyhow, to press on. Our new search for information entered financial fields while Henry found a means at least to get us through the next, that is typesetting stage. It would take a long time, during which something was bound to turn up. This excursion into Micawberism, as will be seen, paid off. Meantime: typesetting.

The printing industry has changed radically since I corrected my first proofs as Editor of *The Wykehamist* in 1936. A typesetter, then, was a craftsman. Now he is a computer operator, often working at home. Computer screens, apart from being bad for the sight, lead everyone to believe that a mistake can be rectified at the touch of a key. The total effect is that mistakes are made too easily; there is a fall in the operator's stamina and morality: he *can* easily remedy an error, but too often he does not bother. When things are too easy, standards fall.

Our typesetting took nearly two years. Printer's errors accounted for at least six months. I would, with good old-fashioned hot metal, have expected 400 to 500 errors. Actually I had to cope with 14,000 primary errors and many secondary ones generated by primary corrections. We had meanwhile designed the volume (in double column), the binding and the dust jacket and got estimates for each. Dust jackets are much more important than their name suggests. Like a company receptionist, the dust jacket is the first thing you see, and this was an especially cogent point when the book was, as it was, a new sort of book. We had to get it right, but what was right? Fanny rummaged all the bookshops within a mile of Fleet Street. Her answer was bright yellow and keep it simple. Nobody else did either. She also proposed a reference to Dr Johnson which we printed on the back. Oliver Turnbull (who printed these dust jackets) suggested that the symbols for our four island nations should go on the otherwise chaste front. Later on, one reviewer mentioned this jacket.

We rather enjoyed this part of the business, but we were now alarmed by the approach of two potential rivals. I will not give them gratuitous help by identifying them (though for purposes of narrative polemics I will call them Tweedle and Twaddle) but their publishers were very big and rich while we were very small and uncertain how to pay the printers' bills. The estimates added up to £41,000. I rustled up £10,000 and lent them to Longcross. We expected, with most of the work already in type to be able to borrow from some financial institution. Bankers, we found, were an uncomprehending as publishers. Among silly incidents was the man who said that they had had to refuse a professor who wanted to publish a 500-copy edition of a special mathematical theory of his own. This proved that they were familiar with academic publishing finance. I was irresistibly reminded of the chorus girl who said 'You can't give Connie a book for her birthday: she's got a book.' Obviously he had been told to say 'no' in advance. Henry had made a wonderful presentation. It made no impression whatever. We left in high dudgeon and a taxi. The real reason for all this obstruction was, I am sure, the one which was never spoken: never do anything unless it has been done before, to which, (on a different issue) Michael Cohen, our admirable accountant remarked that 'in general bankers will lend money only to those who don't need it.'

Some days later, we all met to discuss looking for money. My brother Richard, who lived in Athens, happened to be there. After a while he suddenly said 'How much do you need?' I said '£31,000'. He said 'I'll lend you that. What interest would you be willing to pay?' I did a quick average between bank rates and the yield which he would probably be getting now and said '10%'. So we got our money on better than bank terms and he did better than he was doing at the time. And we all went away rejoicing and got ourselves a printer, Selwood, a branch of Butler and Tanner at Burgess Hill, in Surrey. Our intelligence was that Twaddle would come out nearly a year before us: Tweedle only shortly before. We put our best foot forward. Fortunately the Camera Ready Copy (CRC) was about to be delivered by the typesetters. We financed Selwood's purchase of a suitable paper called *Thinprint*, manufactured by a maker of cigarette papers. Oliver found it. It was so thin that the 1386 pages of the CRC could make a book to be handled easily, yet it was so opaque that one was not distracted by the print on the back. It cost nearly £10,000.

Dies Irae. Twaddle was out! Hatchards had a mound of them. I bought one. Know your enemy. We read it with joy. The authors' bonnets buzzed with bees. Their explanations were sometimes weak: their law poor. Their attitude small. Above all, the number of their entries was only about a third of ours. As we were going to charge £48, ours was better value than theirs at £25. We reckoned that we need fear nothing save powerful commercial publicity. A fortnight later the mound had not diminished.

Next, Fanny and I took the half-hundredweight of CRCs in a brown paper parcel by train to Selwoods. Oh, horror! The paper people had cut the paper the wrong way. Tweedle was imminent. There was no time to send it back and get some more.

The CRCs would have to be turned round and reduced. A 91% page was run off. We squinted at it and decided that the print would just suffice. We prayed, and, interestingly, the only complaint came from Marion von Blumenthal when I gave her a copy on her 80th birthday.

If the typesetters had taken nearly two years, Selwood promised to take no more than seventeen days. Including binding? Oh yes – and delivery. Henry had to scramble. At Tonbridge he found Len Jepp, a splendid character who had a warehouse called *Freight Point* and promised good services. We circularised everyone we knew, promising the Earth (meaning a special pre-publication discount).

We also arranged for a special London stock to be deposited in the crypt of St Dunstan's-in-the-West in Fleet Street. The Temple Church had been bombed during the war and St Dunstan's had been pressed into service. Our children had been baptised there. We gave John Salter, the cosmopolitan incumbent, one of the 200 copies. Meanwhile, with four anchors out of the stern, we waited for the dawn.

And then came a jolt. Butler and Tanner's bindery had made such a mistake as I had never met it in 40 years. They had bound up some signatures in the wrong order. A signature is a fascicule of consecutive pages derived from the same folded sheet and is distinguished at the folded side before binding by a square block-like mark so placed that when you look at all the signatures together, the black blocks look like an uninterrupted staircase. You cannot miss a gap. For many copies to go wrong is infinitesimally rare, and it might be calamitous. Selwood of course took the stock back from Len, and examined and replaced it book by book (it turned out to be about 300 out of 3,200 copies) and they compensated us, but this could not stop the belly-aching which arose from copies no longer in Len's custody.

Meantime and more importantly, we were waiting for reviews. We had published in November 1996. There was nothing for four months, but neither had anything much been said about Tweedle or Twaddle. I suspected that the critics were mentally blocked by the same principle as the publishers and bankers, but I now think that I was wrong. The obstacle was probably the size of the book.

And then the trumpets sounded, beginning in February with John Charmley in the *Daily Telegraph*. Andrew Roberts gave it a five star rating in the *Mail on Sunday*. Ruth Nagley a prolonged shout of joy in the *Hellenic Times* in Athens. There were banner head lines by Simon Heffer in the *Daily Mail*. In January 1999 there was a happy piece by Simon Hoggart in *The Guardian*; in April 2000 a rave in *Heritage*. Sales went up with a bang. Then they fell off again. Elephants always forget. Books do not sell themselves any more than soap, suet or socks. Sales effort is seldom maintained. I persuaded a branch of Dillons behind the London School of

Economics to take a copy. It was a few weeks after publication and they put it where no one could see it. Naturally they still had it when I offered them another copy. I shall return to the other half of this incident.

We now decided to stimulate, as James put it, primary demand. Instead of shops, we approached customers. We wrote a standard, rather restrained letter headed *Progress Report on CBH* with a sample page on the back and we enclosed ten rave-reviews. These were destined for the Good and Great. It was a sweat, involving six processes. Firstly you read an entry in *Who's Who*, decided if it might be suitable and addressed an envelope. Secondly you topped, tailed and dated a letter to him (or her). Thirdly you stuffed letter and reviews into an envelope. Fourthly you sealed the envelope. Fifthly you stamped it and lastly you trotted out and caught the post. Even when Katharine's children Gemma (aged ten) and Tommy (seven) took over stamping and trotting, we had not the strength to send out more than 400 a week, but between October 1998 and September 1999 it remorselessly changed the situation. There are, for example, a lot of professors at the London School of Economics. Quite suddenly that branch of Dillons started to ring us up. And then our bank suddenly asked us if we needed any money. Meantime publishers approached us for rights, and we had some specially agreeable experiences. I must admit that when I enjoy a book it does not occur to me to write to the publishers and say so, but lots of people did. I had one last week (March 2005!).

I will now drop names. A lord promised to ensure that the House of Lords would buy it. They did. Sir Peter Johnson, Baronet of New York, descended from the remarkable eighteenth century Sir William who lived in 'baronial if untidy splendour' and let the Iroquois have the run of his house, said 'Marvellous, and I am enjoying reading whole chunks.' The managing director of L'Oréal in Paris ordered it. The English Speaking Union exhibited it in Moscow. We also bagged five Dukes (17% of the ducal population), seven embassies, the Institute of Policy Studies, a splendid Circuit Judge who ordered two and persuaded a friend to order two more. So did John Clease and Diana Rigg.

Chapter 33

PERSONAL AND PUBLIC TRANSITION

The blomp in the previous chapter reached 2001, but provides an example of the dangers, already remarked, of specialist history. It makes a narrative, but is untrue to life, for, of course, these things did not take up all my time. They would give no more serious picture of me or my life, than you would get it of English History from the biographies of British bird watchers. Much of the life of an unimportant Person is taken up with a routine. From getting up and dressing, a day ambles on until, in the evening one is dozing with Fanny in front of the television. Telephone calls. Bed. Sometimes one goes to church, or stays with someone over the week-end.

This existence is not hum-drum, for the details vary, but it is conventional. Hence unusual episodes – unusual to other people – stand out. One biographical problem, for example for actors and barristers is that actors have acts and barristers have cases, with hardly anything to connect them save their own bodies.

I seem to have moved towards a similar difficulty. If I am able to drum up episodes which might interest somebody, it will not be easy to co-ordinate them. I have visited many places in four continents. These may only be excursions for self-gratification, but there is another admissible side to the statue. I try to look at a place and see what it is, and if I am there for a little time, I try to learn something of the local habits and customs. In Montreal I went on foot from my 23rd-floor bedroom to a 26th-floor restaurant a mile away without ever coming out into the open because the climate makes the open air only intermittently tolerable. At Tangier I saw from a balcony, a lady in ground-sweeping coat and skirts, veil and all. Her maid rang a bell and they both went in. My host said 'she's been visiting her husband's relations. In fifteen minutes she will emerge alone looking like a *parisienne* and go shopping'. And so it fell out. A handsome woman. At a restaurant near Cefalú in Sicily, Fanny, Katharine (aged nine) and I could not get served. After 45 minutes we were nearly desperate, for it had been a long hard climb, and this was the only restaurant in the village. Then somebody asked us across the room whether we were English. We said 'yes'. She spoke to a fat domineering priest sitting at a table. He said something to the waitress, and all was light.

I hope now to solve my problem by barging on regardless, paying only incidental attention to noticeable episodes. I had a second bout of meningitis. The meningitis sequelae included a sexual disturbance. The principal delight of the bed is in coordinating one's love-making so that one maintains one's excitement just below its climax and keeps one's partner's at the height of hers for long periods, preferably for hours. It is a pleasure which is increased by sharing. It needs concentration and observation, sensitivity and self-control. It is a major art, comparable with music.

I surmise that my second attack deranged a tract of my nervous system concerned with self-control. It did not matter what I tried, invariably and helplessly I reached my climaxes so early that I could not give a partner much pleasure. The thing was frustrating to a point of desperation. Fanny seemed quite unable to help. I was spending too little time with her anyway. The unsurprising result was that we pursued differing personal lives. I do not mean that we quarrelled, though we had quarrels of a kind which had not troubled us before, for there remained a substratum of mutual affection; nevertheless it often happened that I came home to an empty house, sometimes from afar. Hope deferred makes the heart sick. In 1973 I had a nervous breakdown. This was the consequence of the combination of the private, the intellectual and the public pressures which I have described. Perhaps, too, it was the lucky sequela of the disease itself, equivalent to Charles Pollitt's suicide. I was off work for six months.

Meanwhile the setting of my professional work was changing. Inflation was creating hydra-headed problems. Authority was being challenged and conventions flouted for the sake of flouting them. Skinheads were smashing up seaside resorts. New and ambitious, sometimes conspiratorial, politicians were breaking surface. The indolent press was inflating occasional murders in Ulster into the dimensions of a civil war. Even the Zoo was being stirred up. Flying pickets, the storm troopers of the left, disrupted work, fomented hatreds or, as at Shrewsbury, destroyed plant. Welsh so-called nationalists were absurdly trying to sabotage reservoirs; Women's Lib: Squatters' Rights, Gay Liberation, the sinister Campaigns for Nuclear Disarmament, and Animal Rights and other mushroom agitations shared one particular feature; they were inspired by a tactical philosophy of intimidation. There was no question of seeking redress of grievances (real or imagined) through agreement or democracy. They meant to bully and sometimes succeeded.

The English used to take politics with a grain of salt, but it is a mistake to think of them as unpolitical. They were not, like the politically incompetent Greeks,*

---

* My Greek sister-in-law Athena quoted a Turkish diplomat. 'You have 5 million clever people and 300 idiots. We have 9 million idiots and 300 wise men'.

obsessed with politics. They did not apply much energy continually to it: rather, they let it simmer in the subconscious and then pop out with the right answer at a crisis. The full time politician was a mistrusted misfit.

So long as such people were rare and restricted in their opportunities, they did no great harm, and English society could, with some amusement, accommodate them. It was organised to manage without permanent and pervasive political movements. Unfortunately the payment, and now the payment of excessive salaries to politicians has founded or funded a professionalism, which encourages the worst.

Of Lenin's many crimes; one of the worst was the creation of that church of lies, the Communist Party. The appropriation of the word 'Party' was itself a lie, for that is precisely what it is not. I can join the Liberals or the Bimetallists by professing their opinions and paying their subscription – if any. I can leave when I like. Free association is of the essence. A real party is open and potentially comprehensive. I cannot join the Communist 'party' in this fashion, or leave it in the same way, for it is a secular priesthood, which disciplines its members and harasses those who try to resign. It is a closed, conspiratorial oligarchy, shut, in non-socialist countries within a self-policed fortress-ghetto, from which it mounts raids into the surrounding society.

The greatest recent change is the infiltration by this alien political professionalism. I first met it at a Fabian houseparty in the late '50s. I was asked to speak on village affairs. These charming clever people were urban-educated left wing intellectuals, with no idea of country living; and the rather trite things which I told them were evidently a revelation. What surprised me, however, was the alienation: These were the rising brains of the Labour Party. So far as I could tell, they had only political interests. In the 1980s we were becoming very familiar with bed-sitter socialists. In the 2000s we see an extended policy of expelling non-politicals from the House of Lords: first the hereditary peers: secondly in 2005 the judges. Now (2007) everyone else.

There is, too, a general trend towards the ossification of jobs. Employers have expected increasingly high qualifications: if you are going to be stuck with somebody for twenty years, he might as well be good. This had in its turn raised the demand for training. The Butler Education Act 1944, the most far reaching social reform of modern times, lengthened school life, invented Further Education and multiplied the Higher element by a factor of over twenty. Brian Keith-Lucas was asked to serve on the managing committee of the Oxford Polytechnic, concealed in the tundra of Headington. He had to take the chair at his first meeting and discovered that he was presiding over something larger than the University of Oxford. It is now called Oxford Brookes University.

As the pressure for entry to such places grew, they raised their exit standards. This required more concentration upon a narrower range of subjects. Exit specialisation soon heightened pre-existing entry specialisation. Potential degree takers are being sorted and sent off down specialist channels, from which escape is not easy, at thirteen or fourteen. The professions, too, are paving their own ways with similar intentions. The Bar, for example, wanted bar students to have a law degree. The proposal was narrowly frustrated so it instituted compulsory training for those already called. We seem to be returning to the Indian caste system which we undermined in its native land. We have almost lost the distinction between education, which makes you a better person, and instruction which may find you a job.

In the high public positions this is very dangerous. Politicians who only politics know become obsessed with the often undignified technicalities and intrigues of their trade. Anyone who has listened much to the House of Commons will recognise the facts behind this assertion: the parochial points; the barracking; the procedural ingenuities; the in-jokes, and the superficiality and vapidity of diction do not assure the bystander that high matters are receiving serious attention.

This is not always the froth on the top. Politics, though an emotionally manipulative activity, is meant to solve problems, but too often they are deliberately created for the sake of distraction, or to enable some faction to survive while others wrestle. One might perhaps think of Harold Wilson and Tony Blair encouraging Welsh and Scots separatism to restrict the choices of their successors, or Ken Livingstone's obviously illegal 'bus subsidy designed to bring the public into collision with the courts.

This was the public life which I found decreasingly congenial. It seemed to me that the Association was beginning to need a different sort of person to manage its affairs.

Chapter 34

SIAM

I suppose that I might pass over my resignation from the National Association as a jolt on a bumpy journey, and leave it at that. Local Councillors were all suffering from post-climax reaction, as after an orgasm. They began to drift and to put off even easy decisions, while I cleaned up routine work such as rewriting and renaming *Parish*, now *Local Council Administration*. The Association could neither adopt a policy nor let me make one, nor finance itself properly at a time when there were fissiparous tendencies such as separate Welsh and Larger Councils' organisations, and the beginnings of a clerks' trade unionism. To put off a decision, they set up a committee to investigate how I ran my office. Fanny thought that this was a gratuitous insult. It did not influence me save as a symptom. Some people, I suppose, can take their living from a virtually purposeless employer, but I am not that sort of person. So I and my family, came to the Annual General Meeting of 1978, and there I advised the Association to find another secretary. They hardly believed their ears. A quarter of a century is a long time, and nobody there had seen me come. Bryan Keith-Lucas said that the wrong person had resigned, but I do not know who he thought that the right one was. Several people threw a dinner that night for the purpose of persuading me to retract, and when I politely refused (it was a good dinner), they wanted me to say that I was retiring for reasons of health, and it was assiduously bruited abroad that I was retiring. I had every intention in my 61st year of getting other work, and I said so.

The Association's rank and file saw through the posturings of its leaders. I had 700 resolutions asking me to stay. Nearly all the county associations invited me to their meetings. They showered me with presents: china, glass, shoes (Northamptonshire of course), a tape recorder, even silver, and somebody, I suspect Ann Rowen, organised a public subscription and raised £2,000, with which, in the autumn of 1979 I went to Siam. It seemed to be one of the countries which had maintained its own way of life. As will be seen, I was only mostly right. Nowadays they officially call it 'Muang-thai' which means 'Land of the Free' and seems to recall the overthrow of the royal autocracy, but in Bangkok they had no objection to 'Siam', and, indeed, there is a Siam Square which is actually, as in Montreal, a square of buildings. It had, I found, a huge restaurant whose menu, in Siamese and English, ran to 80 bound pages – but I anticipate.

I flew to this extraordinary metropolis during the annual floods. From the air the red soil and the unpaved roads made red conventional traces across the green, waterway-divided rice land. Then the plane came down with a bump: you presented your visa, splendidly authenticated with the *Krug*, the legendary royal bird, to the very tough military emigration officer and emerged to see something called the Thai Military Bank, and find your 'bus to Town.

It is a perfectly flat countryside and the straight road runs along the bank of one of the klongs (shallow canals) which one is led to believe, are a feature of the capital. This, unfortunately is no longer true. When King Lert Lah extended Bangkok in about 1810 he dug many klongs from the river Menam, which here has the royal title of Chao Phya, to transport the building materials and food. These lasted until, I suppose, World War II. Then, with a single exception, they were filled in, and the sites used as roads. The loss is great; canals are calm, whereas the confused and uproarious streets are noisy, dusty, and ill kempt. Moreover the water table is only about six inches below the surface. Drainage is much worse. Buildings can have cellars only at great expense, and they rise or spread instead. There were brimming ditches between multi-storey blocks in the centre. This is one reason why I do not wholly believe Anna's account of Victorian Siam. She says that she found a disgraced princess in an underground palace dungeon. I cannot think of a place for a dungeon which would not have been filled with water to the ceiling.

The built-up area is expanding. Its 2,000,000 people take up as much room as 6,000,000 would in the west. My hotel was just off the Sukhumvit Road in an ex-suburb. In the local construction system, which I noticed too late, the materials and skills and willingness to work produce spectacular results. At one place I saw some building skeletons and foundations. When I passed three weeks later it had sprouted into a village with temple and social centre. The Road and the new suburbs stretched for miles beyond. From my bedroom window I could also see an endless green road 200 yards wide in which a single railway track supported slow, almost stumbling diesel-hauled trains. People, often in crowds, walked ceaselessly beside the rails. I could also watch a school where the children, all identically clad and with little individual numbers embroidered on their white shirts, did mass exercises with military precision and grace. I observed too a puzzling display in honour of a Siamese admiral. He, I understand, had the rank of O Pra Sap Di Songkram, which means (I hope) exactly the Gilbertian Lord Who Rules the Water. Three numbered girls were, with great reverence ranging hundreds and hundreds of wooden *elephants* fanwise, facing his pillar, the whole packed display covering an area the size of half a tennis court.

Yet the Siamese are a violent race. I think that their striking politeness and good manners arise from this latent and sometimes patent fury: in 2000 I met a Siamese lady from Chantaburi at Fanny's University Women's Club. She quite spontaneously remarked upon Siamese violence – without their extreme politeness life would become intolerable. To show even a shadow of irritation with someone is the grossest solecism. Conversely boxing, for example, is a great public spectacle. A boxing theatre (one of several) in the Rajdamnön Road holds about 4,000 people and there are bars, restaurants, stalls and shops. The boxers fight unshod with bandaged calves, and use both fists and feet. Each round lasts four ferocious minutes, and a very exciting band of drums, fifes and cymbals urges them on, while bookies walk round taking bets. There are many knock-outs to the head or with a kick to the stomach. I saw a man hit through the ropes. The wrestling, I gather, is just as violent, and you see the odd fight in the streets. They flare up: someone is knocked cold into the gutter, and then the participants move on with the hurrying crowd. These were not muggings.

The reverence, by contrast, manifested itself in all sorts of ways. All lands, for example, are occupied by spirits. These are not ghosts; but if you build upon some plot you are obviously crowding the spirit, and it is polite and desirable to rehouse and pay attention to him. So you put up a residence for him, which is often in the form of a little stone house on a pillar – it looks vaguely like a birdbath – and you leave him food and wine and speak to him daily. Our hotel spirit was of high rank, for he had a palatial six domed residence on several pillars in the car-park. The proprietor used to visit him and talk to him every day. I would like to have found out more, but did not want to intrude. The problem of rehousing spirits in a growing city is considerable, and I saw stonemason's yards which specialised in it.

Nearer the centre, at a cross-roads on the Sukhumvit Road is a garden shrine, fenced off from the street by Victorian iron railings. It is not grand; I first noticed it on my way to an outside breakfast. People going to work were pouring in and out: mostly women, especially typists and bank clerks (who are mostly girls). They would pop in, light an incense stick, say a prayer and go. I found this more impressive than the elaborate and splendidly noisy ceremony with band, choir, robed monks an' all which I found in full jolly blast on another day, and which in no way interrupted the streams of incidental worshippers.

The government encouraged religion; customarily every Siamese male becomes a monk at some time in his life, if only for a few days. This accounts for the numerous saffron yellow robes, but only a few make a permanent vocation, because employers in the rising modernisation are chary of giving people the necessary time off, but the ideal remains as a kind of Confirmation. You get yourself taken into a temple, have your head shaved, renounce sexual indulgence, and after various rites, don the brilliant toga-like robe. You then have to beg your necessaries, especially food, and any food which you get, must be eaten or given away by midday. Monks are therefore not reclusive, or solemn or, normally, old. Their Rule brings them into constant morning contact with the public. Also, apart from contemplative exercises, they practised medicine and teach such things as the Three Rs and music. The Temple of the Tree in Bangkok once had an acupuncture school; its working diagrams still adorn the walls. I got myself massaged there too, while an instrumental class squawked and wailed in the next yard.

King Mongkut (of *The King and I*) had been a monk for 27 years before he succeeded his brother, and was very close to his people. He never got out of the habit, for in the Palace yard is a roofed platform measuring, say, 8ft by 10ft, surrounded by balustrades, and here, as King, he sat daily so that anybody could come to the balustrade and bring his troubles or just talk. The Siamese regard him as a sort of saint, and it seems that the terrible scene, recounted by Anna, when one of his tribute slaves and her monk lover were burned alive for illicit love, did not take place under him or even when Anna was in the country, but in the previous reign.

These monks, by and large, are a cheerful and helpful lot. King Mongkut's artificial hill in the middle of the city, is supposed to show the people in that very flat plain what a hill was like. It is crowned with a temple approached by zig zag paths, but when I climbed up, the gates were shut. I started down, but a monk leaned over the battlement and shouted 'Come back up again. I'll open up for you!' So back I went. He showed me all round this very large establishment, with its galleries and terraces looking out over the endless roofs and streets and traffic – and crematoria – and eventually we came to the largest of the bronze bells, about seven feet high on a stand in a corner of a cloister. He handed me an enormous padded hammer and said 'strike it as hard as you can, for luck.' I said, 'As hard as I can?' 'Yes,' he said, 'to bless the city.' So of course I did, and the deep smooth sound winged its way across the town. It was the only act of worship which he expected of me. It made me feel like the Pope.

The encouragement of religion extends beyond Buddhism. Down the gravelled alley by my hotel there was a Methodist school with little numbered boys and girls as usual, but the chapel, which, apart from Christian symbols, looked exactly like a Buddhist Temple had, I was told, been financed by the government. On a drunken tourist trip in a rice barge on the surrounding country waterways we drank a splendid and salubrious mixture of Mekong (a spirit looking like whisky, but more to my taste) and pineapple juice, and ate endless small bits ranged on a plank. All among the sedges and wild-life and the riparian villages there were two brand-new mosques for the growing Mohammedan population. The Sikh tailor who made me a suit in 36 hours had his *gurdwara* just down the road. There was, of course, a political motive embedded in this natural respect for piety. It was part of the government's policy against Marxist penetration from Viet-Nam and Burma.

Bangkok is modern, and was obviously built in haste and without much order or planning. Enormous traffic jams belched fumes from elderly engines at an unclassifiable mixture of fly-overs, shops, office blocks, humble dwellings, luxury hotels, warehouses, temples, craftsmen's workshops, restaurants, tenements, bars, vegetable markets, brothels, all higgledy-piggledy and often unexpected, like the central snake farm. Snakes are the curse of Siam. 10,000 people a year die of snake-bite, and the only way to combat it is to have the serum available in a refrigerator and regularly renewed in every village, for a victim untreated dies in 90 minutes. The serums are made from the venom of the snakes, and since the quantity needed is very large, there are many snake farms. The Bangkok one was devoted to research, for no one had been bitten in the City for twenty years, but in the country they are directly active. I visited one near Kanburi equipped with shallow pits lined with glass, where they bred a number of varieties. I had no idea until then, how many different sorts there are besides the Cobras and Karaits which figure in Kipling's *Rikki-Tikki-Tavi*. This particular farm, by the way, had a pet mongoose. Do they all? And what is the plural?

The heart of the capital is at the riverside. The Chow Phya is mighty and the city was deliberately sited on the East bank as a protection against the Burmese. In 1767 there had been a great Burmese invasion. They besieged Ayuthia, then the magnificent old capital, occupying some riverine islands in the marshes 50 miles upstream. Eventually they stormed it. The King died of exposure in flight. The royal family was carried away and the city sacked. Its gold now adorns the Shwe Da-gon pagoda in Rangoon. The surviving population was massacred or enslaved. A Burmese inventory of the material and human loot has survived. Even the memory of Ayuthia became quickly dim. There are some large beautiful surviving Stupas, a reclining Buddha in a field and a huge bronze Buddha (which wept the night before the city fell) is now, after nearly two centuries, housed in a building. Otherwise nothing is left.

Archeologists have guessed that there was an open place of worship containing twelve inward facing golden Buddhas, but the Burmese melted everything down and carted it away. More was known about Ayuthia, the richest city in south-east

Asia, from European visitors than from native sources. And then something odd happened. A massive concrete Buddha in a minor Bangkok monastery was being moved to widen a road some years ago. The crane bumped it against a solid object. A corner fell off and revealed a yellow metal. They chipped the concrete off and behold! It was a massive, 30-foot gold statue dating from the twelfth or thirteenth century. There was no record or tradition about it, or how it got there. Nothing at all. Yet, since it is ancient and splendid (I have seen it several times) and, in terms merely of gold, worth more than the National Bank, it can only have come from Ayuthia. Precautions must have been taken against the fall while there was yet time, but everyone in the know must have perished, for the concrete statue was brought downriver and so remained undiscovered by even the Japanese till the post World War II revelation.

The Chao Phya at Bangkok is twice as wide as the London Thames and wider still above and below the city and unbridged; ferries cross it and strings of pot-bellied rice barges with high inboard combings go up and down. Also there are the *rüas*. These are graceful craft, up to 70 feet long but narrow – perhaps six feet wide. There is a canopy, and inward facing seats along the gunwales, and the whole thing, with up to 50 passengers roars along driven by an outboard propeller at the end of a long naked shaft from a Ford V-8 engine mounted above the stern. I went half way to Ayuthia in about 30 minutes and the journey cost me 7 Bahts (5p). Once you leave the City, stilt villages line small creeks. The thatched wooden houses are interconnected by plank-ways along open fronts. Everybody washes, launders, and swims in the water underneath, and everywhere you see four-foot earthenware jars used for collecting rainwater for drinking. Dual water supply, as in Constantinople, is universal; even in the grandest hotels, the drinking water comes in a carboy.

The Palace Compound, not far from the river is rectangular, walled, and about the area of St James's Park, and is divided roughly into four parts. One is a garden; I shall return to the second shortly, another is occupied by some of the ministries; the fourth contains palaces and throne halls, and also a, still guarded, harem housing the now ancient remnant of king Chulalongkorn's many women. He was King Mongkut's son and successor: a modernising monarch like his father, whose first decree, said to have been pronounced at Mongkut's deathbed, abolished the grovelling prostrations of inferiors to superiors including himself. He replaced the 'bullet' currency, suppressed the slave trade, set up a modern educational system, founded universities, overhauled the taxes, and with luck and supple diplomacy prevented the kingdom from being swallowed by predatory French or British imperialists on either side of him – though he had to shake off in the process Kedah and Kelantan to the British and Cambodia to the French. I have noticed continuing signs in Bangkok of claims to Cambodia, such as exhibitions of Cambodian art and architecture, represented as part and parcel of Siamese civilisation.

The King was the father of his country, not least in his philoprogenitiveness: -

> Then Israel's Monarch after Heaven's own heart
> His vigorous warmth did variously impart
> To wives and slaves, and, wide as his command
> Scattered his Maker's image through the land.*

The Royal harem was still an institution popularly inseparable from royalty as such. I have heard various figures for the number of his children: more than 600, less than a thousand. Nearly everyone in public life is descended from him, and as he died as recently as 1910, the relationships are still close.

His successor, Vajiravudha has a bad Western press because he was a homosexual, the target of the limerick: -

> Then up spoke the King of Siam:
> 'For women I give not a damn.
> Give me the joys of my rosy-arsed boys.
> You may call me a bugger. I AM.'

All the same, he left important marks on Siamese life, for he took a learned and energetic interest in the national arts and religious customs, and standardised the calligraphy, spelling and phonology of the language. He or his son (I forget which) was educated at Eton and encouraged the study of English, himself leading the way with translations of three Shakespeare plays. Street names, not only in Bangkok, have long been proclaimed in English as well as Siamese. Incidentally he solved a tiresome problem of social custom, which decrees that you must not use the personal name of your superior, living or dead. Hence no King could ever be mentioned directly by anyone except another King. The royal statues in the Temple of the Jade Buddha had diluted the problem: you called the King 'His Majesty of the latest statue', or his father, 'His late Majesty of the latest statue but one'. Vajiravudha, observing that among their many names, all the Kings of his dynasty were impersonally called Rama, numbered the Ramas. It must have saved a lot of fuss.

Some splendid state rooms are open to the public and remarkable for their craftsmanship. In one throne room, designed I think for the reception of ordinary

---

* Dryden: Absalom and Achitophel II 5-8.

(or fairly ordinary) people, the teak three-tiered throne, upon which the monarch sits cross-legged, is minutely inlaid with closely spaced patterns in mother-of-pearl which give it an unforgettable bluish shimmer. It stands, surmounted by its nine-tiered umbrella, isolated at the crossing of two aisles, so that it is approachable from all directions. I attached myself to the tail of a party of up-country officials on a privileged tour, and saw another throne hall, not publicly accessible, which is used for diplomatic receptions. This had a distantly European flavour and the cloth of estate between its chandeliers might have been in Munich or the Vatican. In a third hall, the throne is used but once in a reign, for the Accession. The King appears in brilliance from a door high up in the end wall, and steps straight to a huge raised golden boat-like altar. At other times he uses a canopied throne on the floor in front.

Since King Prajadipokh, who came next, was driven into exile at Wentworth, the monarchy's ability to compel has been minimal. Its influence, however, seems to be very great.* For one thing, though occupied by a dynasty of recent origin, the throne has always been a religious institution, and this, obviously, is a serious matter in a country where most males become monks.

The enormous Temple of the Jade Buddha, occupies the second quarter of the palace compound. Others may describe the golden profusion of its interior, I found its cloister more remarkable. A rough quadrilateral circuit of about a mile and a quarter contains, I am confident, the biggest fresco in the world. Kings Lert Lah and Nang Klao, the second and third of the present dynasty, faced with having to reconstruct a blasted inheritance, decided to encourage the corporate pride of their nation by an appeal to its traditions. They assembled all the best available artists and designers, and between them they worked out and painted Lert Lah's version of the *Ramayana*, called locally the *Ramakien*. This epic narrative painting with its marble inscriptions covers every flat surface in those cloisters. I spent several half days there, and it is like walking through an oriental *Iliad*, with the *Aeneid*, the *Odyssey*, the *Lord of the Rings*, all the plays of Sophocles and the *War Song of Deborah and Barak* thrown in. You need six months there and good Siamese, and you still see families wandering about it, as the Kings intended, on their day off.

The palace compound, then, is a popular place and crowds come in and out all day past the extremely smart guards. I did not know that it was disrespectful to have one's sleeves rolled up (it was hot), and one sentry scowlingly refused me admittance till I had rolled them down. There is also an endless and beautiful midday bugle call when everyone stands still and officers stand at the salute.

And then one day the King's birthday happened. Hatto Mio! I never saw such a party. The people poured into the city, crammed into or clinging to the outsides

---

* My nephew Alexis von Blumenthal who had a Gap job in the north west says that 'what the King says, goes'.

or roofs of buses, lorries, cars; they came on foot, on bicycles, on motor tricycles, all shouting and cheerful, and moving steadily upon a tree grown space, about eight times the size of Trafalgar Square at the Palace, with a gorgeously vulgar flaring, steam-driven fair. The people, several hundred thousand of them, crowded into this place ever more tightly. I ate things at food stalls and grinned at everyone who grinned at me, until, like Humpty-Dumpty my smile went twice round my head. And then, as night fell, flares and torches were lit and, flamboyantly conducted from a platform by the Prime Minister, the vast concourse sang birthday songs and lullabies to the King and his Queen. I sat on a heap of gravel when I was not eating, or trying to sing, or grinning. It was impossible to edge my way out until about one in the morning.

The streets were now uproarious and crowded with outward traffic. I stood wondering what to do, and a policeman spontaneously, stopped a 'bus for me. I offered to ride on the step, but the packed passengers hauled me inside, sat me down, took my place on the step and in due course stopped the 'bus where I wanted to get off. Then they waved and said things animatedly, and I waved and did so too, and then the 'bus went off cheering fit to bust.

The markets represent another sort of popular concourse. One hears of the floating markets, but I went to the Bangkok city market, which begins near the Palace and runs parallel with, but not along the River. I was certainly not prepared. There is about a mile and a half of it, varying between two and four hundred yards in width on either side of a muddy track. The swarming, chattering traders sell from stalls, baskets, sheds, tents and sometimes in covered halls and they sell anything: Coca-cola, television sets, carved teak, pets, drugs, dolls houses; probably girls and boys; furniture and of course vegetables, rice, fish and fruit in vast amounts and endless variety. The Siamese cuisine is varied and delicious, beautiful to behold but, be warned, they have 200 varieties of chilli, from the large mild paprika to the brilliant yellow grape-like berries which boil your ears, and they have dozens of kinds of vinegar which, with sugar,* all good Siamese use to flavour their food. They are recognisable in South East Asia by this habit. I got quite used to it. The hot spices are collectively called <u>prik</u>. A prim American lady journalist was mischievously asked by a Siamese gentleman what she thought of Siamese *priks*, and left in dudgeon.

You make your way through all this trying to avoid the odd lorry, the chickens and pack animals, and the porters of both sexes with their balancing baskets slung at the ends of shoulder poles, and the jugglers and musicians who still competed with the radio, and seemed to occupy most of the ways. I turned down a side alley leading, I hoped, to a wharf. I had judged it correctly. I sat, as usual, under an

---

* Sugar counteracts chilli heat.

umbrella while a young woman cooked me an admirable lunch over a Bunsen burner. It cost me a shilling.

Then I caught a rüa to Dhonburi, across the river, where, downstream, there is the high pagodaed Temple of the Dawn. This must symbolise something in the national character, for it is represented on stamps, boxes of sweets and almost anything with a national appeal. Strangely, it is faced entirely with Chinese tea cups, dinner plates, broken tea pots, saucers by the thousand, all cemented onto the outside. I asked about this, and was told that several shiploads of pottery had arrived unexpectedly from China in the last century, and that King Nang Klao, enraged by what he considered an insult, had used it as building material.*
I climbed up the steep stone stairs of this pagoda (puff, puff, puff) as high as one could go and admired a very interesting view down on the neatly laid out monks' quarters, the wharves across the River and seawards towards the estuary and the Gulf of Siam. But getting down again backwards was another matter.

Dhonburi has a show-piece floating market, but about 25 miles to the west I found a much more interesting one. It was the exchange point for a large rural area. Several steep-banked channels wound through the usual stilt villages, with their gangways and open fronted houses. The channels were crowded – at some points blocked – with boats, mostly handled by one person, who might be a woman, with a paddle or out-board motor. They have sharp jutting prows and blunt sterns, similar to the Venetian Sandalos; they sell anything inanimate, though as the boats are not canopied, electrical goods are sold from the houses. The occasional craft has a hearth and a fire, and sells cooked food. I shinned down a ladder from a walkway and boarded one of these. The old man was highly amused as I sat on his combing and ate his fresh-water prawns and rice and chicken and beans – and chillies. It was all very matey.

It was on this excursion that I saw palm sugar being made. A man can make a living from 100 closely spaced palms. They grow about 90 feet high and live for about 90 years. He cuts lengths of thick bamboo from below a joint to below the next joint to make a natural if narrow bucket, which he fills with water and palm flowers. These are waxy white, fairly solid and about as big as a banana. After several days he pours the water into a cauldron and chops up the buckets for fuel to boil the cauldron. Evaporation reduces the liquid to a fine whitish powder which is the sugar. It tastes slightly of coconut. The one important overhead arises if this sort of coconut, weighing two to three pounds, falls the 90 feet onto his head.

That was after a bus journey; but several times I went south-west by train on the single-track line down the Isthmus of Kra to Penang. There is a very very holy

---

* I tell this story as it was told to me. There must have been more to it than that.

stupa or pagoda at Kanburi, which houses one of the Buddha's teeth said to be about the size of a number eleven shoe. The stupa is obviously very old, and can be seen about a mile away across the fields. I was on my way to Petchaburi. As the train approached, everyone stood up and solemnly bowed to it. The Siamese regard their religion as their private business, and I had been warned not to imitate them unless invited. So I remained seated... After two more wayside stations, everybody stood up again. I could not see any sacred edifice, but assuming that one would shortly appear, remained seated. Suddenly there was a violent jolt which flung me up almost to the ceiling. Then they all sat down.

Petchaburi is at the edge of the frontier mountains with the now Burmese, province of Tenasserim, on the Bay of Bengal. It is an accident that Tenasserim is Burmese at all. They occupied it in the aforesaid invasion, and the East India Company took it over a generation later. Then the British included it in the governorship of Burma when, in two bites, they swallowed that country, and so now the Burmese have it. It used to export Bird's Nest Soup from two vast caves, to China. Now it infiltrates communism to southern Siam. Petchaburi is the only place where I saw the communist fist salute.

250 miles away south-eastwards across the Gulf of Siam is Pattayá, the much advertised seaside resort up against the frontier foothills of Cambodia. I went there by 'bus through Chantabun so as to be able to say that I had seen it – for I am not fond of seaside resorts – and to see the country in between. The hills had obviously been extracted from Chinese narrative landscapes (*One Hundred and Seventeen Laudable Vistas Between Ping Pong and Fling Po*), and Chantabun was not interesting, but Pattayá certainly has something. Good clean sands look out on a bay partly closed by distant islands. At one end is a group of quite good American style hotels. The beach front is occupied by pleasant night clubs backing onto a pine wood. About half way along is a rare Bo tree, normally found only in temples.

There was also a café under the trees, where I found an elderly American washing up. He said that he liked the climate and they gave him excellent food for his trouble – but there had just been a rush and it looked as if he might miss his date with his girl, who had a couple of hours off in the afternoons. So I offered to help and we got through the chores at a rate of knots and he went off whistling. I wonder if he is still there? He was not a degenerated type: merely a man who had discovered how to enjoy simple pleasures, in which doubtless, the girl loomed large.

At the other end of the beach is a Wentworth style house with an official looking painted sign at the door which says: -

> *Nobody is allowed upstairs unaccompanied.*
> *Unaccompanied persons should apply to the*
> *Receptionist for a Companion.*

I admire the multilateral impartiality of the grammar. It seems that the Siamese did not regard prostitution or deviant sexual tastes with any sense of shame or inhibition. Spouses seem to be naturally faithful to each other's code, whatever it may be, and nobody regarded a prostitute as in any way inferior to any other worker. Some country towns treated the recruitment of their girls into the grander Bangkok brothels as a matter for celebration, the recruiting agents being all women; and a girl returned, richer and at least as marriageable as before, and, of course, well trained. I cannot say for certain whether this is so, but certainly the national attitude seemed freer and easier than I have seen elsewhere even in between-the-wars Paris. I had just unpacked at my Bangkok hotel, when one of the resident ladies rang me. Later I made the acquaintance of the hotel masseuse – and she really was a masseuse – whose good company and charm were irresistible. Women seem to be as respected by men as men by women; this is the effect of Buddhism which seems to assume a fundamental sameness of quality in all creation, while accepting a differentiation of function. If the centipede is my brother, why is my sister very different?

A Bangkok schoolmaster (who also tried to sell me some carpets) explained that it is a tenet of Buddhism, naturally derived from this idea and the moral cycle of transmigration which it expounds, that whatever you do, you should do as well as, perhaps a little better than, you can. I had already noticed that they carve your fruit into beautiful patterns as part of a meal not merely at the Soopradoopa Palace but under the wayside cook's umbrella. The prostitute is respected for her skill.

It is the insensitively vital Western vulgarity which distorts the picture. Bangkok became an American leave centre during the Viet-Nam war, and the Siamese at a price, supplied bedfellows especially in the 200 yard Patpong road. Judging by the journalism, Patpong practically *is* Bangkok. Actually it is less than a sixth of the size of Soho, and the merest fleck on the huge city. There are bigger red light areas elsewhere, but in the aggregate they do not warrant all the shouting. Nor, for that matter, do they deal in vice, for the Siamese, as I have already said, do not regard sex for money as vicious.

I found another aspect of American vulgarity further north at Chieng-mai. When a monastery chapter is in session the monks sit in a horseshoe formation, with their Abbot presiding. Sometimes a *sutra* is read: usually there are long periods of meditational silence. This commonly takes place in a large open ended building, and anyone can look in. Obviously one does nothing to disturb or distract the participants.

As monasteries are entirely male, women are the obvious source of distraction, just as the converse would be the case in the much rarer nunneries. Monks must not look directly at women, and the only nun I encountered (very old and ugly) would not look directly at me.

I found it shaming,* therefore, when an American life-insurance widow marched into such an afternoon chapter, raised her camera to her squarely spectacled face and flashed off in all directions. She was not the only one; and at the Temple of the Swing in Bangkok I heard a raucous female American voice shouting 'Margaret, Margaret, come and look at this'. I expostulated once, and was met with: 'I guess if they'd minded they'd have said so'. I said, 'they were probably too well mannered'. It made no impression whatever. Nothing would penetrate that cocksure thoughtlessness. It is fair to say that if the American male sometimes misbehaves in a night club, he is much better mannered than his woman in a temple.

I now took myself off to Paknam on the Gulf south of Bangkok. It is a very gently sloping plain (a gradient of perhaps two yards in a mile). It is intersected everywhere by six-inch irrigation channels at right angles to the road, and these are fed by hundreds, perhaps thousands, of tiny eighteen-inch windmills. They clatter and shimmer in the wind which sweeps across this immense flat. Somewhere in the middle is a royal pleasance embowered in trees, conspicuous because of their isolation, with bamboos, flowers, and thousands of very large black, red and white butterflies, reminding me distantly of the Swallowtails which my brother and I had hunted at Beatenberg.

This plain is crossed by a single straight road. We were on our way back to the City when, quite suddenly, the 'bus (a public conveyance) lurched off the road into the ditch. This was no accident. Charging at speed in the opposite direction were three huge lorries. A Buddhist abbot was sitting cross-legged on the dignified cab-roof of the first. The rest of his vehicle and the others were occupied by many chanting, incense burning, gong banging, dancing yellow robed monks. Driving into the ditch was the proper way to show respect for a motorised temple.

Chieng-mai, at the headwaters of the Chao Phya, is not far from the Shan areas of north Burma. It was once the capital of a separate kingdom, and has the remains of its moats and walls, and its still very active royal monasteries, but its position in Siamese, international life is equivocal. The adjacent communist controlled Golden Triangle is the main world source of heroin. Chieng-mai is said to be the principal entrepot and currency exchange for this lethal trade. Certainly there is

---

* An Englishman feeling shame because an American misbehaves seems anomalous. I would never feel the same about an Irishman or an Icelander. I suppose that this is a feeling of residual responsibility for a colonial.

a lot of money about. If ever there were a case for an attack on a territory, the Golden Triangle presents it. It should be fire bombed and the crop and lands burnt out: and if a few people get hurt in the process, the punishment would be a good deal less than just.

The lowlands here are extremely fertile and intensively cultivated – sometimes as many as two rice crops and two root crops a year around Lampun since time out of mind. Rice here deserves special attention. In the South-East Asian world the sticky rice of Chieng-mai is well known. It is gently pink before cooking. It is crammed into baskets measuring about eight inches each way, and steamed for hours before being brought to the table in these baskets, and very viscous it is. One could easily cut it with a knife and fork. I got to like it. Though actually rice, it has some of the mechanical properties of the potato.

I am not sure how fertility is maintained, but I saw a harvest in progress and the land was in good heart. Lampun, too, has a furniture and wood carving industry. Brawny ladies with chisels and huge mallets carve the teak into intricate, sometimes pierced patterns at high sped. The motifs, I am afraid, seemed to me conventional and over elaborate. The craftswomen seemed to be taking over from the artists. This is an early stage of decadence, where work is admired for its difficulty or skill rather than for its inspiration. Craft always outnumbers genius, and in a Buddhist society I suppose that there is always a danger of the craft running away with the party. All the same it was a joy to watch.

And then, just to the north the mountains rise abruptly and become jungle, in which nomadic clans wander slowly, practising slash-and-burn cultivation and degrading the primeval forest. The lorry journey was hair-raising. Most of the road was no more than a track of irregular width and doubtful solidity cut into the crumbling mountainside, and eroded by landslides. The vehicle, an ex-American army six-tonner, lurched and snorted and rolled above the precipices. There was a grave risk of spinal injuries by remaining seated and I found an outside step and a pair of overhead handholds, and so travelled in semi-suspension.

Our destination turned out to be a (for want of a better expression) model hamlet. The wandering destructive clans are not controlled by visible frontiers. There is a great belt of Everyman's Land from northern Burma, across Siam into Tong King, and besides the clans and the heroin runners, refugees flee from Communist oppression on both sides. They have no documentation, and even the Siamese cannot, without elaborate interrogation and counter-intelligence, tell them apart. This is a real danger because the Viet-Cong and the Burmese communists slip professional agents in with them; but, on the other hand, the decent souls can merge into local Siamese life instantly, and become an asset to the economy. The

Siamese take this seriously: there are welfare and settlement programmes, and from his country residence in the foothills, the King spends a third of his time investigating cases, advising his advisers and blessing reclamations and modernisations.

There is, too, much American help, and this attracts Americans who might otherwise never have heard of Chieng-mai. They were building some sort of higher institute, and the purpose of the model hamlet in which I was so violently dumped, was to persuade the nomads to settle and support themselves by pursuing their crafts and making things which could be sold to tourists in Chieng-mai. This idea seemed to me unsound. These people, atypically, were dirty and unused to house life. Their artifacts were poor and dull, and they seemed to be submerging their pride in a tourist supported mendicancy, which could easily collapse if tourism were interrupted, as it easily is, by some noisy triviality like a bomb. This was no solution to nomadism: but, as it was concerned with a problem quite different from that of the refugees, I wondered whether there was something wrong with the priorities. How much would it matter if the ex-nomads abandoned the place and returned for a while to their jungle, while the resources used to comfort them were concentrated on the refugees? Or have they lost their jungle skills? And anyway, by what criterion can one judge whether, among these people, a settled life is better than nomadism?

I stayed in a very good hotel on the northern outskirts of Chieng-mai. It was used by guided parties of tourists, many of them French. It also had a huge aviary, an open square fitting into two arms of the building, with nets from ground to roof level four floors above and enclosing several large trees. This was filled with the flash and song of these lovely creatures. I wish that I knew something about birds: though, being able to tell a kingfisher from a crow, I reckon that I know more about them than I do about botany. I also remember the hotel for an incident.

I sat down along the wall for lunch. Apart from two women against another wall, there was no one much about. The head waiter looked faintly embarrassed when he brought the menu, and motioned me to another table opposite. This was on the carpeted part of the room. Then he went away and came back to serve the two ladies himself. He always bowed, served them, bowed again and retreated backwards across the parquet. This, it turned out, was Queen Sirikit and a lady-in-waiting. While they were there the parquet was sacred, and nobody, save the head waiter was permitted to put a foot on it. A French party who came through was meticulously shepherded along the carpet by their guide. I never discovered the reason for this. Was the Queen sensitive to footsteps on wood, or did it represent a sacred enclosure, like fencing Tynwald, or what?

And so we leave (as American travel films say), the rice baskets and heroin, the wandering nomads and the teak-carvers, the tremendous 25-foot-long temple drums of this northern kingdom, but before I go, I must relate my terrifying Filipino experience.

Imagine a night-club in a great dark blue vaulted building with tables on the ground, rows of customers and myself sitting at a table with feet in a pit, while waitresses and men bring food, sticky rice and *Mekong*.

The bells, drums, flutes and one-stringed fiddles strike up their melodious uproar. Expect a boxing match just like the Rajdamnön Road. On come about twenty men and girls with 25-foot bamboo poles each like a scaffolding pole. These are laid out in pairs – three pairs north and south, three east and west across them. One lot holds pairs of poles at each end and clash them together while the band thunders to their rhythm: the other lot step into the opening-and clash-closing clatter squares which the moving poles create. They dance a sort of hopping and tripping measure over the poles. Of course if anyone misses a beat or a step, he may have his ankle crushed between a pair of poles.

A beautiful smiling young woman stood before me in the half darkness. She indicated graphically that I should dance. Well? At the age of 59 what can one do? In the expectant silence she pushed and manoeuvred me into my clatter square. The band and the pole-players were quite ruthless. I hop and trip like my mad-thing partner. I step and leap. I like dancing but this is ridiculous! It seems to go on for ever. I cannot, dare not stop. I have NOT STOPPED. I am still at it now. Suddenly, a stupefied silence. The stupefaction is entirely mine. She says 'Filipino?'. I say 'No'. She says 'Filipino dance'. I say 'You Filipino?' She say 'No'. We kiss passionately to the applause of the bystanders.

Chapter 35

THREE CABLES AND MY FATHER'S SUICIDE

Elephants, being uncommon even in Siam, they make do with substitutes such as the hundreds of little wooden ones paraded before the Lord who Rules the Water, and there is the annual round-up which the King conducts himself, and there are the widespread topiaries which provoked my last Siamese postcard to Henry in the words 'Hephalumpum si requiris, circumspice'. I have, by now, to remind myself for the seventeenth time, that this book is supposed to be about Me not It, but I hope that I have indicated a refreshment of spirit.

So I started to look for work with confidence based on nothing save a little capital, a small pension and an excess of energy. Nothing works out as one expects. Fanny spotted a notice about Traffic Commissioners. Though ignorant of their functions, I applied, and found myself, slightly stupefied in East Anglia as *two* tribunals, holding public inquiries. I will explain about the two a little later; I was at one time as many as eight.

Then, as a constitutional lawyer, I applied for an advertised lectureship in the Law Faculty of the City University. I was interviewed in a pub by quite a different crowd and, indeed, for a subject of which I had never heard, namely Arts Administration. It was new and full of empty spaces. In Traffic Licensing there is something to know, even if I did not know it. In Arts Administration the subject was unexplored. I became a visiting lecturer and then a Visiting Professor.

My life became a twist of three cables: law teaching; traffic licensing and British History, with flitting in and out, courses for vehicle examiners, lectures on architecture, writing this book, and some fun excursions. These all overlapped so frequently that they need to be impossibly described together.

The City University had set up a new and, in a world sense unique Department of Arts Policy and Management, inspired by Anthony Field, Finance officer of the Arts Council, and directed by John Pick. Anthony's point was that the arts institutions, whether concert halls, picture galleries, theatres or anything else cost too much because their management was amateurish. John, a marvellous lecturer, was particularly suitable for his job because he was an ex-actor who had directed an educational institute in Somerset. They listed the subjects in which the managers might need instruction – accounts, marketing, buildings, arts and so forth and came up with – law. This was where I came in, but accidentally I brought something else. A committee to which I belonged debated a subject for a new MA degree in Journalism. The project listed every conceivable art (even presumably barbola work) but not architecture.

Now, of all the arts, architecture is the most pervasive and influential in an urban civilisation. The population lives, works in and sees hundreds of buildings a day. Its outlook is powerfully influenced. When I said so, there was a small silence and then someone said 'Er, would you like to take it on?' The answer was really 'no', but having looked, ever since Winchester took me over Chartres, at hundreds of buildings between Forres and Chieng-mai and read a good deal, I had developed theories; for example that classical architecture was a development in stone of a means to house a God or a bank manager, not congregations or customers; that *Art Nouveau* originated with the advisers of King Ludwig II of Bavaria. I also had some technical knowledge of fortifications, and tried to analyse the engineering differences between Romanesque and Gothic. So, like an idiot, I said 'Yes'. I enjoyed sorting the ideas out. I do not know if my pupils learned anything but at least they asked questions.

Thus on a Tuesday I walked down to the Barbican and harangued my 100-odd law students and on two or three other days of the week I went by train to any of the twelve towns within the quadrilateral formed by Oxford, Southend, King's Lynn and Nottingham. At the Barbican I had to deliver carefully designed lectures to fairly young listeners, mostly women. In the twelve towns I had to sit and listen to applicants and complainants, mostly elderly men. Also at the Barbican I had to *put it across*: in the twelve towns I had always to pass judgement. My life would have been neatly balanced had it not been for those escalating disputes with the Clarendon Press. These students were mature, each with a degree or two. There was even a German perpetual student of 64. Their intellects were to be respected, but they had never done any law before. They had to be taught a good deal of it. It takes seven years to make a good lawyer. I had 40 hours. I devised an approach based on jurisprudence, while I fought the Clarendon Press and considered preventive maintenance at lorry depots. My object was to produce a true picture of the law which might be intelligible to people who had thought little about it and who would certainly be prejudiced by hack journalism. I warned them in the first ten minutes of the dangers, and then plunged in.

My first traffic briefs arrived for some cases at Norwich; – (a) a couple of licensed operators with rattletraps which were apparently falling to pieces and

(b) someone who wanted to be an operator but might not have enough money to be able to keep his lorries in safe repair. Margery Rosenthal, my first pearl of a clerk, knew everything. She organised the whole affair, summarised the business impartially and never hinted at any possible outcome. There I was, on my own, having to take decisions worth millions or several human lives, yet equipped only with the impartiality of ignorance.

I can, as it happens, remember the short era of the pirate 'bus. There would be a regular service along a route marked with 'bus stops. There would be crowds of people rarin' to go. Along would come, not a respectable 'bus called GENERAL in gold, but a steaming oily-smelly brown 'bus called SMITH or JONES, who swore that he was going the same way. Cheaper too. Lots of people piled in. It would leave hurriedly with most of the General's expectations. So the General would have the expense and trouble of regularity, while the pirates skimmed the cream. Result: regulars went bust while the pirates took themselves off when they had made their pile. The public ended up with no service at all. Traffic Commissioners were created to sort this out by a licensing system. On the whole, with hiccoughs, they did.

Then came the lorry, already powerful and getting bigger, and now invading the goods market partly vacated through Dr. Beeching's suspect liquidation of the branch lines. The competition here was not for the routes (there were none) but for custom. There was a temptation to undercut trade rivals by overloading, or skimping on repairs, or exceeding drivers' hours, or driving like mad or all four – or worse. So the Licensing Authority was created to oversee the operators: to force them to prevent accidents by maintenance and inspection in advance; to see that they had enough money to maintain them; to try and exclude criminals and racketeers, and to ensure that the drivers of these monsters knew what they were doing. In a word, to protect public safety.

Hardly any of this was spelled out in the legislation; the Transport Acts were and remain abominably drafted, and are not improved by the importation of EU law which is written in quite a different manner. Not surprisingly I was appealed: actually seventeen times, though overruled in only seven. This was where my being two tribunals may seem only slightly inflated. One set of acts had created the Traffic Commissioners to deal with buses; a second created Licensing Authorities to deal with lorries, but as an afterthought laid down that he who was a Traffic Commissioner should also be the Licensing Authority. I was thus separately both, and when I was temporarily acting for London and the East and the West Midlands with East Anglia, I was $4 \times 2 = 8$.

There is also the Transport Tribunal composed of a County Court Judge and two civil servants, which is a court of appeal from us. Its interpretations were sometimes as questionable as our own. I was once overruled because, with the enormous Oxford English Dictionary plus the case law, I held that 'repute' and 'reputation' meant, as they do, different things. The Tribunal thought that they were the same. Submission to the obviously wrong is an occupational disease. Meanwhile, I travelled. Hardly anything was run-of-the-mill. One operator went into partnership with a printer, and supplied himself with forged international permits. There was another whose defence to overloading was that continental containers had falsified manifests and the weighbridge did not work. He was right on both counts. Somebody at Leicester wanted to start minibus services, and was hotly opposed by Leicester Corporation who spasmodically operated empty double deckers. That one took four days. The minibus man got his licence. One vegetable distributor swore that the operating centre which he was required by law to have, was a house which, on inspection, was boarded up.

The Leicester case was the last in which I sat with lay commissioners. A new Act abolished these valuable colleagues. Then the environmentalists got something in about the disadvantages of depots to the neighbours, so now we had not only to protect public safety but defend private amenity. Since this was what the planning authorities were supposed to be doing, there was further confusion. Their planning departments became notorious in the trade. I do not blame them for misunderstanding this legislative farrago: but I felt entitled to complain if they had not even read it.

The new environmental business began to crowd out the safety side. Neighbours sometimes lodged representations in droves. One lot came in two hired buses. In another case they (all amateurs) supported a well argued case with over a hundred photographs. It takes a long time to see, mark (as exhibits) and inwardly digest a hundred photographs. And sometimes they said strange things. One old age pensioner (who turned out to be younger than I was) considered that he ought to be entitled to sleep until at least eight in the morning. I had had to get up at six to hear him say it. And no matter how much they went on, you couldn't stop them.

I often worked in improvised venues. There was the physiotherapy centre where the evidence was embellished from the next room with piano-accompanied callisthenic dancing. 'What were you, in fact looking for under the vehicle', I was asking the vehicle examiner. 'Left leg UP ladies; left leg DOWN'. Once, having no retiring room I asked everyone to adjourn outside while I sat and wrote. I did not know it was raining. My clerk ferreted them all out of the nearby pubs.

English lawyers have never bothered much with jurisprudence, thus leaving too much in the minds and hands of the politicians, and the abandonment of Roman

Law, by abolishing systematic comparisons, has depressed it to lip service status. What I actually did for my students was to break down the civil legal ideas into *Persons* (whether natural or legal), *Things* (immovable, movable and abstract), and into relationships between persons and things (*Property*) and between persons in conflict (*Tort*) and in agreement (*Contract*). I had not enough time for such subjects as constitutional law and court procedure, but I tried to make up for this by taking them to the courts and Parliament. The principles could be illustrated anecdotally from the facts of leading cases, for these, such as the snail in the ginger beer of *Donohue v Stephenson* or the smugglers of Rye in *Coggs v. Bernard*, attract and illuminate the bewildered, and I am proud that nobody was ever late for my lectures, even if the Orientals tape-recorded them. I sometimes suspect that they danced to them.

In 1985 the Clarendon Press and I decided, politely, to part, and I did other things, including the already mentioned courses for Vehicle Examiners who know how to detect defects in them. The licensing of Heavy Goods Vehicles (HGVs) is impracticable without these experts who lie underneath or tap screws with hammers. They have to give evidence before people like me, but however practical and expert they are, forensically articulate they mostly are not. The purpose of these intensive courses (at Birmingham, Cardington and Bristol) was to teach them how to classify their findings, turn them into words and stand up to cross examination upon them. Each one (they came in tens or dozens) gave evidence individually before a mock inquiry over which I presided, and was filmed so that he could see himself as others see him, and there was also a discussion session after each performance. I used the same standard cases for over twenty years three to six times a year. Believe it or not, no case ever came out the same.

On 24th June 1990 I held a public inquiry at King's Lynn. The next day, being my 72nd birthday, I was too old, and will now go back to an odd episode with a man whom I will call Booh. My Traffic Commissioner boss, the charming and able Ken Peter, had retired and there would be a gap. For the seven months, they put in this man Booh. Fortunately I only cast eyes on him three times, once before Ken left, once after the replacement arrived. Quite enough. He forbade the clerks to send me the papers about my public inquiries, so that I could only find out what they were about in the few minutes before my sittings began. Then he began to write me offensive letters, including one in which he announced it as his policy that there should be no appeals to the Transport Tribunal. As only the operators, not we could appeal, this was beyond our control, but the only possible means of implementing the policy was never to disagree with an operator. I told him in writing. He summoned me to a meeting, where, in the presence of one of his lesser civil servants, he spent two hours in the hostile dissection of all the decisions which I had made in his time. He could not get far because I had been appealed only once. He also told me that he had it in his power to dismiss me. If the contingency had ever arisen, I would have explained to the Secretary of State why he should be dismissed, for he had set the whole Traffic Office by the ears, made everyone miserable, and prevented work from being expedited. He was in fact, a silly bully, and when another Traffic Area had the misfortune to have him, he was reported to have behaved in exactly the same manner.

Let me return for an instant to the inquiries. There are upwards of 2,000 inquiring bodies I believe, and they mostly have to make do with makeshift accommodation: in hotel ballrooms or disused schools, recreation centres or village halls. At Eye in Suffolk we had to sit round a very large table filling in a very small room, and whenever a witness changed, it was like 'when father says turn, we all turn'.

Not surprisingly, people cannot find them, the press cannot be bothered, and though these are supposed to be public hearings, nobody knows what goes on. And yet they daily cope with issues of a magnitude which a High Court judge with his fixed and suitable location, hardly ever sees. If a planning permission is refused, land values may tumble by millions, business goes elsewhere and the locals have to look for new jobs. If I revoke a licence I may put a million pounds worth of hardware off the roads and about 30 people out of work, and disturb deliveries at points anywhere between the Shannon and the Volga. It is wrong that this business should be conducted in such a haphazardly accommodated way.

When I was 79 somebody asked me what my next project was; I said that I had long been sauntering through an effort to translate *The Hunting of the Snark* into German. It now exists as *Die Schnarckjagd:*

> 'Mit Sorge und Fingerhut ist er zu jagen,
> Mit Hoffnung und Gabel verfolgt.
> Du drohst ihn das Leben mit Eisenbahnakte
> Und entzückst Ihn mit Seife und Reiz'

and meanwhile imagine me in splendour in the fourteenth century Guildhall at King's Lynn. The sun streams brilliantly through the vast unshutterable Gothic windows, and blinds and boils the shorthand writer. The clerk says 'court rise, please'. I proceed with dignity round the great panelled hall to my seat. It is a canopied throne three steps above the common herd. 'Please be seated', I say to the deferential mob. I sit down. My throne tips sideways and spills me down the

THREE CABLES AND MY FATHER'S SUICIDE

steps – flump – in a sprawl of limbs and papers. Fortunately I am so August that I can laugh.

This was to have been the final flourish of this book, but to begin in the middle, I sent a copy of *Die Schnarckjagd* to Professor Richard Sheppard of Magdalen College. He had contacted me because he had been commissioned by the Rhodes Trustees to write a piece for their centenary *Festschrift* on the German Rhodes Scholars, and he had found out a good deal about my father and incidentally about Stefan George, and Count Stauffenberg and their friends. And this spreads the story all over Germany.

Schlönwitz was shared between Bob and Elsa as tenants and my father as owner with his second wife Erica Schippel. Until the middle of the Second War Dietrich Bonhoeffer, the heroic Lutheran pastor and theologian also lived in the village where, in that Nazi atmosphere of atheistic barbarism, he kept a congregation of Christians – mostly young – in good and faithful heart. Presumably Bob and Elsa were involved but it is known that my father originally introduced George and Stauffenberg to each other. Stauffenberg was, of course, the central figure in the assassination attempt on Hitler on 30th June 1944; other friends of George's were also implicated and the SS arrested and hanged some 7,000 people in the wake of the explosion. About eighteen months before, however, Bonhoeffer had been arrested: he was still under investigative custody, and therefore had the perfect *alibi*. This did not save him. He was hanged at Flossenburg two days before the Americans arrived. Meanwhile the Russians had overrun Schlönwitz. They summoned his congregation to the school and shot all these young people down. I saw the school when Henry, Nieves and I visited the place. No wonder the *miserere* behind the church pulpit portrays Bonhoeffer as Christ.

At this time my father's sister Nora was living in Marburg. Professor Sheppard tells me that my father had some minor job in the Marburg Nazi party office, but he and I both doubt whether this had any significance. Anyone who wanted work of professional status had to be a registered member of the party, and in the current state of Germany, academic work was probably impossible and a 60-year old man would have had to take what he could get to stay alive. The Professor also tells me that my father's party number was so late and the job so minor, that any denazification tribunal would have pronounced him *entlastet* (exonerated).

The American northward thrust reached his university of Giessen, not far off, on 28th April 1945, and on that day he and his Erica brought their four children, Albrecht, Viktor, Erika and Caroline to Nora and handed them over. They then went out and he shot his Erica and then himself in a cart which they found in the street. As far as I know he left no explanation. Nora, who must have known his intention, said nothing. No Nazi records on the subject have come to light.

There seem to be two opposing possibilities deducible from this grim story. Either he was implicated in the denunciation of Dietrich Bonnhoeffer and feared the vengeance of the Allies, or he was implicated in Stauffenberg's attempt on Hitler and was a late victim of the reprisals. Compulsory suicides were quite common in the Third Reich – Rommel's death is a case in point. The method was to tell the victim to do it himself or have it done in the usual SS fashion by slow self-strangulation with a piano-wire round the neck and the tips of the toes on a roller. He was very little at Schlönwitz throughout the war and a comparison between possible Allied action and certain Nazi cruelty seems to me to make the Stauffenberg alternative the more probable of the two. Indeed his brains and his intimacy with Stauffenberg and the whole Stefan George circle suggest that he may have inspired and taken part in planning the affair. His wartime letters in the *Georgearchiv* at Stuttgart both increasingly reflect George's style and are increasingly gloomy. My cousin Wulf-Werner (the full colonel) said that there had been an epidemic of voluntary suicides in western Germany at this time.

Nora v. Lettow-Vorbeck had one child, Helöise, who became a sort of honorary Blumenthal. I often met her at family gatherings and in Venice. Charming and enterprising – learning English at 75, – she told me much, and particularly that while she and her half-siblings were being brought up together near Lübeck, Nora ran a Scarlet Pimpernel outfit to rescue non-Communists from Communist clutches and get them to the British Zone by rowing across or dodging round the many lakes nearby, and she had told many hilarious stories about it. I asked Helöise to write it all down, but I doubt if she ever did.

In any case, it is a pleasure to record this aspect of Nora's character. A gallant lady.

Chapter 36

FOUR COUNTRIES AND SOME HOSPITALS

I could not complain much when Pofessor Boylan, by then Head of my department at the City University sacked me good humouredly at three days' notice, for I was, at 76, fourteen years over the retiring age. It was the year when I went to Schlönwitz.

Be warned! There will now be an enlarged blomp about travels. I adore them. Snuggling in a sleeper when young. Adding odd days to business trips. Fun travel simply for fun. Weird food.

In 1994 Fanny and I savoured the blessings of Levantine terrorism. The bullets and bombs which enlivened Egypt gave us a week on the Nile in luxury (flights an' all) for about the cost of a weekend in Bournemouth.

Aswan airport was unsophisticated, bureaucratic and cheerful at 104° in the shade. A 'bus showed us a desert. It was very humpy and dark brown, spotted with black stone tussocks, and utterly barren. One could see a long way – probably to Timbuktu and so to the town of Aswan and the NILE at 6.00pm, where our block of floating flats called the goodship *Ra* was coolly throbbing with refreshing red drinks made from Hibiscus flowers call *Karkadeh*, a briefing, dinner, and so to lie unbelievingly on couches on the upper deck and occasionally snooze to traffic noises and a hot wind.

We had been warned that the M/S *Ra* was to sail for Edfu at four in the morning, and the very gentle engine sensation woke us at 5.00am. We were in water bounded by a river bank backed by the greenest vegetation and masses of palm trees of every size and type. The tall coconut palms of Siam are all carefully cultivated. These Upper Egyptian ones are a riot. High, low, medium, fat, scraggy, bushy, leaning, upright, straight, bent and like every riot, disorderly. We saw them giving the impression of depth interspersed with cultivation but though the green seemed to stretch far away, I had an instinct that the riot could not last.

We moved majestically north. We had thought that the *Ra* was one of a small number of these extraordinary craft, which, apart from her four storeys had a flat roof equipped with swimming pool and a bar. The familiar attributes of a boat had been reduced to virtually nothing, because the Nile is always in mirror calm. As you eat in the dining room you see the water gliding past only a foot below the window sill. We soon discovered that we were not an endangered species. Three frequent toots on our sober whistle would be acknowledged by triple salutes of varied musicality: some favoured cacophony, others uproar. Actually there are about 200 of these monsters plying between Aswan and Tell-el-Amarna.

My instinct about the insubstantial nature of the riot proved true. A brown ridge appeared, as distant backing. It got steadily closer driving the green right to the bank, leaving only a few yards of cultivation and some ragged trees. From our portside cabin going north, we saw only the West Bank but from the sun-deck things looked different, for the East Bank seldom mirrored the West. The lush and the barren mostly oscillated between the banks.

During breakfast we went alongside fabled Edfu. The Greeks called it Apollinopolis to which the Romans added Magna.

It is worth describing its large and splendid temple, which is well preserved, adorned with enormous and marvellously energetic bass-reliefs and especially because being typical of the larger monastic temples in general. I can avoid saying much about the others.

There is a vast portal flanked by huge divine or royal statues and sometimes by pairs of obelisks. On each side of the portal is a trapezoid building which may be 150 feet high, perhaps 200 feet wide and as much as 50 feet thick. This is known as a 'pylon' from the Greek for a gate (*pyle*). The word is now inconvenient. Why not simply 'gate'? It is really a sort of screen and often bears bass reliefs of the Pharoah doing hieratic things or making violent exhibitions from a chariot, together with Gods and Goddesses suitable to the temple's dedication.

Inside the gate is a large colonnaded court with chapels built before the temple and which it was considered wrong to remove. I think that this court is the ancestor of the western monastic cloister as well as the coenobitic way of life. There follows another gate with guardian statues and a portal into a large pillared hall, known to the ancients as the Hall of Divine Appearance because a God's statue could be seen through the various open portals as it was carried down the processional aisle. Archeologists have copied the Greeks and call it the hypostyle hall, which only means the hall with big pillars. The pillars are overwhelming and covered, together with the walls, with hieroglyphics illustrated with bass reliefs. They are often as much as eleven feet in diameter and up to 80 feet high.

Next, after several small chapels and store rooms there is a sanctuary, seldom entered by anyone, and this will be enclosed in another chamber so that an ambulatory runs all round it. The outer side of the wall supports a series of cells or storerooms. The whole parallelogrammatic complex is surrounded by a high wall decorated with bass reliefs on the outside and with much hieroglyphic information within, all heavily illustrated. The interior crowded material is fussy in effect but the external surfaces are much barer and, to my eye, aesthetically more impressive, for the main reliefs are not confused by a million muttering inscriptions. Imagine a cathedral covered all over the inside with an illustrated Bible written in characters six inches high. The object of this wall was, I imagine, to keep out prying eyes, and, secondarily thieves. It was not, however, defensible as a fortification.

Edfu town is no great shakes. They took us to our target in *calèches* which bumped and shuddered us agreeably through a myriad pot-holes among open fronted shops unaltered in design since ancient times, and deposited us in a market at the entrance gates, where urgent male business-persons between the ages of 92 and 6 pressed the unique qualities of their wares upon us by getting in the way, pushing them in our faces and extolling their high worth and minimal price: sphinxes, scarabs, brass trays, scarves, *galabeyas*, slippers. Our guide, the admirable and learned Rawiya, told us to bargain and buy, if at all, in the street and never, but never be enticed into a shop. If you were, you would come out poorer and as the owner of something you did not want. She did not know how this happened: she only knew victims.

The temple seems to have superseded another to Horus built by Thothmes III, and is comparatively modern, having been founded by Ptolemy III Euergetes on 23rd August 237 BC and completed on 5th December 57 BC, eighteen months before Caesar's first raid on Britain (the date where I commence my *Companion to British History*), but it has a very holy shrine made from a single 70-ton block of granite, given by Nechtanebo II, the last native Egyptian Pharoah. This Nechtanebo was overthrown by the Persian King of Kings, Cambyses. There are legends of Nechtanebo escaping to Greece, marrying a Macedonian princess and siring the Ptolemaic line, whereby, of course they were really native rulers. They certainly used Egyptian titles and ceremonial, so I would guess that the building of the Edfu temple was a partly political act connected with the shrine of Nechtanebo.

Sand preserved it and David Roberts the Scottish water-colourist, recorded it as it was in 1839, buried up to the capitals and with peasant huts on the roof. Over a hundred of these had to be cleared away when Mariette dug the temple up in the 1860s. If the peasants were at all like the local business persons, I am prepared to guess that they did quite well out of it. The result is quite splendid, and you see the way Egyptian, even if Ptolemaic, Kings wished to be represented as walking with the divine, and smiting their people's enemies.

Some general remarks may not, or may be, out of place. Firstly, the temples, being built of local stone, are now brown. This was not always so, for the ancients painted them brightly using tempera, some of which has survived. In their heighday they must have been brilliant or tawdry. Secondly, the builders never discovered the arch. These constructions, to be roofed, had to have thick pillars with small intervals bridged by sandstone slabs because wood was in short supply and the latter could not reach far without cracking. This created a darkly hieratic effect. Thirdly, though there was some development, temple builders clung to their traditions sculpturally, architecturally and in their records, which as I have already remarked, cover walls and pillars and yield vast amounts of information. It would have been nice, like Rawiya, to read ancient Egyptian as I read French, but aesthetically this has created serious problems.

We were hustled off to lunch and sailed for Esna about four hours away. As a town, Esna is rather more modern than Edfu and once the terminal of a desert trade route. It has the remains of the pillared hall of a great temple to Khnum, a nice God who made human beings on a wheel with clay, and therefore patronises potters. The building was deeply buried in sand, and the unburied part was used as a gunpowder store. In local fighting it was hit by shot and shell but escaped the fate of the Parthenon. The sand having been cleared, it is now at the bottom of a mid-town quarry. The bass-reliefs are very fine and the inscriptions recorded, amongst other things, that someone had been to 360 festivals at different named temples in Egypt. The location, and even the existence of some of these temples is still unknown, but the account is a remarkable indirect record of a widespread religious organisation.

The British built a first dam with 120 sluices and a lock in 1902 to control the water-level for irrigation. The Egyptians built a second dam half a mile lower down for hydro-electricity and abandoned the purposes of the first, which is now used solely as a bridge. I went up onto the sun-deck in the dawn to see us locking through. The lock could have held another *Ra* but actually there was a solitary rowing boat. The whole passage was very efficient and quiet, and we reached Hundred Gated Thebes (otherwise Luxor) just after breakfast.

Luxor (a corruption of an Arabic word meaning The Palaces) comes to the East Bank from a mile or two away and has hotels, casinos, night clubs all in a splendid Afro-Oriental muddle superimposed upon the Hundred Gated with a large temple of its own. About a mile north are the temple complexes of Karnak, while opposite on the West Bank there is the so-called Theban Necropolis. Ammon, the God over everything, lived and worked at Karnak, which was constantly enlarged and improved in a manner appropriate to his rising dignity. The complex covers

62 acres, with temple after temple, sanctuary behind sanctuary, hall upon hall and at least nine gates, connected with the river by an avenue of ram-headed sphinxes and similarly towards Luxor with the temple of Mut, his wife. Every Opet festival He and She proceeded in a flotilla of boats to the temple at Luxor for a ten-day holiday to renew the vital fertility of the World while the population turned out to enjoy itself in imitation. Flute, harp, sack-but, psaltery, dulcimer and all other kinds of musick doubtless anticipated Nebuchadnezzar's famous edict, but were the food of Love and, of course, played on.

The place was established as a capital at the start of the Middle Kingdom and enjoyed its high prosperity between 1600 and 1085 BC. Then the court moved to the Delta. The decline was hastened by the Assyrians under Asshurbanipal ('Sardanapalus'), who sacked it in 672 BC. This could not have been decisive: you only have to look at the place to see that a sack lasting a week or two would have been a mere incident. Actually it cannot have been a clean sweep, for building and activity continued. It remained impressively second-rate even when the Ptolemies took over and ruled from yet further away, at Alexandria; they did not neglect Karnak, for Ptolemy III Euergetes (r 246-221 BC) built a portal there, but people and business were drifting north. I do not believe one statement that by Roman times Karnak was largely in ruins, but the decline of ancient religious observance deprived it of superstitious protection and Christianity was hostile. Those who, as with English monasteries, found it a convenient store of worked building stone were not prevented from quarrying it. Hence I suspect that Karnak became ruinous in the four Christian centuries before the Arab conquest of the 640s AD, and by then the population had declined. Not much more building stone was needed, and there were few people to block the encroaching desert. By Bonaparte's time the archeologists, standing on the sand, put inscriptions on the main gate which were 65 feet above ground level. So at the time 122 of the pillars (each 33 feet in circumference) were probably buried leaving an apparently lone seventeen-foot, ten pillared structure projecting through the surface. Anyway despite sporadic clearances extending over 140 years, some parts of the complex are still unexplored.

As before, we had too short a time here because *Voyages Jules Verne* wanted to show us the Luxor Museum the same morning. The problem of time is insoluble. Karnak could easily warrant a week of tourist scrutiny or three months for an enthusiast, but given A Week on the Nile, a two-thirds morning, if lengthened might be only a theoretical benefit because of the heat, while the museum, if small, is good and cool and, especially, not overcrowded with exhibits. Museum Feet (MF) are inevitable everywhere but SOMEF (Soporific Overcrowded Museum Eye

Flicker) can lead to Zombiism (Z) or Snoring in the Bus (SIB). So we went back for lunch, nursed our MF, siested and flopped till tea, flopped and siested till 7.30pm and then went back to Karnak for a *Son et Lumière*, thereby giving ourselves a second chance.

I have seen several such performances including the original one at Versailles 35 years ago. Portentous, not to say grandiloquent was what this one was, with very hieratic whale music* and a script finely spoken in real English. Here the problem was that the *dramatis personae* were mostly Gods who should not be belittled: fair enough! But I think that script and score could have been toned down so as to let the staggeringly flood-lit buildings make their effect. For staggering they certainly are, both as the Gods take you by the hand through them, and as you later watch from a stand across the sacred lake.

At the corner of the lake there is a red granite scarab as big as three pillows, on a six-foot pillar. If a woman goes round it widdershins seven times she will be married and pregnant within a year; four times clockwise will get you married; three times and you're in luck or divorced. We went round together three times and confidently expect to win the jackpot.

They called us at 5.00am and bundled us across the River at six. Thence by bus to the Valley of the Kings. My narrative sense became somewhat befogged in the heat. There is a lush cultivated plain with villages and ruins, and the Valley, the stoniest and most barren pale brown gulch imaginable, begins abruptly. Rawiya thought that it was a place of royal sepulture because of a pyramid shaped mountain at the end – pyramids in Lower Egypt being then already fifteen centuries old (or so). Very probable, for 68 tombs are known, a 69th has just come to light and they know how many there are to go from temple King-lists. The various rulers obligingly identified themselves with a certain panache (and in cartouches). You know the sort of thing: *I, Ramses the Umpteenth, was the greatest King who ever ruled. My buildings were utterly enormous. My People ate real food. I slaughtered Nubians in heaps. I fathered 5787 children and My Majesty was on back-slapping terms with Amun, Horus, Osiris, Isis and, of course, Min.*

I liked Rawiya's story about Ramses II at the battle of Kadesh. His account appears on some temple wall. His army, tricked by planted information, was divided and Ramses, on the wrong side of the river with the smaller part, charged the enemy. Unfortunately the King's own men all ran away so he prayed to Amun who sent him an army of invisible soldiers with which he routed the enemy and returned in triumph. The more prosaic Hittite archives, however, say that they captured Ramses and let him go on condition that he never invaded Syria again.

---

* A.P. Herbert's useful expression for specially impressive music accompanying an impressive cinematic event such as the appearance of a whale.

There was a difference of outlook between Class I, namely monarchs, their courtiers and family and Class II, those who with their friends, receivers and so forth actually buried them. Class I were dehydrated and embalmed, and having passed the Judgment of Osiris and not been eaten by an infernal Hippocroc, were introduced to the heavenly VIPs and eventually reanimated by divine hydration. Are the cascades of Life Signs represented in the sculpture the origin of the phrase *Water of Life*? The Second Life might, however, not be very enjoyable without furniture, jewels, gold, food, drink, musical instruments and other things conducive to the Good Life. These were crammed into the tomb, which was excavated into the living rock with deceptive side passages, false walls and heavy falls of scree to protect them against Class II. The latter mistrustful of their eternal prospects, or of the Crocotamus, opted for the Good Life here and now. This might be very enjoyable with the things listed above. Having hidden the tombs so carefully, they, and no-one else much, knew exactly where to find them, and with the kind assistance of the police they lived a Good Life. It was a solipsistic situation. If you mistrusted your prospects and robbed tombs, the robberies ensured that the Dilopot would get you. This did not worry them very much and 67 out of the 68 tombs had been robbed. The 68th was Tutenkhamen's.

Obviously the tomb entrances are featureless holes in this soaring, oven-hot stony landscape, but, worse still the priesthood could not hold the proper services and ceremonies to smooth the eternal path, without giving the locations away. Queen Hatshepsut solved the problem. She built a temple into the reverse side of the pyramid mountain, where things could be properly done, without blowing any cover, for all the Kings. As all the orientations were 180° out, much would have to be done backwards, upside down or widdershins, but in the hands of the famously expert Egyptian priests, it would not have been hard, say, to chant your prayers standing on your head.

Queen Hatshepsut was the only native Egyptian Lady Pharoah. I am not sure why her successor hated her: hardly because she opened up the trade route to Punt and imported gold, ivory, incense, apes, peacocks and almug trees. Punt is said to be Somalia, but I wonder if the name included the Yemen and the Hadhramaut opposite, for these countries exported incense in biblical and modern times. Anyway, her name and features were savagely chiselled but, as often happens, he failed to make a proper job of it, so her memory and, one may hope, her Second Life are preserved. Her temple is the model for much modern architecture.

Apart from Tutenkhamen's tomb, we went into two others. I was never very interested in his treasure, but wall paintings in all three were a joy. There was also an ancient tomb-workers' village, filling the end of a valley with stone house walls still up to about four feet. It held about 170 artists with their families. There was a standard method. Subjects were divided up by grid squares so that the artist, having been given a multiplier, could copy from one size to another. This was particularly important in the case of big buildings which, having been built from the bottom up, had to be adorned from the top down.

At the top of this village was a tomb for a famous or head artist. Much smaller than a royal tomb, it was vividly and sometimes amusingly painted. It was said that these workers commuted over the mountain blind-folded, camped in the Valley of the Kings for five or six days and returned to their families blindfolded for the week-end. I find this hard to credit. They, or some of the 170 must have observed the paths and been in a position to sell their knowledge. Try blind-folding 170 men a hundred days a year yourself!

The area is called, like Brookwood Cemetery, a Necropolis. This suggests an organised town of the dead, which it is not. You have to go for miles round the mountain to reach the Valley of the Kings and miles back again for the Valley of the Queens (which also contains the tombs of princes distinguishable by a great plaited lock of hair hanging down over the left ear) and in the area between the River and the mountain there are only about 700 noble tombs now known, with another 150 suspected. This amounts to about one tomb for every ten acres.

There are also a large temple by Amenhotep III, the Colossi of Memnon and several villages. Fanny found the Colossi as she expected and large. To me they seemed surprisingly small and hardly deserving the line *Look upon my works, ye Mighty and despair*. Their desolation is due to isolation. Everything else with which they were associated has vanished leaving them stranded in a field by a roadside. Even the car-park was empty.

Before I leave the Second Life, I must mention the often quoted tomb of Rechmira, occasionally Regent of the Two Lands. His sepulchre is a long wide sloping corridor ending in a burial chamber and inscribed all over with assertions of the brilliance of his administration. These are illustrated with fascinating scenes from life: smiths, potters, masons at work. Farmers. Criminals being beaten. Accountants casting up records (difficult in a barter economy). People paying rent: trapping birds: fishing. Rechmira's family hosting a reception. Boats are in evidence, but nothing on wheels. I would have liked to stay for ages but the snag in popular tombs is the humidity and heat. Tomb visiting is an alternation of dry roasting in the sun, and boiling saunas under ground. An Egyptologist's life must be hard.

With SIB we did three other distinctive things. I mentioned the big Luxor temple in connection with Opet, and we visited it faint but pursuing. It has behind an off-centre main gate, a conventional plan and a *Roman* end-chapel whose inscriptions extol the Pharoah Domitian, he who died on the 'loo observing that he thought that he was turning into a God.

Then Rawya took us to a business which made papyrus. This reed no longer grows naturally in North Africa, but near the Colossi of Memnon I think I saw it being cultivated. It has a juicy stem like a pale yellow stick of rhubarb. You soak it in water (changed regularly) for six days. Then you cut it into thin strips and roll them longer and thinner, thus expelling some of the moisture. with a rolling pin. Next you arrange them into a criss-cross free of gaps to make a sheet the size you want and put it in a press for six days. The result is a perfect sheet of papyrus ready (though darkish yellow) for writing.

We also saw an alabaster business near the Valley of the Queens. I only like simple white alabaster such as a bowl, but could not think what to do with one if I bought it. Men were working the material in the porch using very primitive tools, and the village had only one tap so that black-clad ladies were making long cheerful strides and waving to us, while carrying full buckets of water on their heads. Also the alabaster boss had been on the *Haj* and had painted his house with an enormous picture of the Kaaba together with the aeroplane and camel which took him there. You see such embellishments quite often. Their aesthetic quality may be open to discussion, but they add variety and colour to the mud-tinted groups of architectural boxes which make up the villages.

In Egypt newly married couples do not set up on their own but join the husband's parents, grand-parents and his sisters and his cousins and his aunts, and extra rooms may be added higgledy-piggledy to their already complicated house. On the other hand at Luxor we were tied up opposite an unfinished building, something between a hovel and a bungalow, with an obviously old pile of mud bricks outside together with the family washing machine. At least four men, six women and eight sweet children inhabited it but lived mostly outside under the palm tree. We asked about the unfinished buildings to be seen everywhere and were told that once they were finished they attracted property tax. I expect to see that heap of bricks again.

Now we set sail for Kom Ombo, eating meals as we stemmed the current. No account would be complete without these meals. The po-faced head waiter looked like Colonel Nasser. When at the very first meal he asked what we wanted to drink, I said 'what have you got?' and he silently turned out his pockets. He also warned me that only persons over eighteen were allowed in the bar. Fanny had a sort of hilarious feud with a Nubian because the staff had a tendency to hustle us, and she resisted. This became a ceremony in which napkins, glasses, even half-eaten plates were removed, and after tugs-of-war returned. The food varied from the Anglo-international to Egyptian (not enough of the latter) and there were magnificent and enormous buffets, especially on this evening which was to end in belly dancing.

She was handsome but overdressed, and her mission was, by audience participation, to do as little as possible herself. On the other hand the second part of the show was a man about seven feet high who whirled widdershins in a wide skirt which became a horizontal wheel twelve feet across as the music got hotter, and then suddenly divided upwards into two wheels. I cannot imagine how anyone can whirl like this for ten minutes without falling flat on his face. On the contrary, a few minutes later a stage horse appeared and amused itself and us with energetic and risible antics. After some time its occupants came apart to take their bows; the head was the whirling dervish.

There is an average difference of about three knots upstream and down, the current being stronger than this at Luxor and virtually nil just above the Esna barrage. The long reach towards Kom Ombo is very wide, sometimes more like a lake than a river. The wider the shallower, with sandbanks attracting birds and vegetation and somebody is always rowing a boat trailing a fishing line. Anon the sandbanks would build up and become cultivated, even with trees and huts and defences against flooding. Some are now islands, some so large that they divide the river into separate channels invisible from each other. The two bridges in the 300 miles between Aswan and Luxor are built over such channels. At other points the sandbanks adjoin the bank, which might be a low (say ten-foot) cliff or might slope directly to water-level. These riparian sandbanks are sooner cultivated than the mid-channel ones, and many were used as paddy.

There are plenty of boats, the larger being cargo and feluccas. A well loaded cargo felucca seems to have a freeboard of only a few inches, and they all have centreboards, introduced, I suppose, by the British. Their sails, well shaped, sometimes white, often patched, punctuate the landscape admirably but the method of working them is primitive. A boy usually has to shin up the mast and even along part of the spar to tie or untie something.

This day the manager took us to the engine room, a not very large roaring hell-hole with three engines, yet inaudible in the rest of the ship which glided about like a magic carpet presumably guided by a *djinn*. The heat inside was so intense that the engineers mostly stayed on an adjacent balcony in the open, and listened rather than watched for trouble. This made sense. Any trained man who knows his boat can hear something going wrong at once, and it is as well not to inflict Z in the heat before something happens.

The bridge was back to back with the bar. The manager said that he had a total crew of 60 (compared with a passenger complement of 140 – but we were only 90). I was wrong about the *djinn*. There was a chief pilot and his two assistants. The bridge was equipped with every conceivable sort of navigational electronics, but though the pilots knew how to use them (I saw one do it on request) they never ever did. They relied on their knowledge of the signs and a much quicker sixth sense. The sandbanks shift daily and sometimes hourly and they could tell what had happened often far away. This also applied to other craft. They knew where they were, even a mile off and round a bend, and what they would do, without any radio-telephonic contact. To focus on the echo-sounder, for example, might lose that useful second which made all the difference. Our four-storey block drew just under five feet.

The pilot was a weather beaten steadfast old man in a blue *gallabiyah*, who had a huge illuminated text from the Koran glued down among the instruments. He watched, as I expected, the water with great concentration and at intervals made tiny corrections on his wheel. I think that these were anticipatory; he was reading signs *here* which warned him of a problem which might lie half a mile ahead. The manager said that there was a shortage of pilots: you had to have at least two assistants to be sure that each had had a proper sleep, so the tourist boats in Upper Egypt alone absorbed 600 of them. They were training more. I did not ask how one trained a sixth sense. Anyway, I expect that that old man will – Inshallah – eventually navigate his ship to the Landing Stage of Paradise.

Having danced, disguised as Arabs until the gunpowder ran out of the heels of our boots, we fell into bed. At 4.00am and alongside at Kom Ombo, two gentlemen in turbans and *galabiyahs* were walking off the gangway with a box. They climbed over the wall, put the box on it and proceeded to eat its contents: so none of the buffet was wasted.

The temple is on a mound a hundred yards from the quay. It is a double temple dedicated to Horus and the crocodile god Sobek, because the inhabitants hereabouts were plagued with crocodiles which also ate the cattle. It was decided to set a thief to catch thieves by procuring the services of a crocodile god. Unfortunately Sobek lived in the Fayyum, 800 miles off, so when He arrived, He was quite unknown to the locals, who were used to Horus. The latter obligingly agreed to help, so while Sobek coped with the crocodiles, Horus reassured the congregation. Naturally Hathor, the cow goddess was also represented.

The temple, being unusual, is interesting on that account, but the bass and sunk reliefs are very beautiful and quite a lot of tempera painting is preserved. It was in its day a famous hospital. Inscriptions record royal gifts of medical equipment, and one monarch was cured of an eye infection there. Some Greek islands had temple hospitals, and I wonder whether there was a connection. Apart from its intrinsic interest, there was a second reason why I would like to have stayed longer. The High Dam submerged the country of 100,000 Nubians who were given land around Kom Ombo in compensation, with settlements named after their drowned villages. This New Nubia is a sort of large riverine oasis the size of Rutland which they have developed from the desert. It certainly looked, from the temple mound, prosperously cultivated, and small factory chimneys suggested minor industry. I would have liked to have gone right into it for a long look, for these people are reclaiming land as surely as the Dutch are doing so by pumping out the Zuider Zee, but the latter has a good press whereas Kom Ombo has no press at all.

We got to Aswan during lunch, and embarked on a bus for Philae. This famous place preserved the worship of Isis into the sixth century, long after the Edict of Milan (313). The temple, part Ptolemaic part Roman, stood on an island just above the British Aswan Dam, which first flooded it for three months a year and when raised, for nine months. Finally the High Dam, upstream, combined with the adaptation of the British dam to hydro-electricity would have drowned Philae altogether and it was decided to Do Something About It. They sawed the temple into 13,000 pieces, numbered them and put them together again on a new island; hence, for the first time since 1900 it is visible throughout the year. They had gained experience from moving Abu Simbel, and according to the technicians they did a better job at Philae. Abu Simbel is beginning to have problems.

So we were taken out in large pleasure boats with outboard motors, round capes, rocks and skerries, along the side colonnade to the back of the island where we were let loose. The Ptolemaic-Egyptian part is beautiful but for some reason Trajan's Kiosk has become a widely exploited symbol of it, and it is not really very good. It would be interesting to know the design history and purpose of this inappropriate building. It stands apart from all the rest: perhaps those responsible, had their doubts. Trajan presumably did not design it himself. He would have had more sense: and as it has architraves not arches, the architect was probably a Helleno-Egyptian. Greek architecture was a primitive adaptation in stone of a design system intended for wood, and never progressed. This Kiosk seemed to exhibit the vices of the unadventurous (or decadent) Greek and none of the engineering benefits of the enterprising Roman.

Stop complaining! We wandered about the splendid Egyptian buildings and resolved to return the same evening for the *Son et Lumière* to give ourselves, as at Karnack, a second chance.

Next! The High Dam, which, as seen from the north is an enormous man-made cliff. The occasion of the Suez affair and of the collapse of Britain as an imperial power, this stupendous construction (the base is over half a mile thick and it holds back a lake 300 miles long) was built by 30,000 Egyptians supervised by 2,000 Russians and it is a typically Russo-Communist project, like the Aral Sea, driven through without regard for ultimate consequences. With the old Aswan and other barrages it supplies cheap electricity for everything, where too little was available before. Some Egyptian industries now undercut foreign competition and Rawya said tellingly that where previously village children did their prep: under street lamps, now they do it indoors. The nation has been introduced to washing machines, television and radio, and a more varied, if western, lifestyle. All the same, the Dam has brought controversy and division. The dry climate around Aswan has become humid and, without any advantages of new irrigation, it now endures cloudbursts and flash floods. It has interrupted navigation; even the British five-lock staircase is closed. It has, as I mentioned, caused the transplantation of 100,000 Nubians and submerged hundreds of archeological sites. It is said to have altered the water table as far afield as Tunisia, and the perennial irrigation with which it has replaced the ancient periodic system has deprived middle and lower Egypt of its annual fertilising silt, substituted chemicals and encouraged plant diseases. It is desiccating the Delta, whose falling land-levels are letting in the sea. Dr Greiling, our German geologist friend, called in to advise the government, saw no good long-term prospect unless they blow the dam up. The lake is foreseeably silting up, and by 2020 may be full. What then? It seems that plans are being made for a Parallel Nile, taking off at Abu Simbel and reaching the Mediterranean between Alexandria and El Alamein. Not only might this cope with the silt, but it might fertilise the vast Western Desert and make accessible the metallic deposits such as cobalt said to lie under it. This sounds fine, but 2020, the year of prospective deluge, is just round the corner, and how will this be co-ordinated with Colonel Ghaddafi's Great Libyan River project, abuilding these ten years and with ten years to go?

Meanwhile cheap electricity has spread to all corners of Egypt and there has been a population explosion amounting to about a million births every nine months. The whole complex of factors has led some observers to predict that by 2020 Egypt will be fighting somebody for water: if not the Libyans, the Ethiopians perhaps, or whoever by then is in possession of the headwaters.

Fanny remarked that perhaps we were well out of it after all.

The view from the top, by the way, is magnificent and interesting towards Aswan town and the busy north, but southwards the enormous blue lake stretches beautiful, tranquil and quite dead. Presumably there are fish, but not a single boat or, within sight, any villages. Two years later, we took another boat, the *Prince Abbas*, from the south side of the High Dam all the way to Abu Simbel. She was, so to speak, the *Ra* inside out. Instead of internal passages, all the cabins gave onto an external veranda, from which you could admire the view. We began disappointingly by being stuck for nearly a day between some very blasted desert and a shunting yard on top of the dam. It was slightly enlivened by the cries of a distant *muezzin* and a man who, on hearing them smote his forehead smartly on the ground. A thin entertainment. Eventually we started up the 300-mile stretch, now called Lake Nasser. The deadness and tranquillity returned. It is narrow in parts but sometimes widens out so that you cannot see the coast. In the whole course, I remember no villages and only one town, but there are archeological sites, artificially created by moving temples from the depths to safety. Abu Simbel has had all the press, but there are several others including one which was the scene of the slowest railway journey in history. It had to be moved along the shore. They were short of rails, so, when they pushed the Temple Flyer a hundred yards, they picked up the track left behind and put it down in front. The eight-mile journey took seven months.

On Abu Simbel the paperazzi have served us ill. There are not one but two temples. In the hyped one, with 3½ huge seated open air statues of Ramses II most of the pillars in the main hall are also statues of him. The half outside statue fell down in Ramses' reign. The King left an angry inscription about it, but nobody has ever tried to repair it. So there the bits are, and in that very state it was all jacked up to escape drowning.

The other temple, for Ramses' Queen, is guarded by less spectacular standing goddesses but the interior is much more interesting. There are ceremonial and warlike wall-scenes including a besieged city (Kadesh?) and there is a side suite painted rather like the tombs in the Valley of the Kings. They treated us to a *Son et Lumière* at the King's temple while we sat at the water's edge. Then we dined under the stars in the *Prince Abbas* which went round and round offshore to give us plenty of views of the floodlighting. This was the Captain's civilised idea.

Back two years to our original trip via an unfinished obelisk still in its quarry, and for another *son et lumière* at Philae.

The whale music was, so to speak, a second movement of the Karnak symphony but the script was mostly propagandist tosh. The Gods may not exist, but they should not be patronised, for people venerated them once and, like it or not, they form an element in our civilisation. Fortunately the performance was held together by the wonderful floodlighting of the gorgeous buildings. It was nowhere used, by courtesy of the High Dam, to more breath-taking advantage.

Next day we stopped in Aswan. Aswan is not interesting but we found a shop which, with Arab humour, advertised 'No Hassell. Hassell 10% extra'. Fanny bought gifts for grandchildren. I bought saffron.

I once saw a heap the size of two pianos of alleged powdered saffron in the covered market at Shiraz. Here I bought about two ounces at (even with Hassell 10% extra) about a 50th of the London price.

Then we fought our way through taximen and calèche drivers hassling like mad and who seemed genuinely astonished that we preferred to walk to the Old Cataract Hotel, and drank coffee. I kicked myself later at having forgotten *Karkadeh*, which assuages even the most raging thirst – though thirst as such seldom bothers me: I merely go chuckle-headed or contract Z, a condition not alleviated by an incipient (other kind of) cataract which gave me occasional vertical double vision. Motor cars then have two identical number plates above each other, and the lateen spars of feluccas reach to heaven.

The Old Cataract reminded me of the Shah Abbas at Ispahan. There is a wonderful view from the high terrace over the gardens, across the River and its islands to the Aga Khan's mausoleum and the mountains beyond. Rawya had extolled the pleasures of calm felucca sailing but even she could not raise the wind and our three feluccas had to be pushed or towed by a petrol-smelly river jaunter. On the other hand the Nubian boatman rehearsed us in singing:

'U-u Walele'

until we bellowed it sonorously, and then produced a large (two foot) shallow (four-inch) single-sided drum. He held this in his left hand, tapping out a double rhythm on the parchment with the fingers while he banged a third rhythm with his right hand. He began to chant. I have, frankly, little command of Nubian, but –

Boatman:	My Aunt Aggie had a hat,
Us:	U-u Walele
	Every day she beat it flat,
	U-u Walele!
	She was quite an aristocrat,
	U-u Walele!!
	She always used a cricket bat,
	U-u Walele!!!
	What on Earth do you think of that?
	U-U WALELE

> My Uncle Arthur had a cat,
> U-u Walele.
> It always slept on a coconut mat,
> U-u Walele!
> Actually it was far too fat
> U-u Walele!!
> And never even caught a rat,
> U-u Walele!!!
> What on Earth do you think of that?
> U-U WALELE

Somehow we were dancing under the awning or climbing into the tug to dance there while the litany went uproariously on until the Aga Khan's landing stage.

We disembarked into the usual market and passed through a gate into a walled precinct covering much of the hillside.

> 'Twas brillig and the concrete path
> Did gyre and gimble in the heat';

also it was interrupted by steps which confused one's climbing rhythm. The inventor of steps, I proclaimed to everyone I met, should have his name scrubbed from his tomb. We had of course, to remove our shoes. I like this, but you had to do it outside the building amid a mob and in the direct sun on the pink granite paving. You could have a grilled steak on it, or at least a mutton chop. So I unlatched my sandals and leaped like a young gazelle to the carpet.

That is all there is to be said about the mausoleum. The Begum had already composed her own epitaph in six languages and only awaited Karim to fill in the date. So we fell hastily down the hill and sailed for Kitchener's Island (*U-u Walele*) nearby. This is a quite lovely botanical park in the middle of the Nile. Kitchener, as Sirdar, made Aswan his HQ for several years while organising the reconquest of the Sudan from the Khalifa and his Dervishes. He made this place and filled it with exotic and rare trees, and plants. Perhaps the palms with dead white trunks were almug trees, for there were apes and peacocks. With that moustache one does not think of Kitchener as a modern Queen Hatshepsut, even though she sometimes wore a ceremonial pharaonic beard. It really was an enchanting place. If the Aga Khan was not worth the trouble, Kitchener's Island was worth double. A picnic there would have been perfect. That night the whirling dervish and his horse returned and we danced.

Now for Spain which I have visited several times since Katharine's childhood. In the first place Henry married Nieves, an able and vivacious Basque, at San Sebastian. Basques are not like Spaniards: for one thing they tell each other endless funny stories. The church of San Vicente has a magnificent ceiling-high golden *retablo* but the altar server wore his raincoat throughout. Never mind! When we emerged, there were dancers in white with red and green arches in the porch, all accompanied by fifes, flutes and drums, and then we were driven in a squadron of cars to a mountaintop *bistro* overlooking the islanded bay, where we stuffed ourselves with delicious food and wine and danced enthusiastically till the early morning. The English made a local impression. The locals did not know about top hats, which Henry, his two Nigerian friends and I wore, and I had remembered my miniatures, beginning with Other Buggers Efforts and ending with Haakon VII, also locally unknown.

I have chaotic memories of other middle life Spanish occasions. I was enthusiastic about Avila's walls from a distance but less so when I got inside the town. Toledo, on the other hand is up and down and full of sights and sites. The Plaza del Zoccodovar is where Pedro the Cruel burned unyielding virgins. The Alcazar is splendidly restored after its Civil War siege. Henry told me that the Communists took the Commandant's son, rang up the Commandant and threatened to shoot the boy unless the Alcazar surrendered. They then handed the telephone over to the boy. The following exchange is famous:

'What would you have me do?'

'Do what is right, Papa. Viva España'.

Then, of course, there is El Greco's house. It says worlds for Spanish renaissance taste that with his distorted optical vision he was accepted as Court Painter and must have been very well off. People were genuflecting before the apocalyptic insights of the *Burial of Count Orgaz*. It is less often reproduced than the *Bridge at Toledo*, but the latter is hardly in the same class.

El Greco's Toledo had been rich and splendid for several centuries before his time. The Moors and then the Castilians had made it their capital, famous for swordsmiths. The older Moresque markets still reflect the atmosphere of Islam: the *Geronimo* with its elaborate two-storey cloisters, the affluence of its conquerors. And yet, it is quite a small town. From my hotel Alfonso VI by the Alcazar I walked all over it every day.

The next southward stage was Cordova, of leather fame, which is much bigger. I doubt whether I did the city justice. I spent two days in the vast mosque-cathedral. The first conquering Moors demolished a forum and used 300 of its standard pillars between Moorish arches to support the mosque's flat roof. The worshippers multiplied their increasingly squashed prostrations: a second wave demolished another forum. Its 240 pillars were six feet shorter, so to keep the roof at the same level, they built a six foot platform to support the pillars supporting the new roof. Hence an afforested series of stone arcades, stretching away into the gloom.

Next came the Christians. They built a huge bell-tower into the external cloister and inserted a tall Gothic cathedral choir and some light into the middle of the mosque. Furious critics have attacked this as 'vandalism', 'intolerance', 'insensitivity' and other noises. I do not agree with them. The Gothic intrusion creates a variety without which even under skylights the endless 540 pillars would become monotonous, despite the red and white alternations of the stonework arches. Anyway, if one was to adapt it to Christianity, what else could one do?

Malaga reeked of British banks, fat sun-scorched dowagers and fish-and-chips, but actually I was on my way to a village beyond it where I had for the second time discovered a congenial brothel. You lived in the house. There were lawns, a swimming pool, an amusement wing, the whole surrounded by a high wall. The landlady said of Henrique, a local visitor: 'He wants to screw me, but I won't let him'. I touched up the girl who brought my morning tea and, she being partial to attention, I breakfasted late. The entire party, home and away, having dressed, would lunch in a nearby restaurant. There was a single inclusive and not very high fee, and the whole was activated by conversational English courtesans. This was a week's relaxation!

I will now jump out of bed and lead you on to Ronda. This curious town is in three parts. The easily dismissible one is some middle income housing introduced by a statue to Thrift. Then comes the Old Quarter distinguished by a beautiful eighteenth century bullring and a fairly grand hotel where I decided to lunch. In swept one of those svelte Spanish viragos complete with black Spanish hat and Man. She sent back every bottle and every dish. She stalked round glaring at every seated customer. When I met her eyes I expected her to demand my table, but she shed her blessings elsewhere. I finished my long inquisitive lunch, drawn out by curiosity, and then adjourned to my brand new boarding house called *Nuestra Señora de la Concepcion*.

The Third Quarter is beyond a chasm spanned by a single hugely massive stone arch about 600 feet high. The other side is a separate village with a *plaza* and a cathedral. The *plaza* had been used for bullfights and the west façade of the cathedral still consists of seated galleries for spectators. Ronda has its own bullfighting style, deemed by *aficionados* to be superior to that of Seville.

FOUR COUNTRIES AND SOME HOSPITALS

Despite the distant view of Gibraltar, I did not like Algeçiras, so I pressed back to Granada by 'bus. The scenery on the way is unbelievably rugged, especially a northward rampart *sierra* which prevented a direct *reconquista*, and forced the Castilians to concentrate on the western ports of San Lucar de Barrameda and Cadiz. In that area many town names such as Jerez and Arcos have the suffix *de la Frontera*, – Marcher country; and the *pueblos blancos* (lit: white villages) are mostly sited on cliffs, giving long views of approaching marauders, with a high and difficult *sierra* behind. While the villagers pursued their sparse mountain agriculture, the rival Christian and Moorish cavalries met mostly by accident in the dense cork forests which stretch as far as the Algarve. It was only when the Castilians, well established on the coast, had outflanked the Mountains, that they turned east against Nazirite Granada. Piecemeal attrition led to the late fifteenth century foundation of the exclusively Christian colony of Santa Fé (Holy Faith) only eight miles from the capital itself. It spelled the Moorish doom.

Granada! A person who does not rave about it, cannot be quite right in the head. My hotel consisted of the three top floors of a six storey building, and a dining room full of saleable motor cars. You must stay in Granada as long as you possibly can, and then some. You penetrate the older town towards an elaborate cathedral built triumphantly by *los reyes catolicos* slap in the middle of the still crowded Moorish *souk*. I habitually went further to an open plaza on the river Darro, a pebbly trickle emerging from a huge cleft in the mountain. On the left of the cleft is the Albaicin, a steep occasionally terraced suburb with churches. On the right, almost vertically up a 1,000 foot cliff is the great Watch Tower of the ALHAMBRA with its stone bell-gantry. The sheer pleasure of this sunlit scene, especially from my unpretentious restaurant (serrano ham: manchego cheese) in the plaza, would be unbeatable were it not for the delights to come.

Go right and back through a steep forest resounding with multitudinous waters. Granada is hot, but here one is refreshed. Eventually one comes up a U-turn to the Gate of Judgment and so into the Palace-Capital of the Nazirite Emirs. To your left is the Watch Tower which you saw from below: to your right the famous range of pleasances, beginning, across one's route with the Mirror-like pool, a hundred yards long and leading to the splendours of the Hall of Ambassadors. The Hall is made even more remarkable because through its windows you see that it occupies the top of a squared bastion descending 1,000 feet to the floor of the valley.

The celebrated Court of the Lions, with its basined fountain on their backs is a very delicate cloister with rooms off it to the right and left ceiled with Mudejar honeycombs of incredible elaboration. Before reaching the grisly story about one of these rooms we must visit the Generalife. The backbone of this garden is a straight long water with more fountains leading to a lodge, and nearly at the end on the right among the flowers is an ancient tree. The ceramic inscription says that 'here under this tree the Knight Abencerraces had the Emir Boabdil's wife'. In such a public place Boabdil must have found out very soon. He was annoyed. He summoned the Knight's clan to the Court of the Lions and as they came into the left hand room one by one, his executioner struck off their heads. This was unwise, for the clan was the most powerful of the Emirate, and its demise made Boabdil fatally vulnerable to Ferdinand and Isabella. The last we hear of him is at a sharp bend on the road above the city called the Moor's Last Sigh.

If, with the wings of a bird, you fly from the Hall of Ambassadors across the Darro to one of the higher terraces of the Albaicin, you see the towers and palaces of the Alhambra behind you lining the opposite brow of the great gorge, but some miles behind are the snows of the Sierra Nevada, eternally melting and eternally renewed, making an artesian supply to the thundering streams and fountains of the Palaces and their garden. Water is part of the Mohammedan Paradise. No wonder Boabdil sighed.

'Vandalusia' was the original form of 'Andalusia', but the Vandals all went to Tunis. I had a different later contact with the province, unaffected by sex, human arts or literary romanticism. An interesting advertisement proclaimed that Hugh and Jane Arbuthnott organised comfortable walks among the cork forests and *pueblos blancos*. We were a party of seven and two botanists, plus two mules to carry refreshments and exhausted pedestrians. I was not exhausted, but I fell over things. I recollected that I was 79 and they loaded me onto a mule.

40 years ago I had seen nine pairs of mules hauling ploughs in echelon on a hillside in Old Castile. I think that my Andalusian mule was slightly different. It was as tall as a horse but about six inches shorter with its shoulders and forelegs forming a single vertical column capable of supporting great weights. It hardly noticed my eleven stone. Also its ears were less protrusive, and it was partial to the large, doubtless delicious, acorns shed profusely by the cork oaks. Staying on this animal, which was docile and well behaved, presented problems. I had no reins thank God because I would not have known what to do with them. Sod's law ordained that upward slopes should be steep, so, to avoid falling backwards over its rump I clung to the front of the saddle with my fingers. The same law ordained that I would regularly outdistance the walking party. One would have to stop under the shade of a cork tree for them to catch up. Down would go the mule's head in search of delicious acorns. I could avoid falling forwards over its neck only by hooking my thumbs into the back of the saddle. My hands ached for days.

One feature of these Arbuthnott walks was the wide and vigorous conversation. A spikey barked tree, imported from Guiana, was used to haul recalcitrant slaves down. Should parliamentary adulteries be publicised? Was Spain really an island? How many lives had the chick pea saved during the Great Starvation? Was it really necessary to destroy, as we had seen, most of the vineyards around Jerez? Mules were inclined to flatulence. Jane said that other parties had commented on the conversation. Did walking circulate the blood through the brain and so raise conversational output? Walk and talk.

I left Spain *via* Valladolid, where I changed trains. I had not understood the true significance of a Spanish *Corpus Christi*, but I had four hours to spare. I walked out to the architecturally lavish *plaza* and found my way blocked by a four-mile procession of fraternities (*cofradias*) of respectable citizens carrying crosses, candle sticks, chalices, holy banners and what not. Clinging, so to speak, to their skirts were hundreds of little girls dressed as brides, slightly peppered with little boys in big white arm-bows. Music roared from municipal loudspeakers.

This procession, like all others, had hiccoughs: its slow advance was stopped to permit those at the back to run for their lives. I have never understood the mathematics of this, but I arrived during one such halt. Obviously I should join the stationary *Cofradia de la Santissima Trinidad*, led by a tall tent covering a Pyx or monstrance, or something. I reckoned that it must be going somewhere, and that when it arrived, I would know what to do next. The brethren welcomed me with open arms, though nonplussed by my English dialect. Then we restarted amid clapping. The crowd in the narrow streets was pretty dense. Squash! Our tent battled its way to a clearing in front of the deplorable cathedral, which was equipped, instead of a spire, with an enormous and ugly concrete devotional statue. The brethren now hustled all the little brides and grooms into the cathedral, dismounted their regalia, rolled up their tent and piled as one man into the nearest pub.

So now I knew.

It is not a far cry from Spain to Russia. Henry had a job in Moscow and a flat. Both countries have been victoriously embattled against Islam and the roads to victory have had resemblances, despite the huge contrasts between mountainous Spain and table flat Russia. Each tried, and for different reasons failed to anchor its economy to a stable agriculture. Spanish villages fortified themselves against predatory cavalry: Russian cities built themselves communal *kremlins*, and the Orthodox Church raised fortified monastic refuges with artillery, for the peasantry. I found six of these immense gun bristling monasteries in Moscow itself. The Patriarch has one at Zagorsk, while the Kirilov near the White Lake is about the size of Green Park with double tiers of guns all round. And Spaniards and Russians alike opposed the Mohammedan aridity with the splendours of their liturgies. What are we doing now?

Old Russia developed organically until Peter and Catherine (both Great) with their western education developed new ideas and engrafted, with the aid of Scottish architects, the inorganic Baroque symmetries of St Petersburg upon Holy if higgledy piggledy Russia. Moscow has this combined quality. Henry took us to Bach's *Coffee Cantata*. There is a black monument in the form of a galleon dragged upwards and wasted at the bottom hull. On it scowls the figure, apparently, of Peter the Great. Actually it was designed for Columbus at Miami, but the Miamites did not like it, so Moscow picked it up cheap. The Metro, famous with chandeliers and art work is always punctual, but there are too many stations at the centre and too few in the sticks. It is a public relations success rather than a transport one. I walked the two miles from Novodevychi to Park Culturi because no supplementary bus or trolley bus appeared.

Another western importation came in the form of Marxism, but this was exploited by Lenin the bloodiest criminal genius of the twentieth century. As I have said of Breendonck, the machinery of murder and cruelty is sordid and simple: so now the patient millions endured 70 years of boredom and cruelty, besides perennial corruption. Eventually they, led by Boris Yeltsin, blew the lid off.

In the new freedom the techniques of enterprise had to be relearned. 40 minutes of potholes separated Sheremetevo airport and Moscow. One cabby was an army major in full regimentals because he had not been paid for months. Crime was privatised. On the other hand formerly the people had lunch in state fooderies called TOTs among stacked chairs, surly delays and uneatable grub. Now at Mozhaisk the restaurant was closed but the waitresses happily reopened and served us a delicious Russian lunch with pleasure and charm.

We were on our way to Borodino. The wide battlefield is thickly peppered with granite regimental memorials of the awful 1862 kind. Henry found the spot where our ancestor was mortally wounded. Bonaparte had launched massed cavalry against the steep ramparts of the heavily gunned Russian central redoubt, while Prince Bagration anticipated his errant flanking columns. The imperial bungler was fought to a bloody standstill, but Kutuzov, the Russian field commander had little to do with this, for he sat in a hut a mile back and drank Champagne. A haggard council, with Bagration dying, was held in the hut. After high words Kutuzov imposed a solution. The now slowly retreating army was to abandon Moscow. This could not have been a sudden flash of genius. The great and holy city could not have been abandoned without consulting the Czar, presumably as a contingency.

Later the hut was moved to Moscow and became, like the cockpit of HMS *Victory* a sort of shrine. With the aid of Yuri, Henry's driver, I tried to see it. I was refused because it had been burgled. Someone, I remembered, had stolen Nelson's *chelengk*.

This Yuri, a Ukrainian, had worked in the Soviet Ministry of Foreign Trade in Singapore where he lost his heart and gained an idiosyncratic English (Chinese background, Russian syntax). Besides driving Henry, he was chairman of a finance company. Such phylansterianism was common. Like as not the *local bureau de change* would be owned by the policeman who was its ostensible security guard. 'I tell you good Russian joke', Yuri would say. We would settle down. 'Stalin, Krushchev and Brezhnev are in train. Train stop. They look out of window. No rails. Stalin say "shoot the repair gang and get another". Krushchev say "No. Draw the curtains and sleep. Tomorrow things will be different". But Brezhnev say "I agree with Nikita Sergeivitch about the curtains, but tell the guards to jump up and down so it feels like we are moving"'.

We went to the first private restaurant in Moscow since 1917. A Mexican affair with a combined museum and 'loo in the top of a seventeen-storey hotel. I had never heard of Long Island Iced Tea before. A week later I had it again in a Mongolian restaurant in Oxford. Along the New Arbat, a semi-skyscraper served as the biggest known knocking shop. The owner had just been shot dead on the doorstep. Small but beautiful church choirs are heard everywhere, and an American journalist friend organised a concert for his pianist girlfriend and orchestra. Mostly Bloch. It was in one of the former Tretyakov mansions. These nineteenth century millionaires collected pictures in their double palaces on the Bolshaya Ordinka, but as everybody wanted to see them they pooled the pictures and put them into a vast gallery by our metro station called Tretyakovskaya after it. It also contains two restaurants and a church. Fanny and I spent two days in it looking at nothing but Russian artists and Russian subjects: the *Hanging of the Streltsy* for example.

Oh! And I must include, breathless or not, the Red Square. I had seen a rather pretty double arch with a Holy Water Beneficatory.* Nothing but sky was visible through the arches (rather like looking up the Rue Bonaparte) so I went to investigate. There was the Red Square alright, but it was the wrong way round. This could scarcely have been arranged, even for me. Yes! Lenin's tomb *contra disciplinam socialistam* on the right; hideous old brown GUM opposite. The unmentionable but attractive Kazan Sabor ('cathedral') above it in the corner billowing incense and orthodox harmonies, and worst of all, St Basil's at the bottom. GUM is not a shop but a market, and the inside is made interesting by the bridges which connect opposing storeys. St Basil's is not a church but a stack of about eleven chapels, some rising to the empyrian, some about the size of our

---

* I have just invented this word to avoid calling it a factory. It was crowded with people equipped with bottles and jugs.

bathroom. It had reopened a fortnight ago, but as nobody knew, we had the frescoes to ourselves. Famous and odd, with its tent spires and onion domes, it combines the higgledy piggledy and a mad symmetry in one swell foop. The Russians use the same word for beautiful and for red. Take your pick.

Here is a story which I cannot resist. One used to be allowed to stay only in two Muscovite hotels, because it was too expensive to bug any more. Some Englishmen were holding a drunken party in a bedroom. They talked, naturally, about bugging and took up the floorboards. There, sure enough was a large ringbolt. They turned it until the male screw disappeared. There was a loud crash. Their blow struck, they went to bed. At breakfast the waiters were still dismantling a fallen chandelier.

I suppose that the, mostly disused, St Petersburg-Moscow waterway represented a Stalinist attempt to bring in order. Fanny and I took a Swiss managed fun boat. Our cabin was flooded during a storm in Lake Ladoga. In the theatre at Petrozavodzk funny men, dancers, massed Balalaikas and occarinas, soloists kept going uninterruptedly in Karelian Finnish. It was terrific. We feared that our own scheduled concert the same evening would be an anti-climax. It wasn't. The crew and lovely waitresses were equally vigorous but never trespassed on the same ground. The boat – *The Surkhov* – meanwhile made its way up Lake Onega to the skyscraping wooden cathedral at Kijhi. There was also a tiny shrine to St Lazarus. If you touched it, it cured an ailment. It cured my cold. In the intervening watches we rehearsed. Lord Justice Stewart-Smith was to lead a duck dance. I managed to be both a Volga Boatman in Russian, and a member of the *pas de quatre* in Swan Lake. When Paul, our leader, died with a swanlike thump, the vodka encouraged uproar was heard in Omsk.

At the Northern River Terminal outside Moscow I needed *jetons*, spelled in Russian, to telephone Henry. All the offices in that vast building were closed. I was advised that I had the wrong approach. You got such things at the back 'in a sort of cloakroom' under the steps. Sure enough! But Irina forgot to say, and no one but a Russian would believe that the cloakroom was a combined bar and police station. By the end of our second stay in Moscow, I began to see why Henry liked it so much. *Fais que voudras*, mostly by accident. I had another reason as well: to be 80 is a profession deeply respected by Russians. It even got me through the barrier at Sheremetevo.

Before going, obviously, to Hungary I blew a fuse. I mended it, switched on and blew two fuses. This overstretched my electrical skills so the Temple electricians mended both fuses, switched on and blew everything in the flat. Replacing the century-old wires would entail tearing down the plaster and pulling up the floorboards. The Inner Temple removers (in February 2000) moved us to the opposite side of the garden. Meanwhile we lived by candle power – a bit like Edwardian Flutters Hill.

The move was only a partial success. We now had lovely views across the garden to St Paul's, but an internal muddle which included a corkscrew kitchen so designed that if a second person came in he had to go out backwards. The Temple's removers improved on all this by ignoring our arrangements in favour of speed. They simply cascaded accounts, papers, beds, books, bottles, boots, candlesticks into 160 sofa-sized boxes and then unpacked some of them for tasteful disposition anywhere. I remember particularly three volumes of a twelve-volume encyclopedia held down by an army boot and a dust-pan and brush. In our five months in that flat we never managed to sort it out and we were hotly pursued by the Inland Revenue, and Customs and Excise for returns which, because of the unnecessary confusion, we were unable to supply by the legal deadlines. I had to tell a sob-story, but this one was so extraordinary that I wrung their hearts.

Life, however, had to go on. I had booked an uncancellable package trip to see *The Ring* at Budapesth.... I am NO Wagnerian, and as Bernard Shaw demonstrated, much of his music is incidental to his left-wing theories; but it seemed to me that the Hungarians might take The Ring less solemnly than the Germans. So to Budapesth I flew with some introductions from Munko Orbach, and lodged at the Hotel Raddisson, a place of American grandeur which I would not normally have chosen, but well placed. Of course, I began with Barack Palinka and Dobos, and then they hustled us all off to the *Rheingold*.

Like Covent Garden, La Fenice, The Theatre de la Monnaie an' all, one approaches the State Opera with awe. Those gigantic staircases! Those ceremonial landings! Enormous symbolic ceilings, banks of boxes. We had front row stalls, which clattered down and, despite the embroidery, were as hard as Hell. Shortage of funds, or armoured Magyar bottoms? Never mind: one could see the comings and goings in the orchestra pit.

The introduction gave way to a stage covered in scaffolding and slowly filling with smoke, through which the various characters yelled at us in German, translated by moving fast faery-lights into Magyar. This is a fascinating language full of stops and syllables, which, I am told, are quite unsingable. A clothes shop near my hotel was selling 'puloverek'. Also they write their names backwards.

Presently the scaffolding gave way to a bailey bridge, and the fog began to thin out. A clinker-clanker of industrious dwarves, all hammering cross-legged in chicken cages replaced the singers, drowned the orchestra, and then faded into more Wagnerian drama, through which a huge white staircase moved impressively upon us. The proceedings ended as Wotan, Loge, Brunn – and doubtless Kriem-hilde, Siegfried et al. made their way up to Valhalla with measured tread two steps at a time.

Then I drank too much csopaki with an expensive, but good hotel dinner. White wine seldom suites me.

I went up, of course to the Fischerbastei. The adjacent Matthias (or Coronation) church said that it was performing a ceremonial choral mass; so in I went. We had been warned against muggers who infest Pesth, and against an expected political riot scheduled for Buda. It was the latter warning which naturally inspired my visit to Buda. Not a sign of disorder or policemen. I emerged from the very splendid mass, which had been heavily attended by World War II colonels (perhaps uniformed attendance at mass counts as a riot?). Then I discovered that there was a chamber concert in the conservatoire opposite the church at six.

How to fill in the afternoon?

My description of pre-war Budapest is still mostly valid. From Pesth you get to the Matthias Church end – whoosh – by tram over the long Margaret bridge and round the back to a square now named after Moscow; then you walk up. At the other end, a one-minute funicular takes you up from the Chain (formerly Batthyanny) bridge to a parade ground by the former Royal palace. There is a flamboyant equestrian statue of Prince Eugene on the terrace there. The Russians, of course, smashed the palace up and looted everything in it, and their puppet government set about trying to forget the Proud Past, and changed the names of well known things. The old splendid Royal Guard with their shields and winged helmets disappeared. It was, however, not totally subservient. In Magyar, intelligible to every Hungarian and incomprehensible to Russians (and everyone else) you could bandy the deepest insults and the butt of your venom would smile and bow.

So they had emerged from the battle cellars to restore the old profile above the twin cities; they rebuilt the old palace, but since it could scarcely be re-used as a palace, they sensibly turned most of it into an art gallery. So, I set off across the devastation to look at the pictures. I got an excellent lunch in a deep armchair. The collections are enormous, so I limited myself to local artists and subjects, as in the Tretyakov. The Hungarians are a proud people, isolated by their history as well as language. There was much material on which to feed: *The Women of Szeged Driving Off a Turkish Attack*, for instance.

Then back, with MF, to the Conservatoire. The ground floor had an exhibition of crystals. There was a double staircase like the State Opera. Next came a *Salle des Pas Perdus* backing the concert chamber, and the chamber itself with first-floor windows towards the Matthias Church. The whole thing was very informal. You sat where you liked and when they discovered that they had oversold the tickets, gangs of boys and girls rummaged the building for more chairs.

The chamber orchestra hived off a trio, a quartet, a sextet to play Mozart, Schumann, Beethoven. There were humorous interludes by a lady journalist and her English boy-friend quarrelling noisily. The whole orchestra now burst into full throat – Kodaly; Brahms. Enthusiasm. Two encores! And then we all moved to the Salle des Pas Perdus and were given Champagne and splendiferous chocolates. They were still roistering at 10.30 when I caught my whoosh-tram.

In *The Valkyrie*, another huge staircase the wrong way round was the centre-piece for a batch of fat little valkyries discussing horse management. Afterwards I found a friendly actors' restaurant just round the corner where there were two other theatres. It was as good as in my hotel but half the price. It became my evening habit. By the way, if you want a lunchtime snack, a sausage at the butcher's is delicious and cheap.

Pesth reminded me in 1937 or 1938 of Haussmann's Paris as it then was, and it still does: rings and spokes of boulevards mostly of five and six-storey buildings springing round a small older unplanned centre by the River. The Danube, however, is huge – The Margaret Bridge is half a mile long – quite unlike the Seine, and its islands are outside the settlement, not like the Ile de la Cité at its heart. From Pesth the river makes a curve to the north. Szent Endre is an intimate up-and-down sort of seventeenth century village about fifteen miles out originally settled, as its inscriptions attest, by Croats. There is a colony of artists, an art gallery devoted to the compelling dramatic ceramics of Margit Kovacs, and, of all things, a marzipan museum. I enjoyed the houses, the Tokay shops and the general atmosphere, which is quite unspoiled.

Further north there is Esztergom where the Danube turns from east to south. As the see of the Prince-Primate, it may be called the Canterbury of Hungary, but there the analogy stops. The cathedral is Victorian classical and stands at the top of a long open slope ending steeply at the River, which here forms the frontier with Slovakia. As usual in mainland Europe, the west bank is higher than the east so that you can see far away what the neighbouring country is like from the cathedral terrace. The Hungarian side is an orderly alternation of farms and villages: the Slovak an uncontrolled muddle of villas, allotments and sheds. There has been no effective communication between the two sides for half a century, but the overthrow of Russian communism has its echo. The two governments have agreed to repair the ruined girder bridge. The Habsburg organic world is proving more durable than the artificialities of Marxism.

Hungary is mostly flat, but at Vizegrad nature has built an impressive set of mountain cliffs and rocks to enable the Kings to tax the river traffic from the castle above the pass. Very high and impressive it was, but the February wind froze our ears. The spectacular view from the keep down onto the river almost compensated us for this, and one can see that these mountains form three sides of a box, skirted by the Danube, and that the Hill of Buda is the point at which the third side peters out.

The Pesth parliament house, is a huge mixture of Westminster and Chester Town Hall. I wanted to go in, but the President (on whom be Peace) of Albania was paying a state visit. Whether Gheg or Tosk, I have no real dislike of Albanian presidents, though monarchs would of course be better, but I decided to stay on the river. It is odd in this semi-Marxist Balkan world to observe that Albania, alone of states still flies the double eagle of Byzantine Christendom.

Vast controversies rage about the river. The Slovaks want to build a barrage and appropriate the hydro-electricity. The Hungarians want a share. The wrangle has gone on for years while everyone does without electricity. Then the landbound Hungarians are a fish-eating nation. There are the teaming *fogas* of Lake Balaton and the shoals of torpedo-like carp which swarm or rather swarmed in the Danube. Two days after my arrival an Australian contractor employed by the Roumanian government poured its cyanide waste into the River Theiss, which emptied it into the Danube and killed all the fish for miles. The furious Hungarians spoke loudly of legal proceedings. I hope they win.

Back to the Opera. I tend to conjoin *Siegfried* and *Götterdämmerung*. After twittering and hornblowing in the forest, surprise surprise, the curtain rises upon another staircase, transcending all staircases with a sleeping Brunnhilda surrounded by unearthly flames, half way up. A shortage of building material probably explains the absence of a staircase in the deep forest itself.

As I adumbrated, there was other music. I went to the End of Term symphony concert of the orchestral conservatoire which is right in the middle of Pesth. A charming girl went out of her way to show me there. A crowded audience was full of zest and aspiring soloists. And then I found a folk dance theatre just down the road. In its sophisticated orchestral and dance shows the men are accurately acrobatic, a battery of cymbaloms is hammered in pitch darkness, and the girls were the loveliest and most skilled imaginable. I would have gone again but instead I had a surprise. Mozart's *Requiem* in the Matthias Church. I just happened to see them selling tickets. There was a demo: outside, and a band playing the National Anthem, reputedly the longest in the world and beginning 'Oh Lord, Our enemies attack us on every side'.

I am not deviating (much) from my course if I observe that there are places which have irresistible names. I have spoken of the virtues of *Trollhattan*. I am no stranger to *Ruyton of the Eleven Towns* or *Küssnacht*, but *Bergen-op-zoom* and *Kiskunfelegyhaza* have so far eluded me, so I took a train via *Györ* to *Sopron*, both eighteenth century towns. They sell tickets by the kilometre so that if you were the Bishop of Winchester you would not know where you were going, and, I suspect for ideological reasons, the communal corridors are warmer than the elitist compartments. At any rate you still have to tip your doctor because he is much worse paid than a lorry driver.

Györ is an artificially laid-out place, probably because it was (naturally under the name of *Raab*) a Habsburg fortress. The inner city of Sopron, on the other hand grew organically under the Austrian name of *Ödenburg* and it is utterly charming with well-managed traffic which preserves the calm. In the eighteenth century the local Austrian burghers expelled a lot of protestant immigrants, whose place was slowly taken by Hungarians, and in the disputes over the Bürgenland after World War I, Sopron voted to stay in Hungary and became a national collective hero among the withered sedges of a large shallow, bird-infested lake. It is within easy reach of Vienna and there are good small hotels. I am earmarking it for a second visit. On a different trip I went to nearby Eisenstadt, where Haydn worked and where the Eszterhazys, his patrons, still flourish.

I tend to ignore my health. Walking in Pesth was slower and less painless than usual, so I strode out manfully or used the trams which charge at about 150 miles an hour down the central reservations. Also there is a good underground system. Anyway, whatever my trouble, I returned home to an attack of Sciatica which was a real Lolla-polloozer. I could not stand or walk for seven weeks. At the start I could not sleep for four nights running.

My Middle Temple Lane window was opposite a crow's nest in one of the plane trees. This nest has annually served honeymooning crows. This pair was raising a family. They were young and smart, and so, in due course were their young. I had no idea that crows could be so handsome. I think of them as battered, tramplike creatures vaguely entangled with twigs. Wrong, as usual! They were streamlined, elegant and delicately skilful nest repairers, one on guard while the other foraged.

My compulsory bird-watching ended with the need to get a more convenient habitation, for there seemed to be no prospect of being able to climb many staircases any more. The Inner Temple were sympathetic and offered me one of the few which had a lift. We had another shambolic move. I am writing this eight months later, and we still have not fully sorted ourselves out.

Now in ordinary life none of this would matter much, but my recovery from sciatica was immediately followed by bladder trouble. I must return briefly to my pre-crow period. I had spent a week in Menaggio. I went everywhere by boats, buses and even got landed at Lecco accidentally by train: I began to notice an apparent muscular lassitude which, later, I thought to have been premonitory symptoms of the sciatica, especially when I crawled out of the Luini crucifixion at Lugano and besides, I was woken up one night by a violent blow on the head: when I came to, I discovered that I had fallen out of bed. I couldn't breathe much and had to lean out of the window to do it in the night air over the twinkling lake. Exactly the same thing happened the next night, so in that excellent hotel I stayed awake at night and slept (mostly on steamers) by day. Odd sort of holiday, but still I did not cotton on to anything serious.

Nieves offered to look after me when the bladder trouble developed because Fanny's arthritis was making things difficult even without looking after me. I gratefully accepted. When I arrived, she and Henry took one look at me and insisted that I should see their GP. Their *locum* put me into the hospital at Tunbridge Wells at 40 minutes' notice. Obviously, with hindsight, they saved my life. I had never experienced the interested attention of six doctors and eight nurses, and after ten days I emerged much better but told to come back in two months for another operation with, meantime, a plethora of pills.

My own GP now sent me to a specialist in the Whittington Hospital (complete with Cat), at the foot of the Archway. She said 'Heart trouble'. She would decide in three months' time whether a pacemaker was the answer. During the waiting time, I was sometimes wreathed in wires for electrical tests.

Then came a terrible interval. An agitated telephone call told me to expect very bad news. It was too. My poor secretary, Ann Rowen, friend of 48 years had died suddenly in her sleep, and would I speak at her funeral? Of course I could do nothing less. She was widely liked and people came from all over England to Poole. I nearly burst into tears. She had typed nearly every word which I had written including the million and a half of the *Companion to British History*. She had been an excellent assistant and companion of every kind between Carlisle and Teheran, and in bad times as well as good. She had always turned her hand to any job simply because it had to be done. Her death left a void in my life. 'I am distressed for Thee my sister....'

Next the specialist said that a pacemaker was needed. What was it? I was handed a pamphlet. It seems that everybody but me knows that the heart has a spot from which electrical heart beats are generated. Mine had become unreliable and a mechanism, namely a pacemaker was needed to supplement it. It would be buried in my gallant breast. It was easy. Local anaesthetic. Nothing to it. You'll be out in a day. The place to go was the Middlesex Hospital near the BBC. Whittington would tell Middlesex, and I would get an earful. Month now stumbled after month. I fought telephone battles with these friendly people. I said that I was not in a hurry, but that I would love to plan my life. Erks and doctors seldom realise that other people have lives. Middlesex, on the other hand were most sympathetic, but a fire had disorganised their operations' list. It was my turn to be sympathetic. I was the leading member of the United Society of Fractomachinists and Collapsosperantists. We shook hands on that.

I now realise that my heart must have been giving trouble for two or three years. Everyone overtook me in the street. I had attributed this to age rather than to my heart. Slowness of beat would not have worried me for both my mother (died at 96) and Abimelech (fell down stairs) had had slow hearts. But then I began to hear the irregularities in bed. It sounded like somebody clumping about in the next room; but the sound gaps between footsteps became so long that I began to wonder if I was dead.

The Middlesex fixed an, admittedly distant 15th June. Of course they rang on 7th: they had a vacancy tomorrow. Would I like it? YES. I was commanded to appear at 9.00pm. Fanny and I drank tea, coffee, soup, water with endless hospital food and got worried. At 3.30pm the surgeon appeared. He was very nice. He had a series of emergencies and 'something complicated to work out', but he got me to sign a release of liability in case he accidentally killed me. Evidently The Event would actually happen. More tea, coffee etc. The nurses, mostly Filipino with the usual leavening of Brazilians, could not have been nicer.

At 6.30pm I was trundled down to the basement in my wheeled bed with the ceiling sliding agreeably overhead. The theatre was like a large box-room. Things all over the place. Laughter next door. There was giggled pushing and sliding onto the operating table. Nothing seemed to fit very well. The fire, I suppose. Pause. More laughter next door. Then a witty anaesthetist lady came and, of course, asked me my name just like Buckingham Palace. A legendary Swiss hospital had operated on a patient for piles instead of a verruca. Presently they heaped blankets on me to obstruct the view. Dr Walker now appeared. He was heavily disguised, but I kept my head. I was conscious throughout and felt nothing whatever. He told me what he was doing as he did it. He showed me the burnished cigarette-case-like thing before he slipped it into the pocket which he had dug, and, in the intervals told funny stories to the bystanders. It was a hilarious 40 minutes. I never had any pain or fear: only the boredom of not being allowed to sleep on my left side for three weeks. Meantime I had become a Man of Blood and Iron.

It all ended ten days later when the wound had miraculously healed. We celebrated my 83rd birthday on 25th June by idling about in Kew Gardens, not to avoid strenuous activity but simply because I like the place. It was far worse for Fanny's arthritis, so we tottered slowly from bench to bench and got boiled in the palm house.

Chapter 37

LAST BLAST

It may not be possible to complete an autobiography but one can stop writing it as I did in 2005. Having since then exposed myself to Urbino and Angkor Wat I do not undertake not to start again, but now that I am 88 it seems sensible to look round in case I do not. A hanging card in a German railway carriage quoted Tucholski that 'he who writes his own autobiography has something to hide'. This is of course true. I can think of much which I have left out, but not to mislead people into thinking that I am better or worse than I am: rather to recount the things which have stuck in my memory or struck my imagination, and this necessarily involves admitting defects. And why not? I am not so important that I need a godlike image. Thus, at least, I try to look at a thing and see what it is. Describing it is the difficulty. It has been aptly said that there are four stages in communication: what I meant to say, what I said, what you heard and what you thought it meant.

The circumstances surrounding my life at almost any given moment have forced me to compare This with That, and then That with The Other. At the age of four I had to notice that there were vast numbers of people who spoke, not German but a difficult tongue called English, and later that these vast numbers knew nothing of Berlin or Bavaria, had never heard of Beethoven or sauerkraut, drove on the left, had a passion for sport and ate toast or roast meat. Then, when I had learned to accommodate myself to the contrasting human climates of England and Germany, I discovered that there were other climates. To enter the Latin world from the Teutonic or Anglo-Saxon was like passing from the steppe to jungle. I needed a different technique to get around. I had to grow different antennae.

The habit of comparison was reinforced by the difference of families and schools: between say, the Bakers' cheerful residual urban Edwardianism, and the indirect approaches of the emotional semi-Slav rural v. Blumenthals, or between the sensible logic of Orlando Wagner's arithmetic and the confused Practice of my first prep: school. I very very early took an independent stance because no two grown-ups ever seemed to agree about anything, and some conclusion, any conclusion was necessary in order to get on with life. The famous mathematical textbook writer Clement V. Durrell predicted that I would fail School Certificate Mathematics: to my surprise I got the highest marks in the Kingdom by ignoring his teaching, but on the other hand I got only an Oxford Third by foolishly taking my own line in the philosophy papers when I ought to have larded them with dropped names. One has to keep one's wits about one and remember, especially, that other people may exist. All the same, at 80 I wrote, in German, in the post-preface to *Die Schnarckjagd* that it is utterly impossible to translate from any language into any other. The only way to speak Ruritanian or Afrikaans is to become, for the time being a Ruritan or an Afrikander.

To look at a thing and see what it is, requires realism but not cynicism. Cynicism, the attribution of self-interested motives to all actions, is as much a prejudice as anti-semitism. Common observation shows that it is not true: goodness, in the self-restraint of the tempted or the daily miracles of mother-love or the ministrations of hospital staffs, is very common. Evil comes in when the bad are armed. Typically Stalin asked 'How many divisions has the Pope?' Historical experience shows that evil seldom rules for long. The Third Reich, terrible though it was, lasted not a thousand years but twelve: Marxism, after 70, is cluttering the dustbins.

All the same the firing squads and cremation ovens of fanatic evil can now do so much damage so quickly that their short duration is little consolation or cause for complacency. Vigilance is the price of a decent life, and it is high. The central difficulty in keeping moving towards the star on the horizon is that that we are foolish and lazy and the star is far off. One might have thought that armed wickedness could be neutralised by balancing it with other armed influences or by disarming everyone and resorting to a universal egalitarianism. We have, in the international field, tried the first, but there have been armed conflicts or killing fields in every single year of the twentieth century. It is obvious now, that the second will fail too, because if a democracy is not to be coerced, it will soon be deceived. Lies, if shouted often and loudly enough, become convincing. Truth, if suppressed long enough is forgotten. Government by lies is normal because of the difficulty of getting anything done. The habitual idleness or corruption of the media ensures that too many voters will be misinformed – and that this book will have a bad press.

One thing, however, seems to predominate in our modern scene: this is the concealed concentration of power. Every government in my sentient lifetime has sought to destroy independent sources of power or influence. The greedy Tories had it in for the trade unions. The philistine Margaret Thatcher for the Foreign

Office and the Monarchy. Blair and his social engineers for the independent spirit. I see only one solution to this, for these people seem to be driven by ineradicably inaccurate perceptions of public opinion. Henry quoted the witticism of a German politician: 'Politicians tell lies to the media, and then believe what they read in the newspapers'. This solution, simple to state, is vastly complicated and difficult to apply. It is *less government*.

I could expatiate upon this theme but will confine myself to a few examples. Our vast, burdensome and tangled taxation system not only supports an overmanned administration, but forces us into the hands of some 200,000 chartered accountants, of whom, with their secretaries, receptionists and other hangers-on there are far more than all the armed forces. Most of these talented and admirable people could be advantageously redeployed. Our inactive Quangos do little harm but do we need the hundreds of busy ones? When legal changes were confined to parliament and the courts, we knew roughly where we were because changes were known and relatively uncommon, so governments set up, in delegated legislation an alternative source of law. Some 50,000 statutory instruments have been made in the last ten years, but as this rate of change seems inadequate in the phrenetic political world, local parliaments have been created to add to the volume. Law has become an expensive and unreliable industry, involving, for example constant reprinting and consumption of paper and the felling of forests for it, the employment of thousands of lawyers with *their* clerks, receptionists and hangers on, and all the while the consumption (or waste) of the consumers' immensely valuable and irrecoverable time goes on. We now spend nearly half our working days working for officialdom (I reckon 164 days in the year, Mark Field MP 168). I do not want to work for authority – I would prefer the time off. I think that I could make better use of it than filling in questionnaires. The notion that it is particularly virtuous to pay taxes presupposes that someone else knows my interests better than I do. I take leave to doubt if this is always so. It may seem paradoxical for a lawyer to advocate disobedience of the law (though the Mahatma Ghandi did it very successfully) but I have come to the conclusion that when taxes of all kinds amount to more than 30% of one's resources, one is morally entitled to cheat. Certainly the centralised and increasingly distant and ignorant bureaucracies need to prove that the money is being desirably deployed, but nowadays they substitute lies and force for argument. I for one do not believe that taxes need to be raised to pay for the National Health Service. I think that they are being used under this pretext as a means for social engineering.

The curious fact is that though everyone knows that our administrations have increased, are increasing and ought to be diminished (in Dunning's famous phrase), yet the teeming millions are regularly led or driven by them into situations which nobody in his right mind would accept. Did the *muzhiks* really want the horrors, starvation and typhus of the Russian Revolution? What price Mao Tse Tung's Long March? If it is objected that these were not caused by established bureaucracies, the answer is that they were caused by some bureaucracy or other, each of which ended up in power. This provokes a suspicion that so-called democracy does not exist and egalitarianism is a not very convenient fiction. 'We hold', said the slave owning fathers of the American Constitution 'these truths to be self-evident, that all men are born equal....' The statement is simply false, and it stretches credulity to think that they believed it. I am not as clever as Einstein, or as athletic as Philippides, or as handsome as Marlon Brando, or as rich as Henry Ford, or as good as Jesus Christ, or as evil as Lenin, or as poor as Lazarus, or as ill as Florence Nightingale, or as talented as Sir Winston Churchill or Leonardo da Vinci. These sort of questions can be asked of everybody living and if we are not born equal, are we democratic? Do we decide or are the decisions made for us? The question has only to be asked for the answer to be obvious. Have we an equal chance with our fellows of influencing our future? The answer is equally obvious. And if we deceive ourselves so easily, will we not be deceived even more easily by those who specialise in deception. Let me return to Richard Gatty's furious letter. 'Our business is to purvey lies to the enemy'.

Meantime there is another phenomenon. Our huge and numerous administrations (by which I mean not only government bureaucracies but all those private computer pushers) use larger and larger staffs: to get them in place quickly they have to be trained. Training and education, however, are clean different things. A good education makes a better man: a training merely fits him for a job, which, when the time comes may no longer exist or become disliked or have been snapped up by someone else, yet our schools and universities are getting shorter on education and longer on vocational training. One increasingly burdensome result is that much of our routine administration is carried on, if not by computers, then by people with a fair-weather knowledge of which key to press but not why, and consequently with little understanding of what to do when the wind changes. The charming girls whom I see in the bank, cannot write a proper letter. My account manager seems to have forgotten that economics concerns human beings. We need lots of people who can think rather than accumulate facts. We are, in fact run by the second rate, and are, by way of the computer, acquiring most of the intellectual laziness of slave owners.

The emphasis on vocational training has been accompanied by a refusal to heed experience. We store current knowledge in electronic memories. We cannot do this with history because history involves judgments which machines cannot make. If individuals had, like, say a cockroach, no memory, we could have no experience: we would have to reinvent the wheel or the water closet, even our language every day, perhaps every hour. History is the collective memory of large groups and without it we simply cannot manage our affairs because we would not be able to recollect the mistakes which we ought to avoid. Yet history is downgraded in our educational system, or mutated in the interests of propaganda. One might suspect that our rulers do not want us to look at a thing and see what it is: that the erosion of citizen power is intended; that the beloved ship is being deliberately run onto the rocks.

Meantime my poor Fanny, after a stroke, has been bedridden since 2003, and I have become less a personality and more a collection of spare parts. After two cataract operations, I cannot recognise faces in bright light. A prostate operation has deprived me of my manhood. I hear nothing without hearing aids, but with them I am deafened at a dinner party. I have a walking stick and a pacemaker. My sense of balance is a bit off. Yet my geriatrician says that I have twenty years to go. I do not quite believe him, but I am willing to try, and Fanny's carers Anusha, Hannah, Chinyere and Sheila,* are a constant source of inspiration.

---

* Surnamed Ekanayaka (Sinhalese); Ogunlade (Yoruba); Durueke (Ibo) and Balloomeeah (Mauritian).

CONTINUATION

After about 25 years Fanny wrote to me:

> We have come too far together, love
> To sever now
> Ties made with tears and bombs
> And journeyings together
>
> We didn't notice, the train splits here
> And part stays in a siding
> The other took a loop there
> While one of us was hiding
> From the other.
>
> Change quickly, run like Hell
> There's time to catch another
> Right through: and then – oh well
> Once again we can travel together

30 years later I replied:

> The brilliant platform where the train was waiting
> Gave way too soon to nameless darkened stations.
> Some trains were cold, delayed or soldier-crammed;
> Some missed connections,
>   or
>   We lost our luggage,
> Were carried past an exit in the swirling crowds,
> Or fell exhausted on a sleepless bench.
> Yet still we clung for comfort, love or pleasure
> Bright days we had, and happy nights to measure.
> The double ticket which we bought together,
> Now battered after fifty years' inspections,
> Ne'er promised us a rich or easy ride,
> Nor seats reserved, red carpets, dining cars:
> Only
>   a single one way destination
> Where old, dog-eared, essentially intact
> It may be offered up for cancellation.
>
> Oh yes! Let's run like Hell. We've time to catch it.
> That's one thing clearly printed on the ticket

1st October 2003
Her 85th birthday

Index

Adams, Roland, 285, 286, 287, 294
Alexander, Kathleen, 65, 101
Allen House School, 138, 143–4, 155–6, 162, 287
Arnold-Baker, Fanny, 119, 145, 180, 184, 193, 203–7, 209, 211–2, 213, 222, 225, 226, 229, 235–6, 239, 252, 253, 264, 271, 276, 277, 278, 279, 281, 285, 296, 303, 313, 314, 316, 334, 335, 336, 339, 340, 343, 345, 359, 367, 374, 375, 379, 381, 389, 390, 396, 397, 398, 403, 404
Arnold-Baker, Henry, *see* v. Blumenthal, Henry
Arnold-Baker, James, 322, 334
Arnold-Baker, Katharine, 138, 238, 281, 285, 296, 308, 313, 331, 338, 339, 383
Arnold-Baker, Richard, 66, 203–4, 206, 225, 227, 229, 336, *see also* v. Blumenthal, Werner Gaunt
Arson and Old Hake, 317
Association of Municipal Corporations (AMC), 297, 299, 315, 316

Baker, Percival Richard Arnold ('Pater'), 2, 9, 10, 11, 12, 13, 77, 101–4, 107, 110, 114, 117, 120, 121, 122, 130, 137, 138, 141–2, 143, 144, 151, 152, 154, 156, 157, 158, 177, 179, 191, 199, 203, 205, 209, 213, 225, 226, 271, 276, 277
Baker, Wilhelmine, 2, 3, 4, 8, 9, 11, 12, 13, 20, 23, 24, 25, 27, 28, 46, 49, 50, 51, 53, 56, 58, 61, 62, 65, 66, 69, 70, 71, 72, 73, 75, 76, 77, 79, 60, 81, 82, 84, 85, 87, 89, 90, 91, 92, 93, 94, 96, 98, 99, 100, 101, 102, 103, 104, 105, 107, 114, 117, 118, 121, 126, 130, 134, 137, 138, 141, 146, 147, 195, 225, 226, 271, 272, 277, 314, 315
Battagel, Arthur, 264, 274, 275
Battalion, 7th, 228
Battalion, 8th, 215
Battalion, 10th, 210, 228
Battalion, 70th, 216
Binding, Rudolf, 87, 88, 113
v. Bismarck, Otto, 29, 40, 41, 42, 43, 44, 45, 49, 68
Blumenthal (villages), 30
v. Blumenthal, Albrecht, 2, 20–1, 23–5, 27, 49, 50, 51-3, 58, 61, 62, 66, 69, 71–3, 75, 76, 78–81, 82, 84, 85, 87, 90–1, 93, 96, 99, 101, 102, 103, 104, 105, 107, 110, 121, 126, 134, 135, 136, 141, 154, 179, 365
v. Blumenthal, Christoph Caspar, 35
v. Blumenthal, Cornelia, 46, 51, 58, 59, 60, 66, 105, 106
v. Blumenthal, Elsa, 91, 93, 105, 106, 365
v. Blumenthal, Count Hans Jürgen, 35
v. Blumenthal, Henry, 2, 20, 30, 31, 37, 40, 59, 77, 93, 138, 152, 168, 180, 203, 313, 331, 334, 335, 336, 337, 359, 365, 383, 387, 388, 389, 390, 396, 401, 402

v. Blumenthal, Herrmann, 52
v. Blumenthal, Joachim Frederick, 33, 34, 35
v. Blumenthal, Leonhard, 7, 29, 31, 33, 43, 44, 46, 50, 52, 220
v. Blumenthal, Nieves, 40, 93, 152, 365, 383, 396
v. Blumenthal, Nora, *see* v. Lettow-Vorbeck, Nora
v. Blumenthal, Robert, 14, 31, 48, 49, 53, 91, 93, 105, 106, 107, 365
v. Blumenthal, Ruthger, 35, 105
v. Blumenthal, Vally, 27, 28, 31, 40, 43, 44, 46, 47, 48, 49, 50, 51, 52, 53, 54, 57, 58, 60, 66, 69, 70, 71, 72, 73, 75, 82, 84, 85, 90, 91, 92, 93, 96
v. Blumenthal, Waleska, *see* v. Kleist-Retzow, Waleska
v. Blumenthal, Werner Gaunt, 66, 67, 69, 72, 72, 75, 76, 79, 80, 81, 82, 85, 92, 98, 99, 101, 102, 103, 111, 113, 117, 120, 121, 122, 126, 130, 133, 134, 135, 136, 137, 138, 141, 142, 144, 146, 151, 156, 157, 158, 177, 179, 191, 192, 195, 203, *see also* Arnold-Baker, Richard
v. Blumenthal, Wilhelmine, *see* Wilhelmine Baker
v. Blumenthal, Wolf-Werner, 50, 54, 57, 84, 91, 92, 93, 105
Boltons, the, 1, 2, 109, 145
Bonhoeffer, Dietrich, 365
Brandon, Henry (Lord Brandon of Oakbrook), 144, 218, 277, 285, 287

Buffs, 7th, 212, 228
Buffs, 8th, 212, 215, 228
Buffs, 10th, 210, 212, 215, 225, 228
Buffs, 70th, 105, 216, 219, 241

Chao Phya, 344, 348, 355
Churchill, Sir Winston, 179, 220–1, 258, 265, 314, 331, 402
City University, 189, 333, 334, 359, 367
'Claremont', 7, 11, 92
Companion to British History, The, 1, 220, 317, 329–338, 369, 396
Council for the Preservation (later Protection) of Rural England, 297, 309
County Councils' Association (CCA), 297, 299, 315, 316

Dacey, William, 315, 316
Dewé, Charles, 138, 139, 143

Elmau, 46, 51, 122, 124, 125, 126, 143, 145, 146, 147, 148, 156, 172
Everyman's Dictionary of Dates, 317

Firth, Budge, 173, 174
Flutter's Hill, 103, 117, 118, 151
Forster, Tony, 307, 308

Gatty, Richard, 245, 251, 253, 255, 262, 264, 290, 402
Gaunt, Elizabeth, 3, 7, 8, 11, 12, 13, 14, 20, 73, 91
George VI, King, 196, 199, 238
George, Stefan, 23, 25, 61, 62, 365, 366
Goering, Hermann, 178, 231, 269
Grosvenor, Margaret, 65, 92, 101

INDEX

Haakon VII, King, 75, 273, 383
Hahn, Kurt, 156, 157
Hainsworth, Abimelech, 3, 4, 7–8, 9, 11, 12, 13, 14, 20, 21, 23, 24, 62, 91, 92, 110, 397
Hainsworth, Charles, 3, 4, 11
Hainsworth, Ethel, 3, 11, 92
Hainsworth, Gaunt, 3, 4, 8, 9, 11, 24, 62, 91, 107
Hainsworth, Harriet, 4, 14, 17, 46, 53, 54, 65, 66, 67, 68, 79, 80, 101
Hainsworth, Helena, 3, 4, 14
Hamilton, Ronald, 173
Hampton Court, 313, 314, 315
v. Harnack, Adolf, 147, 148
Hitler, Adolf, 5, 23, 35, 97, 105, 177, 179, 180, 181, 207, 231, 234, 238, 256, 268, 269, 270, 271, 275, 365, 366
Horst, 15, 30, 32, 35, 36, 37, 38, 39, 54
Hothfield Place, 219
Hunt, Cecil, 102, 141, 151, 253
The Hunting of the Snark *see* Die Schnarckjagd

Inner Temple, 226, 235, 285, 288, 391, 395

Jackson, H. A., 173
Josée, 252, 253

Keith-Lucas, Brian, 296, 317, 341, 343
Keyser, Cornelia, *see* v. Blumenthal, Cornelia
v. Kleist-Retzow, Waleska, 49, 69, 71, 91
Krampffer, 36
Krokow, Countess Waleska, 43

Kühne, Erich, 17, 19, 50
Kühne, Irene, 17, 50, 84

Lamont, Colonel, 210, 211, 215
Leeson, Spencer, 169, 170
Lenin, Vladimir Ilyich, 82, 88, 341, 388, 389, 402
v. Lettow-Vorbeck, Nora, 7, 20, 49, 50, 70–3, 75, 77, 90, 91, 93, 365
v. Lettow-Vorbeck, Rudolf (Rudi), 49, 50, 70
Lewis, C. S., 189, 193, 194
Lila, 28, 60, 63, 66, 69, 72
Local Government (Elections) Act 1956, 304, 307
Longcross Press, 321, 335, 336
Low, Toby (Lord Aldington), 163, 164, 271
Ludwig II, King, 76, 124, 145, 360
Lyon, Herbert, 138, 139, 143, 155, 156
Lyon, Hugh, 209

Macfarlane, Bruce, 193, 194
Maclachlan, Donald, 262
Macmillan, Harold, 270
Magdalen College, Oxford, 11, 177, 188, 190, 191, 192, 193, 205, 206, 365
Merthyr, William 3rd Lord, 300–1, 306
Methuen, 308, 320
MI 6, 41, 225, 230, 258, 263, 277, 285, 332
Morris, John, 189, 193
Müller, Johannes, 123, 124, 125, 126, 145, 147, 148

National Association of Parish (later local) Councils, 296, 310

Oeynhausen, Counts, 47
Olweg, 27, 58, 60, 70, 73

Page, Graham, 323, 324, 326
Parish Administration, 308, 313, 317, 320, 343
Parish Councils Review, 321
Parr, Jack, 168, 169
Philby, Kim, 193, 231, 258, 262, 266
Pilgrims (school), 120, 126, 129
Pipit's Hill, 137, 138, 143, 145, 151, 157, 179, 191, 203
PLUTO (Pipeline Under the Ocean), 232, 238
Pollitt, Charles, 295, 321, 340
Max of Baden, Prince, 123, 126, 147, 148, 156, 157

Quackenburg, 39, 43

Read, Sir Herbert, 87
v. Rheinbaben, Gerda, 4, 5, 14, 157
Robinson, Betty, 1, 2, 109, 110, 117, 118, 119
Rowen, Ann, 322, 343, 396
Rural District Council (RDC), 304

Schachen, the, 145, 146
Schlönwitz, 15, 39, 40, 43, 52, 90, 91, 93, 96, 98, 141, 179, 365, 366, 367
Die Schnarckjagd, 331, 364, 365, 400
Searle, Betty, 295, 296, 301
Selli, 27, 51, 58, 59, 60, 63, 69, 72
Sellier family, 66, 75, 76, 126, 145
Sillem, Jim, 41, 258, 281
Spetzgart, 157, 177

Staffelde, 27, 32, 46, 47, 48, 49, 50, 57, 58, 60, 63, 66, 67, 69, 70, 84, 90, 91, 92, 93, 102, 105
Stamp, Dr Dudley, 309
Stauffenberg, Count, 23, 179, 365, 366
Sturdza, Alexander, 147, 148
Suckow, 15, 40, 41, 46

'Tante Su' (Countess Oeynhausen), 48, 55, 84, 105
Taylor, A. J. P., 189, 193, 194
Tennent, Margaret, *see* Grosvenor, Margaret
v. Thadden, Elizabeth, 178
Thompson, Frank, 307
Trollhattan, 278, 279, 282, 395
Turnbull, Oliver, 148, 334, 335

'Uncle Bob', *see* v. Blumenthal, Robert
'Uncle Percy' *see* Percival Richard Arnold Baker

Varzin, 15, 40, 41, 44
Vehlow, 15, 30, 35, 36

Walker, Harold, 172
Wentworth, 5, 77, 110, 137, 195, 226, 350
William II, Emperor, 26, 48, 50, 65
Williams, Dr Alwyn, 169
Winchester (College), 10, 13, 55, 81, 101, 126, 129, 137, 156, 157, 158, 164, 165, 166, 168, 169, 174, 189, 191, 210, 212, 219, 262, 287, 307, 329, 360, 395
Wrotham Camp, 221, 227
Wymondham, 101, 103

Printed in the United Kingdom
by Lightning Source UK Ltd.
120747UK00001B/1-34